THE 100 BEST STOCKS

YOU CAN BUY

2011

PETER SANDER
AND
JOHN SLATTER, CFA

Avon, Massachusetts

Published by
Adams Media, a division of F+W Media, Inc.
57 Littlefield Street, Avon, MA 02322. U.S.A.
www.adamsmedia.com

ISBN 10: 1-4405-0052-5
ISBN 13: 978-1-4405-0052-7
eISBN 10: 1-4405-0890-9
eISBN 13: 978-1-4405-0890-5

Printed in the United States of America.

10   9   8   7   6   5   4   3   2   1

Library of Congress Cataloging-in-Publication Data
is available from the publisher.

This publication is designed to provide accurate and authoritative information with regard to the subject matter covered. It is sold with the understanding that the publisher is not engaged in rendering legal, accounting, or other professional advice. If legal advice or other expert assistance is required, the services of a competent professional person should be sought.

—From a *Declaration of Principles* jointly adopted by a Committee of the American Bar Association and a Committee of Publishers and Associations

Many of the designations used by manufacturers and sellers to distinguish their product are claimed as trademarks. Where those designations appear in this book and Adams Media was aware of a trademark claim, the designations have been printed with initial capital letters.

This book is available at quantity discounts for bulk purchases.
For information, please call 1-800-289-0963.

Contents

Dedication

I continue to dedicate this book to all of you active investors who have the sense of purpose and independence of thought to make your own investing decisions, or at least, to ask the right questions. You continue to be wise enough and inquisitive enough to realize that not all the answers can be found in one place, and smart enough to seek the convenience of a good place to start.

Acknowledgments

Two pairs of eyes are better than one, and so for this 2011 edition I must once again thank my research partner and long time friend and colleague J. Scott Bobo for his prescient analysis and hard work. I must also recognize the good work of Value Line Inc. and their investment survey, which does more than any other investment service I know of to turn piles of facts and figures into a simple readable page. Next, no book happens without the added value of exercise to keep my body in shape and my mind clear, and to that end I offer my thanks to my exercise companions. And of course I must thank my family—wife Jennifer and sons Julian and Jonathan—for taking care of business while I engaged in this enterprise.

PART I

THE ART AND SCIENCE OF INVESTING IN STOCKS

By Peter Sander

The Art and Science of Investing in Stocks

Peter Sander

Congratulations on your purchase of the 2011 edition of *The 100 Best Stocks You Can Buy*.

If you bought this book, you're probably an astute and experienced individual investor who invests in individual stocks in individual companies. Now, that might not seem so profound, but with the some 10,000 mutual funds, 8,000 hedge funds and countless Exchange Traded Funds (ETFs) and index funds out there, it's not inconceivable that the individual stock investor is becoming an endangered species.

But that's just not so. For the better, not only for your own wealth but for the efficient allocation of capital to businesses and ideas that work best, millions still engage in this sort of "pure" investing for all or part of their wealth.

Even if you buy just a few shares of one company, you're an individual investor. You're participating actively in the economy, and you're buying your share of the company with hopes of participating in its success. Like a homeowner choosing to take part in the work of owning a home as a "do-it-yourselfer" you're participating in the individual satisfaction, responsibility, and control that comes with doing it yourself.

If you succeed, you accept the benefits of increased wealth (and reduced fees) along with the satisfaction and sense of accomplishment of doing it yourself. If you fail, true, you'll have no one else to blame but yourself. But at least you won't be forced to drink the poison of having someone else lose your money for you. In the entrepreneurial spirit that so characterizes America and much of the Western world, you'll pick yourself up, dust yourself off, learn from the mistakes, and go out and do it again.

Every edition of *The 100 Best Stocks You Can Buy*, this 2011 edition included, is intended to be a core tool for the individual investor. Sure, it's hardly the only tool available. Today's explosion of Internet-based investing tools has made this book one of hundreds of choices for acquiring investing information. With the speed of cyberspace, our book will hardly be the most current source. So instead, it is intended as a handy guide and core reference for your investing; not as a be-all end-all investing source. Thus, as much as a source of facts and numbers itself, *100 Best Stocks* is intended as a *model* for selecting the best companies and stocks to invest in.

To that same point, *100 Best Stocks* goes well beyond just being a stock screen or a "study" of stocks to invest in. Analysis forms the base of *100 Best Stocks*, but it isn't the rigid, strictly numbers-based selection and analysis so often found in published "best stocks" list. Sure, we look at earnings, cash flow, balance sheet strength and so forth, but we'll also look far beyond those things. We'll look at the intangible and often subtle factors that make truly great businesses—that is, companies—great.

Great companies have good business fundamentals, but what makes them really great is the presence of intangibles and subtleties that will *keep* them great—or make them greater—in the future.

So the selection of the *100 Best Stocks* continues to go far beyond being a simple numbers-based stock screen. It's a selection and analysis of really good businesses you would want to buy and own, not just for past results but for future outcomes. Now, does "future" mean "forever?" No, not hardly, not any more. Nothing is really forever these days—as those who invested in GM or Eastman Kodak or AIG or Bank of America can attest. So while the *100 Best Stocks* list correlates well with the notion of "blue chip" stocks, the discussion proceeds with the harsh reality that "blue chip" no longer means "forever."

As the book title suggests, I feel that the 100 companies listed and analyzed in the pages that follow are the best companies to own for 2011. That said, the word "own" has become a more active concept these days. Gone are the days of "own forever," like the halcyon days where my parents Jerry and Betty Sander, who bought their thirty-five shares of General Motors and lovingly placed the stock certificate in their safe deposit box and henceforth bought nothing but GM cars. Today, there is no forever; the economy, technology and consumer tastes simply change too fast, and the businesses that participate in the economy by necessity change with it. Ownership is a more active concept than it was even ten or twenty years ago.

So going forward, I offer the 100 best companies to own now and in 2011, and that have the best chances of not only surviving but evolving with—or even ahead of—the economy based on their current market position and approach to doing business. But as we all found out during the past two years, nothing is sacred in the business world and can fall apart with astounding speed. What does that mean?

Simply this: you can't take anything you read in the following as "investment advice" or as hard, unwavering truths. The world simply changes too fast, and the analysis of a business and especially the *value* of a business is not a precise science, it is inherently a combination of science and art. True business value is subject to different interpretations and different opinions, and further, we must layer in the pace and effects of change.

What that means is simple and straightforward: you'll have to take the information presented, do your own assessment, reach your own conclusions, and take your own actions. Anything else would go beyond my intentions, and more importantly, stop short of the mark for you.

With that in mind, make the most of what follows, and good luck with your investing!

SO WHY BUY AN INVESTING BOOK THESE DAYS?

The Internet is great, anything you want at your fingertips, practically real time, latest news, latest analysis, latest numbers. News and numbers are great, and they will inevitably help you take the latest facts into consideration and add points and counterpoints to your investment decision. But is the Internet enough?

Consider what a book like The *100 Best Stocks You Can Buy* has to offer. It gives not just facts and figures, but also a mindset. A thought process you can browse through, one you can see applied repeatedly to different situations.

You might not align to the set of 100 stocks I offer here because they are too expensive or don't appeal to your tastes or just don't suit your needs or interests at the moment. That's okay. Even if you don't choose from the 100 stocks offered here, you can follow the thought processes, the choices and decisions made, as a model.

Being an individual investor is rather like being an airplane pilot. You are ultimately in control of his aircraft, you are in control of your finances. And that means taking responsibility for your own decisions, regardless of the information sources—the gauges, charts, ground control folks you have helping you out. So you must develop your own mindset and set of investment knowledge and tools—that's where books come in.

Remember, in investing, like life, it's the thought that counts.

Sophomore Year: 2011

Many of you have bought this book each year for a good long while, and have followed the evolution of the 100 Best lists. Last year more significant changes occurred, as I, Peter Sander, was added to the team as a coauthor to bring a unique value investing perspective and to update the approach to selecting stocks and investing in general.

First, a bit of a biographical sketch (this is review for those who read last year's edition): I am an independent professional researcher, writer and journalist specializing in personal finance, investing and location reference, as well as other general business topics. I have written twenty-four books on these topics, done numerous financial columns and independent privately contracted research and studies. I come from a background in the corporate world, having experienced a twenty-one-year career with a major West Coast technology firm.

I am an individual investor. And have been since the age of twelve, when my curiosity at the family breakfast table got the better of me. I started reading the stock pages with my parents. I had an opportunity during a one-week "project week" in the seventh grade to read about, and learn about, the stock market. I read Louis Engel's *How to Buy Stocks*, then the pre-eminent—and one of the only—books about investing available at the time (it first appeared in 1953, I think I read a 1962 paperback edition). I read Engel, picked stocks, and made graphs of their performance by hand with colored pens on real graph paper. I put my hard-earned savings into buying five shares of each of three different companies. I watched those stocks like a hawk and salted away the meager dividends to reinvest. I've been investing ever since, and in combination with twenty-six years of home ownership and a rigorous, almost sacrificial savings regimen, I have accumulated a net worth exceeding the total *gross* income I received in twenty-one years in the corporate job.

Yes, I have an MBA from a top-rated university (Indiana University, Bloomington), but it isn't an MBA in finance. I also took the coursework and certification exam to become a Certified Financial Planner (CFP®). But I have never worked in the financial profession. That is by design and choice. My goal has always been to share my knowledge and experience in an educational way, a way helpful for the individual as an investor and a personal financier to make their own decisions.

And so I have never made money giving investment advice or managing money for others, nor do I intend to.

An Eye for Value

A few years ago it dawned on me that I really make my living finding value, and helping others or teaching others to find value. Not just in stocks, but other things in business and in life. And what do I mean by value? Simply, the current and potential *worth* of something (or someone) as compared to its price or cost. As it turns out, I've made a career out of assessing the value of people, places, and companies.

My last assignment at the high tech firm was to find value in customers. *People*. My title: Customer Valuation Manager. At the time, around the turn of the millennium, we were building a "customer relationship management" platform, and my job was to segment millions of customers by value, and to assign values to each one to help target messaging and so-called "one-to-one" marketing campaigns. A tricky enterprise, no doubt, because no company can really know what a customer is truly worth, down to the penny, especially going forward. It became an exercise in looking at previous buying behavior, considering other known customer attributes internal and external to the business, assessing the customer's cost (marketing and support costs) making some assumptions, and testing results.

At the time I did not really grasp that the same exact process really applied to investing, too. But a sharp editor at John Wiley & Sons' "Dummies" division put two and two together and hired me to write *Value Investing for Dummies*. The light went on. Whether it's people or stocks, the thought process is the same. Take what you know (fundamentals), add some intuition (intangibles), make some assumptions, proceed carefully, and evaluate the results.

The same publisher—different division—gave me another chance two years later, this time to write a complete reference guide to places to live. Hundreds of places to live appraised for value and ranked top to bottom, best to worst. Value is extremely important in deciding where you would want to live. Sure, the "best" places to live might include Greenwich, Connecticut, Jupiter, Florida or Palo Alto, California. But most of us can't afford them. So the true "best places" for most of us anyway are the places that deliver the most value for the money, now and in the future. The resulting book, *Cities Ranked & Rated—More Than 400 Metropolitan Areas Evaluated in the U.S. and Canada*, and the sister publication *Best Places to Raise Your Family*, finally went beyond the "study" and short list to truly answer the question most of us have—what's the best place to live *for my money*.

The same value approach works in the world of business and stock investing. It isn't just the biggest nor the richest corporations that we should be putting our hard earned money into. If that were the case, we'd simply buy GE or Exxon Mobil and move on. But do these companies represent the best *value* for your investing dollar? Maybe, but maybe not.

Just like customers or places to live, we want companies that produce the greatest return, the highest value, *per dollar invested*. And *for the amount of risk taken.* The amount of risk taken translates into additional dollars an investment might cost, analogous to living in a great place rampant with crime or with questionable schools that might cost you more in the long run. The companies I will identify as among the 100 Best have, in my assessment, the greatest long term *value*, and if you can buy these companies at a *reasonable price* (a factor which I leave out of this analysis because this is a book and prices can change considerably) these investments deliver the best prospects.

Later I'll come back to describe some of the attributes of value that I look for.

A Two-Man Team

As an acknowledgement, and as a partial explanation of how we've gotten to where we are, I continue to employ the services of good friend and colleague J. Scott Bobo as a research assistant. Scott has been huge not only in identifying the 100 Best Stocks but also analyzing them and explaining their pros and cons crisply and in plain English so that you can make the best use of the list. Having Scott on the team allows you get the combined wisdom and observations of two people, not just one, where hopefully one plus one equals something greater than two.

Scott adds a strong analytical touch. But he is most at home as an applications engineer, explaining how a company's products work and how they apply to a customer's needs. As a consequence, and in addition to analytical legwork, Scott really adds an extraordinary and very real-world sense of how a company's products "fit" in the marketplace. Determining whether a company's products are relevant and best-in-class and have a competitive advantage over others is an oft-overlooked core skill for a value investor. Scott brings this skill to the table in a big way.

Going forward, when you see the personal pronoun "we" instead of "I," it represents a thought or evaluation that Scott and I came up with together.

What's Changed for 2011

Last year's edition naturally brought a lot of changes, both with my arrival on the scene and with the wild ride the markets gave us in 2008 and 2009. In 2010 we kept many of the basic tenets of previous editions, including a focus on fundamentals, a long-term horizon, and clearly defined reasons to buy and not to buy. In 2010 we placed more emphasis on "fundamentals that really count," including cash flow, profit margins, and balance sheet strength. We also placed a greater weight on "intangibles"—those hard-to-quantify factors like brand strength, customer loyalty and market position, that seem to over and over separate the winners from the losers. We also shifted toward higher value-add companies and away from low-margin commodity producers subject to the whims of the marketplace and business cycle. Last year, we removed some twenty-six companies from the 2009 list and replaced them with other choices.

In 2011 we continue to evolve, albeit with less change than found in the 2010 edition. First of all, for 2011, we have removed and replaced fourteen companies. These changes came for various reasons and are detailed in Tables 1, 2, and 3.

We also are placing more focus on dividends. More and more, especially in today's volatile markets, we feel that investors should get paid something to commit their precious capital to a company; it's a sign of good faith to investors and provides at least some return while waiting for a larger return in the future—or if things happen to go south later on. "A bird in hand . . . ," as they say. So, as it turns out, some ninety-one of the 100 stocks picked pay at least some dividends. Those that don't, like Apple and Google, are on the list because of other obvious factors of excellence; we can turn our heads the other way on the dividend.

Next, as believers in measuring performance (yes, perhaps it's that engineering background that haunts us) we've added a new section to summarize the performance of the 2010 Best Stocks, if for nothing else than to convince you (and ourselves) that our 100 Best are pretty good.

Finally, in an attempt to have some fun as well as to give a "best of the best" assessment of companies by certain characteristics, we've created five "Stars" lists. These lists cover our Top 10 picks in five categories. Four of the five categories are subjective, the fifth, "Yield," is quite measurable (we also gave the Top 20 instead of the Top 10 for this category). The other four categories are:

1. Safety Stars (solid performers in any market)
2. Growth Stars (companies positioned for above average growth)
3. Recovery Stars (companies that cut costs and are otherwise positioned well for an economic recovery)
4. Moat Stars (companies with significant sustainable competitive advantage)

So, if you're an investor partial to any of these factors, like Safety, these lists are for you.

Wow, What a Year (and a Half)

Who woulda thunk the markets would do what they've done since the fall of 2008? Such a roller coaster. The biggest down cycle in modern times, culminating in a Dow Jones Industrial Average March 9, 2009 low of 6,547, some 54 percent lower than its all time high of 14,167 on October 9, 2007. And then to rebound some 68 percent from that point through April 2010! What's with these markets—losing half their value, then almost doubling back, in a period of less than three years? It used to take years to complete a 50 percent move—now two of them in less than three years? How is one supposed to react to this? And how can anyone gain peace of mind by investing in such madness?

Indeed, it's a challenge. And, my friends, we think volatility is here to stay. These are news-driven markets, and any new news is instantly known around the world, and instantly carries into the stock markets worldwide. Greek debt crisis? Higher or lower unemployment? A failing bank? It's news, and it's out there, and people react.

On top of faster news, the markets themselves are also faster. So-called "high frequency trading," where computers owned by certain investment firms trade with each other at blitz millisecond speed to capture tiny price differentials in the markets, is thought to account for as much as 75 percent of today's exchange volume, especially for larger stocks. Automated trades, thousands per second, thousands and thousands of shares, with no human intervention whatsoever. We saw what happened in the May 6, 2010 "flash crash," where suddenly big players—some knowingly and some unknowingly—turned off their computers. The "demand side" or "bid" side in the market simply dried up, and prices plummeted, some to cents on a dollar for certain stocks and exchange-traded funds. High frequency trading didn't cause the flash crash, but it certainly did amplify its effects.

Anyway, the point is not to scare people off from investing, it is to say that now, more than ever, investors must stay focused on what they invest in. The kind of volatility we've seen recently can actually provide some buying opportunities, so even those really pricey stocks that *everyone* thinks are best to own can be had if the time is right.

Remember that investing in stocks is still about buying shares of a business, and just because there's a "flash crash" doesn't mean that IBM or Johnson & Johnson or Abbott Laboratories are any worse off as companies. It simply means that the market has taken a different approach, probably an irrational one, to evaluating them. It is imperative, as an investor, that you invest in good businesses. If you do, the price of the shares will come out okay in the long term. And if you want to sleep at night, businesses with steady results will tend to be less volatile. Finally, for further insulation against the ups and downs of the markets, we're favoring stocks that pay dividends, because no "flash crash" can take away money you've received and socked in the bank, right?

As we move through the first half of 2010, the year started off well with favorable economic reports on jobs, housing, industrial production, factory orders, and consumer sentiment. In May 2010, the Greek debt crisis (and Spanish and Portuguese and Irish and who knows who else) reminded us that too much debt, whether possessed by consumers, U.S banks, hedge funds or sovereign nations—is too much debt. Plain and simple. The scary part of that crisis was the realization of the importance of the European market for U.S. goods—if Europe goes into a credit clamshell like the United States did in late 2008, and worse, if countries start to default thus poisoning the well for everyone, we might lose Europe as a customer—that would be huge.

So one of our investing tenets has been to shy away from overseas companies because it's harder to understand their businesses and their financial statements. It always seemed better to get international exposure by buying the Hewlett-Packards and Caterpillars of the world, because they *export* sizeable amounts of products to overseas customers—so you get exposure to overseas economies without getting exposure to overseas companies. We still have faith in that tenet, but if Europe implodes, look out below. It's a risk, but far from a certainty.

Meanwhile, back at the U.S. ranch, a funny thing has happened to companies as they've appraised the risky economy, and perhaps more to the point, as they've been literally cut off from being able to borrow funds needed to expand or even to operate. They've gone on the rampage to cut costs. You don't know how many times in the 100 Best Stock write-ups that we've made some reference to the fact the ". . . the company has cut costs dramatically and stands to do well if the economy improves . . . ." Yes indeed, they've done it and done in with a vengeance. We owe our condolences to the many who have lost their jobs as a result, as well as the thousands of small suppliers or owners of commercial real estate space who have fallen victim to this downsizing. It's brutal. But many of these companies have changed their cost structures for good and are not likely to go back to the permanent hiring levels once had. If, as we expect, cost structures stay low, any economic rebound drops to the bottom line. The next few years could be good for stocks *if*—well, if a couple of things—

1. the economy *really does* rebound, and we're concerned about this, as so much of the structural economy and especially the manufacturing economy has moved to China, semi-permanently and
2. we successfully avoid a collapse of international export markets as per the Europe threat mentioned above.

Barring some major structural change (or horrific unforeseen event) the economy will almost surely recover in some way. But it may take a while (debt is something that doesn't go away fast) and it may be oriented toward producing goods and services that barely exist yet—we're probably not going to get fat again as a nation producing domestic cars (at least gasoline-powered ones). Still, any recovery will help, and the best companies are likely to lead the way.

So what does it all mean? It means, as always, stick to your guns and invest smart. That "smart investing" approach combined with the "seed corn" of 100 Best Stocks are the twin essentials of this book.

Let's see how we did with last year's picks.

Report Card: Recapping Our 2010 Picks

We believe that it makes no sense to make stock recommendations, and especially to sell them to the public in book form, unless we step back at least for a second to appraise the collective performance of our recommendations. After all, if our list performs the same as the markets as a whole, you'd save a lot of money and time by simply buying a market index ETF or some similar instrument. And if, like many mutual funds, our picks performed worse, there's little reason to buy our book other than to discover what to avoid.

In that context, we examine the performance of our 100 Best Stocks list for 2010. Since the 2008-2010 period was such a dynamic period in which good defense was at least as important—if not more so—than offense, we will look at our list in two ways:

*   *Up cycle performance.* The markets were strong, as most know, between March 2009 and March 2010; the S&P 500 index as a whole gained some 55 percent as measured by the proxy performance of the S&P 500 SPDR Trust ETF. How did the 100 Best Stocks do between March 1, 2009 and March 10, 2010? Back with that in a second.
*   *Down cycle performance.* A car with a high performance engine may go like a bat out of hell, but what about stopping? What about the brakes?

Similarly, you might ask how the 100 Best Stocks would have fared if you had owned them as the markets *dropped* some 54.8 percent, based on the same proxy, between October 1, 2007 and March 1, 2009.

Evaluating the List

There are many ways to evaluate the performance of a group of stocks over time. Some are simplistic, such as simply averaging the percent gain in each share price. But such a method may not weight a portfolio very realistically, for it assumes you buy the same number of shares of Apple at $273 as you would Duke Energy at $16. We felt, as a result, that it was better to take the approach of an investor with $100,000 to invest—who invested $1,000 in each of the 100 Stocks across the board, regardless of share price. Sure, you end up with some weird quantities of shares in your portfolio, but the portfolio, and thus the performance metrics, aren't weighted in favor of more expensive stocks.

Down Cycle Performance

So we used this approach and hypothetically invested $100,000 in our 100 Best Stocks on October 1, 2007, and sold on March 1, 2009 (the down cycle). Including dividends, our stocks lost some $38,269 (easily calculated and rounded as 38.3 percent.) Pretty bad, right? But, recalling the figure above, it isn't as bad as the S&P 500 overall performance of –54.8 percent, is it? *The 100 Best Stocks proved about 17 percent more "safe" during this rough period.* Table 1 gives the twenty "safest" of the 100 Best Stocks, and the entire list can be found in Part II.

▼ **Down Cycle Performance: The 20 Best of the 100 Best Stocks 2010**
CHANGE IN PRICE, 1/1/2007 THROUGH 3/9/2009

Company	Symbol	Price, 10/1/2007	Price, 3/1/2009	$ Gain/ Loss	% Gain/ Loss
Ross Stores, Inc.	ROST	$25.64	$29.52	3.88	15.13%
Teva Pharmaceutical	TEVA	$44.47	$44.58	0.11	0.25%
Piedmont Natural Gas	PNY	$25.09	$24.14	(0.95)	–3.79%
McDonald's Corporation	MCD	$54.47	$52.25	(2.22)	–4.08%
Perrigo Company	PRGO	$21.35	$20.09	(1.26)	–5.90%
Abbott Laboratories	ABT	$51.37	$47.34	(4.03)	–7.85%
Vulcan Materials Company	VMC	$45.09	$41.41	(3.68)	–8.16%

CHANGE IN PRICE, 1/1/2007 THROUGH 3/9/2009—continued

Company	Symbol	Price, 10/1/2007	Price, 3/1/2009	$ Gain/ Loss	% Gain/ Loss
General Mills, Inc.	GIS	$58.01	$52.48	(5.53)	−9.53%
Baxter International	BAX	$56.63	$50.91	(5.72)	−10.10%
Hormel Foods Corp.	HRL	$35.78	$31.83	(3.95)	−11.04%
Monsanto Company	MON	$85.74	$76.27	(9.47)	−11.05%
McCormick & Company	MKC	$35.97	$31.35	(4.62)	−12.84%
Colgate-Palmolive Company	CL	$71.32	$60.18	(11.14)	−15.62%
Archer Daniels Midland Co.	ADM	$31.73	$26.66	(5.07)	−15.98
The Southern Company	SO	$36.28	$30.31	(5.97)	−16.46%
C.R. Bard, Inc.	BCR	$88.99	$72.38	(16.61)	−18.67%
The Clorox Company	CLX	$60.99	$48.60	(12.39)	−20.31%
International Business Machines	IBM	$117.80	$92.03	(25.77)	−21.88%
Campbell Soup Company	CPB	$34.39	$26.77	(7.62)	−22.16%
Peet's Coffee & Tea	PEET	$27.91	$21.55	(6.36)	−22.79%

Table 1. Down cycle performance, 100 Best Stocks 2010, October 2007—March 2009

As you can see, discount retailer Ross Stores led this list by actually *rising* 15 percent during this period. But only one other stock was in the green; the rest showed modest losses. Strong consumer names like McDonald's and Clorox and such staple providers as McCormick and Campbell Soup held up in the face of adversity.

Up Cycle Performance

Then, of course, we had to measure what happened to our stocks in the "boom" between the market nadir of March 2009 and a snapshot taken on March 10, 2010 near the height of the recovery. *While the S&P 500 advanced an impressive 55.5 percent, our list, including dividends, jumped some 65.5 percent, a 10 percent improvement in performance.* Again, a Top 20 list (and a complete list in Part II):

▼ Up Cycle Performance: The 20 Best of the 100 Best Stocks 2010
CHANGE IN PRICE, 3/1/2009 THROUGH 3/10/2010

Company	Symbol	Price, 3/1/2009	Shares	Invested, 3/1/2009	Price, 3/10/2010	Mkt Value, 3/10/10	$ Gain	% Gain
International Paper Co.	IP	$5.69	175.75	$1,000	$25.11	$4,413.01	$3,413.01	341.3
Lubrizol	LZ	$27.49	36.38	$1,000	$85.85	$3,122.95	$2,122.95	212.3
Johnson Controls	JCI	$11.38	87.87	$1,000	$31.19	$2,740.77	$1,740.77	174.1
Starbucks	SBUX	$9.15	109.29	$1,000	$24.23	$2,648.09	$1,648.09	164.8
Apple	AAPL	$89.29	11.2	$1,000	$224.84	$2,517.52	$1,517.52	151.8
Perrigo	PRGO	$20.09	49.78	$1,000	$50.10	$2,493.78	$1,493.78	149.4
CarMax	KMX	$9.43	106.04	$1,000	$23.29	$2,469.78	$1,469.78	147.0
Wells Fargo	WFC	$12.10	82.64	$1,000	$29.57	$2,443.80	$1,443.80	144.4
FedEx Corp.	FDX	$35.77	27.96	$1,000	$87.26	$2,440.16	$1,440.16	144.0
Caterpillar	CAT	$24.61	40.63	$1,000	$58.78	$2,388.46	$1,388.46	138.9
eBay	EBAY	$10.87	92	$1,000	$25.56	$2,351.43	$1,351.43	135.1
Fair Isaac Corp.	FICO	$10.95	91.32	$1,000	$24.71	$2,256.62	$1,256.62	125.7
Boeing	BA	$31.44	31.81	$1,000	$70.01	$2,226.78	$1,226.78	122.7
Goodrich	GR	$33.13	30.18	$1,000	$71.20	$2,148.46	$1,148.46	114.9
Deere & Co.	DE	$27.49	36.38	$1,000	$58.49	$2,127.68	$1,127.68	112.8
General Dynamics	GD	$36.50	27.4	$1,000	$73.94	$2,026.31	$1,026.31	102.6
Apache Corp.	APA	$53.45	18.71	$1,000	$106.59	$1,993.83	$993.83	99.4
Norfolk Southern	NSC	$27.41	36.48	$1,000	$53.87	$1,965.34	$965.34	96.5
Valmont	VMI	$42.68	23.43	$1,000	$82.59	$1,935.10	$935.10	93.5
Alexander & Baldwin	ALEX	$17.96	55.68	$1,000	$34.44	$1,917.59	$917.59	91.8

Table 2. Up cycle performance, 100 Best Stocks 2010, March 2009—March 2010

Some of the biggest winners were high flyers like Starbucks and Apple. But some were beaten down values like International Paper and Johnson Controls—proving once again that it's always possible to find value in the markets if you look hard enough.

IS 10 PERCENT THAT MUCH BETTER? HOW ABOUT 17 PERCENT?

You may be wondering if it's worth buying this book and doing all this analysis simply to improve performance by factors of 10 percent in an up cycle and 17 percent in a down cycle. In a phrase, you bet it is. Why? Because of compounding. If you avoid a 17 percent loss in a down cycle, then gain 10 percent on the funds you had plus the funds you saved, you could end up with a pile, especially if this cycle repeats. After the roughly three-year period represented by the two cycles, you'd be 28.7 percent ahead. Repeat this 28.7 percent advantage, say, ten times over a thirty-year retirement savings period, and you'd end up with 12.5 times as much money as if you had simply performed alongside the S&P 500 during similar periods.

Sustainable Investing

So with the recent volatility and the speed of change becoming an increasingly permanent characteristic of today's markets, many financial journalists and pundits have recently called the demise of long-term investing, specifically the so-called "buy-and-hold" strategy. Indeed, one wonders when such stalwarts as Citigroup and AIG and such long-term growth and income favorites as Whole Foods and General Electric and BP run into trouble. The speed of change—change in technology and consumer tastes—and, in the case of BP, news-driven change—does indeed bring some concern to the idea of buying shares and locking them away in your safe deposit box. More than ever, you need to stay on your toes and watch for change.

What it really means is that you need to select companies that adapt well to change and can stay in front of changing markets. And it means that a periodic review of your investments—all of your investments—is more important than ever. Every stock you own should be evaluated from scratch—as though you were going to buy it again—at least once a year.

But that doesn't mean that long-term investing is dead. Great companies respond to change and find ways to continue to satisfy customers and make money regardless of the mood and change of the day. Companies like Procter & Gamble reinvent themselves constantly, not with a big housecleaning and restructuring every few years. They get into cosmetics like Olay as the population ages and people become more conscious of their appearance, and as competitive pressure and lack of consumer interest drives profit margins on peanut butter steadily downward. (They did something about this, too, selling their Jif brand to new 100 Best Stocks inductee J.M. Smucker, who knows a thing or two about both peanut butter and jelly.) As aging men become more concerned about their appearance, Procter develops Olay lines for men. You get the idea.

Some companies respond better to changes in the wind than others. Starbucks sailed in front of a huge tailwind, opening store after store until they had so many stores that they cannibalized each other and worse, lost their agility and brand caché. I feel, however, that they learned from this mistake, and have added them to the 2011 list on the basis of brand strength, management excellence, balance sheet strength and core business profitability. The stock doubled in a year. A fault once in a while is okay, but I tend to avoid companies that seem to be "restructuring" or "reinventing" themselves" continuously.

Value—Now More Than Ever

The bottom line is this: For intelligent investors, chasing the latest fad doesn't work, nor does buying something and locking it away forever. Investors must make intelligent choices based on true value and follow those choices through time and change. It all points to taking a "value" oriented approach to investing, and to staying modestly "active" with your investments.

The next obvious task is to define what I mean by a "value" approach. Essentially, it is to think of buying shares in a company as buying the company itself, it is about putting yourself in an entrepreneurial frame of mind, not just an investment frame of mind. Would you want to own that business? Why or why not? That's the first and biggest question that must be answered.

Fundamentally, whether or not you want to own the business depends on two factors: first, the returns you expect to receive on your investment in the near and long term future and second, the risk you'll take in generating those returns. Fortunately, the third factor the prospective entrepreneur must consider—"do I have the time for this?"—isn't typically a consideration.

So you are looking for tangible value—tangible worth—for your precious, scarce and hard-earned investment capital. Now that return doesn't have to be immediate in the form of dividends or a share of the assets, as many in the traditional "value school" suggest. It can come in the form of growth for the longer term. If you realize your return in the form of owning a share of a larger company eventually, that's still a legitimate return. Cash flow received later in the form of a higher share price or a takeover is still cash return, it is just less certain because of the forces of change that may take place in the interim. It is also theoretically worth less because of the nature of discounting—a dollar received tomorrow is worth more than a dollar received twenty years in the future.

The point: many investment experts distinguish between "value" and "growth" investing; in fact, mutual funds are often classified as being one or the other. I dismiss this separation; growth can be an essential component of a firm's value. Indeed, this is the key difference between the original 1930s Benjamin Graham school of value and the more evolved Warren Buffett take.

YOU DON'T NEED TO BE A MATH GENIUS

Calculating "value" can be a daunting task, especially if one goes into the nuances of compounding, discounting and all that business school stuff. Today's value investor doesn't ignore the numbers, but shuns complex mathematical formulas, which in the recent bust, tended not to work anyway; greater forces overtook almost all statistical and mathematical models for stock analysis, leaving many a "quant" scratching his or her head.

Buying companies is not a math-driven process, just like you can't evaluate a school based on its test scores alone. Warren Buffett and Charlie Munger have made this clear over the years and came back to the point with emphasis in the 2009 Berkshire Hathaway shareholders meeting. Buffett mused: "If you need to use a computer or a calculator to make the calculation, you shouldn't buy it." Reading between the lines: the story should be simple and straightforward enough to be obvious without detailed calculations.

Munger, Buffett's relatively more intrepid sidekick, added: "Some of the worst business decisions I've ever seen are those with future projections and discounts back. It seems like the higher mathematics with more false precision should help you, but it doesn't. They teach that in business school because, well, they've got to do something."

No need to read between the lines there.

Indeed, while the numbers are important, savvy value investors try to see where the puck is going. And that means a clear-eyed assessment of the intangible things that make companies great.

Value also implies safety. The safety comes in three forms. First is the fundamental quality and soundness of the firm's financial fundamentals, that is, income, cash flow, and the balance sheet. Value companies have plenty of reserves, a large enough *margin of safety*, to weather downturns and unforeseen events in the marketplace. Second, they have strong enough intangibles—brands, market position, supply chain strength, etc.—to maintain their position in that marketplace and generate future returns.

Thirdly, if you're really practicing value investing principles, you buy these companies at reduced prices, when the markets are down, when the company is out of favor. You're looking for situations where the price is less than what you perceive to be the value, although calculating the value that precisely is elusive. When you "buy cheap" you provide another margin of safety, that margin makes it less likely that the stock will drop further. It gives you room for error if you turn out to be wrong about a choice. Again, it's much like buying a business of your own—you want to pay as little as possible in case things don't turn out as you'd expect.

So taking a value approach provides greater confidence and safety, and is more likely to get you through today's volatile business and investing cycles.

The 100 Best Stocks for 2011: A Few Comments

Almost anybody can make money in a rising market; it is like shooting fish in a barrel. At the risk of mixing metaphors, the rubber really meets the road when it comes to investing in volatile or down markets. Unless you're trading actively (and exceptionally well) or are willing to bet on "short" positions (selling borrowed stock to buy back later on at a lower price) it becomes really important to pick out the really successful companies, the ones that can perform well when the economic tide goes out (sorry, yet another metaphor).

It's amazing how sure-thing sectors like financials, which were quite recently making money hand over fist, paying out great dividends, and flooding the market with a feeling of solidarity, have fallen apart. Even energy, another sure bet for the future, has had a wild ride in prices, really, a bubble. And now the Deepwater Horizon offshore drilling disaster—what next?

This year, among other changes, we reduced the number of industrial and defense stocks. We felt the list was overweighted in industrials in light of the relentless migration of manufacturing to China. We're worried not just about the loss of jobs but the increased cost of manufacturing due to health care, inevitable higher taxes as public finances fail, and the fact that so much manufacturing base has already been lost that economies of proximity and scale will be lost for remaining manufacturers. Who will assemble cars in the United States if all parts must be imported from China? We also thought we were overweighted with defense-oriented issues in light of the new Democratic administration and anticipated efforts to control the deficit, so we removed three defense contractors (General Dynamics, Raytheon, Goodrich) from the list.

So, as shown in Table 5 later on, we shed six industrial companies and two energy companies in the process of shedding and replacing fourteen companies in all.

As just mentioned, we took a hard look at all of our picks. The fact that we only changed fourteen of them reflects the long-term quality we feel to be inherent in the picks made in previous years. Some changed because we just aren't happy with their business models any longer, like eBay or Diebold, or they just got too hard to understand. We lost one due to acquisition (Varian to Agilent Technologies). A few of the others, like Lowe's—well, we just saw more excellence, less economic strife, and less cutthroat competition in Best Buy and Bed Bath & Beyond, so we switched horses accordingly (apologies, another metaphor).

Cutting to the chase, our additions emphasized quality, safety, yield and strong intangibles like brand and competitive advantage

Tables 3 and 4 show the deletions and additions to the 100 Best Stocks list to arrive at the current 2011 version (which can be seen in its entirety at the beginning of Part II. Table 5 categorizes the additions and deletions by sector.

▼ **Companies Removed for 2011**

COMPANY	SYMBOL	CATEGORY	SECTOR
Cintas	CTAS	Aggressive Growth	Industrials
Diebold	DBD	Growth and Income	Industrials
eBay	EBAY	Aggressive Growth	Consumer Discretionary
EnCana	ECA	Aggressive Growth	Energy
Energen	EGN	Aggressive Growth	Energy
General Dynamics	GD	Conservative Growth	Industrials
Goodrich	GR	Aggressive Growth	Industrials
Illinois Tool Works	ITW	Conservative Growth	Industrials
Lowes	LOW	Aggressive Growth	Retail
Piedmont Natural Gas	PNY	Growth and Income	Utilities
Raytheon	RTN	Aggressive Growth	Industrials
United Parcel Service	UPS	Conservative Growth	Transportation
Varian Medical Systems	VAR	Aggressive Growth	Health Care
Vulcan Materials	VMC	Conservative Growth	Materials

Table 3. Companies removed from 2010 100 Best Stocks list for 2011.

▼ New Companies for 2011

COMPANY	SYMBOL	CATEGORY	SECTOR
Bed, Bath & Beyond	BBBY	Aggressive Growth	Retail
Best Buy	BBY	Aggressive Growth	Retail
Bunge, Ltd.	BG	Conservative Growth	Consumer Staples
Chipotle Mexican Grill	CMG	Aggressive Growth	Restaurants
Church & Dwight	CHD	Aggressive Growth	Consumer Staples
Cincinnati Financial	CINN	Income	Financials
Duke Energy	DUK	Income	Utilities
J.M. Smucker	SJM	Growth and Income	Consumer Staples
Kimberly-Clark	KMB	Growth and Income	Consumer Staples
NetApp	NTAP	Aggressive Growth	Technology
Oracle	ORCL	Aggressive Growth	Technology
Pall Corporation	PLL	Conservative Growth	Industrials
Panera	PNRA	Aggressive Growth	Restaurants
Suburban Propane	SPH	Income	Energy

Table 4. Companies added to 100 Best Stocks List for 2011.

▼ Sector Analysis and 2011 Change by Sector

SECTOR	NUMBER ON 2010 LIST	ADDED FOR 2011	CUT FROM 2010
Business Services	1		
Consumer Discretionary	3		−1
Consumer Staples	17	4	
Energy	7	1	−2
Financials	3	1	
Health Care	13		−1
Heavy Construction	1		
Industrials	13	1	−6

▼ Sector Analysis and 2011 Change by Sector

SECTOR	NUMBER ON 2010 LIST	ADDED FOR 2011	CUT FROM 2010
Information Technology	8	2	
Materials	8		−1
Restaurant	5	2	
Retail	11	2	−1
Telecommunications Services	2		
Transportation	3		−1
Utilities	5	1	−1

Table 5. Analysis of 2011 100 Best Stocks changes by sector.

In mid-2010, Standard and Poors (S&P) calculated that 136 of its S&P 500 companies had raised dividends by mid-2010 and only two had reduced or suspended dividends. That compares with 157 increases for all of 2009 feathered in with seventy-eight decreases or suspensions. Upshot: after a dreary year, dividends are back.

What's going on? Well, first, perhaps some companies are getting the message from frustrated shareholders that they, yes, the shareholders themselves, *are* the real owners. Corporate board members are finding themselves generally on the hot seat with such nasty omissions of due diligence like Lehman and others on their collective conscience, plus the threat of increased regulatory scrutiny and fiduciary responsibility, that they are finding themselves becoming more generous with their shareholders. Further, companies have been squeezing expenses and generating cash, without much in the way of really strong ways to deploy the excess capital as the economy remains weak, so why not pay a few dollars more to those poor old shareholders?

Along with many other investment professionals these days, we think dividends are and will be a more important part of the total return for investors. Growth opportunities will be attenuated by the recession and fierce competition in most industries, but the ability to throw off excess cash will remain inherent in most good businesses. Dividends not only become an important part of the investor's expected return, but also a way for the investor to get something out of a company while waiting for the company's prospects or the economy in general to improve. Dividends become a way of being compensated to wait for better days.

Finally, as we stress later on in our value investing tenets section, it is not only today's dividend and yield that are important, it is the *growth* in dividends over time as well. We have a number of companies on the 2011 list that have doubled their dividends, with steady increases, over the past eight years. Repeat that performance for another decade or two, and who knows? You could be earning 50 percent, even 100 percent on your original investment! It's like getting a raise every year—plus exposure to the success and growth of the company and its stock price. A true win-win.

So as a result, ninety-one of the 100 stocks we picked pay a dividend, and the weighted average return using a $1,000 investment in each stock gives an average dividend yield of 2.6 percent, with twenty of our 100 stocks yielding 3.7 percent. That 3.7 percent may not sound like much, but compared to today's sub-one-percent yields on savings instruments, combined with the excellence and growth prospects of a "100 Best Stock," these issues seem like a good deal.

In that light, we present our "Yield Stars" list in Table 6 below—the Top 10 stocks on our 100 Best list by percentage yield as of mid-2010.

▼ Yield Stars

TOP 20 DIVIDEND PAYING STOCKS

Company	Symbol	Dividend	Yield %
Suburban Propane	SPH	3.36	7.3%
AT&T	T	1.68	7.0%
Verizon	VZ	1.90	7.0%
Duke Energy	DUK	0.96	6.1%
Cincinnati Financial	CINF	1.58	6.0%
Southern Company	SO	1.82	5.7%
General Mills	GIS	1.96	5.4%
DuPont	DD	1.64	4.8%
Dominion Energy	DE	1.83	4.7%
Entergy	ETR	3.32	4.6%
ConocoPhilips	COP	2.20	4.4%
Kimberly-Clark	KMB	2.64	4.4%
PayChex	PAYX	1.24	4.4%
Alexander & Baldwin	ALEX	1.26	4.2%

FPL Group	FPL	2.00	4.1%
Heinz	HNZ	1.80	4.1%
Kraft Foods	KFT	1.16	4.1%
Chevron	CVX	2.88	4.0%
Abbott Laboratories	ABT	1.76	3.8%
Johnson & Johnson	JNJ	2.16	3.7%

Table 6. Yield Stars

Dancing with the Stars

Readers have frequently asked us: "Out of your 100 Stocks, what are the best ones? What are your Top 10 picks?" Well, we don't actually rank our 100 Best Stocks 1 through 100. Why? Because different stocks serve different interests, needs, and risk tolerances among other things in a stock portfolio. And we're sure that if we name a "Number One," everyone will follow our lead into it and some dumb thing will happen like the Gulf oil spill or some other more subtle unforeseen change in business conditions. The art and science of stock picking simply do not lend themselves to choosing an overall Number One. Smart investors should buy groups of stocks to build a portfolio much as a diner in an à la carte restaurant picks several dishes to make a meal rather than looking for the single best dish on the menu.

With that in mind, we do believe we can create some value and interest by identifying the Top 10 stocks by certain attributes typically of common interest to investors, especially value-oriented investors. So this year for the first time, we offer Top 10 lists in four categories. We call them our "stars" list, bringing the idea forward from our "Yield Stars" list above. The four categories are Safety Stars, Growth Stars, Recovery Stars, and Moat Stars.

Safety Stars

Safety stars are companies we think will hold up well in volatile and negative stock markets as well as recessionary economies. They have stable products and customer bases, and long traditions of being able to manage well in downturns. They are "sleep at night" stocks when the going gets tough.

▼ Safety Stars

TOP 10 STOCKS FOR SAFETY AND STABILITY

Company	Symbol	Dividend	Yield %
Becton, Dickinson	BDX	1.48	2.1
Campbell Soup	CPB	1.10	3.1
Clorox Company	CLX	2.20	3.5
Ecolab	ECL	0.62	1.3
General Mills	GIS	1.96	5.4
Heinz	HNZ	1.80	4.1
J.M. Smucker	SJM	1.60	2.9
Johnson & Johnson	JNJ	2.16	3.7
Kimberly-Clark	KMB	2.64	4.4
McCormick & Co.	MKC	1.04	2.7

Table 7. Safety Stars.

Growth Stars

Looking at the other side of the coin, we picked ten stocks we feel are especially well positioned to grow, even in a negative economy and especially in a positive one:

▼ Growth Stars

TOP 10 STOCKS FOR GROWTH

Company	Symbol	Dividend	Yield %
Apple, Inc.	AAPL	0.00	0.0
CarMax	KMX	0.00	0.0
Chipotle Mexican Grill	CMG	0.00	0.0
Google	GOOG	0.00	0.0
NetApp	NTAP	0.00	0.0
NIKE, Inc.	NIKE	1.08	1.5
Nucor	NUE	1.44	3.5

TOP 10 STOCKS FOR GROWTH—continued

Company	Symbol	Dividend	Yield %
Peet's	PEET	0.00	0.0
Perrigo	PRGO	0.25	0.4
Tractor Supply Co.	TSCO	0.56	0.9

Table 8. Growth Stars.

Recovery Stars

As we emerge from the 2008–2010 recession (assuming a normal course of economic recovery) we feel that certain companies will do especially well. The assessment is based both on top line revenues and their ability to cut costs during bad times. As good times return, these companies will be particularly well positioned to turn recovery into bottom line returns.

▼ **Recovery Stars**

TOP 10 STOCKS FOR AN ECONOMIC RECOVERY

Company	Symbol	Dividend	Yield %
3M Company	MMM	2.10	2.8
Alexander & Baldwin	ALEX	1.26	4.2
Caterpillar	CAT	1.68	2.9
Deere & Co.	DE	1.20	2.1
Fluor Corp.	FLR	0.50	1.1
Int'l Paper	IP	0.50	2.3
Johnson Controls	JCI	0.52	1.9
Norfolk Southern	NSC	1.36	2.5
PayChex	PAYX	1.24	4.4
Wells Fargo	WFC	0.20	0.7

Table 9. Recovery Stars.

Moat Stars

Finally we get to one of the basic tenets of value investing—the ability of a company to build a sustainable and unassailable competitive advantage. Value investing aficionados call such an advantage a "moat," for it represents a barrier to entry for competitors likely to preserve advantage for some time. The moat can come in the form of technology, the use of technology, a brand, enduring customer relationships, channel relationships, size or scale, or simply a really big head start into a business making it hard or even impossible for competitors to catch up. The appraisal of a "moat" is hardly an exact science; here we give our Top 10 picks based on the size and strength (width?) of the moat:

▼ Moat Stars

TOP 10 STOCKS FOR SUSTAINABLE COMPETITIVE ADVANTAGE

Company	Symbol	Dividend	Yield %
Apple, Inc.	AAPL	0.00	0.0
Boeing	BA	1.16	2.8
CarMax	KMX	0.00	0.0
Fair Isaac	FICO	0.08	0.4
Iron Mountain	IRM	0.25	1.1
McCormick & Co.	MKC	1.04	2.7
Patterson	PDCP	0.40	2.4
Sysco	SYY	1.00	3.4
Valmont	VMI	0.66	0.9
W.W. Grainger	BWW	2.16	2.2

Table 10. Moat Stars.

Tenets, Anyone? The Essentials of Successful Investing

The 100 Best Stocks You Can Buy 2011 is designed to help you get started with picking stocks suitable for you. But rather than simply giving you fish (which may not be the freshest fish by the time they reach you), we feel it is also important to give you some investing groundwork to use in your own investing practice, as well as to help explain some of our guiding principles.

We do not intend to give a complete course on investing, or value investing, here. That probably wasn't the purpose you had in mind when you bought this book, and there isn't space here for a complete discussion anyway. For a more complete treatment of the topic, refer to my title *Value Investing for Dummies* (second edition, Wiley, 2008).

At the risk of sounding "corporate," what makes sense here is to give a high level overview of key investing "tenets" to keep top of mind and back of mind as you sift through the thousands of investment choices. By absorbing these principles, you'll gain a better understanding of the 100 Best Stocks list and take away ideas to help with your own investment choices outside the list.

Buy Like You're Buying a Business

Already covered this one but it's worth repeating: by buying shares of a corporation you are really buying a share of a business. The more you can approach the decision as if you were buying the entire business yourself, the better.

Buy What You Know and Understand

Two of the most widely followed investment "gurus" of our age, Peter Lynch and Warren Buffett, have stressed the idea of buying businesses you know about and understand. This idea naturally follows the entrepreneurial idea of buying stocks as if you were buying a business; if you didn't understand the business, would you be comfortable buying it?

Peter Lynch, former manager of the enormous Fidelity Magellan fund and author of the well known 1989 bestseller *One Up on Wall Street*, gave us the original notion of buying what you know. He suggests that the best investment ideas are those you see—and can learn about and keep track of—in daily life, on the street, on the job, in the mall, in your home. A company like Starbucks makes sense to Lynch because you can readily see the value proposition and how it extends beyond coffee, and can follow customer response and business activity at least in part just by hanging around your own neighborhood edition.

Buffett has famously stuck with businesses that are easy to understand—paint, carpet, electric utilities, with his investments (though he deals with the fantastically complicated businesses of casualty insurance and reinsurance in his core Berkshire Hathaway business). He has shunned technology investments because he doesn't understand them, and more than likely, because their value and consumer preference shifts too fast for him to keep up.

Both approaches make sense, and especially in hindsight, would have kept us farther from trouble in the 2008–2009 crash. Many, many investors didn't understand financial firms as well as they should have; the preponderance of evidence suggests that those financial firms didn't even understand themselves!

Clearly, you won't understand everything about the businesses you invest in—there's a lot of complexity and detail even behind the cooking and serving of hamburgers at McDonalds! Further, a sizeable amount of good knowledge is confidential so you likely won't ever get your hands on it. So you need to go with what you know and realize that a lot of the devil is in the detail. When you analyze a company, if you can say "the more you know the better" instead of "the more you know the more you don't know," you'll be better off.

Greater Trends Are Important

Popular expressions abound about the idea of staying in touch with the big picture when you make any sort of decision. *Don't lose the forest in the trees, keep an eye on the prize,* and so forth. These phrases enjoy no finer hour than tied in with the subject of investing.

We already covered the notion that technologies and consumer tastes change, and with them so do businesses—at least the good ones. Add to this the idea of change brought on by demographic trends (the aging of the population, for instance) and changes in law and policy (toward "green," for instance) and you end up with a wide assortment of "forest" influences that can affect your stock picks.

Sector analysis is employed by many investors as a starting point. Where sector analysis does make sense is in capturing and correctly assessing the larger trends in that sector or industry. The sector thus becomes the arena in which to appraise those trends, often by reading sector analysis published in the media or in trade publications in that sector. One can, and should, learn about the construction industry or health care industry before investing in a company in that industry.

Once the sector trends are understood, a selection of a company, or companies, in that sector can make more sense. A good example is offered by PC makers Hewlett-Packard (a 100 Best Stocks choice) and Dell Computer (not a choice). Dell was the darling of the sector for years, achieving high margins and return on equity, market share growth, and popular marketplace preference for years. The direct sales model seemed unbeatable as a way to reduce costs and avoid obsolescence, and the just-in-time supply chain model, using accounts payable as a primary financing mechanism, all seemed strategically right.

But change was in the air for the PC industry. Lower prices, greater standardization and the migration to laptops all pointed to HP's retail-centric model. No longer was it necessary, or even advantageous, for customers to order direct from Dell. With more standardized computing applications and inexpensive technology, there was less need to customize computers. With laptops, displays, size, and look and feel are more important than simple "speeds and feeds" and people want to see what they were buying. Finally, as costs came down, a PC, laptop or otherwise, was simply something to pick up at a local store. I predict PCs will soon sell in Walgreens, and if you don't believe that, consider that VCRs and DVD players also followed that thought-to-be-impossible path.

So HP ended up in the right place with their emphasis on the retail channel (Dell struggles as a latecomer) and further, was strategically correct in their emphasis on printers and high margin consumables that go with them, and in their emphasis on international markets. Dell has fallen by the wayside on all counts, hence their 80 percent price drop from 2000 and 70 percent drop from their 2005 price peaks, respectively.

So again the lesson, or "tenet," is to understand the greater trends in the economy, in the market, in the sector, and in the industry. If you buy a business, you want to know about the industry, right? Who the competitors are, how they compete, about the market and customer needs and customer tastes, and how companies do business in that market. Right? You want to understand the *future* of that industry and market, right? It's no different when you buy shares.

One more thing to add: most of the time I try to buy what I think to be the best company in the sector—best based on past, current and expected future performance. But sometimes it makes sense, from an opportunity viewpoint, to "play the Avis game," that is, to buy a more nimble, more aggressive, less arrogant or complacent number two competitor. Such a company is leaner, meaner, hungrier, and likely sells for a more reasonable price. Sometimes I'll buy both if I feel the industry or sector is large enough to support two strong competitors, and if there are large enough or strong enough niches available so they won't become cutthroat competitors.

For example, I own Starbucks (a 100 Best Stock) and Caribou Coffee, a much smaller competitor located largely in the upper Midwest. There are two reasons for this choice. One, I felt that the Caribou brand caché would work well in Minnesota and similar places. Second, and more importantly, I liked Caribou's franchising model as a contrast to Starbucks' company owned model (which now may be starting to change with the announcement of franchising for their own subsidiary Seattle's Best). Caribou just might do well capturing business with ambitious franchisees doing the work and understanding local markets best.

Niche and Get Rich

In understanding sectors, industries and markets it's important to consider success opportunities for niche players. A "niche" is a small captive market segment, usually too small for the biggest competitors to profitably consider, but still lucrative for a smaller, more nimble player. Niche players can define and play smaller markets based on product, location or geography, distribution channels or other differentiators like language. Caribou is an example, capturing the franchising niche. Or McCormick & Co. (a 100 Best Stock) capturing the spice niche in a larger food and beverage industry.

For more on niche marketing, see *Niche and Get Rich—Practical Ways to Turn Your Ideas Into a Business* (Entrepreneur Press, 2003), a book I did with my wife Jennifer back in 2003. It is aimed at small business, but (not by design) offers useful material for investing, too.

Stick to the Real Stuff

If you're familiar with accounting or the accounting profession, contrary to public perception, accounting for business assets and activity is not always a precise science. In fact, there can be quite a bit of art involved in accounting, especially for business assets and business income.

Why? Because, while the purchase *price* for most "physical" assets is known, the *value* of those assets over time is a subjective calculation. And there are many assets, like intellectual property, that elude precise evaluation altogether. How much is a patent worth? How much is an acquired business worth? Just like a stock you buy, you know what you paid for it, but how much is it really worth in terms of future returns to the acquiring company? It's a subjective number.

Likewise, reported net income can be fairly subjective, too. How much depreciation expense was taken against assets, and thus against income? How much "expense" was taken to write down intangible assets like patents and other intellectual property? How much "restructuring" expense was incurred? The rules give the accountants and corporate management quite a bit of flexibility to "manage" reported earnings, and asset values as well: what you see may not always be what you get.

The bottom line is this: while assets and income have at least some sub-jectivity in their valuation, debts are quite real, and so is cash. Debts must be paid sooner or later; there is no subjectivity or "art" to their valuation. Likewise, cash is cash, the stuff in the proverbial drawer, and is a take-it-or-leave-it, like-it-or-not fact of life or death for a business.

Thus, as value investors, we look at assets and income as important mea-sures of business activity, but know that there's some subjectivity in those measures. At the same time, we look at debts and cash and cash flow in and out of the business as absolute; neither cash nor debt lie. So we hang our valuation hats on cash and debt where we can.

Now, in particular, cash isn't an absolute measure of business success, either, for there are timing issues. Suppose you are running an airline, and decide this is the year to buy an airplane. A huge cash outflow, possibly matched by a cash inflow from a borrowing. Are this year's cash flow state-ments fully representative of the firm's success or failure? No, because the airplane will be used over a number of years, and the cost of the airplane must be divvied up among those years and matched to airfares collected and other costs to truly understand performance. So that's where conventional income accounting comes in—it helps to do that.

All that said, sharp value investors learn to look for companies that, over time, *produce* capital, in contrast to companies that *consume* it. As judged by the statement of cash flows, a company that produces more cash from opera-tions than it consumes in investing activities (capital equipment purchases mainly) and in financing activities (repaying debt, dividends, etc.) is produc-ing capital. When a company must always go to the capital markets to make up for a deficit in operating or investing cash flow, that's a sign of trouble, which is incidentally borne out by the other absolute measure—debt. If debt is high and especially increasing and especially if it is increasing faster than the business is growing—look out. Or at least, look for a story, like company XYZ is going through a known, understood and rational expansion that needs to be funded. Going to the capital markets to fund operational cash deficits is an especially bad thing to do.

Thus, as an investor, you should always pay attention to assets and income, but even closer attention to cash and debt. This tenet was used in identifying the 100 Best Stocks.

What Makes a Best Stock Best?

So now we get down to brass tacks. Now, the rubber meets the road. Just exactly what is it that separates the wheat from the chaff, the cream from the milk, the great from the merely good? What is it that defines excellence—sustainable excellence—among companies? That's been a topic of considerable debate for years, and with all the study that's gone into it, it's amazing that nobody has hit upon a single formula for deciphering undeniable excellence in a company.

That's largely because it isn't as scientific as most of us would like or expect it to be. It defies mathematical formulas. Take the square of net profits, multiply by the cosine of the debt-to-equity ratio, add the square root of the revenue-per-employee count, and what do you get? Some nice numbers, but not a clear picture of how it works together nor how a company will sell its products to customers and prosper going forward.

Business and financial analysts study such fundamentals, and well they should. Fundamentals such as profitability, productivity and asset efficiency tell us how well a company has done and by proxy, how well it is managed and how well it has done in the marketplace. Fundamentals are about what the company has already achieved, and where it stands right now, and if a company's current fundamentals are a mess, stop right now, there isn't much point in going any farther.

But in most cases, what really separates great from good is the intangibles, the "soft" factors of market position, market acceptance, customer "love" of a company's products, its management, its aura that really make the difference. These features create competitive advantage, or "distinctive competence" as an economist would put it, that cannot be valued. Furthermore and most importantly, they are more about what a company is set up to achieve in the future.

Buffett put it best: Give me $100 billion, and I could start a company. But I could never create another Coca-Cola.

What does that mean? It means that Coke has already established a worldwide brand caché, the distribution channels, the product development expertise that cannot be duplicated at any cost. When companies have competitive advantages that cannot be duplicated at any cost, they have an enduring grip on their markets. They can charge more for their products. They have a "moat" that insulates them from competition, or makes it much more expensive for competitors to participate. They're perceived by loyal customers as being top-line products worth paying more for.

A company with exceptional intangibles can control price and in many cases, can control its costs.

LUV—A GREAT EXPERIENCE. BUT IS IT A GOOD INVESTMENT?

One way to learn a principle is to examine what happens when the principle does not apply. One industry where most of the fundamentals and almost all the intangibles work against it is the airline industry. Airlines cannot control price, because of competition, and because an airplane trip is an airplane trip. Aside from serving different snacks or offering better schedules, there is little an airline can do to differentiate their product, and almost nothing they can do to justify charging a higher price. Further, they have no control over costs—like fuel prices, union contracts and airport landing fees. While some airlines offer good service, there is almost nothing they can do to distinguish themselves as excellent companies or excellent investments. Southwest Airlines (ticker symbol LUV) came closest by offering simplicity, efficiency, a loyal customer base and excellent management, and was rewarded for many years with a market cap greater than all other U.S. airlines combined, but it lands short of being an excellent company to invest in.

Strategic Fundamentals

Without any further ado, let's examine a list of "strategic fundamentals" that define, or keep score of, a company's success. This list can be used as a checklist, although it's hard to find a company that shows excellence in all of these areas.

Are gross and operating profit margins growing?

I like profitable companies; who doesn't? But what really counts is the size of the margin and especially the growth. If a company has a gross margin (sales minus costs of goods sold) exceeding that of its competitors, that shows that it's doing something right, probably with its customers and/or with its costs. But competitive analysis is elusive; there is no dependable source of "industry" gross margins, and comparing competitors can be difficult because no two companies are exactly alike; it's easy to mix apples and oranges.

So I like to see what direction gross margin is moving in—up or down. A growing gross margin also signals that the company is doing something right. That isn't perfect either; as the economy moved from boom to bust many excellent companies reported declines in gross and especially operating margins (sales – cost of goods sold – operating expenses) as they laid off workers and used less capacity. Still, in a steady state environment, it makes sense to favor companies with growing margins. In a declining market, companies that can *protect* their margins will come out ahead.

Does a company produce more capital than it consumes?

Make no mistake about it—I like cash. And pure and simple—I like it when a company produces more cash than it consumes.

At the end of the day, cash generation is the simplest measure of whether a company is being successful, especially over the long term. Sure, if a company buys an airplane or opens a factory or a bunch of stores in a given quarter, it will be cash-flow negative. But that should be a temporary thing; over the long haul, it should produce, not consume cash. Companies that continually have to borrow or sell shares to raise enough cash to stay in business are on the wrong track.

So how do you determine this? You'll have to become familiar with the Statement of Cash Flows or equivalent in a company's financial reports. "Cash flow from operations" is usually positive and represents cash booked from sales less cost of goods sold, with adjustments for non-cash items like depreciation and for increases or decreases in working capital. In simple terms, is the cash going into the cash register from the business.

"Cash used for investing purposes" or similar is a bit of a misnomer, and represents net cash used to "invest" in the business—usually for capital expenditures but also for short-term non-cash investments like securities and a few other smaller items usually beyond scope. This figure is typically negative unless the company sells some part of its infrastructure. Over the long haul, cash generated from operations should well exceed cash used to invest in the business.

Companies in expansion mode may not show this surplus, and that's where "cash from financing activities" comes in. That's the cash generated from issuing debt or selling securities—or paying off debt or repurchasing shares, if things are going well, and dividends are included here as well. Again, a successful company will produce more cash—capital—from the business than it consumes, just as a successful household does the same, else it goes into debt. Smart investors track this surplus over time.

Are expenses under control?

Again, just like your household, company expenses should be under control, and anything else, especially without explanation, is a yellow flag.

The best way to test this is to check whether "Selling, General and Administrative" expenses—so called "SG&A" are rising, and more to the point, rising faster than sales. If so, that's a yellow, not necessarily a red, flag, but if it continues, it suggests that something is out of control, and it will catch up with the company sooner or later. In the recent downturn, companies that were able to reduce their expenses to match revenue declines score more points, too.

Is non-cash working capital under control?

Working capital is a hard concept to grasp—even for small entrepreneurs who live with its ups and downs on a daily basis. Insufficient working capital is one of the biggest causes of death for small businesses, and working capital and especially changes in working capital can signal success or trouble.

Using a simplistic analogy, working capital is the circulatory lifeblood of the business. Money comes in, money goes out, working capital is what circulates in the veins in between. In its purest sense, it is cash, receivables, and inventory, less short-term debts. It's what you own less what you owe aside from fixed assets like plant, stores, equipment.

If receivables are increasing, that sounds like a good thing—more people owe you more money. But if receivables are rising and sales aren't, that suggests that people aren't paying their bills, or worse, the business has to finance more to achieve the same level of sales. Similarly, a rise in inventory without a rise in sales means that it costs the business more money—more working capital—to do the same amount of business. That costs twice, because unless the firm is lucky, more inventory means more obsolescence and potentially more write-offs down the road.

So a sharp investor will check to see that major working capital items—receivables and inventory—aren't growing faster than sales; indeed, a company that generates more sales with a decrease in working capital is becoming more productive.

Is debt in line with business growth?

Like many other "fundamental" items, you can tear your hair out looking at debt figures and trying to decide whether they're in line with asset levels, equity levels and industry norms. A simpler test is to check and see whether long-term debt is increasing or decreasing, and in particular, whether it is increasing faster than business growth. Gold stars go to companies with little to no debt, and to companies able to grow without issuing mountains of long-term debt.

Is earnings growth steady?

I enter the danger zone here, because the management of many companies have learned to "manage" earnings to provide a steady improvement, always "beating the street" by a penny or two. So stability is a good thing for all investors, and companies that can manage toward stability get extra points, and it's worth checking for, but with the proverbial grain of salt.

Still, a company that is able to manage its sales, earnings, cash flow, and debt levels more consistently than competitors, and perhaps more consistently than what would be suggested by the ups and downs of the economy is desirable—or at least more desirable than the alternatives.

Is return on equity steady or growing?

Return on equity is another of those hard to grasp concepts, and another measure subject to subjectivity in valuing assets and earnings. But at the end of the day, it's what all investors really seek, that is, returns on their capital investments.

And like many other figures derived from income statements and balance sheets, a pure number is hard to interpret—does a 26.7 percent ROE mean, in itself, that a company is excellent? The figure sounds healthy, to be sure—it's a heck of a lot better than investing your money in a CD or T-Bill. But because earnings and asset values are subjective, it may not represent true success. In fact, a company can increase ROE simply by borrowing money (yes!) and investing it into the business, even if it isn't invested as productively as other previous funds invested. The math is complicated; I won't go into it here.

So the true test of ROE success is to check whether it is steady or increasing. Increasing—that makes sense. Why *steady*? Because if a company makes profits in a previous period and reinvests them in the business, that amount of money becomes part of equity (retained earnings). If the company reinvests productively, it will produce more returns, and ROE will at least keep up. If the company can't reinvest those earnings productively, ROE will drop—and perhaps it should be paying the earnings to you as dividends instead of investing them unproductively in the business. So if ROE is steady, the company still has good investments to make, and management is probably doing the right thing.

Does the company pay a dividend?

Different people feel differently about dividends, and as shown earlier, we're placing a greater emphasis on dividend paying stocks this year. After all, save for the eventual sale of the company to someone else, a dividend is the only true cash that an investor will realize from buying a stock in a corporation, other than by selling the stock. And, at least in theory, investors should receive some compensation for their investments once in a while.

Yet, most companies tend not to pay dividends, or don't pay dividends that compete very effectively with fixed income yields. So why do investors put up with this? Because, in theory anyway, a company in a good business should be able to reinvest profits more effectively than the investor can (else why would the investor have bought the company in the first place?). And, investors trust that reinvested profits will eventually bring the growth in company value that will be reflected in the share price or eventual takeover or an eventual payment of a dividend or growth in that dividend.

That's the theory, anyway. But there are still lots of companies that get away with paying no dividend in all. Can we tolerate this? Yes, if a company is really doing a great job. But I favor companies that offer at least something to their investors in the short term, some return on their hard-earned and faithfully committed capital. If nothing else, it keeps management teams honest, and shows that management understands that shareholder interests are up there somewhere on the list of priorities.

A dividend is a plus. Lack of a dividend isn't necessarily a showstopper, but it suggests a closer look. A dividend reduction—and there were many in the past year—suggests poor financial and operational health, because the dividend is usually the last thing to go, but in some cases reflects management prudence and conservatism. Best question to ask yourself: would you have reduced the dividend if you were running the company? And down the road, does the company bring back the dividend as times get better? A "no" to either of these questions is troubling.

Finally, dividend payouts should be examined over time. We've seen—and included in our lists—a number of companies that have steadily increased dividends—many for each of the eight previous years. We like this; it's just like getting an annual raise, and if you hold the stock long enough, the percentage return against your original investment can get quite large, even approaching 100 percent per year if the stock is held long enough and the dividend is raised persistently enough. Getting an ever-increasing dividend—and owning a stock that has most likely appreciated because the dividend has increased—is like having your cake and eating it too—a true favorite among investors.

ARE VALUATION RATIOS IN LINE?

One of the most difficult tasks in investing is determining the true value—and per-share value—of a company. If this were easy, you'd just determine a value, compare it to the price, and if the price were lower than the value, push the buy button.

Professional investors try to determine what they call "intrinsic value" of a company, which is usually the sum of all projected future cash flows of a company, discounted back to the present (remember, money received tomorrow is both less predictable and less valuable than money received now). They use complex math models, specifically, "discounted cash flow" or DCF models, to project, then discount, earnings flows. But those models—especially for the individual investor, depend too much on the crystal-ball accuracy of earnings forecasts, and the so-called discount rate is a highly theoretical construct beyond the scope of most individual investors. DCF models require a lot of estimates and number crunching, especially if multiple scenarios are employed as they should be. They take more time than it's worth for the individual investor. If you're an institutional investor buying multimillion-share stakes, I would conclude otherwise.

Valuation ratios are a shorthand way to determine if a stock price is acceptable relative to value. By far and away the most popular of these ratios is the so-called "price-to-earnings" or P/E, ratio, a measure of the stock price usually compared to "ttm," or trailing twelve months' earnings, but also sometimes compared to future earnings.

The P/E ratio correlates well to your expected return on an investment you might make in the company. For instance, if the P/E is 10, the price is 10 times the past, or perhaps expected, annual earnings of the company. Take the reciprocal of that—1 divided by 10—and you get 0.10, or 10 percent. That's known as "earnings yield," the theoretical yield you'd get if all earnings were paid to you as dividends as an owner. Ten percent is pretty healthy compared to returns on other investments, so a P/E of 10 suggests success.

But of course, the earnings may not be consistent or sustainable, or there may be substantial risk from factors intrinsic to the company, or there may be exogenous risk factors, like the total meltdown of the economy. The more risk, the more instability, the lower the expected P/E should be, for the earnings stream is less stable. If you think the earnings stream is solid and stable in the face of the risk, then the stock may be truly undervalued. Look for P/Es that (1) suggest strong earnings yield and (2) are favorable compared to competitors and the industry.

Apart from P/E, the price-to-sales ratio (P/S), price to cash flow (P/CF), and price to free cash flow (P/FCF) are often used as fundamental yardsticks. Like P/E, these measures also have some ambiguities, and it's best to think about them in real-world, entrepreneurial terms. Would you pay three times annual sales for a business and sleep well at night? Probably not—unless it's profit margins were exceptionally high. So if a P/S ratio is 3 or above, look out; and opt for a business with a P/S of 1 or less if you can. Similarly, the price to cash flow ratios can be thought of as true return going into your pocket for your investment; is it enough? Is it enough given the risk? And about the difference between "cash flow" and "free cash flow:" the difference is mostly cash laid out for capital expenditures, so it's worth making this distinction, although the lumpiness of capital expenditures makes consistent application of this number elusive. Incidentally, I don't regard price-to-book value (P/B) ratios as that helpful, because the book value of a company can be very elusive and arbitrary unless most of a company's assets are in cash or other easy-to-value forms.

Companies with high P/E, P/S, P/B, and P/CF ratios aren't necessarily bad investments, but you need to have good reasons to look beyond these figures if they suggest truly inadequate business results.

Strategic Intangibles

When you look at any company, perhaps the bottom line question follows the Buffett wisdom: if you had $100 billion to spend (and we'll assume, the genius intellect to spend it right), could you recreate that company?

If the answer is "yes," it may still be a great company, but it may not be great enough to fend off competition and keep its customers forever. If the answer is "no," the company truly has something unique to offer in the marketplace, difficult to duplicate at any cost. That distinctive competence, that sustainable competitive edge—whatever it is, a brand, a trade secret, a lock on distribution or supply channels, may be worth more than all the factories and high rise office buildings and cash in the bank it could ever have.

What we're talking about are the intangibles, the "soft" factors that make companies unique, that add up to more than the sum of their parts, the factors that ultimately drive future revenues. Intangibles not only define excellence, they define the future, while fundamentals mainly define the past. Seven key intangibles, follow, although you'll think of more, and some industries may have some unique ones of their own, like technology and intellectual property:

DOES THE COMPANY HAVE A MOAT?

A business "moat" performs much the same role as the medieval castle equivalent—it protects the business from competition. Whatever factors, some discussed below, create the moat, ultimately those are the factors that prevent you, with your $100 billion, from taking their business. Moats are usually a combination of brand, product technology, design, marketing and distribution channels, and customer loyalty all working together to protect a company. A moat doesn't just protect the existence of a company, it helps it command higher prices and earn higher profits.

Whether a company has a "narrow" moat, a "wide" moat, or none at all is a subjective assessment for you to make. However, you can get some help at Morningstar (*www.morningstar.com*) whose stock ratings include an assessment of the moat.

Coca-Cola has a moat because of the sheer impossibility of surpassing its brand and brand recognition worldwide. CarMax has a moat because it is farther along in putting retail-style dealerships on the ground and applying management information technologies to its business than anyone else; it would take years for a competitor to catch up. This year, we added a "Moat Stars" list to identify the Top 10 stocks with a solid and sustainable competitive advantage.

DOES THE COMPANY HAVE AN EXCELLENT BRAND?

It's hard to say enough about brand, especially in today's fast moving, highly packaged, highly national and international culture. A strong brand means consistency and a promise to consumers, and consumers sold on a brand will prefer it over any other, almost regardless of price. People still buy Tide, and although there's been a slowdown lately, Starbucks is still synonymous with a high quality and ambience. Good brands command higher prices and foster loyalty and identity and even customer "love." Again, using the Starbucks example, websites appeared soliciting customer appeals to not close stores during the recent store closing initiative; when has anyone (other than a worker) offered so much resistance to closing a U.S. auto plant? Once a company has created a dominant brand (or brands, in the case of P&G) in the marketplace, aside from some major faux pas, they will endure and continue to create value for shareholders for years to come; a good brand is one of the most valuable (yet hard to value) long-term assets around.

Ask yourself if a company has a sought-after brand, a brand customers would pay extra to buy or align with, a brand that would be difficult to duplicate at any cost. Would customers rather fight than switch? Think about Starbucks, Coca-Cola, Heinz, Nike, or the brands within a house, like Frito-Lay (Pepsi) or Tide (P&G).

IS THE COMPANY A MARKET LEADER?

Market leadership usually—but not always—goes hand in hand with brand. The trick is to decide whether a company really leads in its industry. Often—but not always—that's a factor of size. The market leader usually has the highest market share, and the important point is that it calls the shots with regards to price, technology, marketing message, and so forth—other companies must play catch up and often discount their prices to keep up. Apple is a market leader in digital music, Intel is the market leader in microprocessors, Toyota is emerging as the market leader in automobiles.

Excellent companies tend to be market leaders, and market leaders tend to be excellent companies. But this relationship doesn't always hold true—sometimes the nimble but smaller competitor is the excellent company—and will likely assume market leadership eventually. Examples like CarMax, Nucor, Perrigo and Peet's Coffee and Tea can be found on our list.

DOES THE COMPANY HAVE CHANNEL EXCELLENCE?

"Channels" in business parlance means a chain of players to sell and distribute a company's products. It might be stores, it might be other industrial companies, it might be direct to the consumer. If a company is considered a top supplier in a particular channel, or a company has especially good relations with its channel, that's a plus.

Excellent companies develop solid channel relationships and become the preferred supplier in those channels. Companies like Dentsply, Patterson, Fair Isaac, McCormick, Nike, Pepsi, Procter & Gamble and Sysco could all have excellent relationships with their channels through which they sell their product.

DOES THE COMPANY HAVE SUPPLY CHAIN EXCELLENCE?

Like distribution channels, excellent companies develop excellent and low cost supply channels. They are seldom caught off guard by supply shortages and tend to get favorable and stable prices for whatever they buy. This is often not an easy assessment unless you know something about a particular industry.

DOES THE COMPANY HAVE EXCELLENT MANAGEMENT?

Well, it's not hard to grasp what happens if a company *doesn't* have good management; performance fails and few inside or outside the company respect the company. It's not easy for an investor to determine if a management team does a good job or acts in shareholder interests. Clues can include candor and honesty and the ability of company management to speak in accessible, easily understood terms about the company and company performance (it's worth listening to conference calls as a resource). A management team that admits errors and eschews other forms of arrogance and entitlement (i.e. luxury perks, office suites, aircraft) is probably tilting his or her interests toward shareholders, as is the management team that can cough up some return to shareholders once in a while as a dividend.

This may be the most subjective and elusive assessment of all, as few investors work with these folks on a daily basis. Still, over time, you can garner a strong hunch about whether a management team is effective and on your side.

Are there signs of innovation excellence?

This question seems pretty obvious, but it's not just about the products that a company sells. True, if the company is leading the industry in innovation, that's usually a good thing, for "first to market" definitely offers business advantages.

The less obvious part of this question is whether the company makes the best *use* of technology to make operations and customer interfaces as efficient and effective as possible. Again, Southwest Airlines didn't make our list because of the sheer impossibility of achieving excellence in an industry where players can't control prices or costs. But they do make our list in terms of innovation excellence. Why? Simply because, after all of these years, amazingly, they still have the best, simplest, easiest-to-use flight booking and checking flight in the industry. Sometimes these sorts of innovations mean a lot more than bringing new fancy products and bells and whistles to the market. And one can also look to Apple, Google, and CarMax on our list for more obvious examples.

IT PAYS TO FIND A SMART FRIEND IN THE BUSINESS

Most publicly traded companies are required to report their fundamentals on a quarterly and an annual basis. Income statement, balance sheet, statement of cash flows. That's good, because we as investors can easily see how the company is performing; we don't need to get on the phone with the CFO to check the progress of our investment.

But what about the intangibles? Companies are required to report exactly nothing of their brand strength, market position, new product pipeline, or management style. Sure, you may read a lot in an annual report, but it's as much a spin, a marketing message to investors, as it is the real "scoop" about what is or what's going to be.

So how do you fill this information gap? One way is to keep up with the trade press and trade publications of the industry you invest in. Like technology stocks? Read technology magazines and websites and the technology sections of the *Wall Street Journal* and the *New York Times*. But if you really want the inside scoop, make friends with people who work in the industry. They are (or should be) experts in their business. They know the products and the competition. It's not so much that they'll divulge trade secrets about the company they work for; that isn't the point. Instead, they'll help you see where the puck is going for the industry, their company, and other players in their industry. The thousand words you get from a friend in the business can be worth far more than the picture in the annual report.

SIGNS OF VALUE

Following are a few signs of value to look for in any company. Not an exhaustive list by any means, but a good place to start:

- » Gaining market share
- » Loyal customers
- » Growing margins
- » Producing, not consuming, capital (free cash flow)
- » Steady or increasing ROE
- » Management forthcoming, honest, understandable

SIGNS OF UNVALUE

. . . and signs of trouble, or "unvalue:"

- » Declining margins
- » No brand or who-cares brand
- » Commodity producer, must compete on price
- » Losing market dominance or market share
- » Can't control costs
- » Must acquire other companies to grow
- » Management in hiding, off message or difficult to understand

Choosing the 100 Best

So with all of this in mind, just how were this year's 100 Best Stocks list actually chosen? It's probably about time, after pages and pages, to get to that.

The answer is a little more subtle than you might think. If we could give you a precise formula, you wouldn't need this book. You'd be able to do it yourself. In fact, every investor would be able to do it on their own. Our book would simply be the result of yet another stock screener. And every investor would invest in the same stocks. Is that a feasible or practical solution? Hardly. Everyone would scramble to buy the same 100 Best Stocks. The prices would be sky high, and the price of other stocks would melt to nothing.

Fortunately or unfortunately, however you want to look at it, it isn't that simple. There are too many fundamentals and too many intangibles and too many unknown and unknowable weighting factors to combine the fundamentals and intangibles that—well—it just wouldn't work. No screener could recreate the subtle judgment that gets applied to the hard, cold facts. It's that judgment, the interpretation of the facts and intangibles, that makes it worth spending money on a book like this.

While we didn't apply a specific formula or screener to the universe of stocks, we did take a few measurable factors into account to narrow the list from thousands to a few hundred issues. Those factors came from several sources, but at this point we must tip our cap to Value Line and the research and database work they do as part of the Value Line Investment Survey. If you aren't familiar with Value Line, it's worth a look for any savvy individual investor, either online at *www.valueline.com* or, in many cases, at your local library. It is an excellent resource.

Anyway, here are some of the measured factors we looked into, most of which go beyond individual facts or items and instead are measures of strength or performance compiled from a number of factors. In this way, we gain some leverage for not having to deal with lots of little bits of individual data. Here are six metrics we use as a starting point to select and sort stocks for further review:

- *S&P Rating* is a broad corporate credit rating reflecting the ability to cover indebtedness, in turn reflecting business levels, business trends, cash flow, and sustained performance. It's a bit like the credit score you might use or might have used on you to determine your own personal credit risk.
- *Value Line Financial Strength Rating* is used much like the S&P rating except that it goes further into overall balance sheet and cash flow strength. It should be noted that several companies with "B" ratings were selected; these are typically newer companies that will grow into A companies or that may have been hit harder by the recession than others.
- *Value Line Earnings Predictability* is what it sounds like; a calculated tendency of companies to deliver consistent and predictable earnings without surprises.
- *Value Line Growth Persistence* is again what it sounds like—the company's ability to consistently grow even in weaker economic times.

- *Value Line Price Stability* reflects the stability and relative safety of a company. Again, we did not reject a company out of hand due to volatility, rather, if stability was low, we tried to make a case that the business, business model, and intangibles were worth the risk.
- *Dividends and yield.* Companies that pay something are held in higher regard; however, again, it is not by any means an absolute criterion.

With these facts and figures in mind, the evaluation proceeded with a close eye on the "signs of value" and intangibles mentioned above. Some consideration was also given to diversification; we did not want to overweight any sector or industry but instead to give you a healthy assortment of stocks to pick from across a variety of industries.

With these thoughts in mind, you can make more sense of the companies we picked. And of course, full disclosure and full disclaimer—we didn't do *all* the analysis. We couldn't have. It wouldn't have made any sense anyway, for things would have changed from the time we did it, and it might not match your preferences anyway. So it is of utmost importance for you to take our selections and analysis and make them yours—that is, do the due diligence to further qualify these picks as congruent with your investment needs.

The Surgeon General would label this book as "hazardous to your wealth" if you didn't.

Strategic Investing

Although this book is designed to help you pick the best stocks to buy, investing by nature goes well beyond simply buying stocks, just like owning an automobile goes far beyond buying it. Just as clearly, this book isn't about investing strategy, nor about the personal financial strategies necessary to ensure retirement or a prosperous future. That said, I think a few words are in order.

I find that a lot of investors lose the forest in the trees, spending all of their energy trying to find individual stocks or funds without putting enough consideration into their overall investing framework. If they look at the big picture at all, they look at the formulaic covenants of asset allocation, a favorite subject of the financial planning and advisory community, as though the difference between 50 percent equities and 60 percent equities makes all the difference in the world. Sure, it might in the world of pension funds and other institutional investments, where a 10 percent adjustment could move millions into or out of a particular asset class and more or less toward safety, but what about a $100,000 portfolio? Does $10,000 more or less in stocks, bonds or cash make that much difference?

Perhaps not. And of course there's more to that story—doesn't it matter more which equities you invest in than just the fact that you're 60 percent in equities? So while asset allocation models make for nice pie charts, I prefer to approach big-picture portfolio constructs differently.

Start with a Portfolio in Mind

First, I'll make an assumption. That assumption is simply this: you are not a professional investor. You have other things to do with your time, and time is of the essence. You cannot spend forty, fifty, or sixty hours a week glued to a computer screen analyzing your investments.

To that assumption I'll add another: that, as an individual investor, you're looking to beat the market. Not by a ton—20 percent sustained returns simply aren't possible without taking outlandish risks. But perhaps if the market is up 4 percent in a year, you'd like to achieve, 5, 6, perhaps 7 percent without taking excessive risks. Or if the market is down 20 percent, perhaps you cut your losses at 5 or 10 percent. You're looking to do *somewhat* better than the market.

Because of time constraints, and owing to your objective to do slightly better than averages, I suggest taking a tiered approach to your portfolio. The tiers aren't based on the type of assets; they're based on the amount of activity and attention you want to pay to different parts of your portfolio. It's a strategic portfolio approach you would probably take if you were managing a small business—put most of your focus on the products and customers who might bring the greatest new return to your business; let the rest of your slow steady customer base function as it has for the long term.

I suggest breaking up your portfolio into three tiers, or segments. This can be done by setting up specific accounts; or less formally by simply applying the model as a thought process.

We can't go much further without defining the three segments:

THE FOUNDATION PORTFOLIO

In this construct each investor defines and manages a cornerstone foundation portfolio, which is long term in nature and requires relatively less active management. Frequently the foundation portfolio consists of retirement accounts (the paradigmatic long-term investment) and may also include your personal residence or other long-lived personal or family assets, such as trusts, collectibles and so forth. The typical foundation portfolio is invested to achieve at least average market returns through index funds, quality mutual funds, and some income-producing assets like bond held to maturity. A foundation portfolio may contain some long-term plays in

Active Portfolio Segmentation

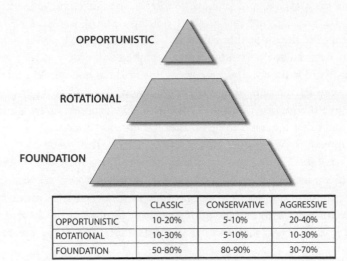

OPPORTUNISTIC

ROTATIONAL

FOUNDATION

	CLASSIC	CONSERVATIVE	AGGRESSIVE
OPPORTUNISTIC	10-20%	5-10%	20-40%
ROTATIONAL	10-30%	5-10%	10-30%
FOUNDATION	50-80%	80-90%	30-70%

commodities or real estate to defend against inflation, particularly in such commodities as energy, precious metals, and real estate trusts. The foundation portfolio is largely left alone, although as with all investments it is important to check at least once in a while to make sure performance—and managers if involved—are keeping up with expectations.

THE ROTATIONAL PORTFOLIO

The second segment, the rotational portfolio, is managed fairly actively to keep up with changes in business cycles and conditions. It is likely in a set of stocks or funds that might be rotated or remixed occasionally to reflect business conditions or to get a little more offensive or defensive. More than the other portfolios, this portfolio follows the rotation of market preference among different kinds of businesses and business assets. The portfolio is managed to redeploy assets among market or business sectors, between aggressive and defensive business assets, from "large cap" to "small cap" companies from companies with international exposure to those with little of same, from companies in favor versus out of favor, from stocks to bonds to commodities, and so forth. Sector-specific exchange-traded funds are a favorite component of these portfolios, as are cyclical and commodity-based stocks like gold mining stocks.

Is this about "market timing"? Let's call it "intelligent" or "educated" market timing. Studies telling us that it is impossible to effectively time market moves have been around for years. It is impossible to catch highs and lows in particular investments, market sectors, or even the market as a whole. Nobody can find exact tops or bottoms. But by watching economic indicators and the pulse of business and the marketplace, long-term market performance can be boosted by well-rationalized and timely sector rotation. The key word is timely. The agile active investor has enough of a finger on the pulse to see the signs and invest accordingly.

While the idea isn't new, the advent of "low-friction" exchange traded funds and other index portfolios makes it a lot more practical for the individual investors. What does "low-friction" mean? They trade like a single stock—one order, one discounted commission. You don't have to liquidate or acquire a whole basket full of investments on your own to follow a sector. We should note that it's been possible to rotate assets in mutual fund families for years with a single phone call, but most funds in these families are less "pure" plays in their sector, and most families do not cover all sectors.

THE OPPORTUNISTIC PORTFOLIO

The opportunistic portfolio is the most actively traded portion of an active investor's total portfolio. The opportunistic portfolio looks for stocks or other investments that seem to be notably under- or over-valued at a particular time. The active investor looks for shorter-term opportunities, perhaps a few days, perhaps a month, perhaps even a year, to wring out gains from undervalued situations.

The opportunistic portfolio also may be used to generate short-term income through covered option writing. Options are essentially a cash-based risk transfer mechanism whereby a possible, but low probability investment outcome is exchanged for a less profitable but more certain outcome. A fee or "premium" is paid in exchange for transferring the opportunity for more aggressive gain to someone else. You collect this fee. Effectively, you as the owner of a stock can convert a growth investment into an income investment, paying yourself a dividend for the ownership of the stock by selling an option. Is this risky? Actually, it is less risky than owning the stock without an option.

Curiously, the main objective of this short-term portfolio is to generate income, or cash. Most traditional investors look at the long-term, more conservative components of a portfolio to generate income through bonds, dividend-paying stocks and so forth. In this framework, the short-term opportunistic portfolio actually does the "heavy lifting" in terms of generating cash income. An active investor might look to trade those stocks with varying degrees of frequency or to sell some options to generate cash. These "swing" trades usually run from a few days to a month or so, and may be day trades if things work out particularly well and particularly fast. It should be emphasized again that day trades are not the active investor's goal nor their typical practice.

ARE RETIREMENT ACCOUNTS ALWAYS PART OF THE FOUNDATION?

The long-term objectives and nature of retirement accounts suggest normal inclusion as part of the foundation portfolio. In fact, retirement assets can be deployed as part of either the rotational or opportunistic portfolio. And in fact, it might make a lot of sense. Why? Because returns generated are tax free, at least until withdrawn. Tax-free returns can compound much faster. Because of the importance of these assets, one should only commit a small portion to an actively managed opportunistic portfolio, but it can be a good way to "juice" the growth of this important asset base.

100 Best Stocks and the Segmented Portfolio

The next natural question is—"So how do I use the 100 Best Stocks to construct my portfolio tiers?" The answer is really that selections from the 100 Best list can be used in all tiers, depending on your time horizon and current price relative to value. If you see a stock on the 100 Best list take a nosedive, and feel that nosedive is out of proportion to the real news and near-term prospects of the company, it may be a candidate for the opportunistic portfolio. If the stock makes sense as a long-term holding (as many on our list do) it's a good candidate for the foundation portfolio. Likewise, if you feel that, say, energy stocks are, as a group, likely to be in favor and are undervalued now, you can pick off the energy stocks on the 100 Best list as a rotational portfolio pick, similarly, if you feel that large cap dividend paying stocks will do well, again you can use the 100 Best list to feed into this hunch.

Not surprisingly, I feel the 100 Best stocks are of the highest quality, and can be used with relatively less risk that most other stocks to achieve your objectives.

When to Buy? Consider When to Sell

If it's hard to figure out when to buy a stock, it's even harder to figure out when to sell. People "get married" to their investment decisions, feeling somehow that if it isn't right, maybe time will help, and things will get better. Or they're just too arrogant to admit that they made a mistake. There are lots of reasons why people hold on to investments for too long a time.

Here's the fundamental truth: buying and selling should be much the same process. Let's look at it from the point of view of selling. When should you sell? Simply, when there's something else better to buy. Something else better for future returns, something else better for safety, something else better for timeliness or synchronization with overall business trends. That something else can be another stock, a futures contract or a house. It can also be cash—sell that stock when . . . when what? When cash is a better investment. Or when you need the money, which is another way of saying that cash is a better investment.

Similarly, if you think of a buy decision as a best-possible deployment of capital, as a buy because there's no better way to invest your money, you'll also come out ahead. It really isn't that hard, especially if you've done your homework. And it's also made easier if you avoid rash overcommitments; that is, you avoid buying all at once in case you've made a mistake or in case better prices come later down the road.

Investing for Retirement

Most of us don't invest just for the sake of investing. We're not so much like players at a poker table who not only enjoy winning money but the process of winning. We're more interested in the result of investing than the process. We may like to invest, like to do research, like to see things come out the way we had in mind. But the main reason we do it is to make money.

And why do we want to make money? Well, for some of us, it's about buying homes, paying for college, or just having a little extra spending money. But for a great many of us, especially those of us for whom there's no defined-benefit pension awaiting us when we retire, we invest because we want a more secure, comfortable retirement years down the road.

So how should one invest for retirement? Should one invest any differently than they would for any of the other objectives I just mentioned? Mostly, investing is investing, and the goal is to make money over the intended period of time one invests. Retirement investing isn't that much different, except there is a greater emphasis on the long term, and for many, a greater need for safety.

The retirement planning process starts with creating a goal, that is, estimating what you will need during retirement to live on. The "what you'll need" is referred to euphemistically as your "number"—an amount that will, with carefully planned withdrawals—service your needs net of government (Social Security) and other pensions until you and your spouse die. There are many ways to calculate this "number," and financial advisers have a bag of tricks and fancy spreadsheets. I like to use a permanent withdrawal rate rule of thumb—that is, you can draw down 4 percent of your asset base each year in retirement. So if you need $2,000 a month (plus Social Security) to live, that's $24,000 a year;

$24,000 a year is 4 percent of what number (multiply by 25)—that's $960,000 you'll need in your retirement account on Retirement Day 1. This number, however, assumes that you want to live strictly off of income, not principal, and that you want to leave the principal intact. Of course, this is a conservative assumption. You can see how complex the calculation can become.

But that's not the point of reading *100 Best Stocks*—the point is to get some tips on where and how to invest to achieve the number. I offer the following:

- *Stay diversified.* You've read about how Enron shareholders had their entire retirement tied up in company stock. If the company fails, you fail twice. It's probably best to not even invest most of your retirement assets in the same industry you work in. A good portfolio of stocks or funds (seven or so different stocks, three or so different funds) is probably optimal. But don't *overdiversify*—you can achieve the same returns at a lot less cost by simply buying an index fund.

- *Think long term.* Obvious, right? Well, today's market can bring some serious surprises to those who think they can simply buy and hold forever and capitalize on the growth of the American Way. The trick here is to buy individual companies that you think will not only be around when you retire, but will be better than they are today. Try to visualize your company ten, twenty, or thirty years from now. And be prepared to bail out when things start to not look like you expected. There are a lot of GM shareholders and bondholders who wish they had done just that.

- *Get at least some dividends.* Future appreciation is nice for retirement, but I believe that a bird in hand is worthwhile, especially if you can reinvest it in the stocks or funds held in your retirement accounts.

- *Dollar cost average.* If you keep reinvesting dividends and/or adding funds to your accounts consistently, you'll buy more shares when prices are low, bringing your average cost down. For most people it's best to keep retirement contributions—and investments—as consistent as possible.

- *Use a portfolio strategy.* Like the one outlined above—create a strong, steady "foundation" and add some opportunistic investments. The opportunistic investments can be used to stretch returns a bit, and they work better in retirement accounts because capital gains taxes are deferred or avoided altogether. That said, you should opportunistically invest only what you can afford to lose. Most of the 100 Best Stocks are suitable for foundation investments, and a few of the "aggressive growth" entries are good for opportunistic investments as well.

So good luck, and I'll come visit you at your beach house.

When and How to Use an Adviser

Individual investors are independent, self-starting, self-driven folks largely capable of accepting responsibility for their own decisions and actions. That's good, and I assume that if you're reading this book, you have at least some of that character. However, the world isn't so simple, and your time isn't so plentiful, and maybe business and investing stuff just isn't your cup of tea, anyway. You don't want to throw everything over the wall to a professional adviser (and pay the fees and lose control and all that) but you may want some help from time to time.

Just remember this—you, you only, and ultimately you are responsible for your own finances, just like a pilot flying an airplane is ultimately responsible for what happens to that airplane and its passengers. You are in charge. You are in charge whether or not you have someone else, like a broker or professional adviser, helping you out. You can (and should) think of advisers as more like a co-pilot, navigator, or air traffic controller—who will give you information and suggestions and help you interpret the information and remind you of the rules when necessary—but ultimately you're in charge.

Financial advisers come in many forms, and I won't go into the details here. What's important is to realize that no matter how much you outsource, you're still at the helm. You need to develop a good, two-way relationship with the adviser where they can bring value and they can help you bring value to the investment decisions and investment strategy. They shouldn't tell you what to do, and they shouldn't just be the "yes man" for everything you want to do. A lively, point-counterpoint discussion of any financial move with an adviser is healthy; two heads are better than one. Remember, if two people think the exact same way, you don't need one of them.

Don't be snowed by fancy terminology and concepts. Investing is a complex subject, but if the explanation sounds more complex than the task itself, look out below. Find an adviser that speaks your language, that is, plain English. Smart, experienced people make things simple, not complex, for others.

Also be clear what you want and what you expect from an adviser. If you aren't, they'll give you the "standard" product, and it may be the same standard product they gave their last client. Say that you want help constructing your portfolio and learning about, say, the tech and health care sectors, which you don't know enough about. Ask them to help you understand the headlines and what's important about them for the banking industry. And so forth.

And of course, as Bernard Madoff has made so clear for so many—make sure you understand what they're doing, if they're managing anything on your behalf. There is nothing worse than thinking everything is okay—when in fact it's completely off in the weeds.

Bottom line, an investment adviser should be a great partner, someone you'd hire into your business if you were trying to create a partnership in the investing business. Look for common sense, look for the adviser to help you most with the things you're least comfortable with. Learn what they do (and have done) with other clients; if it sounds too good to be true, it probably is.

Here's another bottom line: your adviser should make you sleep better at night. If you're waking up at 3 A.M. thinking about your investments, that's bad. If you're waking up at 3 A.M. thinking about your adviser, that's worse. In both cases, they're too risky for you.

Individual Stocks vs. Funds and ETFs

As long as I'm sharing opinions on things like financial advisers and other help you can get with your investing, it makes sense to take a short detour into the world of managed investments. What are managed investments? Simply, they are individual investments where some intermediary buys and repackages individual investments, and sells you pieces of that package.

Intermediaries can be investment companies with professional managers choosing specific investments and otherwise looking after the portfolio. They can also be indexes, where groups of like stocks are accumulated into an index according to some sort of generally fixed formula. Either way, by buying into one of these intermediaries, you're giving up picking individual investments in favor of a packaged and sometimes professionally managed approach.

Of course, like any value proposition, you're giving up something in the interest of gaining something else. The "something else" you're trying to gain by using the packaged approach is usually a combination of the following:

- **Time**—you don't have the time to research individual stocks, or to research individual stocks for 100 percent of your portfolio.
- **Expertise**—in the case of managed funds, you're getting a trained, experienced, investment professional. Some also prefer to hire others to do the work to take the emotion out of investing decisions.
- **Diversification**—by definition, both managed and index funds spread your investments so that you don't have too much wrapped up in a single company; this is generally good unless they diversify away any chance of outperforming the markets. Funds and ETFs also allow you to play in markets otherwise difficult to play in for lack of knowledge or time, e.g. Asian stocks, European currencies, etc.
- **Convenience**—it takes work to build and manage an investment portfolio. With funds you can move in and out of the markets with a single transaction; the administrative work is taken care of.

Of course, with any value proposition comes a downside:

- **Fees**—Not surprisingly, funds, and especially managed funds, charge money for the packaging and services they provide. Actively managed funds can take a half to over 2 percent of your asset value each year, whether they do well or not. If you understand compounding, you know that the difference between a 6 percent return and a 4 percent net return over time is huge. Index funds and ETFs are better in this regard, usually charging 0.25 to 0.75 percent, but it still puts a drag on your outcomes.

- **Tax efficiency**—When ordinary mutual funds sell shares, any gains flow through to you (unless you hold them in a tax-free or tax-deferred retirement account). You cannot control when this happens, and many "active" funds may roll their portfolios frequently, producing adverse tax consequences. Also, you need to watch when you enter the fund—you should buy in after capital gains are paid out, not before, else you'll be paying for someone else's gains. Index funds and ETFs are far less likely to produce "unwanted" gains, for they tie their investments to the indexes, which don't change much.

- **Control**—With funds of any sort, you lose control, and as we said at the outset, there are few things more painful than having someone else lose your money for you. Particularly with managed funds, it is almost impossible to know what they are really doing with your money except in hindsight; I would support any initiative requiring funds to give you a more real time accounting for what they do with your funds.

- **Tendency toward mediocrity**—One of the biggest criticisms of funds over time is the tendency for managers to follow each other and to follow standard business-school investing and risk management formulas. The result is a herd instinct, known in the trade as an "institutional imperative." Worse—and this is the biggie from my perspective—when you buy a fund and especially an index fund, you're getting all the companies in the industry—the mediocre players, the weak hands—not just the best ones.

So I suggest using funds where it makes sense to get some exposure to an industry or a segment of the market otherwise difficult to access or outside your expertise. Use funds to round out a portfolio or build a foundation or rotational portfolio, and to save yourself the time and bandwidth to focus more closely on other more "opportunistic" investments.

Part II

THE 100 BEST STOCKS YOU CAN BUY

The 100 Best Stocks You Can Buy

Index of Stocks by Category

Company	Symbol	Industry	Sector	Category
—A—				
Abbott Laboratories	ABT	Med. Supplies	Health Care	Grow Inc
Air Products	APD	Gases	Materials	Aggr Gro
Alexander & Baldwin	ALEX	Industrials	Transportation	Gro Inc
Apache Corporation	APA	Exploration	Energy	Aggr Gro
Apple	AAPL	Cons Discretionary		Aggr Gro
Archer Daniels Midland	ADM		Cons Staples	Con Gro
AT&T	T	Telephone	Telecomm.	Gro Inc
—B—				
Bard, C. R.*	BCR	Hosp. Products	Health Care	Con Grow
Baxter	BAX		Health Care	Aggr Gro
Becton, Dickinson	BDX	Med. Supplies	Health Care	Con Grow
Bed Bath & Beyond*	BBBY		Retail	Aggr Gro
Best Buy*	BBY		Retail	Aggr Gro
Boeing Company	BA	Aerospace	Industrials	Aggr Gro
Bunge*	BG		Cons Staples	Con Gro
—C—				
Campbell Soup	CPB	Packaged Foods	Cons Staples	Con Grow
CarMax	KMX	Auto, Trucks	Retail	Aggr Gro
Caterpillar, Inc.	CAT	Machinery	Industrials	Aggr Gro
ChevronTexaco	CVX	Gas & Oil	Energy	Gro Inc
Chipotle*	CMG	Restaurant	Industrials	Aggr Gro
Church & Dwight*	CHD	Consumer Staples		Aggr Gro
Cincinnati Financial*	CINF	Financial		Gro Inc
Clorox	CLX	Household Pd.	Cons Staples	Con Grow
Coca-Cola	KO	Beverages	Cons Staples	Con Grow
Colgate-Palmolive	CL	Household Products	Cons Staples	Con Grow
ConocoPhillips	COP	Oil & Gas	Energy	Gro Inc
Costco Wholesale	COST	Wholesale	Retail	Aggr Gro
CVS Corporation	CVS	Pharmacy	Retail	Con Gro

Index of Stocks by Category (continued)

Company	Symbol	Industry	Sector	Category
—D—				
Deere & Company	DE	Farm Equipment	Industrials	Aggr Gro
Dentsply Int'l	XRAY	Dental Products	Health Care	Con Gro
Dominion Resources	D	Gas & Electric	Utilities	Gro Inc
Dover	DOV	Ind. Machinery	Industrials	Aggr Gro
Duke*	DUK	Utilities	Income	Gro Inc
DuPont	DD	Chemicals	Materials	Gro Inc
—E—				
Ecolab	ECL	Specialty Chem.	Materials	Con Gro
Entergy	ETR	Energy	Utilities	Gro Inc
ExxonMobil	XOM	Petroleum	Energy	Gro Inc
—F—				
Fair Isaac	FIC	Business Services		Aggr Gro
FedEx Corporation	FDX	Air Freight	Transportation	Aggr Gro
Fluor	FLR	Heavy Construction		Aggr Gro
FMC Corporation	FMC	Feeding World	Materials	Aggr Gro
FPL Group	FPL	Elect. Power	Utilities	Gro Inc
—G—				
General Mills	GIS	Packaged Foods	Cons Staples	Grow Inc
Google*	GOOG	Technology		Aggr Gro
Grainger, W. W.	GWW	Supplies	Industrials	Con Gro
—H—				
Harris Corp.	HRS	Communications	Inform Tech	Aggr Gro
Heinz	HNZ	Food	Cons Staples	Gro Inc
Hewlett Packard	HPQ	Printers	Inform Tech.	Aggr Gro
Honeywell	HON	Aerospace	Industrials	Aggr Gro
Hormel Foods	HRL	Packaged Foods	Cons Staples	Con Gro
—I—				
Int'l Business Mach	IBM	Computers	Inform Tech.	Con Gro
International Paper	IP	Packaging	Materials	Con Gro
Iron Mountain	IRM	Data Management	Inform Tech	Aggr Gro

Index of Stocks by Category (continued)

Company	Symbol	Industry	Sector	Category
—J—				
Johnson Controls	JCI	Elect. Equip.	Industrials	Con Grow
Johnson & Johnson	JNJ	Med Supplies	Health Care	Grow Inc
—K—				
Kellogg	K	Packaged Foods	Cons Staples	Grow Inc
Kimberly-Clark*	KMB	Paper Products	Cons Staples	Gro Inc
Kraft Foods	KFT	Packaged Foods	Cons Staples	Gro Inc
—L—				
Lubrizol	LZ	Specialty Chem	Materials	Gro Inc
—M—				
Marathon Oil	MRO	Energy		Agg Gro
McCormick & Co.	MKC	Spices	Cons Staples	Con Gro
McDonalds	MCD	Restaurants		Aggr Gro
Medtronic	MDT	Med. Devices	Health Care	Aggr Gro
Monsanto	MON	Industrials		Aggr Gro
—N—				
NetApp*	NTAP	Data Mgmt	Technology	Aggr Gro
Nike	NKE	Clothing	Cons Discretionary	Aggr Gro
Norfolk Southern	NSC	Railroads	Transportation	Cons Gro
Northern Trust*	NTRS	Bank	Financials	Con Gro
Nucor*	NUE	Steel	Industrials	Aggr Gro
—O—				
Oracle*	ORCL	Data Mgmt	Technology	Aggr Gro
—P—				
Pall*	PLL	Gas Filtration	Industrials	Gro Inc
Panera*	PNRA	Food	Restaurants	Aggr Gro
Patterson Companies	PDCO	Dental	Health Care	Aggr Gro
Paychex	PAYX	Payroll Services	Inform Tech	Aggr Gro
Peet's	PEET	Beverages	Restaurant	Aggr Gro
PepsiCo	PEP	Beverages	Cons Staples	Con Grow
Perrigo	PRGO	Pharmacy	Health Care	Aggr Gro
Praxair	PX	Indust. Gases	Materials	Con Grow
Procter & Gamble	PG	Household Prods	Cons Staples	Con Grow

Index of Stocks by Category (continued)

Company	Symbol	Industry	Sector	Category
—R—				
Ross Stores	ROST	Clothing	Retail	Aggr Gro
—S—				
Schlumberger	SLB	Oilfield Services	Energy	Aggr Gro
Sigma–Aldrich	SIAL	Life Science	Industrials	Aggr Gro
Smuckers*	SJM	Packaged Foods	Cons Staples	Gro Inc
Southern Co.	SO	Elect. Serv.	Utilities	Gro Inc
St. Jude Medical	STJ	Medical Devices	Health Care	Aggr Gro
Staples	SPLS	Office Products	Cons Discret	Aggr Gro
Starbucks	SBUX	Food	Restaurant	Aggr Gro
Stryker	SYK	Medical Sup.	Health Care	Aggr Gro
Suburban Propane*	SPH	Gas	Energy	Gro Inc
Sysco Corporation	SYY	Food Distrib.	Cons Staples	Con Grow
—T—				
Target Corporation	TGT	Gen. Merchandise	Retail	Aggr Gro
Teva Pharmaceutical	TEVA	Pharmaceuticals	Health Care	Aggr Gro
3M Company	MMM	Diversified	Industrials	Con Grow
TJX	TJX	Retail	Cons Discret	Aggr Gro
Tractor Supply	TSCO	Industrial Mach.	Retail	Aggr Gro
—U—				
UnitedHealth Group	UNH	Med. Insur.	Health Care	Aggr Gro
United Technologies	UTX	Aircraft Eng.	Industrials	Gro Inc
—V—				
Valmont	VMT	Equipment	Industrials	Aggr Gro
Verizon	VZ	Communication	Telecomm Svcs	Gro Inc
—W—				
Walgreen	WAG	Drug Stores	Cons Staples	Aggr Gro
Wells Fargo	WFC	Divers Bank	Financial	Gro Inc

*New this edition

CONSERVATIVE GROWTH

3M Company

Ticker symbol: MMM (NYSE) □ S&P rating: AA– □ Value Line financial strength rating: A++ □
Current yield: 2.6 percent

Company Profile

The 3M Company, originally known as the Minnesota Mining and Manufacturing Co., is a $24 billion diversified manufacturing technology company with leading positions in industrial, consumer and office, health care, safety, electronics, telecommunications, and other markets. The company has operations in more than sixty countries and serves customers in nearly 200 countries. The company has such a broad reach that it is often looked to as a leading indicator for the general health of the world economy.

3M's operations are divided up among six segments:

■ The Industrial and Transportation segment produces industrial tapes, a wide variety of abrasives, adhesives, specialty materials, filtration products, and products for the separation of fluids and gases. They supply markets such as paper and packaging, food and beverage, electronics, automotive (OEM) and the automotive aftermarket.

■ The Health Care segment serves markets that include medical clinics and hospitals, pharmaceuticals, dental and orthodontic practitioners, and health information systems. Products and services include medical and surgical supplies, skin health and infection prevention products, drug delivery systems, dental and orthodontic products, health information systems and antimicrobial solutions.

■ The Safety, Security and Protection Services segment serves a broad range of markets that increase the safety, security and productivity of workers, facilities and systems. Major product offerings include personal protection, safety and security products, energy control products, building cleaning and protection products, track and trace solutions, and roofing granules for asphalt shingles.

■ The Consumer and Office segment serves markets that include retail, home improvement, building maintenance and other markets. Products in this segment include office supply products including the familiar tapes and Post-It notes, stationery products, construction and home improvement products, home care products, protective material products and consumer health care products.

- The Display and Graphics segment serves markets that include electronic display, traffic safety and commercial graphics. This segment includes optical film solutions for electronic displays, computer screen filters, reflective sheeting for transportation safety, commercial graphics systems, and projection systems, including mobile display technology and visual systems products.

- The Electro and Communications segment serves the electrical, electronics and communications industries, including electrical utilities. Products include electronic and interconnect solutions, microinterconnect systems, high-performance fluids, high-temperature and display tapes, telecommunications products, electrical products, and touch screens and touch monitors.

Financial Highlights, Fiscal Year 2009

FY2009 sales totaled $23.1 billion, down 8.5 percent from 2008, and 2009 net income was $3.31 billion compared to $3.65 billion for 2008. Unit volumes were off 9.5 percent, in line with the overall economy. Broad declines in demand for their products from consumer, commercial, and industrial users tells the tale of 2009.

Like many companies, 3M did a fair amount of restructuring during the slowdowns in 2008 and 2009, resulting in the elimination of 6,400 positions. Charges associated with all the restructuring efforts were absorbed in 2009, with a hit to EPS of $0.17.

The FY2009 results reflected the turnaround in the global economy, with the first through third quarters all showing year-over-year declines, and the fourth quarter showing a nearly 12 percent increase over 2008. Early 2010 results are similarly encouraging and the company is optimistic about its businesses as its industrial customers continue to crawl out of their bunkers.

Reasons to Buy

Last year we said: "3M's leading position as a supplier of specialty materials and consumables to industry make it the canary in the coal mine. And while it's often the first to feel the effects of a recession, fortunately it can also be among the first to recover. FY2009 will be the second down year in a row for 3M, but a turnaround is likely in early 2010; whether the company is a bargain will depend on what's happened with the share price by then."

This year we'll say that last year was a great buying opportunity. The share price has since rebounded to its recent pre-recession trading range, making this stock slightly less attractive, but 3M is still one of the highest-quality issues on the market and deserves serious consideration from every value investor. The company has issued guidance for a 5 to 7 percent increase in organic sales volume increase and earnings of $4.85-$5.00 per share.

Reasons for Caution

The company's share price runs into resistance in the 90–95 range. We're not technical analysts, and don't pretend to be, but even with multiples in the 14–16 range, the shares have stayed mainly in the 75–95 trading range (post-2003 split prices).

SECTOR: **Industrials**
BETA COEFFICIENT: **.80**
10-YEAR COMPOUND EARNINGS PER SHARE GROWTH: **10.5 percent**
10-YEAR COMPOUND DIVIDENDS PER SHARE GROWTH: **6.5 percent**

		2002	2003	2004	2005	2006	2007	2008	2009
Revenues (Mil)		16,332	1,974	18,232	20,011	21,167	22,293	24,462	25,269
Net income (Mil)		23,123	2,403	2,990	3,111	3,851	4,096	3,460	3,193
Earnings per share		2.5	3.09	3.75	3.98	5.06	5.6	4.89	4.52
Dividends per share		1.24	1.32	1.4	411.68	1.84	1.92	2	2.04
Cash flow per share		3.75	4.29	5.07	5.55	6.71	7.29	6.65	6.15
Price:	high	65.8	85.4	90.3	87.4	88.4	97	84.8	84.3
	low	50	59.7	73.3	69.7	67	72.9	50	40.9

3M Center, Building 225-01-S-15
St. Paul, MN 55144–1000
Phone: (651) 733–8206
Website: *www.MMM.com*

Abbott Laboratories

Ticker symbol: ABT (NYSE) ❑ S&P rating: AA ❑ Value Line financial strength rating: A++ ❑ Current yield: 3.0 percent

Company Profile

Abbott Laboratories, founded in 1888 and currently ranked at 80 in the Fortune 500, is one of the most diverse health care manufacturers in the world. Abbott is the third largest producer of pharmaceuticals in the United States, behind Johnson & Johnson and Pfizer and is the largest company in the nutritional products market. The company's products are sold in more than 130 countries, with about 40 percent of sales derived from international operations.

Abbott's major business segments include Pharmaceutical Products (particularly in immunology, cardiology, and infectious diseases), Diagnostic Products (laboratory and molecular diagnostics, diabetes and vision care), Vascular Products (stents and closure devices), and Nutritional Products (infant, adult, and special needs). Pharmaceuticals accounted for just over 56 percent of FY'08 sales.

The company's leading brands include Freestyle (diabetes monitoring), Ensure (nutritional supplements for adults), Humira (rheumatoid arthritis), and Similac (infant formula).

Financial Highlights, Fiscal Year 2009

Abbott's results for 2009 were positive across the board, despite the effects of the continued economic downturn, very unfavorable exchange rates, and the loss of patent protection for a major product (Depakote). Although sales were up a rather modest 4 percent, earnings-per-share rose a very strong 15 percent (to $3.71).

The company's flagship product, Humira, received regulatory approvals for additional indications, the effect of which was to boost sales of the arthritis drug by over 20 percent in the United States and over 40 percent internationally.

The company completed the acquisition of Solvay Pharmaceuticals, which represents $2.9B in annual sales in Eastern Europe, which will add significantly to Abbott's bottom line and should help to moderate the effects of exchange rates going forward.

Reasons to Buy

Abbott sales of vascular stents grew 78 percent in 2009, and their acquisitions of Kos Pharmaceuticals and Guidant Corporation will contribute to their competitiveness in this highly profitable market. Abbott has moved quickly into a leadership position with several of their products, and the Vascular division's profit has more than doubled year-over-year. The company plans to expand product offerings in the drug-eluting stent market and expects continued significant growth in operating profits in the world market for DES products.

Last year we said that the key to Abbott's success is for Humira to remain hot. At the time, the product had a three-year run of 30 percent growth, far outpacing the rest of their product line and straining many investor's expectations for continued success. Well, the fact is that Humira continues to perform like the blockbuster product Abbott had hoped for. In addition to its primary application (the treatment of rheumatoid arthritis), it has also been well received in treatment of Crohn's disease and psoriasis. The company believes that Humira is a platform for a number of future products addressing other autoimmune diseases, which if true, could mean several more years of a very strong product pipeline for Abbott. Humira itself remains on patent protection until 2016.

Due in large part to their in product development, Abbott remains a reliable and stable growth stock. They have raised their dividend every year for the past thirty-seven years while producing long-term (if somewhat cyclical) growth. Even in the very uncertain economic and political/regulatory environment of 2009, the company increased its net margins by 17 percent and increased dividends by 11 percent. ABT has paid consecutive quarterly dividends since 1924.

Reasons for Caution

An agreement with Teva Pharmaceuticals delayed the introduction of Teva's generic version of Abbott's TriCor, but only until March 2011. When generics of Depakote were approved, Abbott saw the revenues for its number two pharmaceutical fall 80 percent. The release of Teva's version of TriCor will negatively impact Abbott's bottom line in 2011, moderated somewhat by the extent to which Abbott is successful in the meantime in migrating patients to the protected TriLipix.

While the long-term effects of the U.S. health care reform legislation passed in early 2010 are unknown, the early returns appear to be fairly neutral to the large pharmaceuticals. Earlier reform of Medicare drug policy under the Bush administration has settled out and seems to be carried forward under the new plan.

SECTOR: **Health Care**
BETA COEFFICIENT: **.60**
10-YEAR COMPOUND EARNINGS PER SHARE GROWTH: **7.5 percent**
10-YEAR COMPOUND DIVIDENDS PER SHARE GROWTH: **9.0 percent**

	2002	2003	2004	2005	2006	2007	2008	2009
Revenues (Mil)	17,684	19,681	19,680	22,337	22,476	25,914	29,528	20,764
Net income (Mil)	3,242	3,479	3,522	3,908	3,841	4,429	4,734	5,745
Earnings per share	2.06	2.21	2.27	2.50	2.52	2.84	3.03	3.69
Dividends per share	0.94	0.98	1.04	1.10	1.18	1.30	1.44	1.60
Cash flow per share	2.83	3.01	3.05	3.42	3.51	4.05	4.32	5.00
Price: high	58.0	47.2	47.6	50.0	49.9	59.5	61.1	57.4
low	29.8	33.8	38.3	37.5	39.2	48.8	45.8	41.3

Abbott Laboratories
100 Abbott Park Road
Abbott Park, IL 60064–6400
(847) 937-3923
Website: *www.abbott.com*

AGGRESSIVE GROWTH

Air Products and Chemicals, Inc.

Ticker symbol: APD (NYSE) ❑ S&P rating: A ❑ Value Line financial strength rating: A ❑ Current yield: 2.6 percent

Company Profile

Air Products and Chemicals produces and sells gases such as hydrogen, helium, nitrogen, and oxygen to industrial manufacturers and commercial end-users worldwide. Gases are vital inputs to many manufacturing processes, and APD is one of the largest global bulk gas sellers. The company operates in more than forty countries and now derives nearly 60 percent of its sales from outside the United States.

After the Q1 2008 divestiture of the Chemicals business, APD reports revenues in four segments:

■ **Merchant Gases**—Industrial and medical customers throughout the world use oxygen, nitrogen, argon, helium, hydrogen, and medical and specialty gases for a wide array of applications. APD supplies most merchant gas in liquid form to small and larger customers delivered via tanker trucks and rail cars. APD provides smaller quantities of packaged gases for customers who require smaller quantities for their processes.

■ **Tonnage Gases**—Air Products supplies gases via large on-site facilities or pipeline systems to meet the needs of large-volume, or "tonnage" industrial gas users. APD either constructs a gas plant near the customer's facility or delivers product through a pipeline from an existing nearby facility. They also design and manufacture cryogenic and gas processing equipment for air separation, hydrocarbon recovery and purification, natural gas liquefaction (LNG) and helium distribution equipment.

■ **Electronics and Performance Materials**—This segment specializes in delivery of products relevant to the electronics industry for the production of silicon, semiconductors, displays, and photovoltaic devices. They also provide performance chemical solutions for the coatings, inks, adhesives, civil engineering, personal care, institutional and industrial cleaning, mining, oil field, polyurethane, and other industries.

■ **Equipment and Energy—**
Designs and sells equipment
for energy production and also
partially owns and operates
several small energy plants
around the world. Equipment
is sold worldwide to customers in a variety of industries,
including chemical and petrochemical manufacturing, oil
and gas recovery and processing, and steel and primary
metals processing.

Financial Highlights, Fiscal Year 2009

APD's customer base is heavily
weighted to industrial uses, more
specifically manufacturing environments, and the first half of FY2009
saw the air going out of their bal-
loons at an alarming rate. Global
manufacturing output declined
11 percent and worldwide silicon
processing dropped 35 percent. As
a result, APD's sales fell 21 percent
and operating income fell 43 percent. The company responded with
a number of cost containment and
cost reduction programs, including
the sale of a number of their businesses and the elimination of some
12 percent of their work force.

In the end, revenues for the
year were off 21 percent on an 8
percent volume decline, 7 percent
in contractual price reductions,
and 6 percent in unfavorable currency treatments. Per share earnings

were off $1.97 from the prior year,
including $1/share in one-time
restructuring charges.

On February 5, 2010, APD
announced a tender offer for the
outstanding shares of Airgas, Inc.
(ARG: NYSE), a producer and distributor of industrial, medical, and
specialty gases based in Radnor, PA.
The offer of $60 per share was a 38
percent premium over ARG's share
price on the day of the offer (valuing
the deal at about $7 billion) with an
initial close date of April 9. This
close date has been extended several
times and is now set to expire in
mid-August. ARG's response to the
offer has been to take a defensive
position; the board unanimously
rejected the offer and recommended
that shareholders not sell, the company has issued an unplanned $250
million in debt, and ARG has filed
suit against APD's current counsel
claiming conflict of interest (counsel used to represent ARG).

Reasons to Buy

The purchase of ARG (assuming
it goes through) will carry a great
deal of leverage for APD. First, it
brings with it a merchant gas operation that APD does not currently
have. Second, APD claims there is
approximately $250 million in cost
reduction potential for the combined companies, which, if fully
realized, would improve operating
margin by some 800 basis points (8

percentage points). Not too shabby, even if the real number tops out at 400 basis points after a few years.

APD's FY2009 second half operating margin was 200 basis points higher than the first half and fourth-quarter sales were sequentially higher. The first half of 2010 has shown increasing strength in revenues and very encouraging growth in earnings. The cost reductions of 2009 were expected to deliver an additional 180 points in operating margin going forward, and in fact, operating income in the second quarter of 2010 is up 40 percent on a 15 percent increase in revenue.

The company remains committed to its goal of achieving 17 percent margin by 2011, and its current cost-cutting efforts have kept it on target.

Reasons for Caution

Organic growth in 2010 will be moderate. Share earnings will be back up to FY2008 levels, but on 10 percent lower revenues. The structural cost savings are real, but revenue growth projections for 2011 are also modest.

The ARG acquisition will be protracted and may get expensive. Keep an eye on that.

SECTOR: **Materials**
BETA COEFFICIENT: **1.10**
10-YEAR COMPOUND EARNINGS PER SHARE GROWTH: **8.0 percent**
10-YEAR COMPOUND DIVIDENDS PER SHARE GROWTH: **10.0 percent**

		2002	2003	2004	2005	2006	2007	2008	2009
Revenues (Mil)		5,401	6,297	7,411	7,768	8,850	10,038	10,415	8,256
Net income (Mil)		525	397	604	712	723	1,036	1,091	866
Earnings per share		2.42	1.78	2.64	3.08	3.18	4.4	4.97	4.06
Dividends per share		0.82	0.88	1.04	1.25	1.34	1.52	1.7	1.79
Cash flow per share		5.03	5.14	5.94	6.49	7.17	8.48	9.36	8.08
Price:	high	53.5	53.1	59.2	65.8	72.4	105	106.1	85.4
	low	40	37	46.7	53	58	68.6	41.5	43.4

Air Products and Chemicals, Inc.
7201 Hamilton Boulevard
Allentown, PA 18195–1501
(610) 481-5775
Website: *www.airproducts.com*

Alexander & Baldwin

Ticker symbol: ALEX (NASDAQ) ❑ S&P rating: BBB+ ❑ Value Line financial strength rating B+ ❑
Current yield: 4.0 percent

Company Profile

An old Hawaiian company with origins dating back to missionary days of the 1830s, Alexander & Baldwin, Inc., together with its subsidiaries, operates in ocean transportation, real estate, and agribusiness. The company offers container ship freight services primarily between Long Beach, Oakland, Seattle and Hawaii, Guam, China, and other Pacific Islands. Its most recognizable carrier is the wholly owned subsidiary Matson Lines.

The company operates some of the fastest container ships in the Pacific Rim; it also has subsidiaries specializing in logistics, stevedoring, and port services in Hawaii but also in China and on the U.S. mainland. The transportation business accounted for 78 percent of revenue, 54 percent of profits and 49 percent of assets in 2009.

The real estate subsidiaries develop and sell residential and commercial property primarily in Hawaii, currently owning over 89,000 acres in the state. In 2009 the real estate business accounted for 15 percent of revenue, 69 percent of profit and 44 percent of assets. The agribusiness segment specializes in sugar and the production, marketing and distribution of coffee, and represents a relatively small share of the company's business at 7 percent of revenue. In 2009 the agribusiness sector operated at a $29 million loss.

Financial Highlights, Fiscal Year 2009

The company earned $1.08 per share in 2009, their lowest tally in over fifteen years. The reasons are understandable and the results could have been worse had the company not responded with cost controls as well as they did. But the agribusiness sector endured yet another season of drought, compounded by low sugar prices, so no candy for A&B in 2009—A&B's revenues were off 20 percent and earnings fell 66 percent compared to 2008.

Transport revenue was off 13 percent, due mainly to reduced net volumes and lower fuel surcharges. Transport profit fell 45 percent to $55 million due mainly to the reduced volumes and some higher terminal costs. Real estate leasing revenues and profits were off 4 and 10 percent, respectively.

The company restructured much of its debt in 2009. It still carries nearly $500 million in long-term obligations, but there are no years with particularly large service requirements in the retirement schedule.

Reasons to Buy

Alexander & Baldwin is a long-term play on the continued growth and importance of trans-Pacific shipping, combined with the growth and value of Hawaii, Hawaiian real estate and agriculture.

The Jones Act provides that no non-U.S. flagged carrier can operate between Hawaii and other U.S. ports, giving Matson, by far the largest carrier serving Hawaii, a virtual monopoly on that business. Matson's fleet is nonetheless also competitive with Chinese carriers servicing routes between Hawaii, Guam, and mainland China.

Many of the larger Pacific carriers have recently laid up capacity in an effort to drive up rates, but as the economic recovery has driven up traffic, smaller players have stepped in to pick the fruit. Matson's utilization is at very high levels and recently negotiated a 25 percent increase in rates over its first quarter level. Matson owns its own port facilities in Hawaii and can respond very quickly to such opportunities.

After its streamlining efforts and other cost reductions, the company exited 2009 with a stronger balance sheet than it started with. Also, it's now trading at just over book value with an attractive dividend.

Reasons for Caution

The longer-term prospects for agriculture (particularly sugar) on Hawaii are not bright. The political support for sugar subsidies appears to be waning, and with the world market price of sugar now at less than 40 percent of A&B's break-even point, A&B has decided that 2010 could be its last year of commercial sugar operations. Potential disposition of the land is unclear at this time, but continuation of its current favorable tax treatment (less than $150/acre) is of vital importance.

As of mid-2009, S&P had a negative credit watch on the company.

SECTOR: **Transportation**
BETA COEFFICIENT: **1.15**
10-YEAR COMPOUND EARNINGS PER SHARE GROWTH: **5.5 percent**
10-YEAR COMPOUND DIVIDENDS PER SHARE GROWTH: **3.0 percent**

	2002	2003	2004	2005	2006	2007	2008	2009
Revenues (Mil)	1,0891	1,232	1,494	1,606	1,607	1,681	1,898	1,405
Net income (Mil)	58.2	81	101	118.7	122	142	132	44.2
Earnings per share	1.41	1.94	2.33	2.7	2.81	3.3	3.19	1.08
Dividends per share	0.9	0.9	0.9	0.9	0.9	1.12	1.24	1.26
Cash flow per share	3.12	3.65	4.19	4.61	4.86	5.54	5.68	3.65
Price high	29.3	34.6	44.7	56.1	54.9	59.4	53.51	35.6
low	2.05	23.5	29	36.8	39.3	44.2	20.6	15.7

Alexander & Baldwin
822 Bishop Street
Honolulu, HI 96813-3924
Phone: (808) 525-6611
Fax: (808) 525-6652
Website: *www.alexanderbaldwin.com*

Apache Corporation

Ticker symbol: APA (NYSE) ❑ S&P rating: A- ❑ Value Line financial strength rating: A ❑ Current yield: 0.6 percent

Company Profile

Established in 1954 with $250,000 of investor capital, Apache Corporation has grown to become one of the world's top independent oil and gas exploration and production companies and currently has a market cap over $30 billion.

Apache's domestic operations focus on some of the nation's most important producing basins, including the Outer Continental Shelf of the Gulf of Mexico, the Anadarko Basin of Oklahoma, the Permian Basin of West Texas, and New Mexico, the Texas-Louisiana Gulf Coast and East Texas.

In Canada, Apache is active in British Columbia, Alberta, Saskatchewan, and the Northwest Territories. The company also has exploration and production operations in Australia's offshore Carnarvon, Perth, and Gippsland basins, Egypt's Western Desert, the United Kingdom sector of the North Sea, China, and Argentina.

Apache's strategy is built on a portfolio of assets that provide opportunities to grow through both grassroots drilling and acquisition activities. The company has seven core areas—two in the United States, and one each in Canada, Egypt, the North Sea (U.K.), Australia, and Argentina.

The company's portfolio is fairly well balanced in terms of gas versus oil, with moderate levels of geologic and political risk, and good reserve life.

Production is split 53/47 between oil/gas—a product mix that provides upside potential in either market. Each core area has significant producing assets and large undeveloped acreage to provide running room for the future, but no single region contributes more than 25 percent of production or reserves. In each core area, the company's goal is to build critical mass that supports sustainable, lower-risk, repeatable drilling opportunities, balanced by higher-risk, higher-reward exploration.

Apache has increased reserves in each of the last twenty-one years and production in twenty-seven of the last twenty-eight years. Management believes the company's portfolio of assets provides a platform for profitable growth through drilling and acquisitions across industry cycles.

Financial Highlights, Fiscal Year 2009

Apache's 2009 revenues fell 30 percent on 9 percent higher production as oil prices declined through the first quarter and gas prices throughout the year. In recognition of the shrinking prices, the company took a non-cash, after-tax adjustment in the carrying value of oil and gas properties of $2 billion in the first quarter. Absent this adjustment, the company earned $1.9 billion for the year, down 52 percent versus FY2008.

Apache entered the year with $4 billion in cash, fully expecting to find attractive acquisition targets. These did not materialize, however, and the company instead retained cash flow for internal expansion, exiting the year with $2 billion on hand. Given the price declines during the year, living within their means turned out to be the better decision.

Reasons to Buy

The recent mobilization for alternative energy sources has revived interest in natural gas. After many quarters of a natural gas glut in the market, large-scale users are taking another look at this low-carbon, low-sulfur source and are starting (and in some cases, re-starting) gas projects that had been on hold through the recession. This renewed interest, coinciding with the development of newer, more cost-effective extraction techniques, has invigorated the market and put some shine on what had been a lackluster business.

Apache has made a specialty of buying up older fields and finding ways to profitably extract additional production. This sort of talent will become increasingly useful as easy oil becomes more and more scarce.

Apache's holdings in the western deserts of Egypt are producing with every new test well. These new finds (in just 200 feet of sand) are expected to bring current production of 8,100 bpd up to 40,000 bpd by the end of 2010. The company owns contractor rights in these fields, so the bottom-line contribution is expected to be excellent.

The Egypt production and expanded capacity in the company's Australian holdings should allow the company to reach its stated 10 percent growth in production for the year. Other projects scheduled to come on line in 2010–2011 will add at least another 15 percent to that total.

Reasons for Caution

On May 28, 2010 the federal government instituted a six-month moratorium on all deepwater drilling in U.S. territorial waters in the wake of the explosion in the Gulf of Mexico of one of BP's deepwater rigs and the subsequent blowout at the wellhead. Given

Apache's recent acquisitions of Mariner's and Devon's deepwater operations in the Gulf, a continuation of the moratorium or an indefinite-term ban on further deepwater drilling would be very detrimental to Apache's long-term plans there.

SECTOR: Energy
BETA COEFFICIENT: 1.20
10-YEAR COMPOUND EARNINGS PER SHARE GROWTH: 32 percent
10-YEAR COMPOUND DIVIDENDS PER SHARE GROWTH: 17.5 percent

		2002	2003	2004	2005	2006	2007	2008	2009
Revenues (Mil)		2,560	4,190	5,333	7,584	8,289	9.978	12,389	8,615
Net income (Mil)		566	1,246	1,670	2,618	2,552	2,812	3,912	1,887
Earnings per share		1.84	3.74	5.03	7.84	7.64	8.39	11.65	5.60
Dividends per share		0.19	0.22	0.26	0.36	0.50	0.60	0.60	0.60
Cash flow per share		4.63	7.36	8.80	12.21	13.19	15.48	19.19	12.72
Price:	high	28.9	41.7	52.2	78.2	76.2	109.3	149.2	106.5
	low	21.1	26.3	36.8	47.4	56.5	63	57.1	51

Apache Corporation
One Post Oak Central
2000 Post Oak Boulevard
Suite 100
Houston, TX 77056–4400
(713) 296–6662
Website: *www.apachecorp.com*

AGGRESSIVE GROWTH

Apple Inc.

Ticker symbol: AAPL (NASDAQ) ❑ S&P Rating: NA ❑ Value Line financial strength rating: A++ ❑
Current yield: NA

Company Profile

Apple Inc. designs, manufactures, and markets personal computers, portable music players, cell phones, and related software, peripherals, and services. It sells these products through its retail stores, online stores, and third-party and value-added resellers. The company also sells a variety of third-party compatible products such as printers, storage devices and other accessories through its online and retail stores, and digital content through its iTunes store.

The company's products have become household names: the iPhone, iPod, and MacBook are just some of the company's hardware products. And while the software may be less well known, iTunes, QuickTime, and OSX are important segments of the business each with their own revenue streams.

The company was incorporated in 1977 as Apple Computer but has since changed its name to simply Apple. The name change in 2007 was the last step in a ten-year retooling that had already changed the company from a personal computer also-ran into one of the most rec-

ognizable and profitable consumer electronics brands in the world.

Apple still sells boxes that sit under your desk and compute, but they are best known for their definition and implementation of successful new product concepts characterized by compelling and state-of-the-art industrial design and a simple, intuitive user interface. These qualities have been instrumental in creating an extremely loyal customer base and a brand cachet unequaled in the consumer electronics business.

Financial Highlights, Fiscal Year 2009

Apple was not completely immune to the effects of the economic downturn, as revenue growth tapered somewhat. The fundamentals remain solid, however, as earnings grew 18 percent, well ahead of revenue.

The iPhone was this year's star performer with revenue growth of 266 percent over 2008. The iPhone still has only a 2 percent market share of new phone sales, but already represents 18 percent of Apple's revenue.

Desktop revenues were off 23 percent due primarily to a shift to lower-priced units, lower average selling prices across the board and a general shift in the market away from desktops and toward portable/laptop machines.

Reasons to Buy

Last year we wrote about the "cool" factor with regard to Apple's products and described how Apple was able to charge a premium for products that did, essentially, the same thing that everyone else's product did. In our "Reasons for Caution" we suggested that a sustained economic downturn might cut significantly into Apple's top line growth, given their position as a "luxury" brand. Well, the top line did suffer somewhat in 2009—"only" 12 percent growth in sales, versus 35 percent the year before. They've clearly weathered the storm, with only desktop unit sales showing any significant ill effects.

Apple has just 7 percent of the total PC market revenue, but they manage to rake in 35 percent of the market's total operating profit (2009 numbers). HP, by contrast, accounted for 25 percent of the revenue but only 17 percent of the segment's profit. Apple, Dell, HP and the rest use many of the same parts, but only Apple doesn't have to pay Microsoft for an operating system. Some point to Apple's OSX operating system as an impediment

to Apple's longer-term growth prospects (which may be true), but for now their proprietary OS is an important contributor to their bottom line. It may seem like a narrow point to make in terms of a Reason to Buy, but a "free" OS has a very positive impact to profitability as market share grows, and Apple has been growing market share steadily over the past five years. And at just 4 percent of global unit market share, there's a lot of room for growth.

Apple's iTunes music sales have grown 60 percent from 2007–2009 and now account for 12 percent of their overall revenue. Given the very high margins associated with this service, iTunes is on track to be a very large, long-term cash cow.

Finally, rumors are rampant at this time regarding Apple-branded television hardware and content. If they manage to integrate this most traditional content delivery system into a compelling product, they could well have another big winner on their hands.

Reasons for Caution

Reviews have been somewhat mixed with regard to Apple's newest product, the iPad. Some say it's too large and does too little to make it really necessary in one's personal digital arsenal. No significant sales figures are available as yet.

At the time of this writing, the stock is trading at an all-time-high.

SECTOR: **Consumer Discretionary**
BETA COEFFICIENT: **1.10**
10-YEAR COMPOUND EARNINGS PER SHARE GROWTH: **45 percent**
10-YEAR COMPOUND DIVIDENDS PER SHARE GROWTH: **Nil**

	2002	2003	2004	2005	2006	2007	2008	2009
Revenues (Mil)	5,742	6,207	8,279	13,931	19,315	24,006	32,479	36,537
Net income (Mil)	117	76	276	1,254	1,989	3,496	4,834	5,704
Earnings per share	0.17	0.2	0.36	1.44	2.27	3.93	5.36	6.29
Dividends per share	0	0	0	0	0	0	0	0
Cash flow per share	0.33	0.26	0.54	1.72	2.59	4.37	5.97	7.12
Price: high	13.1	12.5	34.8	75.5	93.2	203.0	200.3	214
low	6.7	6.4	10.6	31.3	50.2	81.9	79.1	78.2

Apple Inc.
1 Infinite Loop
Cupertino, CA 95014
(408) 996-1010
Website: *www.apple.com*

Archer Daniels Midland Co.

Ticker symbol: ADM (NYSE) ❑ S&P rating: A ❑ Value Line financial strength rating: A ❑ Current yield: 1.8 percent

Company Profile

ADM is one of the largest food processors in the world. They buy corn, wheat, cocoa, oilseeds and other agricultural products and process them into food, food ingredients, animal feed and ingredients, and biofuels. They also resell grains on the open market.

The company owns and maintains facilities used throughout the production process. They source raw materials from sixty countries on six continents, transport them to any of their 230 processing plants via their own extensive sea/rail/road network, and then transport the finished products to the customer.

The company operates in three business segments: Oilseeds Processing, Corn Processing, and Agricultural Services.

The Oilseeds Processing unit processes soybeans, cottonseed, sunflower, canola, peanuts, and flaxseed into vegetable oils and protein meals for the food and feed industries. Crude vegetable oils are sold as is or are further refined into consumer products, while partially refined oils are sold for use in paints, chemicals, and other industrial products. The solids remaining from this processing are sold into a number of applications, including edible soy protein, animal feed, pharmaceuticals, chemical, and paper.

The Corn Processing segment's milling operations (primarily in the United States) produce food products too numerous to list, but include syrup, starch, glucose, dextrose, and other sweeteners. Markets served include animal feeds and the vegetable oil market. Fermentation of the dextrose yields ethanol, amino acids, and other specialty food and feed products. The ethanol is processed for beverage stock or industrial use as the base for ethanol-blended gasolines and other fuels.

The Agricultural Services segment is the company's storage and transportation network. They buy, store, clean, and transport grains to/from ADM facilities. They also resell raw materials primarily for the animal feed and agricultural processing industries.

Financial Highlights, Fiscal Year 2009

ADM's revenues were off 1 percent in 2009 due primarily to decreased worldwide demand for their products across the board. Operating margins were up 20 percent in oilseeds processing, off slightly in Agricultural Services, but were off 81 percent in Corn Processing. Reduced demand for lysine and greatly reduced demand and overcapacity in ethanol accounted for most of the $315 million loss in that segment. Ethanol profits are tied largely to the price and demand for gasoline, and 2009 produced the steepest decline in the demand for gasoline since 1950.

Profits from the wheat, cocoa, malt and sugar operation had an 80 percent decline due primarily to equity losses in its investment in Gruma S.A.B, while the finance division took a loss due to a decline in equity values and poor loan performance.

Stated operating profits for the year were up 15 percent to approximately $3.5 billion, but this figure includes a $520 million one-time, pre-tax credit to reserve inventory valuations. Earnings for the year rose 8 percent to $1.9 billion (also reflective of the accounting change). Absent the accounting adjustment, the company's income was off $90 million from 2008.

Reasons to Buy
The OECD-FAO Agricultural Outlook 2009–2018 predicts that crop demand will increase substantially in the next decade, even surpassing the 2008 highs. Much of the demand will be driven by emerging economies, particularly China, which are already accounting for much of ADM's growth (particularly in the soybean sector). ADM's Asian sales doubled in 2009.

Federal renewable-fuels mandates remain in place and fuel demand through early 2010 appears to be on a rebound to pre-2009 growth levels. ADM is extremely well positioned to provide corn-based ethanol, as 2009 produced another record corn crop and prices are low.

Last-quarter 2009 results showed the company is getting positive results as it continues to stress operational efficiency while recovering from a weak 2009 business environment. Operating margins have improved significantly, and the bioproducts division saw dramatically improved earnings as ethanol fuel demand has begun to increase.

ADM made ten acquisitions last year ($200 million), most in the emerging markets of Asia and South America. Sales growth outside the U.S. has far outpaced domestic growth, and ADM's presence and extensive transportation capability give it a decided advantage over its smaller competitors, many of which are focused only in certain markets or certain industries. ADM's market and geographic breadth reduce its exposure to both climatic and political variables.

Reasons for Caution

ADM is heavily invested in the corn-ethanol-fuel processing chain. China has already said that they will not use corn-based ethanol as a fuel adjunct, and the decreased demand for ethanol-enhanced transportation fuels in the U.S. has dropped dramatically over the past two years. There has been a groundswell of political opposition against corn-based ethanol fuels because of their efficiency and effects on food supply, but remember that ADM is involved in other biofuel products, too. If the trend toward reduced fuel usage and lower gasoline and diesel prices returns, ADM's corn processing unit will suffer.

SECTOR: Consumer Staples

BETA COEFFICIENT: 0.9

10-YEAR COMPOUND EARNINGS PER SHARE GROWTH: 11.5 percent

10-YEAR COMPOUND DIVIDENDS PER SHARE GROWTH: 11.0 percent

	2002	2003	2004	2005	2006	2007	2008	2009
Revenue (Mil)	23,454	30,708	36,151	35,944	36,596	44,018	69,816	69,207
Net income (Mil)	458	438	744	921	1,312	1,561	1,834	1,970
Earnings per share	0.70	0.68	1.16	1.40	2.00	2.38	2.84	3.06
Dividends per share	0.20	0.24	0.27	0.32	0.37	0.43	0.49	0.54
Cash flow per share	1.58	1.68	2.20	2.44	3.00	3.51	3.97	4.21
Price: high	14.9	15.2	22.5	25.5	46.7	47.3	48.9	33
low	10	10.5	14.9	17.5	24	30.2	13.5	23.1

Archer Daniels Midland Co.

4666 Faries Parkway, Box 1470

Decatur, IL 62525

(217) 424-5200

Website: *www.admworld.com*

GROWTH AND INCOME

AT&T Inc.

Ticker symbol: T (NYSE) ❑ S&P rating: A ❑ Value Line financial strength rating: A ❑ Current yield: 6.5 percent

Company Profile

Measured by revenue, AT&T is the world's largest communications holding company. It is the domestic market share leader in local and long-distance voice services, and is the largest provider of consumer and commercial broadband services in the United States. It is also the largest Wi-Fi provider in the United States. Its servers and trunk lines constitute a major part of the global Internet.

Its traditional wireline subsidiaries offer services in thirteen states, and the wireless business provides voice coverage in 220 countries. They have approximately 150 million total Consumer Revenue Connections, with a sales revenue mix of 45 percent wireless, 25 percent wireline data, 25 percent wireline voice, and 5 percent advertising/other.

Financial Highlights, Fiscal Year 2009

AT&T reported decreased revenues in 2009 versus 2008. The decline, while small (0.8 percent), was due in large part to two basic, long-term trends: the decline in advertising revenue and the shrinking voice

(wireline) customer base. Advertising (primarily AT&T Yellow Pages) revenue fell 12.6 percent, while voice revenue 13.4 percent. Of the two, the decline in voice revenue of $5.1 billion had a far greater impact to the bottom line.

Customers are discontinuing voice services at an ever-increasing rate. AT&T is finding that for more and more customers, a cell phone and data services are all that's needed, and traditional legacy voice services are no longer required by residential or commercial users.

On the brighter side, the wireless segment showed steady top-line growth of 8.6 percent and income growth of 19.7 percent, due largely to a 9.4 percent growth in customer base. Sales of Apple's iPhone handsets are responsible for the bulk of this growth.

Reasons to Buy

Last year we talked about how important it was for AT&T to be aggressive in their roll-out of the U-Verse product. The case for haste has been made even more strongly in their 2009 results, where IP data services revenue (U-Verse) grew 17.8 percent and was the only segment in the wireline business to record any growth at all. So why is this a reason to buy the stock? We believe U-Verse is a very attractive product for customers in the digital transition—people who are in the process of rolling over to their first broadband connection, or those who are consolidating voice, data, and TV into one provider. It allows AT&T to retain what would have been lost AT&T customers and also to capture new customers who are discarding their old wired voice service. In the process, AT&T trades one low-value voice connection for a very high value data link, through which they can provide upsells on a daily basis.

If AT&T is able to manage this rollover business well (and so far, it appears that they are), then their dull, boring, unprofitable wireline customers become a field of opportunity. Not only that, but many of the smaller regional ILECs in the country with a similar customer base become attractive buyout opportunities.

AT&T's relationship with Apple appears to be solid. Their exclusivity agreement, always a subject of speculation, is intact, and Apple's iPad will be released with a similar agreement with AT&T. The iPhone and iPad products are far more valuable than simple phones or other data devices, as they are also walking storefronts for applications and other value-added content. AT&T has upgraded their 3G hardware in many metropolitan areas and now offers far better service than other providers, eliminating the main source of frustration expressed by iPhone users.

In the commercial space, AT&T operates one of the largest VOIP (voice traffic over the Internet) networks in the world and can offer seamless integration as new/improved services appear, such as their recent introduction of high-definition video conferencing.

Reasons for Caution

The average service revenue per unit in the wireless sector has been essentially flat for two years. Data revenues have been increasing, but this has been offset by declining voice revenues. Unless AT&T offers more compelling premium services in this channel, their top-line growth in this, their most profitable sector, will be tied simply to the increase in the number of units in service. Growing market share may require them to lower prices.

The wireline services sector will, in all likelihood, continue to be a drag on margins. There are some regulatory initiatives underway that, if approved, should improve the picture somewhat, but the better solution is to convert these customers over to another AT&T product, be it wireless, U-Verse, or commercial VOIP.

SECTOR: Telecommunications Services
BETA COEFFICIENT: 0.75
10-YEAR COMPOUND EARNINGS PER SHARE GROWTH: 1.5 percent
10-YEAR COMPOUND DIVIDENDS PER SHARE GROWTH: 5.0 percent

		2002	2003	2004	2005	2006	2007	2008	2009
Revenues (Mil)		51,755	40,843	40,787	43,862	63,055	118,928	124,028	123,018
Net income (Mil)		7,219	5,051	4,884	5,803	9.014	16,950	12,867	12,535
Earnings per share		2.16	1.52	1.47	1.72	2.34	2.76	2.16	2.12
Dividends per share		1.07	1.37	1.25	1.29	1.22	1.42	1.60	1.64
Cash flow per share		5.14	3.91	3.77	3.42	4.63	5.36	5.56	5.46
Price:	high	41.0	31.7	27.7	26.0	36.2	43.0	41.9	29.5
	low	19.6	18.8	23.0	21.8	24.2	32.7	20.9	21.4

AT&T Inc.
175 East Houston
San Antonio, TX 78205
(210) 821-4105
Website: *www.att.com*

Baxter International, Inc.

Ticker symbol: BAX-S&P rating: A+ ▫ Value Line financial strength rating: A++ ▫ Current yield: 2.8 percent

Company Profile

Baxter International develops, manufactures, and markets bio-pharmaceuticals, drug delivery systems and medical equipment. Their products are used to treat patients with hemophilia, immune deficiencies, infectious diseases, cancer, kidney disease, and other disorders. Based in the United States, Baxter has operations in over 100 countries and operates in three main segments: Bioscience, Medication Delivery, and Renal.

Bioscience produces pharmaceuticals derived from blood plasma. The bulk of the product line is devoted to treatments for hemophilia and its complications. Their ADVATE product is widely used for the control and prevention of bleeding episodes. The company also produces a variety of vaccines with its proprietary Vero cell technology.

Medication Delivery produces a wide range of equipment used to apply, inject, infuse, and otherwise deliver medications to the patient. If it comes in contact with the medication, Baxter probably makes it. Tubes, pumps, valves, syringes, and filters are some of the typical product lines in MD. The company

also sells IV solutions and premixed drugs, as well as anesthetics.

The Renal business is focused on the treatment of patients with kidney failure who are undergoing peritoneal dialysis treatment. They supply a range of products, including home PD machines and all of the accessories and disposables associated with them, as well as equipment and supplies for clinical dialysis facilities.

Product sales are split fairly evenly between the United States and Europe (40 percent each), with the rest of the world making up the balance.

Financial Highlights, Fiscal Year 2009

Baxter had record sales and earnings in 2009, though just barely, with net revenues up just 2 percent. Unfavorable foreign currency exchange rates had a major impact on revenues, cutting 5 percent off the top line growth. Earnings per share did significantly better, growing 14 percent to $3.59. Despite the relatively flat sales performance, the company grew investment in R&D by 6 percent and continued to repurchase shares, adding 3 percent to their EPS.

The growth, however modest, was more or less evenly distributed, with two of the company's three major segments reporting increased revenues and earnings. The Renal segment showed the only downturn, off less than 2 percent due largely to unfavorable currency exchange rates. The earnings growth in the BioScience and Medication Delivery segments was driven largely by improvements in gross margins due to a favorable sales mix of higher-margin products.

The company spent $1.2 billion to repurchase 23 million shares of common stock in 2009 and has an additional $1.9 billion in authorization remaining for further purchases.

In 2009 the company purchased a 40 percent stake in Sigma International for $100 million, including three-year exclusive rights for the distribution of Sigma's infusion pump. The deal also includes provisions for the possible purchase of the remaining 40 percent of the company.

Reasons to Buy

Over the past five years, Baxter's total shareholder return is nearly 85 percent, while the S&P 500's return over the same period is, not surprisingly, down 9 percent. What is surprising is Baxter's performance against the S&P Health Care Sector, which over the past five years is up a rather paltry 5 percent. Why is Baxter beating its

sector index? Baxter's focus on treatments for long-term, chronic, life-threatening conditions has largely insulated them from demand fluctuations, and their international market presence has allowed them to serve the fastest growing markets, and its high market penetrations offer further protection from smaller, local competition.

The company has thirty products in its pipeline with targeted peak sales of $250 million each, and over half of those are already in Phase III clinical trials, including a treatment for some of the most debilitating symptoms associated with Alzheimer's disease. Baxter's steadily improving cash flow (up 18 percent in 2009) looks to be more than sufficient to grow its R&D budget while continuing to fund share repurchase and its steadily growing dividend.

The company's ADVATE product continues to gain momentum and reached sales of $2.05 billion in 2009. It holds leadership positions in the United States, Europe, Japan, and several other markets. Looking forward to continued growth, the company believes that some 70 percent of the world's hemophilia patients are currently undiagnosed and that only 25 percent of the diagnosed are receiving adequate care.

Reasons for Caution

The company continues to have problems with its line of dialysis pumps and has had to augment its funding for the recall of several of its products. Some of its key customers have canceled planned purchases of H1N1 antivirals due to reduced demand on the news that one treatment was sufficient for protection, when two treatments were anticipated. The country of France has an excess of some 50 million doses which it will now be selling, further depressing prices of the drug.

SECTOR: **Health Care**
BETA COEFFICIENT: **0.6**
10-YEAR COMPOUND EARNINGS PER SHARE GROWTH: **9.0 percent**
10-YEAR COMPOUND DIVIDENDS PER SHARE GROWTH: **2.5 percent**

	2002	**2003**	**2004**	**2005**	**2006**	**2007**	**2008**	**2009**
Revenues (Mil)	8,110	8,916	9,509	9,849	10,378	11,263	12,348	12,562
Net income (Mil)	1,188	922	1,040	958	1,464	1,826	2,155	2,330
Earnings per share	1.92	1.52	1.68	1.52	2.23	2.79	3.38	3.8
Dividends per share	0.58	0.58	0.58	0.58	0.58	0.72	0.91	1.07
Cash flow per share	2.71	2.4	2.66	2.46	3.13	3.8	4.52	5.02
Price: high	59.9	31.3	34.8	41.1	48.5	61.1	71.5	61
low	24.1	18.2	27.1	33.1	35.1	46.1	47.4	45.5

Baxter International, Inc.
1 Baxter Parkway
Deerfield, IL 60015
Website: *www.baxter.com*

Becton, Dickinson and Company

Ticker symbol: BDX (NYSE) ◻ S&P rating: A ◻ Value Line financial strength rating: A++ ◻ Current yield: 1.9 percent

Company Profile

Becton, Dickinson is a medical technology company and a supplier to health care institutions, life science researchers, clinical laboratories, industry and the general public. BD manufactures a broad range of medical supplies, devices, laboratory equipment and diagnostic products.

They operate in three worldwide business segments: Medical, Biosciences, and Diagnostics.

BD Medical produces hypodermic needles and syringes, infusion therapy devices, insulin injection systems and pre-fillable drug-delivery systems for pharmaceutical companies.

BD Diagnostics offers system solutions for collecting, identifying and transporting specimens, as well as instrumentation for analyzing specimens. The business also provides customer training and business management services.

BD Biosciences provides research tools and reagents to accelerate the pace of biomedical discovery. Clinicians and researchers use BD Biosciences' tools to study genes, proteins, and cells to understand disease, improve technologies for diagnosis and disease management, and facilitate the discovery and development of new therapeutics.

Financial Highlights, Fiscal Year 2009

The company reported year over year growth in earnings of 9 percent (to $1.22 billion), well ahead of what were basically flat revenues of $7.12 billion. The difficult economic environment, reduced government spending and some unfavorable currency translations were the leading factors in the lower-than-expected revenues. On a volume basis, medical unit sales in Asia and Latin America were up nearly 10 percent. On a currency-neutral basis, U.S. revenues would have been up close to 16 percent.

In spite of the flat revenues, all other indicators for the company were quite good—margins and cash flow were both improved, and the company even raised the dividend and repurchased $550 million in stock. Capital investments and R&D spending for the year totaled nearly $1 billion for the second year in a row. The company completed the acquisition of HandyLab for

$275 million, gaining access to a molecular assay platform to complement BD's existing products.

The company's sales have rebounded well in early 2010, with the Medical and Diagnostic divisions posting strong increases due to the onset of the flu season in North America and caution over other infectious diseases.

Reasons to Buy

Becton, Dickinson appears to be as recession-proof as any stock on our list. The downturn in 2008–2009 certainly affected their stock's performance, but theirs was affected far less than most. People may defer some medical treatments during an economic downturn, but there's a limit to how much and for how long.

Over the past ten years, many medical suppliers have done very well, but BD is one of the more broadly diversified in the field and has a low exposure should any single product perform badly in the marketplace. The bulk of their revenues come from relatively simple, modestly priced supplies and instruments, and their lower-volume, more expensive equipment is built around well-proven and well-understood building blocks.

They're a conservatively run company that responded to the recession by doing what good companies do—cutting expenses, but continuing to invest in itself. You should always invest when it's cheapest to do so.

Erik A. Antonson of Value Line likes Becton Dickinson as well, and sees them closing out 2011 with $8.2 billion in sales and earning $5.60 per share. Specifically, he says: "Demand for the company's broad array of Medical and Diagnostics products will likely remain robust. The Biosciences unit's results should begin rebounding by then, too, owing to an improving economy."

Finally, BD's board recently approved the repurchase of an additional 10 million shares of stock, in addition to the 10 million approved back in 2008 (of which 7 million remain to be bought). This represents a "free" 7.3 percent increase in earnings per share, should the company repurchase these 17 million remaining shares.

The company continues to reinvest in itself, spending nearly $1 billion in 2008 on capital investments and R&D. This is a continuation of a long-term strategy that they have implemented well, and their dedication to maintaining it speaks to their confidence in their current position. Their five-year CAGR is 18.9 percent, compared to the S&P 500 at 5.2 percent and the S&P Health Care Equipment Index at 7.2 percent.

Reasons for Caution

Continued uncertainty surrounding the health care issue in the United States has to be considered when looking at any stock in this sector. Due to the basic and necessary nature of the bulk of their product line, we feel BD is well positioned to sail though these waters without getting swamped, but a re-evaluation of BD would be prudent once the policy issues have been settled.

SECTOR: **Health Care**
BETA COEFFICIENT: **.60**
10-YEAR COMPOUND EARNINGS PER SHARE GROWTH: **13.0 percent**
10-YEAR COMPOUND DIVIDENDS PER SHARE GROWTH: **14.5 percent**

	2002	2003	2004	2005	2006	2007	2008	2009
Revenues (Mil)	4,033	4,528	4,935	5,415	5,835	6,560	7,156	7,160
Net income (Mil)	480	547	582	692	841	978	1,1128	1,220
Earnings per share	1.79	2.07	2.21	2.66	3.28	3.84	4.46	4.95
Dividends per share	0.39	0.4	0.6	0.72	0.86	0.98	1.14	1.32
Cash flow per share	3.06	3.63	4.13	4.60	5.08	5.82	6.60	7.13
Price: high	38.6	41.8	58.2	61.2	74.2	85.9	93.2	80.0
low	24.7	28.8	40.2	49.7	58.1	69.3	58.1	60.4

Becton, Dickinson and Company
1 Becton Drive
Franklin Lakes, NJ 07417–1880
(201) 847–5453
Website: *www.bd.com*

Bed Bath & Beyond Inc.

Ticker symbol: BBBY (NASDAQ) □ S&P rating: BBB □ Value Line financial strength rating: A++ □ Current yield: nil

Company Profile

Founded in 1971, Bed Bath & Beyond and its subsidiaries sell a wide assortment of goods, primarily domestics merchandise and home furnishings, but including food, giftware, health and beauty care items and infant and toddler merchandise. With over 1,100 stores in the United States, Canada, and Mexico, the company has strong geographic coverage—their goal is to be the customer's first choice for the merchandise categories offered. BB&B competes on the breadth and depth of its product offerings, its customer service, new merchandise offerings and low prices.

The company also owns (through acquisition) and operates three other retail chain concepts. Its CTS (Christmas Tree Shops) chain counts sixty-one stores in fifteen states. There are forty-five Harmon stores in three states, and twenty-nine buybuy BABY stores in fourteen states.

The buybuy BABY stores offer over 20,000 products for infants and toddlers, including cribs, dressers, car seats, strollers and highchairs, feeding, nursing, bath supplies and everyday consumables, as well as toys, activity centers and development products. The stores are equipped with private feeding and changing rooms and offer home delivery and setup on everything they sell.

Founded on Cape Cod in 1970, Christmas Tree Shops is a value priced retailer of home decor, giftware, housewares, food, paper goods, and seasonal products. The stores specialize in low cost merchandise with frequent changes in mix to generate continued interest.

Financial Highlights, Fiscal Year 2009

BBBY's blowout fourth quarter (17 percent revenue growth over 4Q2008) led to 9 percent yearly growth in revenue and a 41 percent surge in earnings. Comparable store sales growth was very strong at 11 percent. Profitability has improved as well—net margin was up 180 basis points (1.8 percent) on significantly reduced SG&A.

In 2009 the company opened sixty-seven new stores—thirty-nine BB&B, nine CTS stores, five Harmon stores, and fourteen buybuy BABY stores. FY2009 also marked continued expansion into Canada; the first store opened in early 2008, and there are now sixteen BB&B stores in four Canadian provinces.

Reasons to Buy

Occasionally a retailer hits on a formula that just works. On the upper end, you have Nordstrom's, with their blend of selection, attractive environment, and superior service. At the lower end, you have Wal-Mart, who redefined discount shopping with a clean, well-lit, place in which to buy massive quantities of diapers and ammo under one roof. Bed Bath & Beyond understands that when people are feathering the nest, they enjoy going through as many feathers as possible before selecting just the right one. BB&B stocks more products per category than their competitors and arranges their stores so as to emphasize the number of products per category. They also mimic the display styles of specialty stores by presenting related product groups together in vignette form, reinforcing the perception of wide selection and communicating, if not actually providing, a level of customer service generally associated with those specialty stores. It's a formula they trust and one that seems to work regardless of store size and location.

The BB&B format has not yet reached saturation levels, as there appears to be room for another 500 stores in the United States and Canada. The company's move into other formats, buybuy BABY in particular, comes along at just the right time, as BB&B is generating more than enough cash to fund its own expansion. The company plans to take CTS and buybuy BABY nationwide, and looks to be able to fund the expansion with free cash flow.

The company's gross margins have been extremely stable going back at least twelve years, even as sales have more than tripled and the company has acquired three new chains. This is a very good indicator of a company that has solid control of its costs and pricing.

The exit of Linens 'N Things from the market in 2009 continues to benefit BB&B. Net margin has improved as the company has reduced the frequency of its discount mailers and is seeing better than expected foot traffic in early 2010.

We like the buybuy BABY concept (though not the name) and feel it has terrific expansion prospects. This is a high-margin, non-niche segment serviced by few large specialists. It also has an abundant low-cost supply chain.

Reasons for Caution

There's not a lot of trouble on the horizon. Four large funds hold approximately 40 percent of BBBY's shares, which could lead to higher share price volatility. Due to its rapid expansion plans, the buybuy BABY chain has the burden of high expectations and any stumble in that line may have an inordinately large effect on the share price.

SECTOR: **Retail**
BETA COEFFICIENT: **0.90**
10-YEAR COMPOUND EARNINGS PER SHARE GROWTH: **22.0 percent**
10-YEAR COMPOUND DIVIDENDS PER SHARE GROWTH: **Nil**

		2002	2003	2004	2005	2006	2007	2008	2009
Revenues (Mil)		3,665	4,478	5,147	5,810	6,617	7,049	7,208	7,829
Net income (Mil)		302	400	505	573	611	563	425	600
Earnings per share		1.00	1.31	1.65	1.92	2.15	2.10	1.64	2.30
Dividends per share		-	-	-	-	-	-	-	-
Cash flow per share		1.29	1.61	2.05	2.43	2.68	2.78	2.31	2.98
Price:	high	37.9	45	44.4	47	41.7	43.3	34.7	40.2
	low	26.7	30.2	33.9	35.5	30.9	28	16.2	19.1

Bed Bath & Beyond Inc.
650 Liberty Avenue
Union, NJ 07083
(908) 688-0888
Website: *www.bedbathandbeyond.com*

AGGRESSIVE GROWTH

Best Buy Company

Ticker symbol: BBY (NASDAQ) □ S&P rating: BBB- □ Value Line financial strength rating: A □ Current yield: 1.2 percent

Company Profile

Best Buy is a multinational retailer of technology and entertainment products and services with 3,800 stores in the United States, Canada, Europe, China, Mexico and Turkey. The company's retailers include Best Buy; Best Buy Mobile; Audiovisions; The Carphone Warehouse; Future Shop; Geek Squad; Jiangsu Five Star; Magnolia Audio Video; Napster; Pacific Sales; and The Phone House. The company has 180,000 employees working through retail locations, call centers and websites, and also providing in-home solutions and product delivery.

Founded in 1966, Best Buy's product portfolio is dominated by consumer electronics (about 40 percent) and home office products (about 33 percent). The company operates in two reporting segments, Domestic (all U.S.–based operations in all segments) and International.

The various retailers have up to six different revenue categories each, with U.S. Best Buy and the Canadian Future Shop stores offering the broadest selection of merchandise. Other stores offer a subset of the six categories, which include consumer electronics, home office, entertainment software, appliances, services and "other." The services revenue category consists primarily of service contracts, extended warranties, computer-related services, product repair, and delivery and installation for home theater, mobile audio and appliances.

Financial Highlights, Fiscal Year 2010 (ended February 27, 2010)

FY2010 brought a 10 percent gain in revenues and a 12 percent gain in earnings. The revenue gain was driven primarily by the first full-year's contribution of Best Buy Europe, which was acquired in mid-year FY2009 and the net addition of eighty-five new stores in FY2010. The earnings gain was driven by improved operating income, in turn driven by revenue growth. Operating cash flow increased 17.5 percent in FY2010, and the company exited the year with $1.8 billion in cash and equivalents, compared with $500 million the prior year.

The company acquired Napster, which provides a digital music service that offers digital music downloads and on-demand streaming of user-owned content. The company also purchased the remaining 25 percent of Jiangsu Five Star Appliance Co., one of China's largest appliance and consumer electronics retailers (Best Buy had an earlier 75 percent ownership position).

The company acquired a 50 percent share in Best Buy Europe, a joint venture with Carphone Warehouse (CPW). The business consists of CPW's former retail and distribution business, including over 2,400 retail outlets, and mobile and fixed-line telecom services. The purchase also includes CPW's economic interest in a number of Best Buy operations in Europe.

Reasons to Buy

Best Buy, more than most technology retailers, seems to have grasped the notion that they can increase the size of most tickets if the salesperson applies some expertise to what the customer is saying. The company wants to sell the connectedness of its products, and it seems that they are providing their salespeople with the proper tools and training to do so. The "Geek Squad" offering further supports this notion with an aptly branded configuration and tech support service. More than other retailers, Best Buy sells solutions, and customers have responded well while the company has expanded its margins as a result.

With Circuit City's 2009 exit, Best Buy is gathering market share

and momentum. Their market share is estimated to have grown 240 basis points (2.4 percent) in 2009 and is expected to increase another 100 basis points in 2010. Expansion plans for 2010 include the opening of fifty to fifty-five net large-format stores under the Best Buy brand, the majority of which are in the Domestic segment. They also plan to open seventy-five to 100 small-format stores, primarily Best Buy Mobile stand-alone stores in the United States. In addition, they expect to open ten to fifteen Five Star stores in China.

IDC predicts that global PC shipments will grow 20 percent in 2010, with average selling prices actually increasing as the percentage of netbooks moved through the channel starts to moderate. Emerging markets will see the largest gain, while mature markets will see a more moderate gain of 13.6 percent.

Reasons for Caution

A rumored merger with Radio Shack would potentially create even more outlets for Best Buy's growing mobile business, but we worry that the cost of an integration, coupled with the company's expansion into both Europe and China, might burden cash flow just as gross margins are starting to decline. We seriously question the value of incremental retail phone outlets for any company not named Apple.

SECTOR: Retail
BETA COEFFICIENT: 1.10
10-YEAR COMPOUND EARNINGS PER SHARE GROWTH: 28.5 percent
10-YEAR COMPOUND DIVIDENDS PER SHARE GROWTH: Nil

	2003	2004	2005	2006	2007	2008	2009	2010
Revenues (Mil)	20,946	24,547	27,433	30,848	35,934	40,023	45,015	49,694
Net income (Mil)	622	800	966	1,140	1,377	1,407	1,208	1,342
Earnings per share	1.27	1.63	1.91	2.27	2.79	3.12	2.88	3.15
Dividends per share	-	0.27	0.27	0.31	0.36	0.46	0.53	0.56
Cash flow per share	1.93	2.43	2.82	3.29	3.92	4.84	4.84	5.21
Price: high	35.8	41.8	41.5	53.2	59.5	53.9	53.0	45.6
low	11.3	15.8	29.2	31.9	43.3	41.8	16.4	24.0

Best Buy Company, Inc.
7601 Penn Avenue South
Richfield, MN 55423
(612) 291-1000
Website: *www.bestbuy.com*

The Boeing Company

Ticker symbol: BA (NYSE) □ S&P rating: A □ Value Line financial strength rating: A+ □ Current yield: 2.9 percent

Company Profile

The Boeing Company is the world's largest manufacturer of commercial and military aircraft. They also produce helicopters, ground transportation systems, military communications and missile systems, unmanned aircraft, and develop advanced research for various branches of the U.S. military. Prior to the program's cancellation in early 2010, they were also the prime contractor for the space shuttle. Sales are split 60/40 between U.S.-based (including government) and foreign customers.

Boeing is organized into four major business units: Boeing Capital Corporation, Boeing Commercial Airplanes, Connexion by BoeingSM, and Boeing Integrated Defense Systems. Supporting these units is the Boeing Shared Services Group, which contributes common and infrastructure services that enable the company's business units to concentrate on growth. In addition, the Phantom Works unit provides advanced research and development, including advanced concepts for air traffic management.

Boeing has been the premier manufacturer of commercial aircraft for more than forty years. Today, the main commercial products consist of the 717, 737, 747, 767, and 777 families of airplanes, and the Boeing Business Jet. New product development efforts are focused on the Boeing 787, a high-efficiency model that was expected to be in service in 2008 but has been delayed to late 2010. The company has nearly 13,000 commercial jetliners in service worldwide, which is roughly 75 percent of the world fleet.

Boeing Commercial Aviation Services provides a full range of engineering, modification, logistics and information services to its customer base, which includes passenger and cargo airlines as well as maintenance, repair and overhaul facilities. Boeing also trains maintenance and flight crews in the 100-seat-and-above airliner market through Alteon, the world's largest provider of airline training.

Financial Highlights, Fiscal Year 2009

The company reported sales of $68.3 billion, a year/year increase of 12.2 percent, primarily due to the resolution of a labor strike that affected the production of commercial airframes in the year prior. Earnings for 2009 fell 48 percent, however, due to the difficult capital markets, the reclassification of certain costs associated with the 787 program (three entire airplanes were charged to R&D, a $2.7 billion hit to earnings), and increased development costs for the 747-8 program.

Backlog declined some 10 percent but remains at extremely high levels, with over five years of backlog on the 737 alone.

Reasons to Buy

Worldwide, Boeing forecasts a $3.2 trillion market for new commercial airplanes during the next twenty years and projects a need for approximately 28,600 new commercial airplanes (passenger and freighter), doubling the world fleet by 2026. The vast majority of these new airplanes will be in the single-aisle (ninety seats and above) and twin-aisle (200-400 seats) categories.

Boeing also projects an addressable market of nearly $1 trillion over the next five years in Defense, Space and Security, markets that carry far higher margins than commercial aircraft.

Boeing's remaining backlog of $316 billion ($297 billion of which is contractual) is over four times its current annual revenue. Its backlog of commercial aircraft is over 3,300 units, with a sales value of roughly $250 billion.

The replacement program for the KC-135 tanker is accepting final bids from Boeing and Airbus on July 9, with the award scheduled for November. If you've ever been to the track, you know what to do—watch these two stocks closely and see where the smart money is going.

Reasons for Caution

The current orders for the 787 Dreamliner represent nearly 40 percent of the company's contracted backlog. First customer deliveries, now set for November 2010, are over two years behind schedule. The plane has had its ceremonial first flights—if the delivery of first customer units is delayed yet again, look for more than a few investors to head for the exits. Whether that would represent a warning sign or a buying opportunity would depend on the size of the delay and the size of the exodus.

SECTOR: Industrials
BETA COEFFICIENT: 1.05
10-YEAR COMPOUND EARNINGS PER SHARE GROWTH: 10.5 percent
10-YEAR COMPOUND DIVIDENDS PER SHARE GROWTH: 11.0 percent

	2002	2003	2004	2005	2006	2007	2008	2009
Revenues (Mil)	54,069	50,485	52,457	53,621	61,530	66,387	60,909	68,281
Net income (Mil)	2,275	809	1,872	2,572	3,014	4,074	2,654	1,335
Earnings per share	2.82	1.00	2.30	2.39	3.62	5.28	3.63	1.87
Dividends per share	0.68	0.68	0.77	1.05	1.20	1.40	1.62	1.68
Cash flow per share	4.72	2.82	3.57	4.50	5.78	7.53	5.94	4.13
Price: high	51.1	43.4	55.5	72.4	92	107.8	88.3	56.5
low	28.5	24.7	38	49.5	65.9	84.6	36.2	29

The Boeing Company
100 North Riverside
Chicago, IL 60606
(312) 544–2140
Website: *www.boeing.com*

Bunge Limited

Ticker symbol: BG (NYSE) ❑ S&P rating: BBB- ❑ Value Line financial strength rating B++ ❑ Current yield: 1.4 percent

Company Profile

Bunge Limited is a worldwide player in agriculture and in the food business. The company operates in four segments: Agribusiness, Fertilizer, Edible Oil Products, and Milling Products. The Agribusiness segment is a full-line producer and distributor of food products, including the purchase, storage, transport, processing, and sale of agricultural commodities and commodity products. The Agribusiness segment also provides financial services around these activities, including financing and risk management services. The segment represents 73 percent of the overall business.

The Fertilizer segment engages in mining phosphate-based raw materials and the sale of blended fertilizer products and phosphate-based animal feed ingredients. This segment accounts for 9 percent of the total, and the company recently announced the sale of some Brazilian fertilizer producing operations, although it will remain a retail player. The Edible Oil Products segment involves producing and selling packaged and bulk oils, shortenings, margarine, mayonnaise, and other products derived from the vegetable

oil refining process and represents 15 percent of the business. The Milling Products segment engages in producing and selling wheat flours, bakery mixes, and products derived from corn, including dry milled corn meal, flours and grits, soy-fortified corn meal, corn-soy blend, corn oil, and corn animal feed products, but currently accounts for only 3 percent of the business.

While operations and especially distribution operations are worldwide, Bunge's activities are centered in the Americas—both North and South America. Bunge is the largest processor of soybeans in the Americas and is the world's largest exporter of soybean products. The company continues to expand its international presence with the purchase of Brazilian sugar mills and grain processing plants in locales ranging from Vietnam to the U.S. Pacific Northwest.

Financial Highlights, Fiscal Year 2009

The global recession and stabilizing commodity prices produced a nearly 20 percent drop in top-line revenues for 2009, although as a testimonial to outsized commodity prices in

2008, revenues were still 10 percent ahead of 2007. Earnings suffered as a result, dropping from $7.73 per share to $2.22. More stable commodity prices and currency exchange rates should return the company to its more stable earnings profile of $4.50 to $6.00 per share cash flows running nearly double that.

The company recently announced plans to buy back $700 million in shares, using some of the proceeds from recent sales of fertilizer operations.

Reasons to Buy

We like the international and especially the Americas agricultural plays, including Brazilian sugar/ethanol, which is one of the global strongholds in economically viable ethanol production with a strong domestic market and an emerging export market. Additionally, the company has raised dividends every year since 2002. Cash flow per share is very strong, typically ten times the dividend and nearly twice the reported earnings per share.

In the long term global economy, we like agricultural plays in general, like Bunge as well as Monsanto and ADM, for their products will always be in demand as global food markets expand and in particular as the Chinese adopt a more middle-class lifestyle. The recent floating and strengthening of the Chinese currency should help companies like Bunge. These agricultural companies have been weak through most of 2010, offering good buying opportunities in our opinion.

Reasons for Caution

Like many agricultural producers, especially in recent years, Bunge is susceptible to volatility in commodity prices, As a big international player, Bunge is additionally subject to currency fluctuations, so earnings are less than predictable. But Bunge's track record shows respectable earnings even in a down year like 2009, and "boom" years like 2007 and 2008 show just how far this company can go.

SECTOR: Consumer Staples
BETA COEFFICIENT: 1.35
5-YEAR COMPOUND EARNINGS PER SHARE GROWTH: 7.5 percent
5-YEAR COMPOUND DIVIDENDS PER SHARE GROWTH: 10.5 percent

	2002	2003	2004	2005	2006	2007	2008	2009
Revenues (Mil)	14,074	22,165	25,169	24,275	26,274	37,842	52,574	41,926
Net income (Mil)	278	418	469	530	521	778	1,064	361
Earnings per share	2.88	4.14	4.10	4.43	4.28	5.95	7.73	2.22
Dividends per share	.39	.42	.50	.56	.63	.66	.72	.80
Cash flow per share	4.52	6.03	6.15	6.78	7.04	9.31	11.69	5.41
Price: high	26.3	33.4	57.4	68.0	73.5	125.5	135.0	73.0
low	17.0	23.8	32.8	46.7	47.3	69.9	27.6	38.8

Bunge Limited
50 Main Street, 6th Floor
White Plains, NY 10606
(914) 684-2800
Website: *www.bunge.com*

CONSERVATIVE GROWTH

C.R. Bard, Inc.

Ticker symbol: BCR (NYSE) ❑ S&P rating: A− ❑ Value Line financial rating: A++ ❑ Current yield: 0.8 percent

Company Profile

Founded in 1907 by Charles Russell Bard, the company markets a wide range of medical, surgical, diagnostic and patient-care devices. It markets its products worldwide to hospitals, individual health care professionals, extended care facilities, and alternate site facilities. Most of Bard's products fall into the category of consumables/supplies—intended to be used once and then discarded. The company operates in four core segments—Vascular, Urology, Oncology, and Surgery.

■ **Urology** (28 percent of sales)— The company offers a complete line of urological diagnosis and intervention products including Foley catheters (the market leader and their largest-selling product), procedure kits and trays, urethral stents and specialty devices for incontinence.

■ **Oncology** (27 percent of sales)—Bard's products are designed for the detection and treatment of various types of cancer. Products include specialty access catheters and ports, gastroenterological products, and biopsy devices.

The company's chemotherapy products serve a well-established market in which Bard holds a major market position.

■ **Vascular** (27 percent of sales)—The company's line of vascular diagnosis and intervention products includes peripheral angioplasty stents, catheters, guide wires, introducers and accessories, vena cava filters, and implantable blood vessel replacements. They also sell electrophysiology products such as cardiac mapping and laboratory systems that support sales of the consumables.

■ **Surgical Specialties** (15 percent of sales)—Surgical specialties products include meshes for vessel and hernia repair; irrigation devices for orthopedic and laparoscopic procedures; and topical hemostatic devices.

Bard markets its products through twenty-two subsidiaries and a joint venture in over a hundred countries outside the United States. Principal markets are Japan, Canada, the United Kingdom and continental Europe.

Financial Highlights, Fiscal Year 2009

The company reported year over year sales growth of 3 percent (to $2.54 billion). Vascular sales grew 6 percent to lead all segments, while Urology sales fell 1 percent. Earnings gained a healthy 11 percent to $460 million ($4.60 per share) as the company was very aggressive about cutting costs during the recession. Operating and net margins were up 260 and 150 basis points, respectively. Bard also announced a minor restructuring that is expected to generate pre-tax cost savings of $25 million/year in 2010 and beyond.

The company bought back another 4 percent of its outstanding shares and raised the dividend an additional 6 percent.

The company made two significant acquisitions during the year, acquiring a privately held company whose angioplasty catheter line complement's Bard's own. Bard should now be the market share leader in this growing area. They also acquired worldwide rights to the hernia products business of Brennan Medical, whose technology expanded Bard's offerings and replaced some of Bard's existing devices.

Reasons to Buy

Bard has a broad product line of consumables in a market that has been nearly recession-proof. Health care spending continues to grow ahead of inflation, and the majority of Bard's products fall into the area of non-discretionary purchases.

They have the number one or number two market position across nearly 80 percent of their product line, and their product line recognizes and addresses a number of compelling trends: an aging demographic and the shift to lower-cost, patient-assisted (in-home) therapy.

The company has been successful with recent acquisitions and is well positioned to continue this strategy. They have large reserves of capital and low levels of debt. They have stated their intention to grow their R&D investment by up to 400 basis points (4 percent) through the next two to three years, and acquisitions have been one of their favorite tools.

In March 2010 Bard announced their plan to acquire SenoRx for $212 million in stock. SenoRx makes a minimally invasive breast cancer detection and biopsy sample system, which has been very well received in the market. The company has gross margins in the 70 percent range but is not yet profitable. It looks to be a very good fit for Bard's Oncology operation and the acquisition is estimated to have a fairly small negative impact on Bard's earnings, on the order of ten to fifteen cents per share.

Reasons for Caution

Bard cannot afford to out-research their much larger competitors (St. Jude Medical, Boston Scientific, Johnson & Johnson) and so tends to acquire R&D properties on the open market. This is a more expensive method of funding R&D, to be sure, and it's an operating model that requires far more liquidity than internally developed IP might. The model works for Bard, but if for whatever reason maintaining this high liquidity becomes an issue, it could hamper Bard's top-line growth.

SECTOR: **Consumer Health Care**
BETA COEFFICIENT: **.60**
10-YEAR COMPOUND EARNINGS PER SHARE GROWTH: **17.0 percent**
10-YEAR COMPOUND DIVIDENDS PER SHARE GROWTH: **5.5 percent**

	2002	2003	2004	2005	2006	2007	2008	2009
Revenues (Mil)	1,274	1,433	1,656	1,771	1,985	2,202	2,452	2,535
Net income (Mil)	177	204	263	327	352	406	455	510
Earnings per share	1.68	1.94	2.45	3.12	3.29	3.84	4.44	4.79
Dividends per share	0.43	0.45	0.47	0.5	0.54	0.58	0.62	0.66
Cash flow per share	2.12	2.4	3.03	3.76	4.14	4.85	5.5	6.29
Price: high	32	40.8	65.1	72.8	85.7	95.3	101.6	88.4
low	22	27	40.1	60.8	59.9	76.6	70	68.9

C.R. Bard, Inc.
730 Central Avenue
Murray Hill, NJ 07974
(908) 277–8413
Website: *www.crbard.com*

Campbell Soup Company

Ticker symbol: CPB (NYSE) ❑ S&P rating: B+ ❑ Value Line financial strength rating: B++ ❑ Current yield: 3.1 percent

Company Profile

Campbell Soup Company is the world's largest soup maker. They also produce many other foods and beverages but, at least as far as we know, Andy Warhol never painted a jar of Pace Pineapple Mango Chipotle Salsa, so the company is still best known for its ubiquitous soups. Campbell was incorporated in 1922 but its roots can be traced all the way back to its beginnings in the food business in 1869.

The company has four reporting segments: U.S. Soup, Sauces, and Beverages; Baking and Snacking; International Soup, Sauces and Beverages; and North America Foodservice. Within each segment are the many familiar brands that constitute the business: Swanson, Prego, Pace, V8, Pepperidge Farm, Arnott's, Wolfgang Puck and, of course, Campbell's.

Campbell's products are distributed to 120 countries worldwide and are sold through its own sales force and through distributors. U.S.–based operations accounted for 70 percent of revenue and 80 percent of earnings in FY2009. Products are manufactured in twenty principal facilities within the United States and in fourteen facilities outside the United States, primarily in Australia, Europe, and Asia/Pacific. The vast majority of these facilities are company owned.

Campbell's product strategy centers on three large, global categories—simple meals, baked snacks, and healthy beverages—which they feel are well aligned with broad consumer trends. The company's strategies for sales and earnings growth are similarly focused on a few key concepts: expand the number of brands (within the existing segments), expand the availability of those brands, grow the portfolio through opportunistic acquisitions and partnerships, and improve margins through better price realization and productivity gains.

Financial Highlights, Fiscal Year 2009

Campbell reported net sales of $7.6 billion for FY2009, a decline of 5 percent year to year. The largest category, U.S. Soups, Sauces, and Beverages fell 3 percent with all other categories reporting steeper declines. The bright spots were relatively few, with only the newly launched products making positive contributions to revenue growth. All overseas operations were affected by unfavorable currency adjustments. Earnings fell on reduced volumes, while net margin actually gained 20 basis points on higher average selling prices.

Early 2010 results have generally been positive—the first quarter brought double-digit gains in earnings even as revenues declined. The Q2 revenues were up 1 percent and earnings gained 11 percent. A fair percentage of the earnings increase is due to favorable currency adjustments, but it's clear that the company's cost reduction efforts are paying off.

Reasons to Buy

Campbell owns the number one or number two position in each of the product categories in which it participates. It dominates the $4 billion U.S. soup market with a 63 percent market share.

The company is investing heavily in Russia and China, which together account for half of the world's soup consumption. Russia and China have essentially no premade soups, so there is no in-place competition. Campbell's four largest current markets for pre-made soups (United States, Canada, France, and Germany) account for only 6 percent of the world's soup consumption, so opening up the Russia and China markets would

create a tremendous growth opportunity. Just a 4 percent share of those markets would constitute a unit volume increase of over 10 percent. The company has invested $50 million per year for the past several years and has begun selling concentrated broths in both markets. Campbell expects to be profitable there within three years.

Campbell has a stated long-term EPS growth rate target of 5–7 percent per year and has been able to meet that going back to 2002. This is a fairly defensive stock; non-cyclical, non-financial, low debt, and with a respectable yield. It's a good place to be if you're building a core of safe, well-established businesses that grow conservatively and occupy the top positions in their markets.

Reasons for Caution

It will be difficult for Campbell to organically grow market share for soups in the United States. The market is saturated and Campbell's customer base is an aging demographic that is not quick to adopt the new brands that Campbell will need to introduce to invigorate the portfolio.

Earnings from the North American Foodservice segment are down nearly 60 percent over the past two years and now represent just 3 percent of total company earnings.

SECTOR: Consumer Staples
BETA COEFFICIENT: .60
10-YEAR COMPOUND EARNINGS PER SHARE GROWTH: 1.0 percent
10-YEAR COMPOUND DIVIDENDS PER SHARE GROWTH: 1.0 percent

	2002	22003	2004	2005	2006	2007	2008	2009
Revenues (Mil)	6,133	6,678	7,109	7,548	7,343	7,867	7,998	7,586
Net income (Mil)	625	626	652	707	681	771	798	771
Earnings per share	1.28	1.52	1.58	1.71	1.66	1.95	2.09	2.15
Dividends per share	0.63	0.63	0.64	0.69	0.74	0.82	0.88	1.00
Cash flow per share	2.06	2.12	2.24	2.42	2.41	2.78	3.07	2.87
Price: high	30	27.9	30.5	31.6	40	42.7	40.8	35.8
low	19.7	20	25	27.3	28.9	34.2	27.3	24.8

Campbell Soup Company
1 Campbell Place
Camden, NJ 08103–1799
(856) 342-6428
Website: *www.campbellsoupcompany.com*

CarMax, Inc.

Ticker symbol: KMX (NYSE) ❑ S&P Rating: NA ❑ Value Line financial strength rating: B+ ❑ Current yield: nil

Company Profile

"The Way Car Buying Should Be." That's the slogan used by this clean-cut chain of used vehicle stores and superstores and its new big-box retail-like model for selling cars. CarMax buys, reconditions, and sells cars and light trucks at 100 retail centers in forty-six metropolitan markets, mainly in the Southeast and Midwest. The company specializes in selling cars that are under six years old with less than 60,000 miles; the cars are sold below Blue Book value in a no-haggle environment. The price is the price; the emphasis is on the condition of the vehicles and on a helpful and friendly sales and transaction process. Sales representatives are compensated for cars they sell, but not in such a way that drives them to push the wrong car on a customer. The company sold some 345,465 used vehicles in FY2009 and most reports suggest they are gaining market share in the markets they serve with a high degree of customer satisfaction.

CarMax also has service operations and web-based and other tools designed to make the car selection, buying and ownership experience easier. The offering is, at this time, anyway, unique in the industry, and most think that any potential competitor would have a long way to go to catch up.

Financial Highlights, Fiscal Year 2010

CarMax ends their fiscal year 2010 in February 2010, so most of the results actually cover the calendar year 2009.

FY2010 saw a strong recovery for KMX. After being battered against the rocks for all of a dismal 2008, financial health was restored due to a number of factors. An improved credit market and pent-up demand drove sales through the entire year. The government's "cash for clunkers" program was a godsend for dealers, helping push new car sales, boosting consumer confidence. The sustained low interest rates with improved credit availability boosted financing profits. Tightened internal controls at CarMax reduced SG&A by $100 million on an annualized basis.

The result of the above is that CarMax's sales rebounded to 2006 levels and operating margin nearly tripled. Earnings increased four-fold to $255 million and net margin reached a record high of 3.4 percent. Share price went along for the ride, increasing over 200 percent, making CarMax one of our top performers from last year's portfolio.

Reasons to Buy

Quite simply, CarMax is a stock you buy if you believe the traditional dealer model is broken, and if you believe people will continue to see value in late model used vehicles.

Additionally, CarMax brings the latest in business intelligence and analytic models to the car marketing process, in procurement, merchandising, pricing and selling the vehicles. Do green Jeep Commanders sell well in Southern California? Then let's find some, and put them on the lot there, and set a market-based price. KMX is well ahead of the industry in making analysis-based supply and selling decisions.

In addition, a bigger picture and analytic tools allow CarMax to adjust inventories to business conditions more quickly; in the recent downturn such inventory was reduced by tens of thousands of vehicles. CarMax is one of the biggest players in the used auction market, and some 40 percent of its revenues are generated from wholesaling its inventory.

CarMax plans to resume growth with the planned opening of several new dealerships this year.

And as they grow, their competition is reducing its presence dramatically. There are close to 70,000 new and used car dealerships in the United States, and that number is going to shrink dramatically over the next few years, leaving a clear field of fire for CarMax. With many of its competitors for quality used cars out of business, they should benefit both from opportunities for improved market presence and a reduced cost of goods sold.

The company has barely tapped lucrative markets in the Northeast, Pacific Northwest, Colorado, and many cities in the Midwest. The combination of these new markets and greater consumer acceptance of the concept should provide a strong tailwind for sales once business conditions improve.

Reasons for Caution

CarMax will always be somewhat vulnerable to economic cycles and the availability of credit, and the recent recession has proven to be no exception. There are current and potential customers who will have trouble paying for both an auto loan and a home mortgage, a spillover effect from the recent subprime lending crisis. The 2010 financials spiked somewhat higher as a result of government incentives and an internal accounting adjustment for loan valuations, neither of which are in the plans for 2011.

SECTOR: Retail
BETA COEFFICIENT: 1.20
5-YEAR COMPOUND EARNINGS PER SHARE GROWTH: 18.0 percent
5-YEAR COMPOUND DIVIDENDS PER SHARE GROWTH: NA

	2002	2003	2004	2005	2006	2007	2008	2009
Revenues (Mil)	4,052	4,597	5,260	6,560	7,466	8,200	6,974	7,400
Net income (Mil)	94.8	116.5	112.9	148.1	198.6	182	59.2	255
Earnings per share	0.46	0.55	0.54	0.7	0.92	0.83	0.27	1.15
Dividends per share	0	0	0	0	0	0	0	0
Cash flow per share	0.53	0.64	0.64	0.83	1.08	1.05	0.52	1.4
Price: high	17	19.7	18.5	17.4	27.6	29.4	23	24.8
low	6.4	6.2	9	12.3	13.8	18.6	5.8	6.9

CarMax, Inc.
12800 Tuckahoe Creek Parkway
Richmond, VA 23238
Phone: (804) 747-0422
Website: *www.carmax.com*

Caterpillar, Inc.

Ticker symbol: CAT (NYSE) □ S&P rating: A □ Value Line financial strength rating: A □ Current yield: .5 percent

Company Profile

Headquartered in Peoria, Illinois, Caterpillar is the world's largest manufacturer of construction and mining equipment, diesel and natural gas engines and industrial gas turbines. It is a Fortune 50 industrial company with more than $31 billion in assets. Caterpillar's distinctive yellow machines are in service in nearly every country in the world—nearly 70 percent of the company's revenues are derived from outside the United States.

Caterpillar's broad product line ranges from the company's line of compact construction equipment to hydraulic excavators, backhoe loaders, track-type tractors, forest products, off-highway trucks, agricultural tractors, diesel and natural gas engines and industrial gas turbines. Cat products are used in the construction, road building, mining, forestry, energy, transportation, and material-handling industries.

Caterpillar products are sold in more than 200 countries, and rental services are offered through more than 1,200 outlets worldwide. The company offers service through its extensive worldwide network of 220 dealers. Caterpillar products

and components are manufactured in forty-one plants in the United States and forty-three more plants worldwide. The company has three operating segments: Machinery, Engines, and Financial Products.

Caterpillar's largest segment, the Machinery unit, makes the company's well-known earthmoving equipment. Machinery's end-markets include heavy construction, general construction, and mining quarry and aggregate, industrial, waste, forestry, and agriculture. End markets are very cyclical and competitive. Demand for Caterpillar's earthmoving equipment is driven by many volatile factors, including the health of global economies, commodity prices, and interest rates.

For decades, the Engine segment made diesel engines solely for the company's own earthmoving equipment. Now, Engine derives about 90 percent of sales from third-party customers, such as Paccar, Inc., the maker of well-known Kenworth and Peterbilt brand tractor/trailer trucks. Engine's major end markets are electric power generation, on-highway truck, oil and gas, industrial/OEM, and marine.

The Financial Products segment, which provides 7.6 percent of revenues but 20 percent of operating profits, primarily provides financing to Caterpillar dealers and customers. Financing plans include operating and finance leases, installment sales contracts, working capital loans, and wholesale financing plans.

Financial Highlights, Fiscal Year 2009

You have to feel bad for James Owens. In his last year as CEO of Caterpillar, after nearly forty years of employment with the Big Cat, the company ran into the worst year in its financial history since the 1940s. Caterpillar closed 2009 with a 37 percent decline in sales, and a stunning 75 percent decline in earnings.

Last year we referred to Caterpillar's "trough" business model, wherein the company shifts gears and focuses on cash flow, cost savings, and protecting the balance sheet. The air-raid sirens began sounding at Caterpillar in late 2008 and the company operated through most of 2009 in this trough mode. There were layoffs, major production cuts, plant shutdowns, and for the first time in the company's history, dealers were allowed to cancel orders.

Reasons to Buy

Results for early 2010 have been encouraging. Although sales are still below 1Q2009 levels, earnings are well ahead of pace as a result of the significant cost reductions taken in 2009. The company is positive with regard to their prospects and the economic environment in general. They have revised their outlook for 2010—they now expect sales in the range of $40 billion and a per-share net of $2.50–$3.25.

Caterpillar is the world's largest supplier of heavy equipment. They make to stock, and make to order, equipment that no other company can provide. Their brand is well known and well regarded throughout the world. Even during the recession the company continued to invest in R&D, spending $1.4 billion in 2009 to develop new products and technologies, earning 450 patents in the process. They are the unquestioned alpha dog in the heavy equipment market, and their brand and reputation have tremendous value in a business where product reliability and support are foremost in a purchasing decision.

Caterpillar took pains to protect their dealers during the recession with financial services to the dealers and special terms to end customers, as well as allowing them to cancel orders when necessary. As a consequence, Caterpillar's reputation with their customers remains intact and the company will have a healthy and established dealer network through which to sell and service their products.

Caterpillar apparently sees a brighter future for rail in the United States. In June 2010 they entered into an agreement to buy Electro-Motive Diesel, a manufacturer of locomotives, for $820 million in cash. This puts Caterpillar at the top-tier of rail suppliers in North America, with a full portfolio of locomotives, locomotive and railcar services, and engineering and track services. There's $857 billion in tax incentives out there for mass transit providers, and Caterpillar stands to benefit.

Reasons for Caution

Caterpillar is still carrying a very large debt load. At the end of FY2009 total debt was $31.6 billion, with nearly $10 billion due in the coming year. On the upside, the company managed to reduce this debt last year and has put new controls in place to reduce its previous inventory costs.

SECTOR: Industrials
BETA COEFFICIENT: 1.30
10-YEAR COMPOUND EARNINGS PER SHARE GROWTH: 10.5 percent
10-YEAR COMPOUND DIVIDENDS PER SHARE GROWTH: 11 percent

	2002	2003	2004	2005	2006	2007	2008	2009
Revenues (Mil)	20,152	22,763	30,251	36,339	41,517	44,958	51,234	32,396
Net income (Mil)	798	1,099	2,035	2,854	3,537	3,541	3,557	895
Earnings per share	1.15	1.57	2.88	4.04	5.17	5.37	5.71	1.43
Dividends per share	0.7	0.72	0.78	0.96	1.2	1.32	1.62	1.68
Cash flow per share	2.93	3.62	5.00	6.46	8.03	8.64	9.25	5.17
Price: high	30	42.5	49.4	59.9	82	87	86	61.3
low	16.9	20.6	34.3	41.3	57	58	32	50.5

Caterpillar, Inc.
100 N. E. Adams Street
Peoria, Illinois 61629–5310
(309) 675-4619
Website: www.cat.com

Chevron Corporation

Ticker symbol: CVX (NYSE) ❑ S&P rating: AA ❑ Value Line financial strength rating: A++ ❑ Current yield: 3.7 percent

Company Profile

Chevron is the world's fourth largest publicly traded, integrated energy company based on oil-equivalent reserves and production. It is engaged in every aspect of the oil and gas industry, including exploration and production, refining, marketing and transportation, chemicals manufacturing and sales, and power generation.

Active in more than 180 countries, ChevronTexaco has reserves of 11.9 billion barrels of oil and gas equivalent and daily production of 2.6 million barrels. In addition, it has global refining capacity of more than 2 million barrels/day and operates more than 22,000 retail outlets (including affiliates) around the world. The company also has interests in thirty power projects now operating or being developed.

Its downstream (Refining/ Retailing) businesses include four refining and marketing units operating in North America, Europe and West Africa, Latin America, Asia, the Middle East and southern Africa. Downstream also has five global businesses: aviation, lubricants, trading, shipping, and fuel and marine marketing.

The company's global refining network comprises twenty-three wholly owned and joint-venture facilities that process more than 2 million barrels of oil per day. Gasoline and diesel fuel are sold through more than 22,000 retail outlets under three well-known consumer brands: Chevron in North America; Texaco in Latin America, Europe and West Africa; and Caltex in Asia, the Middle East and southern Africa.

Chevron is the number one jet fuel marketer in the United States and third worldwide, marketing 550,000 barrels per day in eighty countries. The company's fuel and marine marketing business is a leading global supplier and marketer of fuels, lubricants and coolants to the marine and power markets, with about 500,000 barrels of sales per day.

Financial Highlights, Fiscal Year 2009

Sales in 2009 for Chevron fell 36.8 percent to $167 billion, while net income fell 56.2 percent to $10.5 billion. Ouch. The overall decline in the worldwide economy drove down volumes significantly, leading to a large oversupply of both petroleum and gas products. As a result, benchmark prices for West Texas Intermediate crude fell 38 percent (full-year average) and natural gas prices experienced a similar decline, with prices falling 58 percent. If you're a vertically integrated oil company, those numbers pretty much tell you how your year is going to go.

As crude prices rose slowly through 2009 Chevron's refining operations got squeezed between higher input costs and reduced retail demand for gasoline. As a result, the downstream operations saw dramatically reduced earnings, falling from $3.5 billion in 2008 to $500 million in 2009.

Reasons to Buy

Chevron will be following the lead of Exxon with regard to its less-profitable downstream business. The company will limit its refining business to forty markets, down from ninety-three markets in 2009. Overall, Chevron is cutting refining capital expenditures 23 percent this year and will be combining their refining and chemical operations in 2010 to better leverage costs. They also plan to reduce the number of retail filling stations from 3,200 down to 1,900. Upstream operations are more profitable (and are becoming evermore expensive), so the money is better spent there.

Successful production has begun at several new fields, including Angola (142,000 bpd), Brazil (72,000 bpd), and the United States (135,000 bpd). New finds during the year include significant deposits in Angola, the United States, and the Republic of the Congo. In Australia, Chevron has finalized delivery agreements for the output of a very large liquid natural gas platform in Western Australia that should produce on the order of 8.6 million metric tons of LNG annually.

Chevron is one of the world's largest producers of heavy crude oil, which represents about one-third of the world's hydrocarbon reserves. Industry production of heavy oil is projected to grow by 30 percent by the end of this decade.

Reasons for Caution

The April 2010 blowout of a BP well in the Gulf of Mexico and the consequent loss of life, the sinking of a TransOcean floating rig and the ongoing (at the time of this writing) environmental damage have cast a pall over the entire industry. BP's exposure is yet to be determined, but at the moment their stock is down nearly 40 percent compared to the day of the incident (interestingly, over the same period, Chevron is down only 10 percent and has outperformed the S&P 500). We expect that this incident will substantially increase the cost of any and all future deepwater operations in the Gulf and could substantially damage the value of the leases there. Chevron has halted two deepwater exploration wells and will have to reconsider two others that were scheduled for later in 2010. Chevron currently derives 10 percent of its production from the Gulf.

SECTOR: **Energy**
BETA COEFFICIENT: **.90**
10-YEAR COMPOUND EARNINGS PER SHARE GROWTH: **18.0 percent**
10-YEAR COMPOUND DIVIDENDS PER SHARE GROWTH: **7.0 percent**

	2002	2003	2004	2005	2006	2007	2008	2009
Revenues (Mil)	98.9	121.8	150.9	198.2	210.1	220.9	273	172.6
Net income (Mil)	1.1	7.2	13	14.1	17.1	18.7	23.9	10.5
Earnings per share	0.54	3.48	6.14	6.54	7.8	8.77	11.67	5.24
Dividends per share	1.4	1.43	1.53	1.75	2.01	2.32	2.53	2.66
Cash flow per share	2.98	5.9	8.67	8.96	10.09	12.11	16.69	10.95
Price: high	45.8	43.5	56.1	66	76.2	95.5	104.6	79.8
low	32.7	30.7	41.6	49.8	53.8	65	55.5	56.1

Chevron Corporation
6001 Bollinger Canyon Road
San Ramon, CA 94583–2324
(925) 842–5690
Website: *www.chevrontexaco.com*

AGGRESSIVE GROWTH

Chipotle Mexican Grill

Ticker symbol: CMG (NYSE) ❏ S&P rating: not rated ❏ Value Line financial strength rating: B++
❏ Current yield: nil

Company Profile

Chipotle Mexican Grill develops and operates Mexican-inspired fast-food restaurants. As of June 2010 they have just over 1,000 stores in the United States and Ontario, Canada. The company was founded in 1993 and in early 2010 opened their 1,000th store. McDonald's Corporation held a 91 percent stake in the company until January of 2006, when the company had its IPO. The company sold 7.77 million shares for $22 each, and four months later sold another 4.2 million shares for $61.50 each. McDonald's completed its divestiture in October of 2006.

The concept for the stores is "fast-casual," with fresh ingredients carefully prepared and served quickly in an attractive and modern environment. In general, Chipotle offers better ingredients than those found in most fast-food chains, albeit with a much smaller menu. Instead of rice, beans and an entrée served in the scores of combinations that you find in the typical Mexican restaurant, Chipotle offers a burrito, a bowl (basically a burrito without the tortilla wrap), and recently, soft tacos. The customer can choose among different ingredients for those three dishes, but there are no other options for entrées. Salads, chips and guacamole round out the menu.

Sixteen years after their founding, Chipotle is still in the top ten fastest growing restaurant chains in the United States. The stores tend to be located in urban/suburban areas with strong residential and daytime population. Their preferred traffic generators include residential, office, retail, university, and hospitals. The company makes a point of using ingredients that are sustainably grown and naturally raised. Their motto is "Food with Integrity," and Chipotle is already the largest restaurant seller of naturally raised meat and the largest restaurant buyer of locally grown produce in the United States. Chipotle supplies its restaurants through twenty-two independently owned and operated distribution centers.

Financial Highlights, Fiscal Year 2009

Chipotle grew revenues 14 percent in 2009 largely on the strength of 121 new store openings. Comparable store sales were up 2.2 percent due to menu price increases, partially offset by fewer customer visits and smaller tickets per visit.

Menu price increases were also significant in the 62 percent earnings growth, as net margin grew 250 basis points or 2.5 percent, a huge gain in the typically low-margin fast food business. The company has held the line on expenses, with no significant increases in basic costs as a percentage of revenue versus 2008.

Reasons to Buy

Chipotle is gaining mindshare. Given their menu, their success in western and southwestern states is not at all surprising. Even the "message" that comes with the food seems tailored to the left-coast social zeitgeist (not a criticism, just an observation). As it turns out, however, after California, the state with the greatest concentration of Chipotle restaurants is Ohio. Ohio is not a hotbed of refined Mexican-food palates. We speak from some experience here when we say that Ohio has more bad Mexican restaurants per capita than anyplace south of Hudson Bay. We think if Chipotle can make it there, as they say, they can make it anywhere.

The company expects to open between 120 and 130 new restaurants during the year. We expect revenue gains from the new stores to be even stronger in 2010 due to an improved economic environment.

The company built its 2010 plan around an expectation for flat comps, but so far in 2010 the comps are coming in around 4 percent higher, strictly on improved volumes with no pricing changes. The company has since revised its estimate and is now predicting mid-single digit growth in comps for the year.

Chipotle has funded its growth almost entirely internally with its own cash flow. Their cash flow remains strong and should easily support an accelerated new store growth rate for the 2011-2013 period. As an indication of its finances, the company, in addition to opening 120 new stores in 2010, plans to buy back nearly 10 percent of its outstanding shares. The company has negligible long-term debt.

Reasons to be Cautious

CMG is a hot, trendy pick currently trading at a price and multiple higher than most every issue in our book. Tastes can change, and Chipotle's menu may fall out of favor even before we publish. Share growth will depend greatly on the company's ability to open new stores in profitable locations, and to sustain or even grow interest in its menu offerings.

SECTOR: **Industrials**
BETA COEFFICIENT: **1.00**
10-YEAR COMPOUND EARNINGS PER SHARE GROWTH: **NA**
10-YEAR COMPOUND DIVIDENDS PER SHARE GROWTH: **Nil**

	2002	2003	2004	2005	2006	2007	2008	2009
Revenues (Mil)	-	-	471	628	823	1,086	1,332	1,518
Net income (Mil)	-	-	7.8	37.7	41.4	70.6	78.2	127
Earnings per share	-	-	-	1.43	1.28	2.13	2.36	3.95
Dividends per share	-	-	-	-	-	-	-	-
Cash flow per share	-	-	-	2.02	2.33	3.46	3.98	5.62
Price: high	-	-	-	-	67.8	155.5	150.0	148.9
low	-	-	-	-	40.9	54.6	36.9	86.0

Chipotle Mexican Grill
1401 Wynkoop Street
Suite 500
Denver, CO 80202
(303) 595-4000
Website: *www.chipotle.com*

AGGRESSIVE GROWTH

Church & Dwight

Ticker symbol: CHD (NYSE) □ S&P rating: BBB- □ Value Line financial strength rating: A □ Current yield: 0.8 percent

Company Profile

Church & Dwight is the world's largest producer of sodium bicarbonate. Their most well-known products are marketed under the Arm & Hammer® brand, used across several product categories. The company has sold this iconic product continually since its founding in 1846; the product's longevity owing to its versatility. Sodium bicarbonate is used in the chemical industry, the baking industry, the cleaning industry, agriculture (as both a soil and feedstock amendment), and the paper industry. It's an abrasive, a deodorizer, a leavening agent, a water purifier, a dialysate (treatment for kidney failure), a blowing agent for plastics ... the list goes on and on.

Sodium bicarbonate is not the company's only product, but it is at the core of most of its businesses. These businesses are divided into two basic groups, Consumer and Specialty, with the Consumer group further divided into Domestic and International segments. The Domestic Consumer segment accounted for 74 percent of the company's FY2009 net sales, Consumer International 16 percent, and Specialty the remaining 10 percent.

The company has eight key brands that constitute 80 percent of its Consumer sales. These include Arm & Hammer®, Trojan®, Oxiclean®, Spinbrush˙, First Response®, Nair®, Orajel®, and Xtra®. Of the eight brands, all but Arm & Hammer have been added since 2001 through acquisition, and all except Xtra occupy the top position in their product segment. The company claims the Arm & Hammer brand appears in more grocery aisles than any other brand, and that the brand appears in over 90 percent of American homes.

Financial Highlights, Fiscal Year 2009

FY2009 was another very good year for this growing presence in the consumer products segment. Organic sales rose 5 percent, earnings rose 23 percent, and cash flow was up to a record $400 million. Excluding restructuring charges, gross margin increased 430 basis points to 44.8 percent. And even after a 20 percent increase in global marketing expenses (on top of a 15 percent increase in FY2008), net margin rose 160 basis points to 9.9 percent.

Reasons to Buy

Ten years ago Church & Dwight had one iconic consumer brand and its net sales were less than $1 billion. They now have over eighty brands and $2.5 billion in annual sales. The growth in their base of core brands has accelerated over the past five years and the company is in terrific position for further acquisitions. They've done an excellent job of integrating the acquired brands into the core business, as well as leveraging their core brand into new products. If they can repeat this sort of performance they could start acquiring even larger and stronger brands.

The company's largest segment is also its most profitable, by a fair margin. FY2009 income before taxes in Consumer Domestic was 18 percent of sales, while the corresponding figures for Consumer International and Specialty were 10 percent and 6 percent respectively. This is particularly compelling as the company is planning on rolling out a significant number of new brands and core brand expansions in Consumer Domestic in 2010 and 2011.

The company's brand base is split 60/40 between premium and value brands, providing a fair amount of protection during shifting economic environments.

C&D feels there is room for further growth in its gross margin and has several supply chain initiatives underway to make improvements through 2011.

Reasons for Caution

As they grow in brand count they will likely start spending a greater percentage of operating capital in SG&A and will also start to run into shelf-space pressure. And this is not a reason for caution, but it has to be said: for a consumer-focused organization, C&D has one of the least effective websites of any large company we've seen. The company would benefit from spending a little more to promote its brands, in our opinion.

SECTOR: Consumer Staples
BETA COEFFICIENT: 0.60
10-YEAR COMPOUND EARNINGS PER SHARE GROWTH: 19.0 percent
10-YEAR COMPOUND DIVIDENDS PER SHARE GROWTH: 6.5 percent

	2002	2003	2004	2005	2006	2007	2008	2009
Revenues (Mil)	1,047	1,057	1,462	1,737	1,946	2,221	2,422	2,521
Net income (Mil)	67.3	78.5	88.8	123	143	169	201	249
Earnings per share	1.07	1.24	1.37	1.83	2.07	2.47	2.86	3.48
Dividends per share	0.20	0.21	0.23	0.24	0.26	0.26	0.34	0.46
Cash flow per share	1.59	1.78	2.02	2.64	2.97	3.41	3.89	4.73
Price: high	24.3	27.7	33.7	39.6	43.6	57.2	65.5	62.4
low	17	18.4	25.6	32.1	32.7	42.4	47.6	45.4

Church & Dwight Co., Inc.
469 N. Harrison St.
Princeton, NJ 08543
(609) 683-5900
Website: *www.churchdwight.com*

Cincinnati Financial

Ticker symbol: CINF (NASDAQ) ❑ S&P rating: BBB+ ❑ Value Line financial strength rating: B++
❑ Current yield: 5.9 percent

Company Profile

Cincinnati Financial Corporation, founded in 1968, is engaged primarily in property casualty insurance marketed through independent insurance agents in thirty-seven states. The company, one of the twenty-five largest property and casualty insurers in the nation, operates in four segments: Commercial Lines Property Casualty Insurance, Personal Lines Property Casualty Insurance, Life Insurance, and Investments.

At year-end 2009, the Company owned 100 percent of three subsidiaries: The Cincinnati Insurance Company, CSU Producer Resources Inc. and CFC Investment Company. In addition, the parent company owns an investment portfolio and the headquarters property, and is responsible for corporate borrowings and shareholder dividends.

Its standard market property casualty insurance group includes two subsidiaries: The Cincinnati Casualty Company and The Cincinnati Indemnity Company. This group writes a range of business, homeowner and auto policies.

The two non-insurance subsidiaries of Cincinnati Financial are CSU Producer Resources, which offers insurance brokerage services to CFC's independent agencies so their clients can access CFC's excess and surplus lines of insurance products; and CFC Investment Company, which offers commercial leasing and financing services to CFC's agents, their clients and other customers.

Financial Highlights, Fiscal Year 2009

The company uses a measure of goodness they refer to as the value creation ratio, which is the rate of growth in book value per share, plus the ratio of dividends declared per share to beginning book value per share. How's that for a non-GAAP measure? While this is technically a sum of ratios rather than a ratio, we think we see where they're going with this. They're weighting equally the growth in assets and the cash spun off by those assets, which is a reasonable way to look at things when you're managing to a long-term target.

Against this measure, FY2009 was a much better year than was either 2008 or 2007. The VCR for FY2009 came in at a positive 19.7

percent, versus -23.5 percent in 2008 and -5.7 percent in 2007. A rolling five-year average of VCR correlates with other GAAP measures of performance, with FY2009 coming in at 1.7 percent, 2008 at -1.3 percent, and 2007 at 6.3 percent.

In February 2009, the company sold its entire holding in Fifth Third Bancorp. They also raised their indicated dividend rate for the forty-ninth consecutive year.

Reasons to Buy

The company has given priority to premium growth in the coming years, both through geographic expansion and diversification of premium sources. In 2009 they added eighty-seven new agencies in their current operating territories and have targeted an additional sixty-five agencies in 2010 writing an aggregate $1 billion in annual property casualty premiums. Since 2008, the company has added Colorado, Wyoming and Texas to its coverage areas and has given strong indications that it plans to add more western states in the future. By mid-2010, the company has added Texas agencies that write a total of $750 million in policies across all carriers.

The company has diversified its premium sources by entering the excess and surplus lines market. The company already has agents that write $2.5 billion worth of these policies with other carriers, and CFC is optimistic about its ability to address a significant share of that business. The first two years in this market have provided very encouraging results. The company is also expanding the number of states in which it offers personal lines, adding nine new states in the past two years.

Measured by premium volume, the company is ranked as the number one or number two carrier among 75 percent of the agencies that have represented them for the past five years. Working to improve that measure further, the company during 2009 rolled out three major new technology platforms for their writers, with the goal of improving efficiency in quoting, billing, and payment across all business and personal lines.

Reasons for Caution

Interest rates on the industry's traditional investment instruments have been in decline over a period of several years. Coupled with a decline in top-line growth, CFC's earnings have been under significant pressure. The full-year results from 2010 will provide a solid indication of the effectiveness of CFC's recent initiatives.

SECTOR: **Financial**
BETA COEFFICIENT: **0.95**
10-YEAR COMPOUND EARNINGS PER SHARE GROWTH: **5.0 percent**
10-YEAR COMPOUND DIVIDENDS PER SHARE GROWTH: **10.5 percent**

	2002	**2003**	**2004**	**2005**	**2006**	**2007**	**2008**	**2009**
Revenues (Mil)	14,059	15,509	16,107	16,003	17,222	16,637	13,369	14,440
Net income (Mil)	300	386	524	562	496	610	344	215
Earnings per share	1.67	2.17	2.94	3.17	2.82	3.54	2.10	1.32
Dividends per share	0.81	0.91	1.00	1.21	1.34	1.42	1.53	1.57
Loss / Prem Earned	.76	.71	.63	.63	.64	.59	.73	.77
Price: high	42.9	38.0	53.5	45.9	49.2	48.4	40.2	29.7
low	29.4	30.0	36.6	38.4	41.2	36.0	13.7	17.8

Cincinnati Financial Corporation
6200 S. Gilmore Road
Fairfield, OH 45014
(513) 870-2000
Website: *www.cinfin.com*

The Clorox Company

Ticker symbol: CLX (NYSE) □ Fiscal year ends June 30 □ S&P rating: A □ Value Line financial strength rating: B++ □ Current yield: 3.3 percent

Company Profile

A leading manufacturer and marketer of consumer products, Clorox markets some of consumers' most trusted and recognized brand names, including its namesake bleach and cleaning products, Green Works™ natural cleaners, Armor All® and STP® auto-care products, Fresh Step® and Scoop Away® cat litter, Kingsford® charcoal, Hidden Valley® and K C Masterpiece® dressings and sauces, Brita® water-filtration systems, Glad® bags, wraps and containers, and Burt's Bees® natural personal care products. With approximately 8,300 employees worldwide, the company manufactures products in more than two dozen countries and markets them in more than 100 countries.

The company's home care cleaning products are primarily comprised of disinfecting sprays and wipes, toilet bowl cleaners, carpet cleaners, drain openers, floor mopping systems, toilet and bath cleaning tools, and pre-moistened towelettes.

Clorox also provides professional products for institutional, janitorial, and food service markets, including bleaches, disinfectants, food-storage bags, and bathroom cleaners. Its auto care products consist of protectants, cleaners and wipes, tire- and wheel-care products, and automotive fuel and oil additives.

In addition, the company offers food products, including salad dressings, seasonings, sauces, and marinades. Clorox sells its products to grocery stores and grocery wholesalers primarily through a network of brokers; and through a direct sales force to mass merchandisers, warehouse clubs, and military and other retail stores in the United States. It also sells its products outside the United States through subsidiaries, licensees, distributors, and joint-venture arrangements with local partners.

The company was founded in 1913 as Electro-Alkaline Company. It has been known as The Clorox Company since 1957.

Financial Highlights, Fiscal Year 2009

Sales grew 3 percent to $5.5 billion, generating earnings of $537 million. Earnings rose 16.5 percent year over year, led by the Household and Lifestyle business segments. In light of the business conditions extant in their June-June fiscal year, these are significant results. Most businesses, particularly in the consumer goods sectors, did not do nearly as well.

Although commodity and energy-related costs rose by nearly $110 million in 2009, these increases were more than offset by an aggressive cost savings program that reduced COGS by $118 million.

Cash flow rose 8 percent to a record $738 million, funding debt reduction and an increase in the dividend of 9 percent.

The company recently bought Caltech Industries, a maker of disinfecting bleaches, adding over 1,000 hospitals to its existing base of 600 commercial customers.

Reasons to Buy

Even in a slowing consumer market, Clorox, due to its strong brand position (number one or two positions in the market with 88 percent of its products) was able to increase prices again in FY2009. Clorox continues to compete well against store brands and expects to do even better as many stores simplify and rationalize their offerings.

Clorox has delivered on total shareholder return. Even over the past two years of recessionary pressures, the company has increased its dividend by 25 percent while maintaining a share price well within its five year rolling average. The company has allocated another $725 million for share repurchase and has restated its commitment to

dividend increases. The dividend is now a healthy 3.3 percent and we feel share value increases are built in, as the company has made (and continues to make) significant changes to its cost structures.

The company's Economic Profit metric appears to be paying off. This measure, which tracks the profit generated over and above the cost of profit-generating capital, focuses its businesses on their use of capital and their costs. They anticipate that by 2013 they will be able to show year/year double-digit growth of this measure, which they refer to as "true north" as they feel it corresponds with shareholder value creation. The measure was up nearly 4 percent this year, despite the negative impacts of foreign exchange rates and rising commodity prices.

The brands appear to be quite robust. In response to the rising commodity prices, Clorox took more than fifty price increases in its products but maintained and grew market share across most of its lines.

Reasons for Caution

Less than 20 percent of CLX's revenue is generated internationally, and the company has more exposure to a weakening dollar than do most of its competitors. Also, 80 percent of its revenue is derived from a relatively saturated domestic market, making it relatively expensive to capture additional market share.

SECTOR: **Consumer Staples**
BETA COEFFICIENT: **.65**
10-YEAR COMPOUND EARNINGS PER SHARE GROWTH: **9.0 percent**
10-YEAR COMPOUND DIVIDENDS PER SHARE GROWTH: **9.5 percent**

	2002	2003	2004	2005	2006	2007	2008	2009
Revenues (Mil)	4,061	4,144	4,324	4,388	4,644	4,847	5,273	5,450
Net income (Mil)	322	514	546	517	443	496	461	537
Earnings per share	1.37	2.33	2.43	2.88	2.89	3.23	3.24	3.81
Dividends per share	0.84	0.88	1.08	1.1	1.14	1.31	1.66	1.88
Cash flow per share	2.3	3.3	3.49	4.66	4.17	4.55	4.82	5.22
Price: high	47.9	49.2	59.4	66	66	69.4	65.3	65.2
low	31.9	37.4	46.5	52.5	56.2	56.2	47.5	59

The Clorox Company
1221 Broadway
Oakland, CA 94612
(510) 271-2270
Website: *www.clorox.com*

ONSERVATIVE GROWTH

The Coca-Cola Company

Ticker symbol: KO □ Listed: NYSE □ S&P rating: A+ □ Value Line financial strength rating: A++ □ Current yield: 3.0 percent

Company Profile

The Coca-Cola Company is the world's largest beverage company, although most of what they produce you wouldn't want to drink as-is. The company mainly produces concentrates and syrups that it then sells to bottlers worldwide. These bottlers add water (still or carbonated, depending on the product), sugar and other (often local) ingredients, then bottle and distribute the products to restaurants, retailers, and other distributors. The company owns the brand and is responsible for consumer brand marketing initiatives, while the distributors handle all downstream merchandising. The company operates in over 200 countries and markets nearly 500 brands of concentrate. These concentrates are then used to produce over 3,000 different branded products, including Coca-Cola.

The total numbers are staggering: 570 billion servings per year, 1.6 billion beverages consumed per day, 18,000 servings per second, unit growth in 2008 equivalent to the entire Japanese market, processed through over 300 bottlers and all handled through the world's largest beverage distribution system.

The company-owned bottling businesses handle 22 percent of the bottling volume, while 78 percent is done by independent, licensed bottlers in which the company has no controlling or equity interest.

Financial Highlights, Fiscal Year 2009

Coke's relatively weak close to 2008 continued through 2009 and the first part of 2010. Unit volumes were up 2 percent in 2009, but revenues were off 3 percent, due almost entirely to the impact of unfavorable currency fluctuations. Gross margin was essentially flat at 64.2 percent and SG&A declined 4 percent. In almost every other significant measure, 2009's financial results look very much like 2008's.

Given the state of the world economy through much of 2009, flat performance year/year may not be all that bad. In fact, PepsiCo has an identical story to tell—basically unchanged year/year in its beverage operations with flat revenues and earnings.

Early in 2010 the company, in a non-cash transaction, acquired the North American distribution assets of Coca-Cola Enterprises, an independent bottler in which the company already had a 34 percent interest. Coca-Cola now controls the distribution of over 90 percent of its products in North America. Coke's main rival, PepsiCo, had been making similar acquisitions over the past few years and Coke's move was seen partially as a defensive gesture, although it will also provide Coke greater flexibility in pricing and greater leverage in raw materials purchasing.

Reasons to Buy

Coca-Cola has global category leadership in soft drinks, juices and juice drinks, and ready-to-drink coffees and teas. They're number two globally in sports drinks, and number three in packaged water and energy drinks. In Coca-Cola, Diet Coke, Sprite and Fanta, they own four of the top five brands of soft drink in the world. They're everywhere, and with so many popular brands the local bottlers can "test the waters," choosing among hundreds of products for the right ones for their area.

Although the company has lagged the market in terms of non-CSD (carbonated soft drink) product offerings, the growth of those products in Coke's developing markets is very encouraging. Coke has targeted for much stronger growth in the second half of 2010 and moving forward, particularly in the growing economies of India, Indonesia, and China. The growth in the consumption of non-alcoholic ready-to-drink beverages tracks the per-capita growth in disposable income, and the company has identified key cities with the most promising demographics for its marketing efforts.

The Coca-Cola name is probably the most recognized brand in the world, and is almost beyond valuation. Warren Buffett once famously said "If you gave me $100 million and said take away the soft drink leadership in the world from Coke, I'd give it back to you and say it can't be done."

Coke has traditionally been a steady hedge stock, and at its current price it's beginning to look more like it's well positioned for growth—its current P/E ratio is the lowest it has been in more than fifteen years.

Reasons for Caution

Coke's customer base in its most profitable market (the United States) is aging and is buying fewer carbonated beverages. Unit volume in the United States has been flat for the past six years, and Coke needs to address this issue. Profits from the U.S. market finance the development of the new, growing markets that Coke wants to engage, so if they fall behind the curve in the United States they face setbacks worldwide.

SECTOR: Consumer Discretionary
BETA COEFFICIENT: 0.60
10-YEAR COMPOUND EARNINGS PER SHARE GROWTH: 6.0 percent
10-YEAR COMPOUND DIVIDENDS PER SHARE GROWTH: 9.5 percent

	2002	2003	2004	2005	2006	2007	2008	2009
Revenues (Mil)	19,564	21,044	21,962	23,104	24,088	28,857	31,944	30,990
Net income (Mil)	4,100	4,790	5,014	5,196	5,568	5,981	7,050	7,145
Earnings per share	1.65	1.95	2.06	2.17	2.37	2.57	3.02	3.05
Dividends per share	0.8	0.88	1	1.12	1.24	1.36	1.52	1.64
Cash flow per share	1.99	2.31	2.45	2.59	2.81	3.08	3.58	3.6
Price: high	57.9	50.9	53.3	45.3	49.3	64.3	65.6	59.4
low	42.9	37	38.3	40.3	39.4	45.6	40.3	37.4

The Coca-Cola Company
One Coca-Cola Plaza
Atlanta, GA 30313
(404) 676-2121
Website: www.coca-cola.com

Colgate-Palmolive Company

Ticker symbol: CL (NYSE) □ S&P rating: AA- □ Value Line financial strength rating: A++ □ Current yield: 2.5 percent

Company Profile

Colgate-Palmolive is the second-largest domestic manufacturer of detergents, toiletries, and other household products. They're also one of the leaders in the pet nutrition market; their Hill's pet food brand represents 17 percent of their total sales.

Colgate is also strong in the global consumer products market, with a presence in over 200 countries and territories under such internationally recognized brand names as Colgate® toothpastes and brushes, Palmolive® soaps, Mennen® deodorants, Ajax®, Murphy Oil Soap®, Fab®, and Soupline/Suavitel®, as well as the Hill's® brands. For 2009, over 80 percent of its revenue came from sales outside the United States, with particular strength in Latin America.

Financial Highlights, Fiscal Year 2009

Colgate reported basically flat revenue growth for 2009. While this is not great news for a company whose sales had grown steadily (if not spectacularly) for over a decade, it's not all that bad. Given the overall economic trends in consumer spending

and the challenging currency environment, Colgate's numbers were actually pretty encouraging. Strong, high-quality earnings growth was the result of favorable pricing, cost-cutting measures and other structural initiatives that yielded improvements in gross margin of 250 basis points and net margin of 210 basis points.

In fact, organic sales growth (absent currency effects) was up 6.5 percent for 2009, but Colgate's international exposure led to currency exchange problems, the upshot of which was to completely offset those gains for a net of zero growth.

Earnings were up across all geographic and most product reporting segments, with particular strength in Latin America, where toothpastes and brushes did exceptionally well. Weakest sales growth was seen in Europe/South Pacific and in the Hill's pet food segment, where growth was essentially flat.

Reasons to Buy

Colgate is the predominant global market leader in toothpastes. Nearly half of all toothpaste sold worldwide in 2009 was a Colgate product.

Market acceptance for toothpaste in the United States is nearly 100 percent, but outside the United States, toothpaste is still a rapidly growing market. Analysts suggest that worldwide, consumer oral care products are barely at 50 percent market penetration. Given this healthy potential for market growth, along with the improving demographics of a health-conscious and appearance-conscious pool of consumers, globalization gives a Colgate investor a lot to smile about.

The first full-year results of the company's four-year restructuring plan are in and they look good. The improvement in gross margin, in particular, is very impressive given the recent uncertainty in most commodity markets and rising energy costs. In our recommendation last year we paid special attention to this aspect of Colgate's long-term strategy, as we felt the company was saying all the right things with regard to a massive streamlining of its supply chain. We're glad to see that it's starting to pay off, and we expect even more good news from this program next year.

The company's board has approved the repurchase of another 40 million of its outstanding shares, amounting to 8 percent of its common stock. The dividend was recently bumped another 20 percent (not reflected in the Current Yield, above), with hints recently of further increases in the offing. The cash flow to support the buyback and the dividends is certainly there, and then some—cash flow is up some 40 percent over the past three years and is expected to continue to grow at this rate well into 2012.

Reasons for Caution

In 2009 Venezuela represented 7 percent of the company's overall sales. Early in 2010, in order to address the rampant inflationary conditions in effect at the time, Colgate designated the U.S. dollar as the functional currency for its Venezuelan subsidiary. Venezuela has since initiated a program of fixed exchange rates, differing for essential and non-essential goods. While Colgate has already "baked-in" the more conservative rate and taken additional hedges in the currency markets, the situation bears watching, simply because of the company's relatively large revenue exposure there. As it is, the impact to earnings in 2010 is expected to be as much as ten cents per share, but the confidence in this figure can shift with the political winds in Venezuela.

SECTOR: Consumer Staples
BETA COEFFICIENT: .55
10-YEAR COMPOUND EARNINGS PER SHARE GROWTH: 11 percent
10-YEAR COMPOUND DIVIDENDS PER SHARE GROWTH: 11 percent

	2002	2003	2004	2005	2006	2007	2008	2009
Revenues (Mil)	9,294	9,903	10,584	11,397	12,238	13,790	15,330	15,327
Net income (Mil)	1,288	1,421	1,327	1,351	1,353	1,737	1,957	2,291
Earnings per share	2.19	2.46	2.33	2.43	2.46	3.2	3.66	4.37
Dividends per share	0.72	0.9	0.96	1.11	1.28	1.44	1.56	1.72
Cash flow per share	2.92	3.2	3.18	3.42	3.71	4.21	4.54	5.29
Price: high	58.9	61	59	57.2	67.1	81.3	82	87.4
low	44.1	48.6	42.9	48.2	53.4	63.8	54.4	54.5

Colgate-Palmolive Company
300 Park Avenue
New York, New York 10022–7499
(212) 310-2291
Website: *www.colgate.com*

ConocoPhillips

Ticker symbol: COP (NYSE) □ S&P rating: A □ Value Line financial strength rating: A++ □ Current yield: 4.0 percent

Company Profile

ConocoPhillips is the third-largest integrated energy company in the United States based on market capitalization and proven reserves and production of oil and gas. It is also the second largest petroleum refiner in the U.S. and the fifth largest refiner in the world. ConocoPhillips has the eighth-largest stock of proven petroleum reserves in private hands. Their businesses span the hydrocarbon value chain from wellhead through refining, marketing, transportation and chemicals.

ConocoPhillips is best known for its technological expertise in deepwater exploration and production, reservoir management and exploitation, 3-D seismic technology, high-grade petroleum coke upgrading, and sulfur removal.

Headquartered in Houston, Texas, ConocoPhillips operates in more than forty countries with about 30,000 employees worldwide and assets of $152 billion.

The company has five core activities worldwide:

■ Petroleum exploration and production. This segment primarily explores for, produces, transports and markets crude oil, natural gas and natural gas liquids on a worldwide basis.

■ Petroleum refining, marketing, supply and transportation. This segment purchases, refines, markets and transports crude oil and petroleum products, mainly in the United States, Europe and Asia.

■ Natural gas gathering, processing and marketing. This segment gathers, processes and markets natural gas produced by ConocoPhillips and others, and fractionates and markets natural gas liquids, predominantly in the United States and Trinidad. The midstream segment primarily consists of a 50 percent equity investment in DCP Midstream, LLC but also includes a 30.3 percent interest in Duke Energy Field Services, LLC.

■ Chemicals and plastics production and distribution. This segment manufactures and markets petrochemicals and plastics on a worldwide basis. The chemicals segment consists of a 50 percent equity investment in Chevron Phillips

Chemical Company LLC (CPChem).

■ LUKOIL Investment. This segment consists of an equity investment in the ordinary shares of OAO LUKOIL, the largest oil company in Russia and the second largest producer in the world. On December 31, 2009, ownership interest was 20 percent based on issued shares.

Financial Highlights, Fiscal Year 2009

The company grew sales 28.4 percent to $241 billion. Reported earnings came in at a loss of $17 billion due to recorded impairments (see below), without which the income would have been $15.8 billion positive (32.8 percent growth year over year).

The company recorded noncash impairments of $34 billion in 2008, including $7.4 billion to their LUKOIL investment and a $25.4 billion impairment to their Exploration & Production business as a function of decreased commodity prices.

The company announced its intent to divest itself of $10 billion of its current asset base and use the proceeds for share buyback. They have not yet said what precisely would be up for sale, other than to note they would be "non-core,

non-strategic" assets. The company will maintain their interest in several emerging businesses—fuels technology, gas-to-liquids, power generation and emerging technologies—that provide current and potential future growth opportunities.

In early 2010, Conoco announced their intention to sell off, over a period of three years, their 20 percent share in LUKOIL. The announcement was not met with joyous acclaim by the Russian government, but the government has said they will not attempt to block or hamper the sale in any way. This sale is independent of Conoco's other planned asset sale.

Reasons to Buy

Oil and gas stocks have historically been cyclical with long-term growth as a trend. This is one of the better opportunities in recent years to pick up a solid performer at a low point in the price cycle. Oil demand will rise as the world economies come out of recession, and Conoco's vertical integration and enormous refining capacity make it one of the better rebound plays.

The company plans to use half of the proceeds from its asset divestiture to repurchase shares on the open market. Here's an opportunity to front-run a lot of big trades—at current prices, a $5 billion stake would buy about 8 percent of Conoco's outstanding common stock.

Reasons for Caution

We're hoping Conoco's divestiture plans include their stake in the Canadian oil sands projects, whose economic viability has still not been proven at significant volumes.

SECTOR: Energy
BETA COEFFICIENT: 1.10
10-YEAR COMPOUND EARNINGS PER SHARE GROWTH: 22.0 percent
10-YEAR COMPOUND DIVIDENDS PER SHARE GROWTH: 9.5 percent

	2002	2003	2004	2005	2006	2007	2008	2009
Revenues (Bil)	56.75	104.2	135.1	179.4	183.7	187.4	240.8	149.3
Net income (Bil)	1.51	4.59	8.11	13.64	15.55	11.89	15.86	5.35
Earnings per share	1.56	3.35	5.79	9.55	9.66	9.14	10.66	3.59
Dividends per share	0.74	0.82	0.9	1.18	1.44	1.64	1.88	1.91
Cash flow per share	2.73	5.91	8.28	10.27	14.19	14.86	16.8	9.85
Price: high	32.1	33	45.6	71.5	74.9	90.8	96	57.4
low	22	22.6	32.2	41.4	54.9	61.6	41.3	34.1

ConocoPhillips
600 North Dairy Ashford
Houston, TX 77079–1175
(212) 207-1996
Website: *www.conocophillips.com*

Costco Wholesale Corporation

Ticker symbol: COST (NASDAQ) ❑ S&P rating: A+ ❑ Value Line financial strength rating A: ❑ Current yield: 1.2 percent

Company Profile

Costco Wholesale Corporation operates an international chain of membership warehouses, mainly under the "Costco Wholesale" name, that carry brand name merchandise at substantially lower prices than are typically found at conventional wholesale or retail sources. The warehouses are designed to help small-to-medium-sized businesses reduce costs in purchasing for resale and for everyday business use, but as most know, the individual consumer has been their big growth driver. Costco is the largest membership warehouse club chain in the world based on sales volume and is the fifth largest general retailer in the United States.

Costco carries a broad line of product categories, including groceries, appliances, television and media, automotive supplies, toys, hardware, sporting goods, jewelry, cameras, books, housewares, apparel, health and beauty aids, tobacco, furniture, office supplies, and office equipment. The company also operates self-service gasoline stations at a number of its United States and Canadian locations.

Additionally, Costco Wholesale Industries, a division of the company, operates manufacturing businesses, including special food packaging, optical laboratories, meat processing, and jewelry distribution.

Costco is open only to members of its tiered membership plan. As of March 2010, Costco has 566 locations, 413 in the United States and Puerto Rico, seventy-seven in Canada, thirty-two in Mexico, twenty-one in the U.K., twenty-two in Asia and one in Australia.

Financial Highlights, Fiscal Year 2009

Costco felt the effects of the worldwide recession and turned in their first-ever year-over-year decline in revenues, down 1.5 percent versus 2008. Most of this was due to a decrease in comparable sales, partially offset by sales at new warehouses. Net sales were very negatively impacted by unfavorable foreign currency exchange and gasoline price deflation, which together accounted for a reduction of nearly 6.5 percent.

Earnings were down 15 percent largely as a result of lower sales volume, the impact of foreign currency exchanges, and a pre-tax charge for ongoing litigation.

Membership fees increased 1.7 percent, to $1.53 billion, primarily due to new membership sign-ups at warehouses opened in 2009. Selling, general and administrative expenses as a percentage of net sales increased 58 basis points (0.58 percent) over the prior year, primarily due to a 20 percent spike in health care costs.

The numbers have turned around nicely since the company closed the books on 2009 in August of that year. Through the first half of fiscal 2010, comparable sales are up 3 percent in the United States and 19 percent at international warehouses, for a combined 6 percent increase year/year.

Reasons to Buy

Costco derives much of its operating income from membership fees, and the company has the best membership retention in the industry at 87 percent. Total membership at the end of FY2008 was 56 million.

Costco actually gained market share during the recession. They moved up two places in the ranking of U.S. retailers, from third to fifth, and remain the ninth-largest retailer in the world.

Costco's model of drawing visits with lower prices is still valid. During a period of the lowest consumer confidence in memory (4Q2008), Costco's sales grew 13 percent, driven primarily by a 9 percent increase in comparable store sales. Because of its price leadership, the company tends to fare well in both strong and weak economies.

New warehouses (those open less than one year) have been turning in impressive numbers, with an average of over $100 million each on an annualized basis. These are the highest first-year numbers in a decade. Also, the recent openings in Asia and Australia have gone very well. The Tokyo warehouse had 47,000 new members signed up by the first day, and the Australian store did $841,000 on its opening day—the highest ever for any store.

The company is more optimistic about expansion than it has been in the last two years, saying that they would like to get back to a rate of thirty to forty openings per year, if conditions permit.

Reasons for Caution

Without the excellent performance of the newest stores, Costco's numbers over the last eighteen months would be far less impressive. To the extent that Costco needs new locations to plump up the bottom line, anything that delays their expansion plans could have a broader impact to ongoing operations.

SECTOR: Retail
BETA COEFFICIENT: .75
10-YEAR COMPOUND EARNINGS PER SHARE GROWTH: 12.5 percent
4-YEAR COMPOUND DIVIDENDS PER SHARE GROWTH: not meaningful

	2002	2003	2004	2005	2006	2007	2008	2009
Revenues (Mil)	37,993	41,693	48,107	52,935	60,151	64,400	72,483	71,422
Net income (Mil)	700	721	882	989	1,103	1,083	1,283	1,086
Earnings per share	1.48	1.53	1.85	2.03	2.3	2.37	2.89	2.57
Dividends per share	0	0	0.2	0.45	0.49	0.55	0.61	0.68
Cash flow per share	1.48	1.53	1.86	2.03	2.31	2.63	2.89	4.16
Price: high	46.9	39	50.5	51.2	57.9	72.7	75.2	61.3
low	27.1	27	35	39.5	46	51.5	43.9	38.2

Costco Wholesale Corporation
999 Lake Drive
Issaquah, WA 98027
(425) 313-8203
Website: *www.costco.com*

CONSERVATIVE GROWTH

CVS/Caremark Corporation

Ticker symbol: CVS (NYSE) □ S&P rating: A □ Value Line financial strength rating: A □ Current yield: 1.0 percent

Company Profile

Stanley and Sid Goldstein were distributing health and beauty products in the early 1960s when they decided to branch out into retailing, opening their first Consumer Value Store in Lowell, Massachusetts in 1963. The CVS chain had grown to forty outlets by 1969, the year they sold the business to Melville Shoes. Melville underwent a restructuring in the mid-1990s, spinning off CVS and other retail units.

CVS Corporation is now the largest domestic drugstore chain, based on store count. CVS operates over 7,000 retail and specialty pharmacy stores in forty states and the District of Columbia. The company holds the leading market share in thirty-two of the 100 largest U.S. drugstore markets, more than any other retail drugstore chain.

Stores are situated primarily in strip shopping centers or free-standing locations, with a typical store ranging in size from 8,000 to 12,000 square feet. Most new units being built are based on either a 10,000 square foot or 12,000 square foot prototype building that typically includes a drive-thru pharmacy. The company says that about one-half of its stores were opened or remodeled over the past five years.

The Caremark acquisition in 2007 transformed CVS from a retailer into the nation's leading manager of pharmacy benefits, the middlemen between pharmaceutical companies and individuals with drug benefit coverage.

CVS's purchase of Long's Drugs in 2008 vaulted the company into the lead position the U.S. drug retail market, ahead of Walgreen's. Long's is only the most recent in a series of acquisitions by CVS in recent years, including MinuteClinic, Osco Drugs and Sav-On Drugs in 2006, Caremark (for $26.5 billion) in 2007, and finally Long's (for $2.6 billion) in 2008. Earnings over the period have nearly tripled, although per-share earnings have grown a somewhat more modest 55 percent.

Financial Highlights, Fiscal Year 2009

CVS's revenue for the year was $98.7 billion, up 12.9 percent versus FY2008. Net earnings rose 15.1 percent to $3.7 billion, while per-share earnings from continuing operations rose 11.6 percent to $2.59. The company added just over 100 net new stores during a period of what was for CVS very moderate growth. The company plans to add 200-300 more stores in 2010 and similar growth is anticipated for 2011.

In August 2008 CVS closed on their purchase of Long's Drugs, a 521-store chain based primarily in California, which brought with it Long's PBM operation with 8 million prescription members and 450,000 Medicare beneficiaries. The 2009 results reflect the full-year's effects of that incremental revenue, specifically $6.6 billion incremental to sales and $1.1 billion to gross profit. The Long's contribution to gross profit actually reduced CVS's gross margin.

Reasons to Buy

Looking at the U.S. population, approximately 39 million people are sixty-five or older today. That number is projected to climb to 47 million by 2015, and prescription drug use is expected to rise substantially within this demographic. With leading market positions in California, Florida, and other sun-belt states, CVS feels they stand to benefit from this trend to a greater extent than most other pharmacy players.

The recent federal health care overhaul left basically untouched Medicare Part D, which at the end of 2009, provided prescription coverage to 27 million Americans who would otherwise not be eligible. Medicare Part D also encourages caregivers to use generic drugs whenever possible, and generics, while cheaper overall, generate higher margins for the pharmacy. Over the next five years, over $50 billion in branded drugs will lose patent protection, creating further opportunities for generics and driving pharmacy margins even higher.

In November 2009 the company authorized the repurchase of an additional $2 billion of its outstanding common stock, $500 million of which it exercised immediately.

Reasons for Caution

The PBM business ($50 billion/ year) will face a difficult year. In addition to losing some $5 billion in expiring contracts, they are still struggling to maintain margins. During 4Q2009, when revenues were up almost 15 percent year/ year, their operating profit fell 70 basis points.

SECTOR: Retall
BETA COEFFICIENT: 0.80
10-YEAR COMPOUND EARNINGS PER SHARE GROWTH: 14.5 percent
10-YEAR COMPOUND DIVIDENDS PER SHARE GROWTH: 10 percent

	2002	2003	2004	2005	2006	2007	2008	2009
Revenue (Mil)	24,182	26,588	30,594	37,006	43,814	76,330	87,472	98,729
Net income (Mil)	719	847	959	1,225	1,369	2,637	3,589	3,803
Earnings per share	0.88	1.03	1.15	1.45	1.6	1.92	2.44	2.63
Dividends per share	0.12	0.12	0.13	0.14	0.16	0.24	0.26	0.3
Cash flow per share	1.29	1.49	1.75	2.15	2.5	2.59	3.37	3.73
Price: high	17.9	18.8	23.7	31.6	36.1	42.6	44.3	38.3
low	11.5	10.9	16.9	22	26.1	30.5	23.2	23.7

CVS/Caremark Corporation
One CVS Drive
Woonsocket, RI 02895
(914) 722-4704
Website: *www.cvs.com*

Deere & Company

Ticker symbol: DE (NYSE) □ S&P rating: A− □ Value Line financial strength rating: A++ □ Current yield: 1.9 percent

Company Profile

Deere & Company, founded in 1837, grew from a one-man blacksmith shop into a worldwide corporation that today does business in more than 160 countries and employs more than 40,000 people around the globe. Deere has a diverse base of operations reporting into two broad categories following last year's restructuring: Equipment Operations and Financial Services.

Equipment Operations includes the former separate segments of Agricultural Equipment, Construction and Forestry Equipment, Commercial and Consumer Equipment, and Power Systems, which produces diesel engines and powertrain systems for Deere and OEM applications.

Financial Services includes their former Credit Operations and Health Care segments.

Deere has been the world's premier producer of agricultural equipment for nearly fifty years. If it's used on a farm and requires an engine, Deere likely offers it. Deere is also the world's leading manufacturer of forestry equipment, and a major manufacturer of heavy construction equipment (Caterpillar being the market leader in the heavy

construction segment). They're also the world leader in premium turf-care equipment and utility vehicles in both the commercial and consumer markets.

John Deere Credit is one of the largest equipment finance companies in the United States, with more than 1.8 million accounts and a managed asset portfolio of nearly $16 billion. It provides retail, wholesale and lease financing for agricultural, construction and forestry, commercial and consumer equipment, including lawn and ground care, and revolving credit for agricultural inputs and services. These services are available in all of Deere's largest markets, including Argentina, Australia, Brazil, Canada, France, and Germany. Their Health Care operations provide health care management services to about 4,400 employer groups and cover more than 515,000 members.

Financial Highlight, Fiscal Year 2009

Fiscal 2009 was a year that Deere & Company saw coming but couldn't outrun. For Deere (as well as for other capital equipment manufacturers), 2009 was one of the most dramatic downturns in the capital equipment market's history. Deere saw a 19 percent decline in sales and a whopping 57 percent fall-off in earnings. Most of the declines were concentrated in their Construction and Forestry segment and Financial Services.

Construction and Forestry's woes were driven by volume, as they took a 45 percent hit to sales, representing some 70 percent of the company's overall top-line decline. Despite top-line growth of 2 percent, Financial Services was unable to generate earnings due to increased credit losses and uncertainty in the capital markets.

The company measures its internal programs and its financial health against what they refer to as Shareholder Value Add, which is a fairly rigorous and conservative measure that is most appropriate for longer-term projects and programs, as it tends to negate the effects of variation in the short-term cost of capital. Deere adopted this tool throughout the corporation in 2001 and feels it has been a powerful contributor to their success since then. Measured against this standard, the company's SVA for the year was only slightly negative, with fairly encouraging results in the Agriculture and Turf segments.

Reasons to Buy

When we wrote about Decre a year ago it seemed fairly clear that they

had already dodged most of the boulders that rolled across the road leading from 2008 toward 2010 and what was left to do was check for dents and maybe slap on a new coat of paint. Their top-line had firmed up, they still had record levels of cash, and the economic landscape was much clearer than it had been. The company's shares, which were trading in the high thirties at the time, are now in the low sixties. This hardly makes them unique in the broader view of the market, as many stocks have rebounded more than 100 percent over the same time. What's unusual about Deere's recovery is that sales remain largely depressed, and yet the company is turning in surprisingly strong numbers.

Sales in the first half of 2010 are still down 8 percent over 1H2009, but earnings are up 20 percent. The restructuring appears to have been effective in reducing costs without negatively impacting delivery of product or taking too large a bite out of the company's underlying finances. Cash flow is up, debt and inventories are down, and the company was able to spend a record $1 billion on research and development. When sales turn around, the company is positioned to produce very solid bottom line growth. Most analysts have pegged FY2010 earnings at $4 per share, up almost 40 percent over 2009.

Deere's products are competitive worldwide. The company sells over 50 percent of its units outside the United States and Canada—they've recently begun sales operations in Russia, and their market share in India continues its solid growth.

Reasons to be Cautious

The U.S. economy is still sluggish, and Deere's sales have not yet turned around. In addition, the growing U.S. deficit has many in Congress looking hard at the country's policy of farm subsidies.

SECTOR: Industrials
BETA COEFFICIENT: 1.45
10-YEAR COMPOUND EARNINGS PER SHARE GROWTH: 10.0 percent
10-YEAR COMPOUND DIVIDENDS PER SHARE GROWTH: 9.0 percent

		2002	2003	2004	2005	2006	2007	2008	2009
Revenues (Mil)		11,703	13,349	17,673	19,401	19,884	21,489	25,804	20,756
Net income (Mil)		319	643	1,406	1,447	1,453	1,822	2,053	1,198
Earnings per share		0.67	1.32	2.78	2.94	3.08	4.01	4.7	2.82
Dividends per share		0.44	0.44	0.53	0.61	0.78	0.91	1.06	1.12
Cash flow per share		1.49	2.02	3.54	3.85	4.09	5.12	6.01	4.05
Price:	high	25.8	33.7	37.5	37.4	50.7	93.7	94.9	56.9
	low	18.8	18.8	28.4	28.5	33.5	45.1	28.5	24.5

Deere & Company
One John Deere Place
Moline, IL 61265
(309) 765–4491
Website: *www.deere.com*

Dentsply International, Inc.

Ticker symbol: XRAY (NASDAQ) □ S&P rating: A− □ Value Line financial strength rating: B++ □
Current yield: 0.6 percent

Company Profile

Dentsply is the largest dental products company in the world. The company designs, develops, manufactures and markets a broad range of products for dentists, orthodontists, and dental laboratories, including dental prosthetics, precious metal dental alloys, dental ceramics, endodontic instruments and materials, pastes, sealants, scalers, and crown and bridge materials. They are the leading United States manufacturer and distributor of dental x-ray equipment, dental handpieces, intraoral cameras, dental x-ray film holders, film mounts, and bone substitute/grafting materials. Finally, they are also a leading worldwide manufacturer or distributor of dental injectable anesthetics, impression materials, orthodontic appliances, dental cutting instruments, and dental implants. In all, the company produces or resells over 120,000 SKUs, protected by more than 2,000 patents.

Dentsply has a presence in more than 120 countries, though its main operations take place in the United States, Canada, Germany, Switzerland, the U.K., Japan, and Italy. The company has an extensive sales network of over 2,100 sales representatives, distributors, and importers. Its products are manufactured in or distributed from facilities around the world and include well-established brand names such as Caulk, Cavitron, Ceramco, Dentsply, Detrey, Midwest, R&R Rinn, and Trubyte.

Financial Highlights, Fiscal Year 2009

Dentsply's net sales declined 1.5 percent in FY2009. This is Dentsply's first year-over-year decline in sales in over fifteen years, although the shortfall was small enough that when precious metal content is removed from calculation (precious metal costs are passed through to customers without margin), sales were essentially flat. Gross margin fell 200 basis points (2 percent) as a result of unfavorable product mix and unfavorable currency movements.

The company put expense controls in place in response to the downturn in the economy and was able to shave 100 basis points off of SG&A. Additional savings were gained via headcount reduction and restructuring, but in the end earnings fell 2 percent, or four cents per share versus 2008. As bad years go, though, this was not all that bad.

Dentsply's board has authorized the repurchase of 5 million shares of Dentsply stock. This represents approximately 3.5 percent of the outstanding shares.

Current business development programs, including acquisitions and new partnerships, added nearly $90 million in new sales in 2009, or 4.5 percent of total sales.

Reasons to Buy

The company maintains a robust pipeline and continues to fund R&D at a healthy clip. In 2009 Dentsply released over thirty new products.

Demographics, at least in the domestic market, are working in the company's favor. Older people tend to spend more on dental care, and every office visit, whether it be for a simple cleaning or full endodontic repair, uses Dentsply consumables. A larger percentage of the population are retaining their natural teeth, and are doing so far longer than they used to. People with their natural teeth tend to visit the dentist far more often than those with no remaining natural teeth.

Trends in the global economy also favor Dentsply. As per-capita and discretionary incomes rise in the emerging nations of the Pacific Rim, Latin America and Eastern

Europe, improved health care, and dental care in particular, become a priority. Dental care spending in India and China is growing far faster than in the mature U.S. market. International sales represent 63 percent of Dentsply's total sales; this trend is increasing, and Dentsply is responding with increased presence in the developing markets.

The company feels strongly that there are further cost reductions possible in its current structure and is committed to leveraging far more of its overhead expenses with broader technology implementations.

They are nearly debt-free and have cash to support both share repurchase and acquisitions, should opportunities arise.

Reasons for Caution

Dentistry in North America and Western Europe has changed focus over the years from treating pain, infections, and poor overall dental health toward a practice with an increased emphasis on preventive care and cosmetic dentistry. Cosmetic dentistry includes many high-value procedures, but cosmetic procedures are elective in nature and are often not covered under insurance programs. When unemployment is high and the economy is lagging, these procedures can be deferred indefinitely and Dentsply's top line will suffer as a result.

SECTOR: Health Care
BETA COEFFICIENT: .85
10-YEAR COMPOUND EARNINGS PER SHARE GROWTH: 13.5 percent
10-YEAR COMPOUND DIVIDENDS PER SHARE GROWTH: 10.0 percent

	2002	2003	2004	2005	2006	2007	2008	2009
Revenues (Mil)	1,514	1,571	1,694	1,715	1,810	2,010	2,194	2,160
Net income (Mil)	146	173	196	216	224	260	286	276
Earnings per share	0.92	1.07	1.2	1.34	1.41	1.68	1.88	1.84
Dividends per share	0.09	0.1	0.11	0.12	0.14	0.16	0.19	0.2
Cash flow per share	1.21	1.38	1.52	1.69	1.8	2.03	2.3	2.32
Price: high	21.8	23.7	28.4	29.2	33.8	47.8	47.1	36.8
low	15.7	16.1	20.9	25.4	26.1	29.4	22.8	21.8

Dentsply International, Inc.
P.O. Box 872
221 West Philadelphia Street
York, PA 17405–0872
(717) 849-4243
Website: *www.dentsply.com*

Dominion Resources, Inc.

Ticker symbol: D (NYSE) □ S&P rating: B+ □ Value Line financial strength rating: B++ □ Current yield: 4.7 percent

Company Profile

Dominion is one of the nation's largest producers of energy, with 27,000 megawatts of power generation, 6,000 miles of electric transmission lines, 12,000 miles of natural gas transmission, gathering and storage pipeline, and 1.3 trillion cubic feet equivalent of natural gas reserves. Included in these assets is the nation's largest underground natural gas storage system with about 942 billion cubic feet of storage capacity serving retail energy customers in twelve states. Dominion's strategy is to be a leading provider of electricity, natural gas and related services to customers in the energy-intensive Midwest, Mid-Atlantic and Northeast regions of the United States, a potential market of 50 million homes and businesses where 40 percent of the nation's energy is consumed.

As of March 2010, Dominion operates in three reporting segments:

Dominion Generation includes the generation operations of Dominion's merchant fleet and regulated electric utility, as well as energy marketing and price risk management activities for their generation assets. Their utility generation operations primarily serve the supply requirements for the Dominion Virginia Power segment's utility customers. Their generation mix is diversified and includes coal, nuclear, gas, oil, and renewables. DG produced 60 percent of the company's earnings in 2009.

Dominion Energy includes Dominion's Ohio regulated natural gas distribution company, regulated gas transmission pipeline and storage operations, regulated LNG operations and Appalachian natural gas E&P business. Dominion Energy also includes producer services, which aggregates natural gas supply, engages in natural gas trading and marketing activities and natural gas supply management and provides price risk management services to Dominion affiliates.

The gas transmission pipeline and storage business serves gas distribution businesses and other customers in the Northeast, Mid-Atlantic and Midwest.

Dominion Virginia Power is responsible for all regulated electric distribution and electric transmission operations in Virginia and North Carolina. It is also responsible for Dominion Retail and all customer service, as well as their non-regulated retail energy marketing operations. DVP's electric transmission and distribution operations serve residential, commercial, industrial and governmental customers in Virginia and northeastern North Carolina.

Financial Highlights, Fiscal Year 2009

Dominion's net revenue declined 5 percent primarily due to a charge ($614 million) for the proposed settlement of Virginia Power's 2009 rate case proceedings and an $86 million decrease in sales of gas production from E&P operations. Lower fuel expenses offset these negatives somewhat, as did the positive impact ($158 million) of the 80 percent expansion of the Cove Point storage facility.

The company added 31,000 new customer accounts to its Dominion Virginia Power (DVP) business, placed its expanded Cove Point LNG facility into operation, and received approval for its Appalachian Gateway Project, a natural gas pipeline project linking the West Virginia and Pennsylvania production with storage fields and pipelines in Pennsylvania.

The company achieved a 93 percent capacity factor at its nuclear generation facilities, the highest average level since 2005 and much higher than the 90 percent average for the U.S. nuclear industry as a whole.

Reasons to Buy

Dominion has exited the natural gas exploration and production business, having sold off its remaining assets in early 2010 (the divestiture began in 2006). The company felt that the business, although profitable, was too volatile and so was viewed as a negative among the traditional utility and large institutional investors. The company felt that its contributions would never be fully reflected in the price of the stock. We agree, and although the price Dominion got for the most recent assets was 15 percent lower than expected, the company is more attractive as a distribution and storage player than as a utility with E&P operations.

The company plans to raise its payout ratio, reflecting its greater reliance on regulated businesses as income sources. The ratio, which was 50 percent in 2009, will be raised to 60 and 65 percent in 2010 and 2011.

Virginia Power's most recent rate request was approved, allowing it an 11.9 percent ROE. This is 1 to 2 percent higher than most other utilities.

Reasons for Caution

In March 2010 the company reaffirmed its earnings guidance for $3.20 to $3.40 per share, but recent (June) announcements indicate that some "downward flexibility" exists in those numbers. Some retirement and benefit charges may be much larger than anticipated.

SECTOR: **Utilities**
BETA COEFFICIENT: **.70**
10-YEAR COMPOUND EARNINGS PER SHARE GROWTH: **7.5 percent**
10-YEAR COMPOUND DIVIDENDS PER SHARE GROWTH: **2.0 percent**

	2002	**2003**	**2004**	**2005**	**2006**	**2007**	**2008**	**2009**
Revenues (Mil)	10,218	12,078	13,972	17,971	16,482	15,674	16,290	15,131
Net income (Mil)	1,378	1,261	1,425	1,033	1,704	1,414	1,781	1,585
Earnings per share	2.41	1.96	2.13	1.5	2.4	2.13	3.04	2.64
Dividends per share	1.29	2.58	1.3	1.34	1.38	1.46	1.58	1.75
Cash flow per share	4.45	3.97	4.18	3.71	4.91	5.08	5.07	4.82
Price: high	33.6	33	34.5	43.5	42.2	49.4	48.5	39.8
low	17.7	25.9	30.4	33.3	34.4	39.8	31.3	27.1

Dominion Resources, Inc.
P.O. Box 26532
Richmond, VA 23261–6532
(804) 819–2156
Website: *www.dom.com*

AGGRESSIVE GROWTH

Dover Corporation

Ticker symbol: DOV (NYSE) ❑ S&P rating: A ❑ Value Line financial strength rating: A ❑ Current yield: 2.2 percent

Company Profile

Dover Corporation is a diversified industrial conglomerate made up of thirty-four operating companies engaged in specialized industrial products and manufacturing equipment. Dover acquires and develops platform businesses marked by growth, innovation, and higher-than-average profit margins. Traditionally, the company bought entities that could operate independently. Over the past ten years, though, Dover has put increased emphasis on also acquiring businesses that can be added to existing operations.

Dover operates as a decentralized corporation, but provides resources as necessary and implements best practices company-wide as appropriate. The company measures all of its businesses against a set of metrics it refers to as "Performance Counts." These metrics include:

- Eight or more inventory turns per year
- 10 percent or greater annual earnings growth
- 15 percent or greater operating margins
- 20 percent or less working capital as a percent of assets

- 25 percent or greater after-tax return on investment

The companies are organized into four reporting segments: Electronic Technologies, Engineered Systems, Fluid Management, and Industrial Products.

The corporation targets 8 to 10 percent of revenue annually for acquisition capital. Their acquisition criteria are fairly specific. They seek high value-added, engineered industrial products for mission-critical applications that have defensible differentiation and whose markets have high barriers to entry. They focus on industrial components and products sold to a broad customer base of industrial and/or commercial users and prefer longer product life cycles with low or moderate market revenue and market volatility.

In other words, dot.coms need not apply.

They also look for companies with existing regional or national distribution systems and with potential for global distribution. They strongly prefer to keep existing management in place whenever possible, as they are buying for the long term.

Financial Highlights, Fiscal Year 2009

Dover's fiscal 2009 was not a memorable year, unfortunately. Most of Dover's revenues are tied to heavy manufacturing and infrastructure programs, and very few sectors of the economy fared worse during the recession than did those two. Revenues fell 24 percent and earnings were off 47 percent from FY2008. As it happens, 2008 was a record year for Dover in terms of revenue and earnings, so the bar was set fairly high.

It wasn't all bad news—free cash flow grew 120 basis points (supporting a 13 percent increase in the dividend), and the operating margin held at a fairly robust 14.8 percent. The company also reduced its already low debt and managed to exit the year with significantly improved working capital.

Reasons to Buy

The last time Dover had this sort of decline was during the worldwide credit crunch following the 2001 tech collapse. Dover recovered very nicely in that situation by doing exactly what they did last year when they saw the most recent problems coming: they concentrated on maximizing what they could control. The company focused on margin maintenance and cash flow generation, with the goal of making funds available for continued internal and external investments.

Dover's recovery, starting in 4Q2009, has been very encouraging. Revenue and earnings will not get to 2008 levels in 2010, but as of mid-year they're already 40 percent of the way there. We look for continued growth through 2011 and beyond. Margins are already on the mend and should be ahead of 2008 levels by a few hundred basis points, because . . . .

Dover in 2009 opened their new China Regional Headquarters in Shanghai, with the goal of integrating their various current Asian supply chains out of one location. Cost savings are expected to be in the $75 to $100 million range by 2011. Frankly, we think this is something that could have (and should have) happened several years ago, but better late than never. Dover is also moving its corporate HQ operations to Chicago to integrate operations with the segment management. "Synergy" (we don't like that word) may or may not result, but it will certainly save some money (which is a word we do like).

Dover has survived and done well by growing carefully and profitably while focusing on a few key markets where they have core competencies. This is a conservatively run operation that just happens to generate over 10 percent free cash flow, year in and year out.

Reasons for Caution

Industrials, in general, are still on the mend and will likely trail most other areas of the economy in the recovery. Also, some of Dover's current businesses have likely suffered significant damage to their customer base, their supplier base, or both. Reinvigoration of the industrial sector will take some time, and this is a stock that will require (and reward) patience.

SECTOR: **Industrials**
BETA COEFFICIENT: **1.15**
10-YEAR COMPOUND EARNINGS PER SHARE GROWTH: **7.5 percent**
10-YEAR COMPOUND DIVIDENDS PER SHARE GROWTH: **7.5 percent**

		2002	2003	2004	2005	2006	2007	2008	2009
Revenues (Mil)		4,184	4,413	5,488	6,078	6,512	7,226	7,569	5,776
Net income (Mil)		211	285	413	510	562	661	695	373
Earnings per share		1.04	1.40	2.00	2.50	2.73	3.26	3.67	2.00
Dividends per share		0.54	0.57	0.62	0.65	0.71	0.8	0.9	1.02
Cash flow per share		1.84	2.15	2.80	3.22	4.02	4.63	5.14	3.38
Price:	high	43.6	40.4	44.1	42.2	51.9	54.6	54.6	43.1
	low	23.5	22.8	35.1	34.1	40.3	44.3	23.4	21.8

Dover Corporation
280 Park Avenue
New York, NY 10017–1292
(212) 922-1640
Website: *www.dovercorporation.com*

Duke Energy

Ticker symbol: DUK (NYSE) ❑ S&P rating: A- ❑ Value Line financial strength rating: A ❑ Current yield: 5.8 percent

Company Profile

Duke Energy Corporation is a utility provider and operator operating primarily in the Southeast and Midwest but with operations outside those areas. The company has three segments: U.S. Franchised Electric and Gas, Commercial Power, and International Energy. The company was reformed into a new company in 2007 after spinning off most of its gas business into a new company called Spectra Energy.

The Franchised Electric and Gas segment generates, transmits, distributes, and sells electricity in central and western North Carolina, western South Carolina, southwestern Ohio, Indiana, and northern Kentucky including the Greater Cincinnati area; and transports and sells natural gas in southwestern Ohio and northern Kentucky. This segment supplies electric service to approximately 4 million residential, commercial, and industrial customers with approximately 151,600 miles of distribution lines and a 20,900 mile transmission system. The company is relatively heavily invested in nuclear power, with

some 35 percent of its power provided this way (55 percent coal, 10 percent other).

The Commercial Power segment offers onsite energy solutions and utility services for large customers. This segment owns, operates, and manages power plants; and handles all procurement and services around these plants; it also develops customized energy solutions for these customers.

The International Energy segment operates and manages power generation facilities, and sells and markets electric power and natural gas outside the United States. This segment provides services and consulting for retail distributors, electric utilities, independent power producers, marketers, and industrial and commercial companies. It also develops, owns, and operates a fiber optic communications network, primarily in the Southeast U.S, serving wireless, local, and long-distance communications companies, as well as Internet service providers, and other businesses and organizations. The company was founded in 1916 and is based in Charlotte, North Carolina.

Financial Highlights, Fiscal Year 2009

Since the 2007 spinoff, it's hard to connect recent history to early operating results. Like most utilities, the company took a small revenue hit in 2009 as consumer and especially commercial customers contracted due to the recession. Earnings, however, were up slightly to $1.13 per share due mainly to cost-cutting and a moderation in source energy costs. In the quarter ended March 31, 2010, the company resumed a modest uptrend in revenue and income. The company just raised the dividend to $0.245 per quarter per share, keeping its record of steady annual raises intact albeit with half the raise of previous years. Investors were warned that this might be the case.

Reasons to Buy

Duke has always been a well-managed utility operating in solid markets with a growing customer base. The North Carolina customer base is diverse and especially attractive as more companies and individuals move there to enjoy lower costs of living and costs of doing business. The company should also stand to benefit, perhaps more than peers, from an economic recovery.

We actually like its nuclear exposure as we do think nuclear power will return to the electricity generating stage in a bigger way. Duke will have the advantage of experience and existing infrastructure. Because it's a relatively new concern in its current form, and perhaps because if its nuclear exposure, the dividend is more than 1 percent higher than the average for similar companies. That said, it is well covered by current cash flows.

Reasons for Caution

For many, nuclear power is a reason for caution, and we certainly would want to diversify utility holdings to avoid overexposure to utilities with nuclear facilities. Like most utilities, Duke depends on regulatory rate relief to grow revenues, and so the regulatory environment is critical. The company is currently building three new plants, and cost overruns may be an issue.

SECTOR: **Utilities**
BETA COEFFICIENT: **0.65**
10-YEAR COMPOUND EARNINGS PER SHARE GROWTH: **NA**
10-YEAR COMPOUND DIVIDENDS PER SHARE GROWTH: **NA**

	2002	2003	2004	2005	2006	2007	2008	2009
Revenues (Mil)	-	-	-	-	10,607	12,720	13,207	12,731
Net income (Mil)	-	-	-	-	1,080	1,522	1,279	1,461
Earnings per share	-	-	-	-	.92	1.20	1.01	1.13
Dividends per share	-	-	-	-	-	.86	.90	.94
Cash flow per share	-	-	-	-	2.62	2.70	2.45	2.53
Price: high	-	-	-	-	21.3	20.6	17.9	17.5
low	-	-	-	-	16.9	13.5	11.7	15.9

Duke Energy Corporation
526 South Church Street
Charlotte, NC 28202-1803
(704) 594-6200
Website: *www.duke-energy.com*

E. I. DuPont De Nemours

Ticker symbol: DD (NYSE) ❑ S&P rating: A ❑ Value Line financial strength rating: A++ ❑ Current yield: 5.0 percent

Company Profile

Founded in 1802, DuPont is a world leader in science and technology in a range of disciplines, including biotechnology, electronics materials and science, safety and security, and synthetic fibers. They refer to their business as "market-driven science," reflected in 2009's introduction of over 1,400 new products and over 2,000 patent grants.

In 2009 the company strategically realigned its businesses into six market- and technology-focused growth platforms:

- Agriculture and Nutrition
- Safety and Protection
- Electronic and Communications
- Performance Chemicals
- Performance Materials
- Performance Coatings

The company has operations in eighty countries worldwide and about 60 percent of consolidated net sales are made to customers outside the United States. Worldwide subsidiaries and affiliates of DuPont conduct manufacturing, seed production, or selling activities, and some are distributors of products manufactured by the company.

DuPont has one of the largest R&D budgets of any company in the world. In 2008, DuPont spent $1.4 billion on research and development, representing a spending level which has been fixed at 5 percent of net sales from 2006–2009, enabling the company to bring more than a thousand new products to market per year. DuPont operates more than fifty R&D centers around the world, aiming to attract the best available scientific talent and take advantage of the regional knowledge necessary to create products that cater to the varying needs of customers in every market. DuPont's research is concentrated at its Wilmington, DE facilities. DuPont's modern research is focused on renewable bio-based materials, advanced biofuels, energy-efficient technologies, enhanced safety products, and alternative energy technologies.

Financial Highlights, Fiscal Year 2009

Revenues fell 14 percent in 2009 as customers for their engineered materials had already scaled back new development programs and reduced requirements for existing products. DuPont responded with cost cutting; capital programs were zero-based, working capital was minimized and spending was reduced overall. The company also restructured its product lines, reducing headcount and redundant administration.

Profits still suffered, down in 2009 by 28 percent versus 2008. There's only so much you can do to respond to rapid market changes when you're running a research-heavy company with relatively low cash turnover and revenues heavily tied to streams from patented products. Many of DuPont's products serve the construction, automotive, and industrial sectors, and those markets remain depressed even as the consumer markets are starting to turn around.

Reasons to Buy

DuPont is a major supplier to the automotive industry. Although the automotive sector remains depressed, DuPont's agricultural and safety segments (which constitute 42 percent of operating income) continue to grow throughout the recession.

Like many stocks, DuPont did well during the recovery, and our recommendation of DuPont last year was based on our assertion that the stock was simply undervalued, which is our position this year as well. The product pipeline is full, individual product margins remain

strong, and the company's biggest money-makers still dominate their markets. Share price grew over 60 percent from last year's recommendation and our opinion of the company's prospects remains high.

The company's plan for future growth is built on major initiatives: improving worldwide food production, reducing dependence on fossil fuels, and growth in emerging markets. We feel there are great synergies between these goals and the initiatives of other major industrial and governmental programs. Concentrating on these goals, the company is targeting a revenue CAGR of 14 percent through 2012 which would yield revenue in 2012 50 percent higher than the peak in 2008.

Ignoring the effects of the recession, it's been a decade since DuPont stock has traded outside the twenty-point range of $35 to $55. If their business returns soon to pre-recession levels (and we think it will), then the current price of $34 looks very attractive.

Reasons for Caution

It's also been a decade since DuPont has surprised on the upside. It's not clear that they have the products, company, or management to produce a breakout year in the foreseeable future. The days when they could count on Detroit to buy millions of gallons of paint per year are long gone, and there are no new cash cows on the immediate horizon.

SECTOR: Materials
BETA COEFFICIENT: 1.1
10-YEAR COMPOUND EARNINGS PER SHARE GROWTH: −0.5 percent
10-YEAR COMPOUND DIVIDENDS PER SHARE GROWTH: 2.5 percent

	2002	2003	2004	2005	2006	2007	2008	2009
Revenues (Mil)	24,006	26,996	27,340	26,639	28,982	30,653	30,529	26,109
Net income (Mil)	2,012	1,607	2,390	2,100	3,148	2,988	2,477	1,769
Earnings per share	2.01	1.65	2.38	2.32	2.88	3.22	2.73	1.93
Dividends per share	1.4	1.4	1.4	1.46	1.48	1.52	1.64	1.64
Cash flow per share	3.54	3.19	3.75	3.97	4.4	4.89	4.25	3.4
Price: high	49.8	46	49.4	54.9	49.7	53.9	52.5	35.6
low	35	34.7	39.9	37.6	38.5	42.3	21.3	16

E. I. DuPont De Nemours
1007 Market Street
Wilmington, DE 19898
(800) 441-7515
Website: *www.dupont.com*

Ecolab, Inc.

Ticker symbol: ECL (NYSE) □ S&P rating: A □ Value Line financial strength rating: A □ Current yield: 1.4 percent

Company Profile

Ecolab is the global leader in commercial products and services used for cleaning, sanitizing, food safety and infection prevention. Founded in 1923 and headquartered in St. Paul, Minnesota, Ecolab serves customers in more than 160 countries across North America, Europe, Asia Pacific, Latin America, the Middle East and Africa, and employs more than 26,000 associates. The company delivers comprehensive programs and services to industries such as foodservice, food and beverage processing, hospitality, health care, government and education, retail, and facilities maintenance.

The company conducts its domestic business under these segments:

■ Institutional Division is the leading provider of cleaners and sanitizers for utensils, laundry, kitchen cleaning and general housecleaning, product-dispensing equipment and dishwashing racks and related kitchen sundries to the foodservice, lodging, and health care industries. It also provides products and services for pool and spa treatment.

■ Food & Beverage Division offers cleaning and sanitizing products and services to farms, dairy plants, food and beverage processors, and pharmaceutical plants.

■ Kay Division is the largest supplier of cleaning and sanitizing products for the quick-service restaurant, convenience store, and flood retail markets.

Ecolab also sells janitorial and health care products, textile care products for large institutional and commercial laundries, vehicle care products for rental, fleet, and retail car washes, and water-treatment products for commercial, institutional, and industrial markets. Other domestic services include institutional and commercial pest elimination and prevention, and the commercial kitchen equipment repair services.

The company operates directly in nearly seventy countries. In addition, the company reaches customers in more than 100 countries through distributors, licensees and export operations, with more than fifty state-of-the-art manufacturing and distribution facilities worldwide.

Financial Highlights, Fiscal Year 2009

FY2009 was a rough period for the restaurant and hospitality industries, which are two of Ecolab's core markets. As a result, Ecolab turned in mixed results when compared with 2008. Revenues were down 4 percent, but earnings gained 3 percent due mainly to cost-cutting measures taken during the year. On a constant currency basis, revenues would have been flat, with a 3 percent decrease in unit volume offset by a 3 percent pricing increase. Gross margin rose by 70 basis points (0.7 percent) but operating income actually fell 4 percent due to special charges, mainly for restructuring. Per-share earnings fell 3 percent, again impacted heavily by special charges—minus these, EPS would have increased 7 percent compared to 2008.

Ecolab increased their dividends 11 percent to $0.62/share for 2010, marking the eighteenth consecutive annual dividend rate increase and the seventy-third consecutive year of dividend payments.

Reasons to Buy

Ecolab entered 2010 leaner and cleaner than it was at the beginning of 2009, and the first half of 2010 has been bright indeed. First quarter per share net rose 24 percent over 1Q2009, and international operations in particular are recovering quickly.

Ecolab is the largest participant (with a 10 percent share) in what is estimated to be a $45 billion global cleaning and sanitation market, and Ecolab's operating margin is three times that of its largest competitor, DiversyJohnson. Overall, the market is not especially cyclical and has a built-in growth component as governments improve and modify regulations regarding cleanliness for public and private institutions and commercial buildings.

The company is not simply a distributor as many other smaller players tend to be—they have over 4,500 patents on their branded products. Many of their products are cleaning systems which, once in place, tend to stay in place and then require Ecolab branded consumables throughout their life.

In light of several well-publicized food contamination incidents over the past two years, Ecolab's customers have a renewed focus on cleanliness and sanitation in food preparation and serving, which is the heart of Ecolab's Institutional business. Ecolab is leveraging this positive attention by growing their presence in mainland China, where they have found a receptive customer base and huge opportunity.

Reasons for Caution

The stock has recently been trading at multiples in the mid-20s while the stock has been flirting with all-time highs. It's good if there's support for those valuations, but your eventual purchase price should be considered carefully so as not to overspend for this well-regarded issue.

SECTOR: **Materials**

BETA COEFFICIENT: **0.8**

10-YEAR COMPOUND EARNINGS PER SHARE GROWTH: **12.5 percent**

10-YEAR COMPOUND DIVIDENDS PER SHARE GROWTH: **10.5 percent**

	2002	**2003**	**2004**	**2005**	**2006**	**2007**	**2008**	**2009**
Revenues (Mil)	3,404	3,762	4,185	4,535	4,896	5,470	6,138	5,901
Net income (Mil)	210	277	310	320	369	427	464	447
Earnings per share	0.8	1.06	1.19	1.23	1.43	1.7	1.86	1.99
Dividends per share	0.27	0.29	0.33	0.35	0.4	0.52	0.52	0.56
Cash flow per share	1.79	1.96	2.18	2.27	2.54	2.87	3.38	3.43
Price: high	25.2	27.9	35.6	37.2	46.4	52.8	52.3	49.7
low	18.3	23.1	26.1	30.7	33.6	37	29.6	40.7

Ecolab, Inc.

370 Wabasha Street North

St. Paul, MN 55102–1390

(651) 293-2809

Website: *www.ecolab.com*

GROWTH AND INCOME

Entergy Corporation

Ticker symbol: ETR (NYSE) □ S&P rating: BBB □ Value Line financial strength rating: A □ Current yield: 4.0 percent

Company Profile

Entergy Corporation is an integrated energy utility engaged primarily in electric power production and retail electric distribution operations. Entergy owns and operates power plants with approximately 30,000 megawatts (MW) of electric generating capacity and provides electricity to 2.7 million utility customers in Arkansas, Louisiana, Mississippi, and Texas.

The company operates primarily through two business segments: U.S. Utility and Non-Utility Nuclear.

The U.S. Utility segment generates, transmits, distributes, and sells electric power in a four-state service territory that includes portions of Arkansas, Mississippi, Texas, and Louisiana, including the City of New Orleans. It also operates a small natural gas distribution business.

Non-Utility Nuclear owns and operates five nuclear power plants located in the northeastern United States and sells this electric power primarily to wholesale customers. This business also provides maintenance services to other nuclear power plant operators. These five plants make Entergy the second largest nuclear electric generator in the United States, behind Exelon.

In mid-2007, Entergy filed notice of its plans to spin off its non-regulated nuclear generation business. In mid-2008, the NRC gave its approval for the proposed plan, but Entergy later put the plan on hold, citing "complete disarray" in the credit markets, which would have made the sale too expensive. In early 2009, Entergy seemed prepared to proceed with the plan, but in March 2010 the New York State PSC voted to reject the proposal and in April 2010 Entergy scrapped the spinoff plan altogether.

Financial Highlights, Fiscal Year 2009

Entergy's operating revenues fell 18 percent to $10.7 billion in 2009, while net income grew 0.8 percent to $1.23 billion. Diluted EPS grew 1.6 percent to $6.30. Cash flow gained another 3 percent and is now up more than 100 percent over the past eight years.

The utility sector was hit especially hard, with revenues from residential off 16 percent, commercial off 23 percent, and industrial off 33 percent. Non-utility nuclear revenues were basically flat.

Reasons to Buy

For the past eleven years of its current management, Entergy has held to a fairly aggressive goal of providing total shareholder return in the top quartile of its peer group every year. With the exception of 2009, they've met this goal and have over the period generated a return of 277 percent, versus 87 percent for utilities as a whole and 10 percent for the S&P 500. The company currently projects 5 to 6 percent compound annual net income growth through 2014.

Entergy is seeking rate hikes in both Arkansas and Texas, citing parity for risk/return as compared to their competitors in those areas. Both requests are based on an 11.5 percent ROE; their combined contribution to 2011 revenue would be approximately $420 million.

Carbon caps and a federal cap-and-trade plan seem likely in the Obama administration's energy plan at this point. Depending on the implementation, this plan could be a windfall to electric utilities in the United States, as it would make them the largest players in the world's largest commodity market. A windfall is not the most likely outcome, but there seems little doubt that however the plan is implemented, generators like Entergy will have a new and profitable arena in which to compete.

The company in 2010 added an additional $750 million to its authorized share repurchase pool, raising 2010's projected buyback to 5 percent of the company's outstanding shares. The company also indicated that, under the current longer-term plan, as much as $5 *billion* will be returned to shareholders over the next five years in the form of combined dividends and share buybacks. As an indication of where things are going, the company early in 2010 raised its dividend by 11 percent to $3.32/share.

In spite of this year's setbacks, we can't say enough good things about the company's management. In 2008 and again in 2009, despite two of the worst years on record in the capital markets and the uncertainty of the spinoff, Entergy received a perfect 10 rating from *GovernanceMetrics International*, one of fewer than fifty companies to receive such a score of the 4,200 companies reviewed. Similarly, *Institutional Shareholder Services Corporate Services* awarded Entergy its top position for electric utilities and ninth place among all companies reviewed. And for the eighth year in a row, Entergy was named to the *Dow Jones Sustainability Index*, placing Entergy in the top 10 percent of the largest 2,500 companies in the world, based on "long-term economic, environmental, and social criteria." In the past four years only one other U.S. utility was mentioned in the index.

Reasons for Caution

The failure of the spinoff has left Entergy with a bit of a blank slate. The company is well-funded, well-managed, and has solid prospects for its core businesses, but the longer-term plan for integrating both new operations and (potentially) a greatly modified regulatory environment has just been reset. Expect extraordinary (but minor) costs as Entergy winds down the remaining spinoff effort.

Entergy's public utility operations are located in hurricane territory, along the Gulf coast of the United States. In 2008, Hurricanes Gustav and Ike and major ice storms reduced cash flow by $314 million due to costs from downtime and system repairs. As a result, Entergy carries higher reserves and pays higher insurance premiums than other similar operators.

SECTOR: **Utilities**
BETA COEFFICIENT: **.70**
10-YEAR COMPOUND EARNINGS PER SHARE GROWTH: **10.5 percent**
10-YEAR COMPOUND DIVIDENDS PER SHARE GROWTH: **6.5 percent**

		2002	**2003**	**2004**	**2005**	**2006**	**2007**	**2008**	**2009**
Revenues (Mil)		8,305	9,195	10,124	10,106	10,932	11,484	13,094	10,746
Net income (Mil)		878	874	933	943	1,133	1,135	1,241	1,251
Earnings per share		3.68	3.69	3.93	4.4	5.36	5.6	6.2	6.3
Dividends per share		1.34	1.6	1.89	2.16	2.16	2.58	3	3
Cash flow per share		7.62	7.43	8.33	8.18	10.69	11.73	12.89	13.29
Price:	high	46.8	57.2	68.7	79.2	94	125	127.5	86.6
	low	32.1	42.3	50.6	64.5	66.8	89.6	61.9	59.9

Entergy Corporation
639 Loyola Avenue
New Orleans, LA 70113
(504) 529-5262
Website: *www.entergy.com*

ExxonMobil Corporation

Ticker symbol: XOM (NYSE) ❑ S&P rating: AAA ❑ Value Line financial strength rating: A++ ❑ Current yield: 3.0 percent

Company Profile

ExxonMobil is the world's largest publicly traded oil company. They are engaged in the exploration, production, manufacture, transportation, and sale of crude oil, natural gas, and petroleum products. It also has a stake in the manufacture of petrochemicals, packaging films, and specialty chemicals.

Divisions and affiliated companies of ExxonMobil operate or market products in the United States and some 200 other countries and territories. Their principal business is energy, involving exploration for, and production of crude oil and natural gas, manufacture of petroleum products and transportation and sale of crude oil, natural gas and petroleum products.

The company is a major manufacturer and marketer of basic petrochemicals, including olefins, aromatics, polyethylene, and polypropylene plastics and a wide variety of specialty products. It also has interests in electric power generation facilities.

ExxonMobil conducts oil and gas exploration, development and production in every major accessible producing region in the world. They have the largest energy resource base of any non-government company and are the largest non-government natural gas marketer and reserves holder. They're the world's largest fuels refiner and manufacturer of base stocks used for making motor oils. They have refining operations in twenty-six countries, 42,000 retail service stations in more than 100 countries and lubricants marketing in almost 200 countries and territories. They market petrochemical products in more than 150 countries, and 90 percent of the company's petrochemical assets are in businesses that are ranked number one or number two in market position.

Financial Highlights, Fiscal Year 2009

ExxonMobil's 2009 was the downturn year that we all expected. Oil prices for the first half of 2009 were half of what they were for the first half of 2008, and the drop in revenue for the year was about what most had imagined—revenues were off 35 percent, while earnings fell nearly 58 percent. Total earnings for the year were "just" 19.3 billion, with $17 billion of that coming from upstream operations. Chemicals actually earned more than down-stream, coming in at $2.2 billion versus $1.8 billion for downstream.

In December the company announced a deal to acquire XTO Energy in a stock swap valued at $41 billion. XTO's holdings are expected to add 10 percent to Exxon's current total resource base.

Flush from a record FY2008, the company invested $27 billion in exploration and capital projects in 2009, repurchased 250 million shares of stock, and raised the dividend 7 percent.

Reasons to Buy

First quarter 2010 earnings came in at 6.3 billion, up 38 percent over 1Q2009, due largely to higher crude realizations and much improved margins on chemicals.

The XTO acquisition is a strong indication of Exxon's shift toward more profitable upstream operations. XTO is one of a number of players in unconventional oil production, specifically shale deposits. XTO has large holdings in U.S. shales such as the Marcellus, Haynesville, and Bakken basins. These areas are currently producing natural gas but also contain large deposits of oil shales. The U.S. deposits of oil shales constitute 62 percent of the worldwide deposits. The deal works well for XTO as natural gas prices have been depressed for some time and futures have dropped as well.

Exxon also provides development capital for XTO's holdings.

Exxon is the largest publicly traded oil company in the world, and in the oil business there are strategic advantages that accrue to size. Having the resources to bring to bear on an opportunity can mean the difference between winning and losing an exploration or develop-ment award.

Exxon's return on upstream capital employed (16.3 percent in FY2009) is nearly 70 percent higher than the industry average. They get far more revenue in return for each exploration/development/produc-tion dollar spent than their compet-itors. And since upstream represents over 75 percent of earnings, they have significant cost advantages over their competition.

Reasons for Caution

In the first quarter of 2010, poor refining margins led to a down-stream revenue decline of $1.1 bil-lion—the segment barely broke even for the quarter. Exxon has already begun to sell off its retail outlets, and should downstream demand deteriorate further Exxon may have to accelerate this process. Since January 2007 the monthly average gallons of finished petro-leum products supplied per U.S. resident has fallen from its thirty-year average of 2.56 gallons per day to 2.22 gallons per day.

SECTOR: **Energy**
BETA COEFFICIENT: **.75**
10-YEAR COMPOUND EARNINGS PER SHARE GROWTH: **17.0 percent**
10-YEAR COMPOUND DIVIDENDS PER SHARE GROWTH: **6.5 percent**

		2002	2003	2004	2005	2006	2007	2008	2009
Revenues (Bil)		179	211	264	328	335	359	425	276
Net income (Bil)		11	17	25.3	36.1	39.1	40.6	45.3	19.3
Earnings per share		1.69	2.56	3.89	5.71	6.62	7.28	8.69	3.98
Dividends per share		0.92	0.98	1.06	1.14	1.28	1.37	1.55	1.66
Cash flow per share		2.88	3.97	5.48	7.19	8.82	9.82	11.58	6.60
Price:	high	44.6	41.1	52	66	79	95.3	96.1	82.7
	low	29.8	31.6	39.9	49.2	56.4	69	56.5	61.9

ExxonMobil Corporation
5959 Las Colinas Boulevard
Irving, TX 75039-2298
(972) 444–1538
Website: *www.exxonmobil.com*

Fair Isaac Corporation

Ticker symbol: FIC (NYSE) □ Fiscal Year ends September 30 □ S&P Rating: NA □ Value Line financial strength rating: B++ □ Current yield: 0.4 percent

Company Profile

Fair Isaac Corporation provides decision support analytics and solutions to help businesses improve and automate decision making. The most well known of these solutions is the "FICO score"—an analytic single-figure estimate of a consumer's creditworthiness used in the credit industry and for other purposes such as employment and insurance.

The company operates through four segments: Strategy Machine Solutions, Scoring Solutions, Professional Services, and Analytic Software Tools. The Strategy Machine Solutions segment (52 percent of revenue) offers preconfigured decision management applications for marketing, customer management, fraud prevention and insurance claims management. The Scoring Solutions segment (21 percent) engineers and manages the FICO scoring model and offers it to loan originators and other financial institutions. The Professional Services segment (20 percent) provides consulting services to help customers develop their own analytics and applications of those analytics, while the

Analytic Software Tools segment (7 percent) offers end-user software products that businesses use to build their own tailored decision management applications.

About 76 percent of the company's revenues are derived from transaction and unit-priced products, such as the access and sale of a FICO score. About 71 percent of revenues are derived from the consumer credit, financial services and insurance industries. Overseas revenue has grown from 29 percent to 33 percent of total revenues in the past three fiscal years.

Financial Highlights, Fiscal Year 2009

On the heels of an already tough 2008 business environment for most of FIC's customers, 2009 saw a continuation of poor performance overall for the lending and financial services industries. As a result, orders for FIC products fell some 15 percent in 2009 versus 2008. Not surprisingly, the Professional Services business saw the biggest decline, dropping 25 percent, due in part to the company's decision to stop pursuing some lower-margin consulting services business.

Whenever the economy takes a sharp negative turn, the first reaction by most large companies is to institute controls on discretionary spending such as travel, conferences, etc. As the downturn extends, large technology projects are often put on ice until such time as a recovery is imminent. This is what has happened to FIC's business of the last eight quarters. FIC's customers have simply delayed (or canceled) the implementation of new programs that require the purchase of products and services of the type provided by FIC.

In June 2009, the company sold the assets associated with its LiquidCredit for Telecom (LCT) and RoamEx product lines. LCT and RoamEx solutions were included primarily in its Strategy Machine segment.

Reasons to Buy

Whatever the outcome of the current administration's financial reform proposals, it seems reasonable to assume that the world of credit analysis, risk assessment, and financial decision management in general will become more complex rather than simpler. As a result, we see the need for products and services such as FIC can provide becoming more widespread, with an even greater need for industry specialization and sophistication in financial modeling software.

Over three-quarters of FIC's revenue is tied to commercial transactions and transaction processing. As consumer spending and the need for credit checking and reporting services increases, we expect FIC's revenues to return to pre-2007 levels.

International demand for FIC's products continues to grow. Although the percentage of revenue generated from international orders has remained relatively flat, at approximately one-third of total revenues over the last three years, new products, a growing market acceptance of analytics and a focus on the international market is expected to provide increased leverage here.

Although revenues and earnings have fallen for two consecutive years, the company is well capitalized and has maintained respectable operating margins, due in large part to effective cost controls and restructuring efforts. And although the company has divested itself of some operations and is a bit leaner, its core businesses are well funded and well positioned for growth as the smoke clears from the recent recession.

Reasons for Caution

The Credit Card Act of 2009 takes effect mid-2010, and although its consequences to FIC's customer base are undetermined as yet, the bottom lines of many card issuers are likely to be negatively impacted. Furthermore, Congress is considering additional new regulations for the financial industry, which could lead to delays in orders for new FIC products.

SECTOR: **Business Services**
BETA COEFFICIENT: **1.10**
10-YEAR COMPOUND EARNINGS PER SHARE GROWTH: **14.5 percent**
10-YEAR COMPOUND DIVIDENDS PER SHARE GROWTH: **13.0 percent**

	2002	2003	2004	2005	2006	2007	2008	2009
Revenues (Mil)	392.4	629.3	706.2	798.7	825.4	822.2	744.8	630.7
Net income (Mil)	61.3	107.2	108.9	134.5	103.5	104.7	81.2	65.1
Earnings per share	1	1.41	1.49	1.86	1.5	1.82	1.64	1.34
Dividends per share	0.04	0.05	0.08	0.08	0.08	0.08	0.08	0.08
Cash flow per share	1.21	2.18	2.24	2.91	2.57	3.03	2.49	2.15
Price: high	29.6	43.1	41.5	48.5	47.8	41.8	32.2	24.5
low	19.4	28	23.7	32.3	32.5	32.1	10.4	9.8

Fair Isaac Corporation
901 Marquette Avenue Suite 3200
Minneapolis, MN 55402-3232
Phone: (612) 758-5200
Website: *www.fairisaac.com*

FedEx Corporation

Ticker symbol: FDX (NYSE) ❑ Standard & Poor's rating: BBB ❑ Value Line financial strength rating: B++ ❑ Current yield: 0.5 percent

Company Profile

FedEx Corporation is the world's leading provider of guaranteed express delivery services. The corporation is organized as a holding company, with individual businesses that compete collectively and operate independently under the FedEx brand. The company offers a wide range of express delivery services for the time-definite transportation of documents, packages and freight. Commercial and military charter services are also offered by FedEx.

The company's operations include:

- The world's largest express transportation company (FedEx Express)
- North America's second-largest ground carrier for small-package business shipments (FedEx Ground)
- The largest U.S. regional less-than-truckload freight company (FedEx Freight)
- A "24/7" option for urgent shipments, providing nonstop, door-to-door delivery in the contiguous United States, Canada, and Europe (FedEx Custom Critical)

- The largest-volume customs filer in the United States, providing freight forwarding, advisory services, and trade technology (FedEx Trade Networks)

The infrastructure supporting these businesses is enormous. For example, the FedEx Express business alone operates 51,000 ground vehicles and 654 aircraft and employs 275,000 people. In addition, they maintain over 700 World Service Centers, over 1,800 FedEx Office locations, nearly 7,000 authorized ShipCenters, and over 43,000 Drop Boxes. They serve over 375 airports in over 200 countries. The rest of the businesses under the FedEx brand have additional resources, and the numbers become staggering pretty quickly.

Financial Highlights, Fiscal Year 2009

FedEx's revenue declined 6 percent versus FY2008 primarily due to the downturn in the worldwide economy, partially offset by the exit of DHL express from the market. FedEx believes they captured 50 percent of DHL's former volume, but that the yields were below FedEx's average yield.

Operating margin fell 180 basis points (1.8 percent) on reduced recovery of volume-driven costs partially offset by lower fuel expenses. Net margin fell 150 basis points to 3.3 percent, off from 5.9 percent just two years ago.

The company took non-cash charges in FY2009 totaling $1.2 billion associated with the 2004 acquisition of Kinko's and the 2006 acquisition of Watkins Motor Freight. The bulk of the charges were impairments to goodwill associated with Kinko's $810 million. Added to last year's similar impairment, FedEx has now discounted some $1.7 billion in value from the $2.4 billion Kinko's acquisition.

Reasons to Buy

Results in 2010 have been encouraging, particularly in International shipments. Indications are that the most recent quarter's results could show a doubling in earnings versus a year ago. We expect margins to improve as volumes return, but earnings growth will be incremental through 2011.

The company has initiated a new round of cost-cutting measures that it believes will improve operating profit by $1 billion. Over the past five years the company has reduced its debt by $1 billion and added over $5 billion to shareholder equity.

FedEx has grown its international priority service at a compound annual growth rate (CAGR) of over 15 percent over the last nine years. In the process, the business has grown its revenue contribution from 17 percent to 24 percent of the company's overall sales. The company has invested heavily in China and is now number two in market share.

While the dividend yield is still modest, we do like the company's record of steady increases and the inclusion message that sends to longer-term investors.

Reasons for Caution

On July 3, 2010 the U.S. Congress is scheduled to vote on a reconciliation version of an FAA funding bill that might or might not contain language that would reclassify FedEx employees so as not to be covered under the 1926 Railway Labor Act. This act, which currently governs employees of FedEx, requires that employees of railroads, airlines, or express services, if organized under a labor union, be organized systemwide, preventing the possibility of some small local striking and shutting down the entire network. This systemwide requirement makes it far more difficult for unions to organize a company like FedEx.

If a bill containing the revision language (heavily supported by both the Teamsters and FedEx rival UPS) passes through Congress and is signed into law by President Obama, CEO Fred Smith has promised to reduce FedEx Express operations "to subsistence levels." We doubt Mr. Smith will follow through on his threat, but the unionization of the 95 percent of FedEx' workforce that is currently non-union will certainly impact earnings going forward.

SECTOR: Transportation
BETA COEFFICIENT: 0.95
10-YEAR COMPOUND EARNINGS PER SHARE GROWTH: 11.50 percent
10-YEAR COMPOUND DIVIDENDS PER SHARE GROWTH: No dividend prior to 2002

	2002	2003	2004	2005	2006	2007	2008	2009
Revenues (Mil)	20,607	22,487	24,710	29,363	32,294	35,214	37,953	35,497
Net income (Mil)	710	830	838	1,449	1,885	2,073	1,821	1,173
Earnings per share	2.39	2.74	2.76	4.82	5.98	6.67	5.83	3.76
Dividends per share	-	0.20	0.24	0.29	0.33	0.37	0.40	0.44
Cash flow per share	7.00	7.31	8.15	9.74	11.13	12.39	12.13	10.09
Price: high	61.4	78	100.9	105.8	120	121.4	99.5	92.6
low	42.8	47.7	64.8	76.8	96.5	89.5	53.9	34

FedEx Corporation
942 South Shady Grove Road
Memphis, TN 38120
(901) 818–7200
Website: www.fedex.com

Fluor Corporation

Ticker symbol: FLR (NYSE) □ S&P rating: A- □ Value Line financial strength rating: A++ □ Current yield: 1.1 percent

Company Profile

Fluor is one of the world's largest publicly owned engineering, procurement, construction, maintenance and project management companies. They provide infrastructure and infrastructure services primarily for five industry segments:

■ Oil & Gas, where they serve "all facets" of the upstream, downstream, and petrochemical markets, including oilfields, refineries, and pipelines. Oil & Gas operations account for 58 percent of the company's overall revenue
■ Industrial and Infrastructure, their most diverse organization, includes transportation, mining, life sciences, telecom, manufacturing, and commercial and institutional projects. I&I accounts for 15 percent of the company's revenue.
■ Government, addressing the U.S. Departments of Energy, Defense, and Homeland Security.
■ Global Services, providing operations and maintenance, supply chain, equipment services and contract staffing, generates 12 percent of the company's revenue.
■ Power, which designs, builds, commissions, and retrofits electric generation facilities based on coal, natural gas, and nuclear fuels.

Financial Highlights, Fiscal Year 2009

Fluor's revenues fell 2 percent year/year while earnings rose by the same percentage. Margins remain healthy and cash flow grew over 5 percent. Overall, ongoing operations were in good shape and well managed. However, since many of Fluor's projects can span several years, an important measure of the health of their business is the state of their backlog, and here's where the news gets a little dark, as backlog dropped a full 20 percent, down to just over 15 months of current revenue.

Fluor ended 2009 with approximately $2.1 billion in cash and securities, with negligible long-term debt. They posted a record return on total capital of 23.2 percent.

Reasons to Buy

Obviously, these are not great times for the capital project market. Fluor's main customer base (oil and petrochemical) have seen sharp price declines following the recent commodity boom. The recent failure of a large floating oil rig in the Gulf of Mexico may dampen whatever enthusiasm was generated in the exploration business by the President Obama's recent moves toward loosening the restrictions on offshore drilling. The capital market decline has had perhaps its greatest impact on just the sort of projects that Fluor specializes in. Nonetheless, Fluor has significant levels of capitalization and remains optimistic for a continued recovery in the global financial markets. The loss of backlog, although significant in year/year terms, should be viewed in terms of "the weakest orders die first." The remaining backlog appears firm.

Fluor is more diversified than many of its competitors and is spread across more highly profitable businesses. Less than half of Fluor's backlog is in Oil & Gas, and the rest of their operations actually contribute more to earnings per unit of revenue. A revival of construction of nuclear power plants, now in its early stages, may also be a bonus for Fluor.

Fluor still has the highest credit rating of any company in the sector.

This doesn't guarantee access to capital, it keeps them at the front of the line and ahead of their competition.

Finally, although we're not necessarily bargain hunters, it doesn't hurt that Fluor's stock is trading nearly 15 percent under its year-ago price, even though its 2009 performance provided far better performance at the bottom line.

Reasons for Caution

During 2009, Fluor's backlog declined some 20 percent, all of it in Oil & Gas, where the hit was close to 50 percent. The company expects to turn 60 percent of its backlog into revenue during 2010, and with refining capacity in the United States more than adequate to meet projected demand for some time, we would not anticipate Fluor's backlog in Oil & Gas to recover rapidly. Fluor's revenue in 2010 will be down some 10 percent, and a full recovery to 2008 revenue levels is not anticipated until 2012. This stock is a quality issue but it will take some time to recover.

Finally, this is a stock that needs to be closely monitored. One significant contract delay or cancellation, or a couple of disputed claims or cost overruns can have a measurable impact on Fluor's stock price even in the best of times. Flour is an excellent company but this is a stock that may not be for the faint of heart.

SECTOR: Heavy Construction
BETA COEFFICIENT: 1.35
10-YEAR COMPOUND EARNINGS PER SHARE GROWTH: 12.5 percent
10-YEAR COMPOUND DIVIDENDS PER SHARE GROWTH: 1.5 percent

	2002	2003	2004	2005	2006	2007	2008	2009
Revenues (Mil)	1,274	1,433	1,656	1,771	1,985	2,202	2,452	2,199
Net income (Mil)	170	180	178	227	264	410	673	685
Earnings per share	1.07	1.12	1.08	1.31	1.48	2.25	3.67	3.75
Dividends per share	0.32	0.32	0.32	0.32	0.32	0.4	0.5	0.5
Cash flow per share	1.53	1.58	1.58	1.9	2.21	3.14	4.61	4.85
Price: high	22.5	20.4	27.6	39.6	51.9	86.1	101.4	50.5
low	10	13.3	18	25.1	36.8	37.6	28.6	41.7

Fluor Corporation
6700 Las Colinas Blvd
Irving, TX 75039
Tel: (469) 398-7000
Website: *www.fluor.com*

FMC Corporation

Ticker symbol: FMC (NYSE) □ S&P rating: BBB+ □ Value Line financial strength rating: A □
Current yield: 0.9 percent

Company Profile

FMC Corporation is a diversified chemical company serving global agricultural, industrial and consumer markets. The company, founded in 1883, employs some 4,800 people throughout the world. FMC operates its businesses in three segments: Agricultural Products, Specialty Chemicals and Industrial Chemicals.

FMC Agricultural Products provides crop protection and pest control products for worldwide markets. The business offers a portfolio of insecticides and herbicides, and is considered an industry leader for its innovative packaging.

In the Specialty Chemicals Group, FMC BioPolymer is the world's leading producer of alginate, carrageenan and microcrystalline cellulose. FMC Lithium is one of the world's leading producers of lithium-based products and is recognized as the technology leader in specialty organolithium chemicals and related technologies.

In the Industrial Chemicals Group, FMC Alkali Chemicals is the world's largest producer of natural soda ash and is the market leader in North America. Downstream products include sodium bicarbonate, sodium cyanide, sodium sesquicarbonate and caustic soda. FMC Hydrogen Peroxide is the market leader in North America with manufacturing sites in the United States, Canada and Mexico. FMC Active Oxidants is the world's leading supplier of persulfate products and a major producer of peracetic acid and other specialty oxidants. Based in Barcelona, Spain, FMC Foret is a major chemical producer supplying customers throughout Europe, the Middle East, and Africa with a diverse range of products including hydrogen peroxide, peroxygens, phosphates, silicates, zeolites and sulfur derivatives.

Financial Highlights, Fiscal Year 2009

Given FMC's large customer base of industrial users, it's no surprise that revenues were down 9 percent overall versus 2008. Agricultural Products and Specialty Chemicals were basically flat, but Industrial Chemicals was down 21 percent, hurt by lower volumes across the board and major price declines in phosphates.

Earnings were off 25 percent, including restructuring and other charges of about $75 million. Absent these charges, earnings fell 13 percent. Earnings in Agricultural Products were up 18 percent due to the popularity of new products and improved market conditions in Brazil. Specialty Chemicals also turned in positive numbers, up 5 percent on the strength of the BioPolymers unit. This wasn't enough, though, to offset the declines in Industrial Chemicals, where earnings fell 55 percent due to reduced volumes.

Reasons to Buy

The 2009 results were dominated by the losses in the phosphate market, which were driven by a combination of market factors—reduced worldwide demand, a sudden drop in certain agricultural futures prices, and the ability of Chinese buyers to source nutrients in eastern Europe at far below the then market price. Analysts agree that the outlook for 2010 is far brighter than last year. Most doubt the ability of the Chinese to hold the market price at its current lows.

FMC's BioPolymers unit has performed extremely well in what has been a weak market for industrial chemicals. These products are used primarily as food adjuncts—fat substitutes, stabilizers, thickeners, and the like. BioPolymers has been able to raise prices and increase unit volumes in the face of market headwinds due to the performance of the products and broad customer acceptance. Look for FMC to continue their acquisition strategy here, as it has paid off well for them in the last two years.

FMC is well positioned as the leading supplier of lithium-based compounds used in the lithium-ion battery industry. Lithium batteries are used extensively in technology products such as laptops, music players, and soon, electric cars. Every hybrid car currently in production uses nickel metal hydride (NiMH) battery chemistry, but lithium batteries appropriate for automobile usage are not far off. Lithium's unparalleled power-to-weight ratio and rapid recharge cycle time make cars lighter and more amenable to typical usage patterns.

FMC is a key player in a broad consortium of U.S.-based companies working to establish a dominant domestic lithium battery industry. Lithium battery technology is the key to the future of the automotive industry, and some have said that the country that makes the batteries will make the cars.

Reasons for Caution

FMC is up against some very aggressive pricing from Chinese producers of soda ash, a key component in the manufacture of glass. Prices for ash are expected to remain low for quite some time, at least throughout 2010.

SECTOR: **Materials**
BETA COEFFICIENT: **1.25**
10-YEAR COMPOUND EARNINGS PER SHARE GROWTH: **3.50 percent**
10-YEAR COMPOUND DIVIDENDS PER SHARE GROWTH: **NM**

		2002	2003	2004	2005	2006	2007	2008	2009
Revenues (Mil)		1,853	1,921	2,051	2,150	2,347	2,633	3,115	2,826
Net income (Mil)		87.5	67.5	135.2	171.9	216.4	132.4	351	305
Earnings per share		1.28	0.95	1.60	2.20	2.74	3.40	4.63	4.15
Dividends per share		-	-	-	-	0.36	0.42	0.48	0.50
Cash flow per share		2.94	2.72	3.64	4.00	4.54	5.25	6.55	6.00
Price:	high	21.2	17.4	25.3	31.9	39	59	80.2	63.3
	low	11.5	7.1	16.5	21.6	25.9	35.6	28.5	50.8

FMC Corporation
1735 Market Street
Philadelphia, PA 19103
(215) 299-6000
Website: *www.fmc.com*

FPL Group, Inc.

Ticker symbol: FPL (NYSE) ❑ Standard & Poor's rating: A- ❑ Value Line financial strength rating: A ❑ Current yield: 4.3 percent

Company Profile

FPL Group is a leading clean energy company with 2009 revenues of more than $16 billion, approximately 42,700 megawatts of generating capacity, and more than 15,000 employees in twenty-seven states and Canada. Headquartered in Juno Beach, FL, FPL Group's principal operating subsidiaries are NextEra Energy Resources, LLC, and Florida Power & Light Company, one of the largest rate-regulated electric utilities in the country. FP&L serves 4.5 million customer accounts in Florida. Through its subsidiaries, FPL Group collectively operates the third largest U.S. nuclear power generation fleet.

NextEra Energy, LLC (formerly FPL Energy, LLC), FPL Group's competitive energy subsidiary, is a leader in producing electricity from clean and renewable fuels. The generating assets of NextEra represent over 18,000 megawatts of capacity. FPL FiberNet, LLC, provides fiber-optic services to FPL and other customers, primarily telecommunications companies in Florida.

FP&L is recognized as one of the "cleaner" producers in the United States, with just over half of its generation coming from natural gas, and less than 15 percent coming from coal and oil. By contrast, coal makes up 50 percent of the fuel mix for electricity generation nationwide. NextEra Energy is the largest owner and operator of the wind generating facilities in the U.S.

Financial Highlights, Fiscal Year 2009

Revenues in FY2009 declined 1.9 percent versus FY2008, while earnings declined 1.5 percent over the same period. Earnings are split roughly 50/50 between FPL and NextEra, with corporate costs accounted for independently.

The decline in revenue is due primarily to the decrease in usage by residential customers. Going back to FY2000, FPL's average annual customer growth has been 1.8 percent, but starting in 2007 that growth has essentially stopped, likely due to the credit/housing crisis that affected many fast-growth real estate markets such as south Florida. FPL's inactive and low-use accounts peaked in mid-2009 but declined slightly in the fourth quarter. None the less, FPL's earnings increased 5.5 percent in 2009, primarily due to a base rate increase granted back in 2005.

NextEra's earnings declined 7.3 percent, reflecting the negative impacts of weather (2009 turned out to be a bad year for wind—it happens) and higher expenses to support growth in infrastructure. NextEra Energy sells the majority of its output on the wholesale market as a hedge against price volatility, and it can be forced to buy capacity on the open market in order to meet its contractual obligations.

Reasons to Buy

The Recovery Act of 2009 contains a number of tax incentives for the deployment and use of renewable and nuclear sources, and NextEra is well positioned to take advantage here—they have a total pipeline of 30,000 megawatts of wind projects and added 1,170 megawatts of new wind projects in 2009. Their total current investment in wind resources is over $8 billion, and they plan to add 1,000 megawatts of wind generation in 2010, and 1,000 to 1,500 megawatts in each of 2011 and 2012.

FPL is the largest provider in a growing energy market, and has been one of the best-performing stocks in the utility market over the past several years. Since 2002, measured by total shareholder return, FPL has outperformed 84 percent of the companies in the S&P Utility Index and 85 percent of the companies in the S&P 500 Index. During the period, total return was 127 percent, compared with 32 percent for the total utility index and negative 10 percent for the S&P 500 Index.

Reasons for Caution

FPL's March 2009 petition to the Florida regulators asking for rate adjustments in 2010 and 2011 was basically denied. The requested amounts for the two-year period totaled $1,250 million, and the FSPC granted them just $150 million on an ROE 20 percent lower than requested. Florida's economy and unemployment rate at this time are apparently not amenable to supporting investments of the type envisioned by FPL. Without the rate concessions, FPL's ability to attract capital may be severely hampered and many of FPL's long-term programs could be delayed indefinitely as a consequence.

SECTOR: **Utilities**
BETA COEFFICIENT: **.75**
10-YEAR COMPOUND EARNINGS PER SHARE GROWTH: **7.0 percent**
10-YEAR COMPOUND DIVIDENDS PER SHARE GROWTH: **5.5 percent**

	2002	2003	2004	2005	2006	2007	2008	2009
Revenues (Mil)	8,311	9,630	10,522	11,846	15,710	15,263	16,410	15,646
Net income (Mil)	710	883	887	885	1,761	1,312	1,639	1,615
Earnings per share	2.01	2.45	2.46	2.32	3.23	3.27	4.07	3.97
Dividends per share	1.16	1.2	1.3	1.42	1.5	1.64	1.78	1.89
Cash flow per share	4.51	5.36	5.6	6.18	6.77	6.85	8.03	8.75
Price: high	32.7	34	38.1	48.1	55.6	72.8	73.8	60.6
low	22.5	26.8	30.1	35.9	37.8	53.7	33.8	41.5

FPL Group, Inc.
700 Universe Boulevard
Juno Beach, FL 33408
(561) 694-4697
Website: *www.investor.fplgroup.com*

GROWTH AND INCOME

General Mills, Inc.

Ticker symbol: GIS (NYSE) ❑ S&P rating: BBB+ ❑ Value Line financial strength rating: A+ ❑
Current yield: 2.9 percent

Company Profile

General Mills is the second-largest domestic producer of ready-to-eat breakfast cereals and the sixth-largest food company in the world. Their sales are broken out into three major segments: U.S. Retail ($9.1 billion), International ($2.6 billion), and Bakery and Food-stuffs ($2.0 billion). They also have unconsolidated net sales in the Joint Venture segment ($1.2 billion).

Major cereal brands, most of which bear the Big G label, include Cheerios, Wheaties, Lucky Charms, Total, and Chex cereals. Other consumer packaged food products include baking mixes (Betty Crocker and Bisquick); meals (Betty Crocker dry packaged dinner mixes), Progresso soups, Green Giant canned and frozen vegetables); snacks (Pop Secret microwave popcorn, Bugles snacks, grain and fruit snack products); Pillsbury refrigerated and frozen dough products, frozen breakfast products and frozen pizza and snack products; organic foods and other products, including Yoplait and Colombo yogurt. The company's holdings include many other brand names, such as Haagen-Dazs frozen ice cream and a host of joint ventures.

The company's international businesses consist of operations and sales in Canada, Europe, Latin America, and the Asia/Pacific region. In those regions, General Foods sells numerous local brands, in addition to internationally recognized brands, such as Haagen-Dazs ice cream, Old El Paso Mexican foods, and Green Giant vegetables. Those international businesses have sales and marketing organizations in thirty-three countries.

Financial Highlights, Fiscal Year 2009

For the fiscal year ended May 31, 2009, General Mills net sales grew 8 percent to $14.7 billion, while year-to-year earnings growth was up 10 percent. Diluted earnings per share (EPS) totaled $3.98, up 10.3 percent from $3.52 in 2008. Overall sales gains were two points from volume and eight points from net price realizations, offset by two points of negative foreign currency exchange.

Cost of sales as a percentage of net sales was flat, while gross margin grew 7 percent as a result of improvements in operating leverage, cost structures, and net price realization, offsetting input cost inflation.

Particularly encouraging was the rebound of the top three revenues segments. Big G, Meals, and Pillsbury all experienced 5 percent sales growth in 2008, but turned in sales gains of 11 percent, 8 percent, and 12 percent respectively in 2009.

Reasons to Buy

The company met its internal operations goals: low single-digit growth in net sales; mid single-digit growth in total segment operating profit; high single-digit growth in EPS; and a 50 basis point annual increase in return on average total capital. The company feels that performance in these areas, coupled with an attractive dividend will result in long-term value creation for stockholders. This is a very conservative approach, and similar to what Kellogg's does, but after all, we're talking about cereal here.

The company has gained market share against all of its competitors beginning in 3Q2009 since starting a new advertising campaign. Advertising and marketing costs have risen 19 percent, but the push helped the company generate operating profits of 29 percent in 2009.

Sales in 2010 have so far been 2 to 3 percent higher, in line or slightly above the company's guidance. Wheat and corn prices have stabilized at much lower levels over the past nine months, creating pricing and discounting opportunities.

The company has continued its policy of share repurchase, further reducing the number of outstanding shares by 2.5 percent. The company also raised the dividend 10 percent. General Mills is most attractive as a stable, steady growth component to your overall portfolio.

Reasons for Caution

The company carries a significant debt load (over 90 percent long-term debt/equity). In part a legacy of the purchase of Pillsbury in 2002 and in part due to other more recent acquisitions, their debt is the highest in the industry. Even though working capital for the last decade has been financed through debt, the only material effect seems to have been the attenuation of dividends.

SECTOR: **Consumer Staples**
BETA COEFFICIENT: **.50**
10-YEAR COMPOUND EARNINGS PER SHARE GROWTH: **8.0 percent**
10-YEAR COMPOUND DIVIDENDS PER SHARE GROWTH: **4.0 percent**

		2002	2003	2004	2005	2006	2007	2008	2009
Revenues (Mil)		7,949	10,506	11,070	11,244	11,640	12,442	13,652	14,691
Net income (Mil)		581	917	1,055	1,100	1,090	1,144	1,288	1,367
Earnings per share		1.70	2.43	2.85	2.74	2.90	3.18	3.52	3.98
Dividends per share		1.10	1.10	1.10	1.24	1.34	1.44	1.57	1.72
Cash flow per share		2.39	3.69	3.94	4.18	4.25	4.59	5.00	5.55
Price:	high	51.7	49.7	50	53.9	59.2	61.5	72	72.1
	low	37.4	41.4	43	44.7	47	54.2	51	46.4

General Mills, Inc.
Post Office Box 1113
Minneapolis, MN 55440–1113
(763) 764-3202
Website: *www.generalmills.com*

Google, Inc.

Ticker symbol: GOOG (NASDAQ) ❑ Value Line financial strength rating: A++ ❑ S&P Rating: NA (no debt) ❑ Current yield: NA (no dividend)

Company Profile

Google operates the world's leading Internet search engine. The vast majority of its income, however, is derived not from the ubiquitous "Google" taskbar, but from the delivery of targeted advertising through Google AdWords and Google AdSense. The licensing of its search technology (Google Search Appliance) to other companies generates a tiny fraction of its revenue. Advertising delivery has generated the bulk of Google's revenue throughout its history, and generated 97 percent of Google's revenue in 2009.

The revenue model is pretty simple. Google's AdWords scans the HTML code that's displayed on a user's screen, searching for keywords. When keywords are found, ads relevant to the keywords are displayed on the page as well. Advertisers select their own target keywords and pay when customers click on their ads. Google and the advertiser are notified of every click, and other tracking information relevant to the click is transmitted as well.

Advertisers get targeted ads without much up front cost, and the ads appear on pages from Google's large roster of partners, from AOL to the *Washington Post*. Partners in turn receive a share of the advertising revenue when ads on their pages are clicked.

The company also provides, free of charge, a number of worthwhile programs. Google Docs, for example, mimics most of the popular commercial office suites. They also provide, at no charge, their own browser, 3D modeling software, image manipulation software, website authoring software, mapping software, mail portal, and personal search engine. They own and operate YouTube, one of the most popular social media sites on the Internet. They also provide a service that allows you to view, in fairly high resolution, nearly any location on Earth.

Finally, they have recently developed and licensed an operating system for a line of smartphones designed to compete directly with Apple's iPhone.

Financial Highlights, Fiscal Year 2009

Google's share price rebound in 2009 was easier to understand than most any other stock here. Simply grow revenue 9 percent, add 23 percent to earnings, bump operating margins by 350 basis points and throw off cash like a printing press on tilt and market watchers are bound to notice eventually.

The company remains debt-free. They increased their cash position by over 50 percent (to $24.5 billion) and remain in position to fund nearly any conceivable initiative they should choose to take on.

Reasons to Buy

Google recently bought AdMob, a leader in mobile display ad technology, which should help to accelerate Google's efforts to be the first and best in this market. The $750 million price represents about one month of cash flow.

Google has the most popular media portal on the planet in You-Tube, and they have begun a pilot program of distributing movie content through it. However, Google is widely thought to be working on a plan to become not just a portal but a content provider for online entertainment. Given the size of their war chest, it's not at all inconceivable that they could buy one or more existing movie or television studios and produce and distribute ad-supported content. It's widely suspected that Apple is considering a similar model.

Google bid against Verizon for wireless spectrum space and bowed out after the price got too high. In the process they convinced the government to include common-carrier provisions in the licensee's agreement that benefited Google's follow-on plan: to develop a mobile platform that would guarantee support for context and location sensitive search and ad placement. That platform is the Android operating system and is now being deployed on nearly 1.5 million units per month. The Android platform, unlike Apple's iPhone, is an open-source project that encourages the rapid development of low-cost applications, which Google then monetizes with ads.

Reasons for Caution

Google recently had a dust-up with the Chinese government, the result of which was Google's decision to stop censoring politically sensitive content for the Chinese market. Whether or not this was the Chinese government's plan all along (in order to support the Chinese-based Baidu search engine) is probably neither here nor there, but Google's decision may not have been the wisest financial move, considering the size of the Chinese market. One could argue that western-based advertisers might have been less willing to pay for Chinese views anyway, but in the long run, Google will have to reconcile its business model with local mores if it wishes to index the planet, as they have stated more than once.

SECTOR: Technology
BETA COEFFICIENT: 0.9
10-YEAR COMPOUND EARNINGS PER SHARE GROWTH: NA
10-YEAR COMPOUND DIVIDENDS PER SHARE GROWTH: NA

	2002	2003	2004	2005	2006	2007	2008	2009
Revenues (Mil)	440	1,465	3,189	6,138	10,604	16,594	21,795	23,650
Net income (Mil)	100	106	406	1,518	2,941	4,204	5,299	6,519
Earnings per share	0.45	0.41	1.49	5.20	9.50	13.29	16.69	20.41
Dividends per share	-	-	-	-	-	-	-	-
Cash flow per share	0.50	0.64	1.93	5.97	11.12	16.00	20.66	24.45
Price: high			201.6	446.2	513	747.2	697.4	626
low			85	437	331.5	437	247.3	282.8

Google, Inc.
1600 Amphitheatre Parkway
Mountain View, CA 94043
(650) 253-0000
Website: *www.google.com*

W. W. Grainger, Inc.

Ticker symbol: GWW (NYSE) ❑ S&P rating: AA+ ❑ Value Line financial strength rating: A++ ❑
Current yield: 1.8 percent

Company Profile

Grainger is North America's largest supplier of facilities maintenance products. They sell more than 300,000 different products through a network of over 600 branches, eighteen distribution centers, and several websites. Grainger also offers repair parts, specialized product sourcing and inventory management. Grainger sells principally to industrial and commercial maintenance departments, contractors and government customers. The company has nearly 2 million customers, primarily in North America.

Their Canadian subsidiary is Canada's largest distributor of industrial, fleet and safety products. They serve their customers through 166 branches, five distribution centers, and offer bilingual websites and catalogs. Grainger, S.A. de C.V. is Mexico's leading facilities maintenance supplier, offering customers more than 40,000 products.

Grainger's customer base includes governmental offices at all levels, heavy manufacturing customers (typically textile, lumber, metals, and rubber industries), light manufacturing, transportation (shipbuilding, aerospace, and automotive), hospitals, retail, hospitality, and resellers

of Grainger products. Grainger owns a number of trademarks, including Dayton motors, Dem-Kote spray paints, and Westward tools.

Many of Grainger's customers are corporate account customers, primarily Fortune 1000 companies that spend more than $5 million annually on facilities maintenance products. Corporate account customers represent about 25 percent of Grainger's total U.S. sales. Both government and corporate account customer groups typically sign multi-year contracts for facilities maintenance products or a specific category of products, such as lighting or safety equipment. In 2009 the company averaged 95,000 transactions per day.

Financial Highlights, Fiscal Year 2009

Grainger's FY20098 sales fell 9.1 percent year-over-year (to $6.22 billion), while earnings over the same period declined 13.3 percent (to $475 million). These results were not entirely unexpected, given the steep decline in the business levels of the majority of Grainger's customers. Sales saw a volume decline of over 14 percent, led by the heavy manufacturing segment, partially offset by higher prices.

The company took on $500 million in debt, ostensibly to finance further expansion/acquisitions. It has no other significant long-term debt.

Grainger's Lab Safety Supply (LSS), a leading business-to-business direct marketer of safety and other industrial products in the United States and Canada, was folded into the Grainger Industrial Supply brand, and its products will be carried alongside Grainger's main lines at Grainger distribution centers.

Reasons to Buy

Grainger has added over 70,000 new products since the beginning of FY2009, expanding their coverage in many growth sectors. Incremental growth from new products has been a profitable growth driver for Grainger since 2006 and the company projects continued positive results from this strategy.

Grainger has already modified their earlier guidance to analysts with regard to their 2010 EPS, raising it ten percent to $6.00, nearly matching 2008's actuals.

Grainger is far and away the biggest presence in the MRO (maintenance, repair, and operational) world. Their only broad-line competitor is one-quarter their size and the rest of the market is highly fragmented (Grainger has 4 to 5 percent market share). They also have the deepest catalog by far. It's estimated that 40 percent of purchases in the MRO market are unplanned, so having the broadest inventory and having it in stock is a big advantage for Grainger.

Over the last five years Grainger has repurchased over 20 percent of its outstanding shares, and they plan to continue the practice in the coming years. Over the same period, the dividend has been increased 125 percent. Return of shareholder value is one of the stated goals of the company, as they have no R&D expenses and their growth continues to be entirely self-funded. They have negligible long-term debt, and 2009's cash flow was off just under 8 percent, in spite of the much larger retreat in sales. They ended 2009 with $460 million in cash, and have over the last five years averaged free cash flow of 15 percent of earnings.

Reasons for Caution

Grainger's customer base is still on the mend and may be so for some time. Also, this customer base is mainly in North America—we expect growth in the developing economies will be more attractive, and Grainger has not announced plans for significant growth there.

Grainger acquired a few smaller companies in 2009, bought Alliance Energy in early 2010, and will continue to make acquisitions over the course of 2010. Acquisition and integration costs will depress operating margins somewhat in the current year.

SECTOR: Industrials
BETA COEFFICIENT: 0.95
10-YEAR COMPOUND EARNINGS PER SHARE GROWTH: 9.5 percent
10-YEAR COMPOUND DIVIDENDS PER SHARE GROWTH: 10.5 percent

		2002	2003	2004	2005	2006	2007	2008	2009
Revenues (Mil)		4,644	4,667	5,050	5,527	5,884	6,418	6,850	6,222
Net income (Mil)		236	227	277	346	383	420	479	402
Earnings per share		2.5	2.46	3.02	3.78	4.25	4.94	6.09	5.25
Dividends per share		0.72	0.74	0.79	0.92	1.16	1.4	1.55	1.78
Cash flow per share		3.59	3.47	4.14	4.97	5.79	6.95	8.28	7.60
Price:	high	59.4	53.3	67	72.4	80	98.6	94	102.5
	low	39.2	41.4	45	51.6	60.6	68.8	58.9	59.9

W. W. Grainger, Inc.
100 Grainger Parkway
Lake Forest, IL 60045
(847) 535-0881
Website: *www.grainger.com*

Harris Corporation

Ticker symbol: HRS (NYSE) ❑ S&P rating: B+ ❑ Value Line financial strength rating: BBB+ ❑ Current yield: 2.0 percent

Company Profile

Harris is an international communications and information technology company serving government and commercial markets in more than 150 countries. Founded in Ohio in 1895, the company was primarily a supplier of printing equipment until the mid-1950's when it began to focus on electronics. Over the next two decades the electronics segment grew much faster than the print segment, and the company exited the printing business entirely in 1983. Now headquartered in Melbourne, Florida, the company has over 15,000 employees, including nearly 7,000 engineers and scientists. Harris develops communications products, systems, and services for global markets, including government communications, RF communications, broadcast communications, and wireless transmission network solutions.

Its major business units include:

■ Government Communications Systems conducts advanced research studies, develops prototypes, and produces and supports communications and information systems for mission-critical applications for military and government customers. These activities also provide a research base for commercial products and services. GCS accounts for approximately 50 percent of revenue.

■ RF Communications supplies tactical radio communication products, systems and networks to military and government organizations, and provides high-security encryption solutions. These solutions address the requirements of U.S., NATO, and Partnership for Peace Forces, as well as government agencies and embassies around the world. RFC accounts for approximately 40 percent of revenue.

■ Broadcast Communications provides content delivery solutions, including advanced digital transmission, automation, asset management, digital media, network management and video infrastructure solutions to commercial broadcasters in radio, television, and digital satellite broadcast markets. BC accounts for approximately 10 percent of revenue.

Financial Highlights, Fiscal Year 2009

Harris's FY2009 revenue declined 5.5 percent to $5 billion, largely as a result of its divestiture of Stratex Systems. Comparing continuing operations, revenue grew 9.1 percent year-over-year. Earnings fell 31.1 percent as a result of a one-time non-cash goodwill impairment of $255 million to the Broadcast Communications segment. Absent that adjustment, earnings from operations grew 25 percent. Net margin grew 260 basis points, or 2.6 percentage points.

Reasons to Buy

Over the past five years Harris has doubled its share of the ground-based tactical radio market to 42 percent. This is a $3.8 billion dollar worldwide market that is growing at 11 percent/year.

The RF addressable radio market, currently valued at $8 billion, is expected to grow to nearly $18 billion in calendar year 2012, of which Harris's current and planned products are expected to cover over 90 percent.

The company has been able to translate acquisitions and design wins into income at an impressive rate. Over the past five years, Harris' earnings CAGR is 35 percent,

and products introduced in the past three years have revenue CAGR of 49 percent.

The company has great cash flow (up 12 percent for 2009) and a sound capital structure. In addition to funding nearly $1 billion in R&D in 2009 ($250 million internal, $750 million under government contract), the company bought back 2 million shares of stock and raised the dividend 33 percent (to $.80). They're well positioned for their acquisition plans and will continue to repurchase shares and boost dividends.

In June 2009 the company rejected preliminary buyout offers in the neighborhood of $10 billion, saying that it was under an expected offer of $75–$85/share. The company is currently (June 2010) trading at an 11 multiple, which is quite cheap give the company's recent solid record of earnings and its relatively low volatility.

Reasons for Caution

Questions remain about the eventual value of the F-35 strike fighter contract. Actual delivered quantities may be far lower than originally discussed. Harris is the prime contractor for three of its avionics and communication subsystems, with a projected value of $4 billion over the life of the program.

SECTOR: Information Technology
BETA COEFFICIENT: 1.05
10-YEAR COMPOUND EARNINGS PER SHARE GROWTH: 12.5 percent
10-YEAR COMPOUND DIVIDENDS PER SHARE GROWTH: 3.5 percent

	2002	2003	2004	2005	2006	2007	2008	2009
Revenues (Mil)	1,876	2,093	2,519	3,001	3,475	4,243	5,311	5,005
Net income (Mil)	83	90	126	202	310	391	462	513
Earnings per share	0.63	0.68	0.94	1.46	2.22	2.8	3.39	3.87
Dividends per share	0.1	0.16	0.2	0.24	0.32	0.44	0.6	0.80
Cash flow per share	1.04	1.1	1.36	2.06	3.07	4.06	4.75	5.27
Price: high	19.3	19.7	34.6	45.8	49.8	66.9	66.7	48.3
low	12	12.7	18.9	26.9	37.7	45.9	27.6	26.1

Harris Corporation
1025 West NASA Boulevard
Melbourne, FL 32919
(321) 727-9383
Website: *www.harris.com*

H.J. Heinz Company

Ticker symbol: HNZ (NYSE) ❑ S&P rating: BBB ❑ Value Line financial strength rating: A+ ❑ Current yield: 3.9 percent

Company Profile

H. J. Heinz Company manufactures and markets food products such as condiments and sauces, frozen food, soups, desserts, entrées, snacks, frozen potatoes, appetizers, and others for consumers and commercial customers. The company's best known product, its ketchup, has a 60 percent market share in the United States, 70 percent in Canada, and nearly 80 percent in the U.K. Condiments and sauces (including ketchup) accounts for approximately 42 percent of the company's revenue, with meals and snacks producing 45 percent, and Infant/Nutrition making up the remainder.

The Heinz portfolio includes 150 brands that hold either the number one or number two market share positions in their categories, with presence on five continents and in over fifty countries. The company sells its products through its own direct sales organizations, through independent brokers and agents, and to distributors to retailers and commercial users. The company has operations in North America, Africa, Latin America, Europe, the Asia Pacific, and the Middle East.

Heinz' laboratories develop the company's recipes, which are then duplicated at one of the seventy-nine company-owned factories or one of several leased factories. Most of the bulk raw products are sourced locally when possible, and are purchased against futures contracts in order to stabilize pricing, while other ingredients are purchased on the spot market.

Heinz operates in five segments—four defined by territory of service, and one by customer base. The North American Consumer Products includes all operations for all consumer product lines in the United States and Canada. Europe, Asia/Pacific, and Rest of World run operations parallel to NACP, but targeting only their geographies. U.S. Foodservice also serves the United States but only the commercial and institutional customers.

Financial Highlights, Fiscal Year 2010

In the nine months ended January 27, 2010, sales increased $275 million, or 3.7 percent, to $7.77 billion, reflecting net price increases of

4.2 percent, offset by a net volume decline of 2.3 percent. Operating income increased 4.3 percent to $1.21 billion.

Per-share earnings from continuing operations were $2.27, down 3.4 percent versus the prior year. Including discontinued operations, net income was $673 million, or $2.11 per diluted share, compared with $748 million, or $2.34 per diluted share a year ago. EPS movement for the year was unfavorably impacted by $0.33 by currency movements.

The third quarter has shown a very favorable upward trend, with double-digit organic sales growth in all the geographies, and only Food Service showing a moderate decline of 3 percent, although operating profit for the segment was up nearly 20 percent. Restaurant traffic is still down, but at least commodity prices have stabilized. The year-end results are not final, but overall the company has reversed the trend of the first half and has turned in earnings that nearly match the previous year, with the deficit assignable to currency fluctuations. Asia/Pacific turned in results that were especially encouraging, with new acquisitions providing a much needed bump to earnings.

Reasons to Buy

The resilience of Heinz's strong brands was apparent during the recession as the company maintained growth in sales and earnings over each of the past three years, although tapering significantly in 2009. Even in 2009, though, the company's top fifteen brands (which account for 70 percent of its sales) were able to maintain price and increase volumes 7 percent in the second half of the year. The FY'10 third quarter was the nineteenth consecutive quarter of organic sales growth.

Heinz has been successful recently with its new brand introductions, leveraging its Global Innovation and Quality Center. Part of the company's product development goal is to derive 15 percent of revenues from products introduced within the previous thirty-six months.

Heinz's emphasis on emerging markets is paying off. Acquisitions and increased marketing efforts delivered significant growth in 2009, and now this segment accounts for 15 percent of total sales. Heinz believes growth to 20 percent is possible through 2012 with more new products and better market penetration.

Heinz is committed to the value of shareholder return, and has increased its dividend in 2009 and has committed a value, continues to emphasize its dividend and will likely increase it over the next few years. At mid-2009 share prices it yields 3.9 percent.

Reasons for Caution

Growth in emerging markets will come at a cost. Many of the brands we take for granted will require large investments in marketing to establish presence and familiarity. Heinz can also expect to see higher acquisition costs for established local brands as competitors move into this arena.

SECTOR: Consumer Staples

BETA COEFFICIENT: 0.7

10-YEAR COMPOUND EARNINGS PER SHARE GROWTH: 2.5 percent

10-YEAR COMPOUND DIVIDENDS PER SHARE GROWTH: 2.0 percent

		2002	2003	2004	2005	2006	2007	2008	2009
Revenues (Mil)		8,236	8,414	8,913	8,643	9,002	10,070	10,148	10,605
Net income (Mil)		713	779	823	750	792	845	923	905
Earnings per share		2.03	2.2	2.34	2.18	2.38	2.63	2.9	2.85
Dividends per share		1.49	1.08	1.14	1.2	1.4	1.52	1.66	1.68
Cash flow per share		2.64	2.86	3.11	3.06	3.28	3.63	3.82	3.80
Price:	high	43.5	36.8	40.6	39.1	46.8	48.8	53	43.8
	low	29.6	28.9	34.5	33.6	33.4	41.8	35.3	30.5

H.J. Heinz Company

One PPG Place

Pittsburgh, PA 15222

(412) 456-5700

Website: *www.heinz.com*

Hewlett Packard

Ticker symbol: HPQ (NYSE) □ S&P rating: A □ Value Line financial strength rating: A++ □ Current yield: 0.6 percent

Company Profile

Hewlett-Packard is a global technology solutions provider to consumers, businesses and institutions. The company's offerings span IT infrastructure, services, business and home computing, and imaging and printing.

The company is organized around six reporting segments:

- Personal Systems Group is the world's leading provider of personal computers based on unit volume shipped and annual revenue. PSG provides commercial PCs, consumer PCs, workstations, handheld computing devices, calculators and other related accessories, plus software and services for the commercial and consumer markets.
- Imaging and Printing Group is the leading imaging and printing systems provider in the world for consumer and commercial printer hardware, printing supplies, printing media and scanning devices. IPG is also focused on imaging solutions in the commercial markets, including managed print services solutions, commercial printing, industrial applications, outdoor signage, and the graphic arts business.
- Enterprise Storage and Servers provides solutions for both the enterprise and the small business markets. ESS provides products in a number of categories, including entry-level and mid-range servers, and business-critical systems such as the fault-tolerant Integrity servers.
- HP Services is HP's consulting arm, providing multi-vendor IT services, technology services, consulting and integration and outsourcing services. HPS also offers industry-specific services for communications, media and entertainment, manufacturing and distribution, financial services, health and life sciences and the public sector, including government services. HPS collaborates with the HP business units as well as with third-party system integrators and software and networking companies to bring solutions to HP customers.

- HP Software is a leading provider of enterprise and service provider software and services, including IT management software, business reporting solutions, and integrated voice/data development platforms.
- HP Financial Services offers leasing, financing, utility programs and asset recovery services, as well as financial asset management services for large global and enterprise customers.

Financial Highlights, Fiscal Year 2009

HP announced its plans to acquire 3Com, a maker of network infrastructure products, for $2.7 billion. The acquisition is expected to be completed in the first half of 2010 and will move HP into the upper tier of networking suppliers.

Revenues were off 3.4 percent versus 2008, and earnings were down 8 percent as the company continued to absorb restructuring and acquisition costs. Operating margin was off only 10 basis points. The first full-year's results of the EDS acquisition were impressive. Earnings in their sector improved 57 percent on a 14.5 percent increase in revenue over 2008's nine-month contribution.

Reasons to Buy

CEO Mark Hurd's cost-reduction efforts continue to pay off for HP.

The printer group (IPG) saw greatly diminished revenues, but earnings were up 260 basis points due to greatly improved inventory and expense control. Overall, the company's revenues were off, but SG&A fell 120 basis points compared to 2008. The company plans to continue its cost-cutting with a goal of saving $2 billion over the next two years.

HP's acquisition of EDS in 2008 was a major positive factor in HP's revenue and margin picture in 2009 and looks to have been the right deal at the right time. HP was able to retain 99.5 percent of EDS's top 200 clients, and the EDS client base gives HP entry to a new customer base for its current hardware product line.

HP is a much healthier company than it was three years ago. They've had real success in leveraging the supplier base for their consumer and commercial PC and server lines. The addition of EDS has given them a high-margin business that more closely aligns them with IBM's high value-add consulting model, and the purchase of 3Com immediately creates opportunities for single-provider deals that didn't exist before. 3Com's product line also fills holes in HP's current networking offerings.

HP has emerged a winner in head-to-head competition with Dell after years of lagging; it is also coming out on top versus Lexmark and other names in the printing and imaging business. HP is better positioned for growth in emerging markets than many of its rivals, and HP has once again assumed the role as the lead IT brand worldwide.

Reasons for Caution

The 3Com acquisition has not been met with wild enthusiasm by Cisco, the 800-lb. networking gorilla. HP and Cisco had been close partners on many deals in the past, but we do not expect this to continue. "We're seeing the dissolving of a long marriage between the two," said Zeus Kerravala, an analyst with the Yankee Group. "They're looking for opportunities, and it has to come from somewhere." HP also continues to lag behind other technology companies in bringing to market true breakthrough innovations in their marketplaces.

SECTOR: Information Technology
BETA COEFFICIENT: 0.95
10-YEAR COMPOUND EARNINGS PER SHARE GROWTH: 7.5 percent
10-YEAR COMPOUND DIVIDENDS PER SHARE GROWTH: 1.0 percent

	2002	2003	2004	2005	2006	2007	2008	2009
Revenues (Mil)	72.35	73.06	79.91	86.67	91.66	104.3	118.4	114.5
Net income (Mil)	2,409	3,557	4,067	4,708	6,198	7,264	8,329	7,660
Earnings per share	0.79	1.16	1.33	1.62	2.18	2.68	3.25	3.14
Dividends per share	0.32	0.32	0.32	0.32	0.32	0.32	0.32	0.32
Cash flow per share	1.49	2	2.22	2.49	2.97	3.86	4.84	5.26
Price: high	24.1	23.9	26.3	30.3	41.7	53.5	51	52.9
low	10.8	14.2	16.1	18.9	28.4	38.2	28.2	25.4

Hewlett-Packard Company
3000 Hanover Street
Palo Alto, CA 94304
(866) 438-4771
Website: *www.hp.com*

Honeywell International, Inc.

Ticker symbol: HON (NYSE) □ S&P rating: A □ Value Line financial strength rating: A+ □ Current yield: 2.7 percent

Company Profile

Honeywell is a diversified technology and manufacturing company, developing, manufacturing and marketing aerospace products and services (40 percent of sales); control technologies for buildings, homes and industry (31 percent); automotive products (15 percent) and specialty materials (14 percent).

Honeywell operates in four business segments: Aerospace, Automation and Control Solutions, Specialty Materials, and Transportation Systems.

The Aerospace segment primarily makes cockpit controls, power generation equipment, and wheels and brakes for commercial and military aircraft. It also makes jet engines for regional and business jet manufacturers. Demand for the company's aircraft equipment is driven primarily by expansion in the global jetliner fleet, particularly jets with 100 or more seats. Since 1993, the global airliner fleet has grown at a 3 percent annual pace. The Aerospace segment is also a major player in the $35 billion global aircraft maintenance, repair and overhaul industry, which is growing at a 2.2 percent annual rate.

Honeywell's Automation and Control Solutions segment is best known as a maker of home and office climate controls equipment. It also makes home automation systems, lighting controls, security systems and fire alarms.

The Specialty Materials operation makes specialty chemicals and fibers, which are sold primarily to the food, pharmaceutical, and electronic packaging industries.

The Transportation System segment consists of a portfolio of brand name car-care products, such as Fram filters, Prestone antifreeze, Autolite spark plugs, and Simoniz car waxes. The unit also manufactures braking systems for large trucks and service vehicles.

Financial Highlights, Fiscal Year 2009

Honeywell's sales for FY2009 fell 15 percent primarily due to volume declines, as prices remained firm. Operating margin improved slightly, due primarily to reduced COGS in the Specialty Materials segment. All four segments experienced the decline in sales, with Transportation getting the worst of it with a 27 percent drop and

Automation and Control Systems performing best with only a 10 percent decline.

The company's overall 23 percent decline in earnings was concentrated mainly in Aerospace and Transportation, with Transportation's earnings falling 61 percent. Automation and Control, by contrast, saw only a 2 percent decline.

In early 2010 the company paid $1.2 billion for a maker of protective clothing and equipment—the purchase is expected to be accretive to earnings in 2011. The company also announced a partnership with DuPont on the development of a new refrigerant. The companies will produce and market the product independently.

Reasons to Buy

We like where Honeywell is positioned with regard to the growing awareness of the value of energy efficiency. Over the next few years we see a lot of movement toward green practices in building design and use, and no one has a stronger portfolio of lighting and temperature control systems than Honeywell. Over half of the company's portfolio, across all four segments, is in the area of energy efficiency. The company also has a valuable distribution network and existing customer base, as they've been in this business longer than anyone else. If Honeywell can leverage their position here with the

right message (and assuming the construction market begins to turn around), the company could experience strong growth, particularly in the Automation and Controls segment.

Honeywell will be part of the consortium responsible for the development and deployment of the next-generation air traffic control system commissioned by the FAA. This is a long-term program and Honeywell is not the primary contractor, but this system will likely be the model for the modernization of air traffic systems worldwide.

The company has a solid balance sheet and has seen a healthy uptick in orders during the first half of 2010, including a 33 percent uptick in the lagging Transportation segment. They have revised their earnings guidance upward through the end of the year ($.05) and participate almost exclusively in high-margin businesses. Economic recovery will further accelerate HON's earnings growth.

Reasons for Caution

The company's highest-revenue segment (Automation and Controls) is closely tied to the construction industries. And while there is evidence of a recovery in that segment of the economy, signs of a significant turnaround are not yet there.

SECTOR: **Industrials**
BETA COEFFICIENT: **1.15**
10-YEAR COMPOUND EARNINGS PER SHARE GROWTH: **3.5 percent**
10-YEAR COMPOUND DIVIDENDS PER SHARE GROWTH: **6.5 percent**

	2002	2003	2004	2005	2006	2007	2008	2009
Revenues (Mil)	22,274	23,103	25,601	27,653	31,367	34,589	36,556	30,908
Net income (Mil)	1,644	1,344	1,281	1,736	2,083	2,444	2,792	2,153
Earnings per share	2.00	1.56	1.49	1.92	2.52	3.16	3.75	2.85
Dividends per share	0.75	0.75	0.75	0.83	0.91	1.00	1.10	1.21
Cash flow per share	2.71	2.25	2.27	2.93	3.59	4.39	5.03	4.07
Price: high	40.9	33.5	38.5	39.5	45.8	62.3	63	41.6
low	18.8	20.2	31.2	32.7	35.2	43.1	23.2	23.1

Honeywell International, Inc.
101 Columbia Road
P. O. Box 2245
Morristown, NJ 07962–2245
(973) 455-2222
Website: *www.honeywell.com*

Hormel Foods Corporation

Ticker symbol: HRL (NYSE) ❑ S&P rating: A+ ❑ Value Line financial strength rating: A ❑ Current yield: 2.1 percent

Company Profile

Founded by George A. Hormel in 1891 in Austin, Minnesota, Hormel Corporation is a multinational manufacturer of consumer-branded meat and food products, many of which are among the best known in the food industry. The company, according to management, "enjoys a strong reputation among consumers, retail grocers, and foodservice, and industrial customers for products highly regarded for quality, taste, nutrition, convenience and value."

The company's business is reported in five segments: Refrigerated Foods, Grocery Products, Jennie-O Turkey Store, Specialty Foods, and All Other. The company's products include hams, bacon, sausages, franks, canned luncheon meats, stews, chilies, hash, meat spreads, shelf-stable microwaveable entrees, salsas, and frozen processed meats. These products are sold in all fifty states by a Hormel Foods sales force assigned to offices in major cities throughout the United States. Their efforts are supplemented by sales brokers and distributors.

Hormel's headquarters and its Research and Development division and flagship plant are all located in Minnesota. Company facilities that manufacture meat and food products are situated in Iowa, Georgia, Illinois, Wisconsin, Nebraska, Oklahoma, California and Kansas. In addition, custom manufacturing of selected Hormel Foods products is performed by various companies according to corporate guidelines and quality standards.

Hormel has thirty-four brands in the number one or two market positions. They develop and release new products on a continuous basis; nearly 25 percent of their revenues come from products introduced in the last eight years. Their goal is to reach (by 2012) $2 billion in annual sales from products introduced since 2000.

Financial Highlights, Fiscal Year 2009

Hormel closed out 2009 with a nice recovery to what had been shaping up to be a down year overall. As it turned out, the company's cost-cutting measures allowed them to construct something close to a silk purse with earnings up 20 percent on a 3 percent decrease in revenue.

The revenue fall-off was across all the company's lines and reflected both volume and per-unit declines driven by lower commodity costs. The company also exited its joint venture with Carapelli Oils late in the year, which accounted for some of the shortfall.

The company also announced the inception of its MegaMex foods joint venture (with Herdez del Fuerte, based in Mexico City) in which the company will distribute (and may manufacture) well-known Mexican brands such as Embasa and La Victoria in the United States. Initial incremental revenue is expected to be on the order of $200 million.

Fully diluted per-share earnings came in at $2.53, up 12 percent from FY2008. Like the sales declines, the earnings gains were also broad-based, with all segments reporting margin percentage gains from ongoing operations. The company bought back 1 percent of its shares and raised its dividend $.02, maintaining its moderate yield.

Reasons to Buy

The company is in a strong cash position with no debt and is well positioned for some significant growth. Some of that cash will go to support the extensive roll outs of new products over the next eighteen months that the company expects will account for approximately $2 billion in incremental revenue. We expect there will be several acquisitions in key growth areas as well, likely targeting ethnic markets.

The MegaMex venture is starting relatively small, but we expect Hormel will exercise its clout in the retail space to capture market share in the rapidly growing Hispanic foods category. If Hormel begins manufacturing the products as well, the earnings growth could be a nice surprise.

Commodity prices have been trending toward stability at fairly low levels, allowing Hormel (with their volume) to lock in some attractive hedge pricing.

Hormel has shown that they can operate at an attractive level of profitability even on reduced unit volumes and under pricing pressure. We expect they will recover from the recession as well as any and certainly better than most, but even if it's another six quarters before a full recovery is in effect, Hormel seems to be just fine.

Reasons for Caution

Hog prices have been trending up slightly through early 2010, and pork is Hormel's largest input. Producers, while not exactly wallowing in red ink, had seen their prices depressed for over two quarters but are now able to support higher pricing. If prices spike as they did in 2009, it's not clear how quickly Hormel might be able to raise product prices in response, given the state of the consumer market.

SECTOR: **Consumer Staples**
BETA COEFFICIENT: **.65**
10-YEAR COMPOUND EARNINGS PER SHARE GROWTH: **10.0 percent**
10-YEAR COMPOUND DIVIDENDS PER SHARE GROWTH: **8.0 percent**

	2002	2003	2004	2005	2006	2007	2008	2009
Revenues (Mil)	3,910	4,200	4,780	5,414	5,745	6,193	6,755	6,534
Net income (Mil)	189	186	232	254	286	302	286	343
Earnings per share	1.35	1.33	1.65	1.82	2.05	2.17	2.08	2.53
Dividends per share	0.39	0.42	0.45	0.52	0.56	0.6	0.74	0.78
Cash flow per share	1.97	1.98	2.27	2.67	2.97	3.13	3.06	3.52
Price: high	28.2	27.5	32.1	35.4	39.1	41.8	42.8	40.5
low	20	19.9	24.9	29.2	31.9	30	24.8	29.2

Hormel Foods Corporation
1 Hormel Place
Austin, MN 55912–3680
(507) 437-5007
Website: *www.hormel.com*

CONSERVATIVE GROWTH

International Business Machines

Ticker symbol: IBM (NYSE) □ S&P rating: A □ Value Line financial strength rating: A++ □ Current yield: 1.8 percent

Company Profile

Big Blue is the world's leading provider of computer hardware and services. IBM makes a broad range of computers, mainframes, and network servers. The company also develops software (it is number two, behind Microsoft) and peripherals. The company continues to innovate and invent, and has for the last sixteen years led the world in the number of U.S. patents issued.

In 2009, IBM derived over 75 percent of its revenue and 82 percent of its income from the Software and Services businesses. The company continues to design and produce mainframes and has its label on five of the top ten supercomputers in the world. They also produce high-margin commercial servers and enterprise-level installations, but they have exited the lower-margin hardware businesses, such as consumer PCs, laptops and hard drives.

Financial Highlights, Fiscal Year 2009

The company reported a year/year decline in net revenue of 7.6 percent, while earnings actually rose 8.8 percent. Per-share earnings were up a whopping 12.6 percent, making 2009 the seventh consecutive year of double-digit EPS growth at IBM. IBM's shift to higher-margin businesses accounted for the higher earnings in the face of declining sales.

IBM has traditionally had strong cash flow, and 2009 was no exception. Free cash flow was up 5.5 percent. The 2008 free cash flow is up nearly 85 percent over the last six years. Over the last nine years, Big Blue has generated over $100 billion in free cash flow and exited 2009 with $14 billion in cash and liquid securities, even after spending $7.4 billion in share repurchase and distributing $2.9 billion in dividends.

Gross margins were up in the three largest business segments and off slightly in the three smallest segments. The biggest gains were in Global Technology Services Software (240 basis points), Global Business Services (150 basis points), and Software (60 basis points). The largest decline was in Global Financing, largely due to fluctuation in currency markets. The company's shift to higher-margin businesses is (happily) accompanied by greater focus on the financial performance of those businesses.

Reasons to Buy

Once viewed as a teetering giant of the computer industry, with a massive intellectual property portfolio but with an uncertain product strategy, IBM has over the last decade successfully re-invented itself as a powerhouse in the Software and Services sector. While their gross margins in hardware remain healthy (but shrinking) at 38 percent, their margins in the much larger Services arms are at 30 percent and growing, and Software generates 14 percent more revenue than hardware at margins of over 85 percent.

Not long ago, many companies felt they had to have in-house information technology departments to service their IT needs. Now, most have found that it's far more efficient to contract those services out to someone who can provide data warehousing, website development and maintenance, regional/national/global IT infrastructure, etc., without requiring a commitment in fixed assets. This is where IBM has leveraged their expertise, and as this trend continues and as businesses grow their reliance on these services, IBM benefits.

They've successfully implemented a global focus to their growth. Revenue growth outside of U.S./Europe/Japan was double the growth of IBM's "major markets" and now represents 19 percent of their total revenue. Their focus is on high-margin, long-term global infrastructure and services, a model that has proven to be very successful over the last decade.

They continue to innovate and are in a great position to acquire whatever technology they choose not to develop internally. They have world-class semiconductor design and production facilities and license design, manufacturing, and packaging services and products.

Their services income is largely based on long-term contracts, which are not as subject to the vagaries of the world economy as would be sales of hardware.

Reasons for Caution

IBM has carved out a very large chunk of the outsourced IT business. Innovation in this area can be rapid and disruptive, and margins can shrink precipitously as a result. IBM will have to stay ahead of the curve with innovative and compelling products and defensive product strategies in order to maintain revenue growth.

Competition in the services area is heating up, with Hewlett-Packard's purchase of EDS and Oracle's acquisition of Sun Microsystems. These two moves have created competitors with strong synergies and a compelling sales pitch to new and existing customers.

SECTOR: **Information Technology**
BETA COEFFICIENT: **0.90**
10-YEAR COMPOUND EARNINGS PER SHARE GROWTH: **9.5 percent**
10-YEAR COMPOUND DIVIDENDS PER SHARE GROWTH: **14.5 percent**

	2002	2003	2004	2005	2006	2007	2008	2009
Revenues (Mil)	81,186	89,131	96,503	91,134	91,424	98,786	103,630	95,758
Net income (Mil)	3,579	7,583	8,448	7,934	9,492	10,418	12,334	13,425
Earnings per share	3.07	4.34	4.39	4.91	6.06	7.18	8.93	10.01
Dividends per share	0.6	0.66	0.7	0.078	1.1	1.5	1.9	2.15
Cash flow per share	6.53	7.27	8.24	8.71	9.56	11.28	13.28	13.9
Price: high	124	94.5	100.4	99.1	97.4	121.5	130.9	132.3
low	54	73.2	81.9	71.8	72.7	88.8	69.5	81.8

International Business Machines Corporation
New Orchard Road
Armonk, New York 10504
(800) 426-4968
Website: *www.ibm.com*

CONSERVATIVE GROWTH

International Paper Company

Ticker symbol: IP (NYSE) □ S&P rating B+ □ Value Line financial strength rating B+ □ Current yield: 0.4 percent

Company Profile

International Paper Company (International Paper), incorporated in 1941, is a global paper and packaging company complemented by a North American merchant distribution system with primary markets and manufacturing operations in North America, Europe, Latin America, Russia, Asia and North Africa.

During the year ended December 31, 2009, the company operated twenty-one pulp, paper and packaging mills, 146 converting and packaging plants, nineteen recycling plants, and three bag facilities. During 2009, the production facilities in Europe, Asia, Latin America and South America included nine pulp, paper and packaging mills, fifty-two converting and packaging plants, and two recycling plants.

The company operates in six segments: Printing Papers, Industrial Packaging, Consumer Packaging, Distribution, Forest Products, and Specialty Businesses and Other. International Paper produces uncoated printing and writing papers. Uncoated papers business produces papers for use in copiers, desktop and laser printers, and digital imaging. Market pulp is used in the manufacture of printing, writing and specialty papers, towel and tissue products and filtration products. Pulp is also converted into non-paper products such as diapers and sanitary napkins.

International Paper is the largest manufacturer of containerboard in the United States. Its products include linerboard, medium, white-top, recycled linerboard, recycled medium and saturating kraft. About 80 percent of its production is converted domestically into corrugated boxes and other packaging by the 137 United States container plants. The company's coated paperboard business produces coated paperboard for a variety of packaging and commercial printing end uses.

Xpedx, the company's North American merchant distribution business, provides distribution services and products to a number of customer markets. Xpedx supplies commercial printers with printing papers and graphic pre-press, presses and post-press equipment, building services and away-from-home markets with facility supplies, and manufacturers with packaging supplies and equipment.

Financial Highlights, Fiscal Year 2009

FY2009 was a year like no other for International: a 55 percent decline in earnings; a 700 percent swing in the stock price; a 70 percent drop in the dividend; and over $1.4 billion in restructuring charges. In fact, however, 2009 was in many ways a continuation of a process begun in FY2008 as the company continued to redefine itself after divesting of nearly all of its considerable forestry operations. They ended 2008 with order cancellations, customer liquidity issues, high currency volatility, and rising input costs. The first half of 2009 was clearly going to be worse than the last half of 2008, as bad as that was.

What went right for IP during 2009? Well, like many of the capital-intensive companies in our list, IP took the opportunity to maximize cash and put it to use in the current year, and as a result the company's balance sheet finished FY2009 $4.3 billion to the good. Benefits from the late-2008 Weyerhauser acquisition accrued more quickly than anticipated, and a large part of the $500 million decline in overhead was attributed to successes here. Related to that, the company turned in a top-quartile ROI against its peers and industry-leading pre-tax earnings.

The picture brightened considerably in the second half as the economy woke up and the capital markets returned to life. Customer run rates turned around, inventory replenishment orders appeared and steady-state orders returned to nearly pre-recession levels.

Reasons to Buy

The caption under the photo of International's FY2009 is "The market hates uncertainty." IP entered the year with a lot of questions still hanging around from 2008 regarding their acquisition of Weyerhauser's packaging operation, their divestiture of the bulk of their forestry operations, and the large restructuring begun in that year. Then, in 2009, add in the collapse of the capital markets, another even larger restructuring, and it's not at all surprising that investors started looking around for the nearest exit row. Was $4/share ever an appropriate price for IP in 2009? No, not even close. But the fear, uncertainty, and doubt had taken hold. And nine months later, IP was trading at seven times its low for the year.

The Weyerhauser packaging acquisition is paying off better than planned. The company generated more than $500 million in incremental revenue in 2009 as a result of the effectiveness of the integration process.

The smoke has cleared. International is in great shape financially with a healthy customer base and a leaner operational profile than it's had in the last decade. You can pick this stock up on the cheap and never look back.

Reasons for Caution

IP's customers will need some time to recover fully from the recession. The economy needs several more quarters to catch up.

SECTOR: Materials

BETA COEFFICIENT: 1.45

10-YEAR COMPOUND EARNINGS PER SHARE GROWTH: 4.0 percent

10-YEAR COMPOUND DIVIDENDS PER SHARE GROWTH: -2.5 percent

	2002	2003	2004	2005	2006	2007	2008	2009
Revenues (Mil)	24,976	25,179	25,548	24,097	21,995	21,890	24,829	23,366
Net income (Mil)	540	382	634	513	635	1,168	829	378
Earnings per share	1.12	0.80	1.30	1.06	2.18	2.70	1.96	0.88
Dividends per share	1.00	1.00	1.00	1.00	1.00	1.00	1.00	0.33
Cash flow per share	4.44	4.21	4.51	3.85	3.63	4.15	5.02	4.27
Price: high	46.2	43.3	45	42.6	38	41.6	33.8	27.8
low	31.3	33.1	37.1	27	30.7	31	10.2	3.9

International Paper Company

400 Atlantic Street

Stamford, CT 06921

(901) 419-4957

Website: *www.internationalpaper.com*

Iron Mountain Incorporated

Ticker symbol: IRM (NYSE) □ S&P rating: BB- □ Value Line financial strength rating: B □ Current yield: 1.0 percent

Company Profile

Iron Mountain is the world's leading provider of record, document, and information-management services. Businesses that require or desire off-site, secure storage and/or archiving of data in physical or electronic form contract with IRM for whatever level of service meets their needs.

In general, IRM provides three major types of service: records management, data protection and recovery, and information destruction. All three services include both physical and electronic media.

Revenues accrue to the company through two streams—storage and services. Storage revenues consist of recurring per-unit charges related to the storage of material or data. The storage periods are typically many years, and the revenues from this service account for just over half of IRM's total revenue over the last five years. Service revenue comes from charges for any number of services, including those related to the core storage service and others such as temporary access, courier operations, secure destruction, data recovery, media conversion, and the like.

IRM's client base is deep and diverse. They have over 90,000 clients, including 93 percent of the Fortune 1000 and over 90 percent of the FTSE 100. They have over 900 facilities in 165 markets worldwide, and they are six times the size of their nearest competitor.

Financial Highlights, Fiscal Year 2009

IRM's revenues were basically flat year/year, while earnings rose 28 percent on significantly improved gross margins. Reduced capital expenditures and improved operations led to a record free cash flow of $336 million, leading to the initiation of the company's first ever dividend ($.25 quarterly). In addition, the board approved a $150 million share repurchase program.

IRM has said that they are de-emphasizing acquisitions (at least partially due to their debt load), but in the fourth quarter they announced their plans to acquire Mimosa Systems for $112 million. Mimosa's technology provides its customers with on-site, enterprise-class data archiving, which complements IRM's existing off-site and cloud-based storage.

Growth rates in the storage business have been very steady over the last eight quarters, but service revenue declined again in 2009, down 4 percent from 2008. Service revenues are far more discretionary and client spending levels are impacted to a greater extent by economic downturns, which is reflected in these results.

Reasons to Buy

Iron Mountain's business strategy for the last fifteen years has been one of acquisition and integration, buying smaller businesses and consolidating their operations and, more importantly, their customer base. Customers in this business tend to stay with a known quantity, and over the years no one has become more known than IRM. This strategy has worked very well for them, and now IRM is the clear market leader. Their large, predictable revenue stream gives them the flexibility to maintain their policy of strategic acquisition while funding the resulting restructuring internally.

A common observation of IRM's critics is that paper records are dying off and most data is now generated and stored electronically, creating opportunity for competitors like IBM and EMC. This is true, but it ignores a couple of facts: Existing paper still needs to be stored for a long time, and there's a lot of it. Nearly 75 percent of IRM's revenue comes from paper storage, but this percentage is declining as IRM's customers are storing far more electronic data now.

It also ignores a number of other important points. For one, IRM's current customers would need a very good reason to split their data storage business between two vendors, one doing only electronic storage and the other doing electronic storage plus everything else as well. Second, if competitors for the electronic storage business become a problem, IRM can price their electronic storage below market and still be quite profitable. And last, for the customer base that IRM serves, this is not a burdensome expense. Changing vendors could likely cost them more than they might ever hope to save. For now, IRM has a pretty good moat.

Reasons for Caution

Non-discretionary service revenues are expected to decline slightly again through 2010, even as the recurring storage business begins to pick up following the recession. Since the service revenues bring higher margins, Iron Mountain's earnings will be under some pressure at least until 2011.

SECTOR: Information Technology
BETA COEFFICIENT: 0.95
10-YEAR COMPOUND EARNINGS PER SHARE GROWTH: 55.4 percent
10-YEAR COMPOUND DIVIDENDS PER SHARE GROWTH: NM

	2002	2003	2004	2005	2006	2007	2008	2009
Revenues (Mil)	1318	1501	1817	2078	2350	2730	3055	3,014
Net income (Mil)	67	84.6	94.2	114	129	153	152	195
Earnings per share	0.35	0.44	0.48	0.57	0.64	0.76	0.78	0.96
Dividends per share	-	-	-	-	-	-	-	-
Cash flow per share	0.92	1.12	1.32	1.52	1.69	2.01	2.19	2.55
Price: high	15.2	18.1	23.4	30.1	29.9	38.8	37.1	24.9
low	9	13.4	17.2	17.8	22.6	25	16.7	21.3

Iron Mountain Incorporated
745 Atlantic Avenue
Boston, MA 02111
Website: *www.ironmountain.com*

CONSERVATIVE GROWTH

Johnson Controls, Inc.

Ticker symbol: JCI (NYSE) ❑ S&P rating: BBB+ ❑ Value Line financial strength rating: A ❑ Current yield: 1.6 percent

Company Profile

Johnson Controls is a large manufacturer of automotive, heating ventilation and air conditioning (HVAC) controls and energy controls and products. Their products are found in over 200 million vehicles, 12 million homes and 1 million commercial buildings. Their business operates in three segments: Automotive, Building Efficiency, and Power Solutions.

Their automotive business is one of the world's largest automotive suppliers, providing seating and overhead systems, door systems, floor consoles, instrument panels, cockpits and integrated electronics. Customers include virtually every major automaker in the world. The business produces automotive interior systems for original equipment manufacturers (OEMs) and operates in twenty-nine countries worldwide. Additionally, the business has partially owned affiliates in Asia, Europe, North America and South America. In fiscal 2009, the automotive business accounted for 42 percent of the company's consolidated net sales.

Building Efficiency is a global leader in delivering integrated control systems, mechanical equipment, services and solutions designed to improve the comfort, safety and energy efficiency of non-residential buildings and residential properties with operations in more than 125 countries. Revenues come from facilities management, technical services and the replacement and upgrade of controls/HVAC mechanical equipment in the existing buildings market. In fiscal 2009, building efficiency accounted for 44 percent of the company's consolidated net sales.

The Power Solutions business produces lead-acid automotive batteries, serving both automotive original equipment manufacturers and the general vehicle battery aftermarket. They also offer Absorbent Glass Mat (AGM), nickel-metal-hydride and lithium-ion battery technologies to power hybrid vehicles. Sales of automotive batteries generated 14 percent of the company's fiscal 2009 consolidated net sales.

Financial Highlights, Fiscal Year 2009

There aren't a lot of highlights for JCI in FY2009. It was a rough year all the way around, with sales off 26 percent, earnings down over 80 percent (even recording a loss in two quarters) and cash flow down over 60 percent. No question about it, it was a bad year to be a large supplier to the automotive and construction industries.

Early 2010 results, however, are very encouraging, with double-digit sales growth overall and per-share earnings that beat estimates by over 50 percent. Management estimates for 2010 EPS are $1.75, up 400 percent over 2009.

Reasons to Buy

In March 2009 the company announced the second in a series of comprehensive restructuring plans that would be substantially complete by the end of 2010. The goals of both plans are basically to downsize the company to better align it with the anticipated demands for its products going forward. Targeting primarily the automotive and power solutions businesses, the plans include reductions in manufacturing capacity (both through consolidation of facilities and the sale of others) and reduction of operating costs through plant relocation to lower labor cost environments. Accompanying these moves will be a reduction in workforce of approximately 16,300 employees.

These are tough steps for any company to have to take. Many companies (in fact, several of JCI's customers) missed the opportunity to take these steps and paid an even greater price later on partly as a result of their inaction. JCI's share price bottomed out in early March 2009 (as did the share prices of the vast majority of the issues on the NYSE). Since then, the shares have nearly quadrupled in price and are trading just about where they were two years ago. We feel the actions taken by JCI were both necessary and prudent, and have reaffirmed the company's future as a valued supplier to the automotive and construction industries.

JCI will be a major participant in the coming automotive applications of lithium battery technology. They are already in the 2009 Mercedes S-class hybrid and are the exclusive suppliers to the upcoming (2012) Ford plug-in hybrid for its battery and battery controls. Johnson's joint venture with Saft Advanced Power Solutions (JCS) is also providing lithium-ion batteries to the Dodge Sprinter development program. JCI's subsidiary Varta has set up a JCS development center in Hanover, Germany to support the European market.

Reasons for Caution

JCI is a leader in the race for the next automotive power technology, but there's no guarantee that lithium will be the clear winner. Other technologies are making progress as well, and the politics of lithium sourcing are far from settled.

SECTOR: **Industrials**
BETA COEFFICIENT: **1.25**
10-YEAR COMPOUND EARNINGS PER SHARE GROWTH: **11.5 percent**
10-YEAR COMPOUND DIVIDENDS PER SHARE GROWTH: **12.5 percent**

	2002	2003	2004	2005	2006	2007	2008	2009
Revenues (Mil)	20,103	22,646	25,363	27,883	32,235	34,624	38,062	28,497
Net Income (Mil)	601	683	818	909	1,028	1,252	1,400	281
Earnings per share	1.09	1.2	1.41	1.5	1.75	2.09	2.33	0.47
Dividends per share	0.22	0.24	0.28	0.33	0.37	0.44	0.52	0.52
Cash flow per share	2.08	2.28	2.5	2.6	2.95	3.34	3.63	1.48
Price: high	15.5	19.4	21.1	25.1	30	44.5	36.5	28.3
low	11.5	12	16.5	17.5	22.1	28.1	13.6	8.4

Johnson Controls, Inc.
P. O. Box 591
Milwaukee, WI 53201–0591
(414) 524-2375
Website: *www.johnsoncontrols.com*

Johnson & Johnson

Ticker symbol: JNJ (NYSE) ❑ S&P rating: A+ ❑ Value Line financial strength rating: A++ ❑ Current yield: 3.2 percent

Company Profile

Johnson & Johnson is the largest and most comprehensive health care company in the world, with 2009 sales of $62 billion. JNJ offers a broad line of consumer products, over-the-counter drugs, as well as various other medical devices and diagnostic equipment.

The company has three reporting segments: Consumer Health Care, Medical Devices and Diagnostics, and Pharmaceuticals. In those segments, Johnson & Johnson has more than 200 operating companies in fifty-four countries, selling some 50,000 products in more than 175 countries. One of Johnson & Johnson's premier assets is its well-entrenched brand names, which are widely known in the United States as well as abroad. And as a marketer, JNJ's reputation for quality has enabled it to build strong ties to commercial health care providers.

The company has a stake in a wide variety of health segments: anti-infectives, biotechnology, cardiology and circulatory diseases, diagnostics, gastrointestinals, minimally invasive therapies, nutraceuticals, orthopaedics, pain management, skin care, vision care, women's health, and wound care.

The company's well-known trade names include Band-Aid adhesive bandages, Tylenol, Stay-free, Carefree and Sure & Natural feminine hygiene products, Mylanta, Pepcid AC, Neutrogena, Johnson's baby powder, shampoo and oil, and Reach toothbrushes.

Financial Highlights, Fiscal Year 2009

As if 2009's recession needed another bellwether, consider this: in 2009, Johnson & Johnson posted their first year-over-year sales decline in seventy-six years. The downturn in revenues led to a number of reactive cost-cutting measures, including headcount reductions, but the company reported downturns in most measures. Earnings were off almost 6 percent, spending on R&D fell nearly 8 percent, and EPS declined 4 percent.

Not all the news was bad, as total shareholder return for the year, including dividends and share repurchase, totaled 11.3 percent. The Q4 results far outpaced Q3, and the company was able to recognize all of the current restructuring costs in the current year. Still, the year was a disappointing one for a company used to consistently reporting year-over-year top line growth.

Pharmaceuticals were off 8.3 percent, primarily due to the loss of patent protection for Topamax® in March 2009, and Risperdal® June 2008. This is the second consecutive year of decline for the Pharmaceutical unit. The company has moved to bolster the business through continued acquisition, picking up Cougar Biotechnology for its oncological portfolio, and a key license from Elan Corporation.

The company continued to expand its global footprint, building new research and manufacturing operations in Brazil, Russia, India, China, and other developing markets. The company also received a nice $1 billion bump from a legal settlement with Boston Scientific in January 2010, and expects to receive $700 million more in January 2011 from the same settlement, which was a patent infringement case involving cardiac stents.

Reasons to Buy

The loss of patent protection for Topamax® and Risperdal® resulted in $3 billion in lost sales in 2009, but J&J's pharmaceuticals still have ten brands each producing over $1 billion in annual revenue. They launched five new drugs in 2009 and have a pipeline of some promising candidates, although applications for their potential anti-convulsant Comfyde have been withdrawn.

Their Medical Devices and Diagnostics segment has been a solid performer even through the recession. Their weakest businesses were in consumer markets where out-of-pocket medical spending was depressed. The economic recovery currently underway and broadened health care coverage are expected to address the bulk of 2009's issues in this area.

The company's five-year compound annual growth rate (CAGR) for international sales is 13.6 percent, and J&J's International sales now make up over 50 percent of the total. As standards of medical care rise internationally and as the potential for health care funding reform in the U.S. increases, J&J's growth outside the United States is particularly appealing. The world health care market is expected to grow 5 percent per year over the next five years, and J&J participates in over 30 percent of those markets.

The company exited 2008 with nearly $14 billion in cash and exceptional free cash flow, so more acquisitions, further dividend increases, and continued share repurchase look to be more than fully funded.

Reasons for Caution

Johnson & Johnson compete in research-intensive businesses that require steady cash flow to support new product development. Bringing a new drug to market requires, on average, $800 million and ten years of development and testing, interruptions in free cash flow over a period of several years can cripple the product pipeline. J&J need to maintain cash flow growth year-to-year to keep the pipeline robust.

SECTOR: Health Care
BETA COEFFICIENT: .60
10-YEAR COMPOUND EARNINGS PER SHARE GROWTH: 13 percent
10-YEAR COMPOUND DIVIDENDS PER SHARE GROWTH: 14.5 percent

	2002	2003	2004	2005	2006	2007	2008	2009
Revenues (Mil)	36,298	41,862	47,348	50,514	53,324	61,095	63,747	61,897
Net income (Mil)	6,651	7,197	8,509	10,411	11,053	10,576	12,949	12,906
Earnings per share	2.18	2.4	2.84	3.35	3.73	4.15	4.57	4.63
Dividends per share	0.82	0.93	1.1	1.28	1.46	1.62	1.8	1.93
Cash flow per share	2.85	3.36	3.84	4.25	4.6	5.23	5.7	5.7
Price: high	65.9	59.1	64.2	70	69.4	68.8	72.8	65.9
low	41.4	48	49.2	59.8	56.6	59.7	52.1	61.9

Johnson & Johnson
One Johnson & Johnson Plaza
New Brunswick, N.J. 08933
(800) 950-5089
Website: *www.jnj.com*

GROWTH AND INCOME

Kellogg Company

Ticker symbol: K (NYSE) □ S&P rating: BBB+ □ Value Line financial strength rating: A □ Current yield: 2.8 percent

Company Profile

Founded in 1906, Kellogg is the world's leading producer of breakfast cereal and a leading producer of convenience foods, including cookies, crackers, toaster pastries, cereal bars, frozen waffles, meat alternatives, pie crusts, and cones.

The company's brands include Kellogg's®, Kcebler®, Pop-Tarts®, Eggo®, Cheez-It®, Nutri-Grain®, Rice Krispies®, Special K®, Murray®, Austin®, Morningstar Farms®, Famous Amos®, Carr's®, Plantation®, and Kashi®.

The company operates in two segments: Kellogg North America (NA) and Kellogg International, with NA generating two-thirds of the company's revenue. NA operations are further divided into Cereals, Snacks, and Frozen/Specialty categories. International operates as three regional entities: Europe, Latin America, and Asia Pacific. The company produces more than 1,500 different products, manufactured in nineteen countries and marketed in more than 180 countries around the world.

Kellogg is a conservatively run company, emphasizing long-term thinking and leveraging existing brand strengths while keeping a sharp focus on cost savings. They've created and manage to several internal measures of financial performance that are geared toward sustainable long-term growth.

Financial Highlights, Fiscal Year 2009

Reported revenues declined 1.9 percent, but the company still managed to return an 80 basis point increase in net margin, to 9.8 percent. Revenues were off due to reduced unit volume (who can forget the Eggo waffle shortage? Not us!), and production changes in Russia and China. In spite of the global economic downturn, the company generated record operating profit, EPS and cash flow.

The company took advantage of 2009's advertising downturn by spending a record $1.1 billion to promote their brands at a rate significantly above the industry average.

The company continues to provide accelerated shareholder return in recent years through dividend increases and stock buyback programs—dividends and EPS have five-year CAGR of 7 and 8 percent, respectively.

Reasons to Buy

Kellogg owns just over a third of the U.S. market for ready-to-eat cereals, which makes them the market leader in probably the most mature food category in the world. But, having invented it over a hundred years ago, they continue to respond to customer demand for new and interesting products. Last year, for instance, they released Special K Chocolatey Flakes, and added dietary fiber to Corn Pops, Apple Jacks, and Froot Loops. Don't tell the kids.

Last year Kellogg began full-scale implementation of a cost-cutting program that had piloted very well. Results through 2009 have saved 26 cents of EPS putting them well over their target of $1 billion in total savings through the end of 2011.

Kellogg's strategy since 2001 has been to "win in cereal and expand snacks," meaning "hold onto market share in the mature segment and grow the newer segment with product innovation." This has worked well for them, as 25 percent of their revenues are from cereals and snacks have grown (organically and through acquisition) to 30 percent of overall revenue. If they continue to succeed

with this strategy we can expect to see continued steady growth in both top and bottom lines.

We like Kellogg's growth in international markets. As discretionary income rises, so does consumption of prepared foods, and the international markets will reward companies that have the right products. Special K, for example, is growing at double-digit rates internationally and at triple-digit rates in India.

The company has a compelling history of slow but steady growth. Year after year they target low single-digit growth and year after year, with very few exceptions, they hit the target. They're also committed to dividend growth and year after year they deliver (current yield is about 3 percent). This is a stock that will let you sleep at night.

Reasons for Caution

Frozen and specialty foods have had two disappointing years in a row and the company is already taking some cost hits as they pare away some brands; further extraordinary costs may be in store. Particularly in a soft economy, Kellogg faces threats from generic and store-branded products, especially on the cereal aisle.

SECTOR: Consumer Staples
BETA COEFFICIENT: .60
10-YEAR COMPOUND EARNINGS PER SHARE GROWTH: 6.0 percent
10-YEAR COMPOUND DIVIDENDS PER SHARE GROWTH: 3.5 percent

	2002	2003	2004	2005	2006	2007	2008	2009
Revenues (Mil)	8,304	8,812	9,614	10,177	10,907	11,776	12,822	12,575
Net income (Mil)	711	787	891	980	1,004	1,103	1,148	1,212
Earnings per share	1.73	1.92	2.14	2.26	2.51	2.76	2.99	3.17
Dividends per share	1.01	1.01	1.01	1.06	1.14	1.24	1.3	1.43
Cash flow per share	2.6	2.83	3.15	3.39	3.41	3.78	3.99	4.35
Price: high	37	38.6	45.3	47	51	56.9	58.5	54.1
low	29	27.8	37	42.4	42.4	48.7	35.6	35.6

Kellogg Company
One Kellogg Square
P. O. Box 3599
Battle Creek, MI 49016–3599
(269) 961-6636
Website: *www.kelloggcompany.com*

GROWTH AND INCOME

Kimberly-Clark

Ticker symbol: KMB (NYSE) □ S&P rating: A □ Value Line financial strength rating: A++ □ Current yield: 4.2 percent

Company Profile

Kimberly-Clark develops, manufactures and markets a full line of personal care products, mostly based on paper and paper technologies. Well known for their ubiquitous Kleenex brand tissues, KMB also is a strong player in bath tissue, diapers, feminine products, incontinence products and others.

The company operates in four segments: Personal Care, Consumer Tissue, K-C Professional & Other, and Health Care. The Personal Care segment provides disposable diapers, training and youth pants, and swimpants; baby wipes; and feminine and incontinence care products, and related products. Brand names include Huggies, Pull-Ups, Little Swimmers, GoodNites, Kotex, Lightdays, Depend, and Poise. The Consumer Tissue segment offers facial and bathroom tissue, paper towels, napkins, and related products for household use under the Kleenex, Scott, Cottonelle, Viva, Andrex, Scottex, Hakle, and Page brands. The K-C Professional & Other provides paper products for the away-from-home, that is, commercial/ institutional marketplace under Kimberly-Clark, Kleenex, Scott, WypAll, Kimtech, KleenGuard, Kimcare, and Jackson brand names. The Health Care segment offers disposable health care products, such as surgical drapes and gowns, infection control products, face masks, exam gloves, respiratory products, pain management products, and other disposable medical products.

To give an idea what drives growth at KMB, in the first quarter of 2010, Personal Care sales grew 8.1 percent, Consumer Tissue grew 2 percent, K-C Professional and other products grew 12.1 percent, and Health Care products grew at a 23.2 percent rate.

The company sells its products to a variety of retailers, mass merchandisers and distributors. Wal-Mart accounts for some 13 percent of sales. Sales have been centered in the United States but the company is reaching out to foreign markets. The company was founded in 1872 and is headquartered today in Dallas, Texas with a historical, technology and manufacturing base in the Fox River Valley in Wisconsin.

Financial Highlights, Fiscal Year 2009

Kimberly-Clark reported a rare drop in revenues in 2009 as consumers became more thrifty and steered clear of premium brands. Price increases and strong international sales help stem the tide, but the real story was cost cutting; the company achieved some $240 million in cost cuts through the year. Much of the savings was in productivity improvements, as raw pulp costs actually increased during the period, so KMB should be relatively well positioned for a recovery. Fourth quarter revenues actually increased 8 percent vs. 2008, a healthy sign, and earnings were up 16 percent in the quarter. Results for the first quarter of FY10 were a bit disappointing due to currency fluctuations and higher pulp costs, but the company stuck by its forecasts.

Reasons to Buy

Kimberly-Clark has shown itself to be a steady business in all kinds of economic climates. The high yield and strong track record of raising dividends is a definite plus—the company has almost doubled the dividend in the last eight years. Strong cash flow has also been turned into a healthy share buyback program, as well as funding international expansion and enhanced marketing efforts.

Compared to some peers, especially Procter & Gamble, the company is less inclined to go for "glamour" markets such as cosmetics, choosing instead to add to margins through operating efficiencies and scale. Safety-oriented investors may find this approach preferable. In addition, Value Line gives the company an "A++" for financial strength and a top rating for safety, the latter of which it has maintained since 1990.

Reasons for Caution

While the paper products business is steady, it isn't easy to see where growth would come from. The company, rightly so, is targeting international expansion, but competition and currency fluctuation make the results far from certain. The cost of pulp and paper raw materials can also be highly volatile. Investors should focus on income and safety with this issue; any growth would be a plus.

SECTOR: Consumer Staples
BETA COEFFICIENT: 0.55
10-YEAR COMPOUND EARNINGS PER SHARE GROWTH: 5.0 percent
10-YEAR COMPOUND DIVIDENDS PER SHARE GROWTH: 8.5 percent

	2002	2003	2004	2005	2006	2007	2008	2009
Revenues (Mil)	13,566	14,348	15,083	15,903	16,747	18,266	19,415	19,115
Net income (Mil)	1,748.5	1,716.7	1,800.2	1,803.7	1,844.5	1,861.6	1,698.0	1,884.0
Earnings per share	3.36	3.38	3.61	3.78	3.90	4.25	4.14	4.52
Dividends per share	1.20	1.36	1.60	1.80	1.96	2.08	2.27	2.38
Cash flow per share	4.81	4.91	5.39	5.74	6.10	6.34	5.98	6.40
Price: high	66.8	59.3	69.0	68.3	68.6	72.8	69.7	67.0
low	45.3	42.9	56.2	55.6	56.6	63.8	50.3	43.1

Kimberly-Clark
P.O. Box 619100
Dallas, TX 75261
(972) 281-1200
Website: *www.kimberly-clark.com*

GROWTH AND INCOME

Kraft Foods Inc.

Ticker symbol: KFT (NYSE) □ S&P rating: BBB □ Value Line financial strength rating: A+ □ Current yield: 3.8 percent

Company Profile

Kraft is the second largest food and beverage company in the world and the largest in the United States. Their products are manufactured in 168 different facilities in seventy countries and distributed in over 150 countries. Many of their brands are recognizable around the world, such as their nine "billion-dollar" brands: Kraft®, Jacobs®, LU®, Maxwell House®, Milka®, Nabisco®, Oreo®, Philadelphia®, and Oscar Mayer®.

The company operates in eight segments, with Europe and Developing Markets constituting 40 percent of revenue, and U.S. Beverages, U.S. Cheese, U.S. Convenient Meals, U.S. Grocery, U.S. Snacks, and Canada & North America Foodservice evenly dividing the remaining 60 percent.

In early 2010 the company sold off its frozen pizza brands DiGiorno and Tombstone, two manufacturing facilities and a number of other properties to Nestlé for $3.7 billion in order to raise cash for the $19.5 billion purchase of Cadbury Plc. The purchase of Cadbury, which was met with a great deal of pre-sale resistance in the U.K., progressed from friendly, to hostile, and then back to friendly after the purchase price was increased $2 billion. The purchase is expected to add approximately $12 billion to Kraft's 2010 revenues.

Financial Highlights, Fiscal Year 2009

Kraft's revenues fell 5 percent to $40.3 billion in 2009 due marginally to volume declines across most reporting segments, but primarily because of nearly $2 billion in unfavorable currency adjustments. Operating income was up due largely to broadly higher pricing and the absence of over $1 billion in restructuring costs in 2009 versus 2008. North American beverages were modestly profitable, but in general most businesses reported flat revenue and earnings growth (absent currency effects).

Financial comparisons by segment and geography will be complicated moving forward as significant consolidation of assets is expected as the Cadbury integration proceeds.

Reasons to Buy

Kraft now has eleven brands each with over $1 billion in sales and over seventy brands with over $100 million in sales. Over 80 percent of its revenue is generated by brands that hold the top market share position. These are powerful retailing positions, particularly in the prepared foods segment, where brand is pre-eminent (sometime more important than the actual taste, in our humble opinion). In any case, these top positions are key to getting preferred shelf positions and floor space at markets, so having the bulk of your revenue coming from the all-star team is a good position to be in.

The company has completed a five-year restructuring program designed to significantly reduce corporate cost structures and to locate the resources involved in product-line decisions closer to the markets served. The 1Q2009 net profits were up 10 percent over the year ago quarter, due primarily to reduced SG&A, so things seem to be working. Expect net margins to continue to recover through 2010.

The Cadbury purchase does a number of good things for Kraft. First, they now have access to the best snack-food distribution system in Europe. Kraft has been trying to increase its market penetration there for the better part of five years, and now they have the tools to do so. Second, cost savings from facility consolidations in the United States and Europe is expected to save $650 million in the first few years alone. Third, the Cadbury brand has enormous loyalty in Europe and has been making real headway in the United States. Kraft's market clout and distribution system here can only help. Finally, Cadbury's has been building its brand in developing markets, and Kraft has targeted developing markets as an area of strategic focus for growth.

Reasons for Caution

The Cadbury purchase and frozen pizza business sale have received some criticism from none other than Warren Buffett, who referred to the actions as "dumb moves." He was especially mystified by the pizza sell-off, wondering how a $280 million contributor to the bottom line could be sold for $2.7 billion (after taxes).

SECTOR: **Consumer Staples**
BETA COEFFICIENT: **0.65**
10-YEAR COMPOUND EARNINGS PER SHARE GROWTH: **5.5 percent**
5-YEAR COMPOUND DIVIDENDS PER SHARE GROWTH: **16.5 percent**

		2002	2003	2004	2005	2006	2007	2008	2009
Revenues (Mil)		29709	31010	32168	34113	34356	37241	42777	40386
Net income (Mil)		3505	3452	3205	3183	3203	2906	2844	3021
Earnings per share		2.02	2.00	1.87	1.88	1.94	1.82	1.88	2.03
Dividends per share		0.54	0.63	0.75	0.85	0.94	1.02	1.10	1.16
Cash flow per share		2.44	2.48	2.39	2.43	2.51	2.48	2.61	2.67
Price:	high	43.9	39.4	36.1	35.7	36.7	37.2	35	29.8
	low	32.5	26.3	29.5	27.9	27.4	30	24.8	20.8

Kraft Foods Inc.
Three Lakes Drive
Northfield, IL 60093
(847) 646-2000
Website: *www.kraft.com*

GROWTH AND INCOME

Lubrizol Corporation

Ticker symbol: LZ (NYSE) ❑ S&P rating: BBB ❑ Value Line financial strength rating: B+ ❑ Current yield: 1.7 percent

Company Profile

Lubrizol produces and supplies specialty chemicals and other materials that improve the quality and performance of its customers' products in the global transportation, industrial, and consumer markets. Typical applications include additives for engine oils, gasoline, and diesel fuel, machine lubricants, and additives for pharmaceuticals and specialty materials.

The company is geographically diverse, with global manufacturing, supply chain, technical, and commercial infrastructure. They operate production and/or laboratory facilities in twenty-seven countries, in key regions around the world. They derive about 48 percent of consolidated total revenues from North America, 28 percent from Europe, 18 percent from the Asia/Pacific and the Middle East regions, and 6 percent from Latin America. Lubrizol sells its products in more than 100 countries.

The company reports results from two segments—Lubrizol Additive and Lubrizol Advanced Materials. For 2008, the revenue split between the two was 70/30, respectively. Operating income, however,

was split 83/17. Versus FY 2007, revenue growth from Additives was 17 percent against only 1 percent growth from Advanced Materials.

The company's key strategic focus to achieve top line and earnings growth includes driving organic growth and product innovation, new products and new applications. The company will also focus on selective acquisitions either in specialty chemicals or industrial fluids, complementing Lubrizol's existing business lines.

Financial Highlights, Fiscal Year 2009

The company reported a top-line decline of 9 percent largely on reduced unit volume as a result of the global recession and customers reducing their normal inventory levels. There was a significant demand recovery in the second half, however.

Earnings rose an astounding 82 percent as a result of aggressive cost controls and a 17 percent decline in average material costs. COGS fell 21 percent versus the revenue decline of only 9 percent, driving the gross margin increase of 1,100 basis points to 33 percent.

As a result of the decreased volumes and inventory reduction initiatives cash flow increased significantly, rising nearly 50 percent to $10.09 per share.

Reasons to Buy

Somebody greased the skids at Lubrizol. Last year we said: "Given the challenges of 2008 and Lubrizol's response, we're confident that they are well-positioned for improved profitability over the next three to four years. In addition, the company has traditionally generated dividend yields in the low 3 percent range—although 2008's yield was only 2.5 percent, that should increase."

Boy, were we wrong. The yield actually went down. Way down, in fact, as the stock, which had been trading in the low $20s at the time we wrote the article recently traded above $97. We apologize to anyone who bought LZ hoping for yield improvements, but maybe you can live with a 300 percent gain on your investment.

Forgive us a bit of chest thumping—as someone once said: "You can't gloat when you lose." Besides, Lubrizol is far from out of gas. Even at its current price of $86, the stock is trading at only 9.8 times trailing earnings and in May 2010 the company turned in earnings of $2.35 for the quarter on revenue of $1.32 billion, both numbers well ahead of projections. The dramatic increase

in its operating margin freed up yet more cash, and the company repurchased 1.2 percent of its outstanding shares and raised the dividend 16 percent.

So far in 2010 the recovery from 2009 looks pretty remarkable, but we feel confident that sustained growth is in the cards, and other analysts agree. The consensus estimates for Lubrizol's top-line growth seems to be 12.5 percent annually for the next four to five years.

The specialty chemicals market has been abuzz recently with talk of consolidation, and in April Lubrizol confirmed that they have been in discussions with the German chemicals maker Cognis for a potential offer in the $4.1 billion range. BASF has also been rumored to have been in discussions with Cognis as well. If Lubrizol does not acquire Cognis they will certainly be on the lookout for other opportunities—Lubrizol has always had exceptional cash flow, but right now they're a well-oiled machine.

Reasons for Caution

There aren't a lot of bumps in the road that we can see. Additives are a moderate-growth segment, but are very profitable at the moment. This could change if oil prices spike up, but as long as material costs remain reasonable and Lubrizol is effectively hedged, the company's cost structure looks solid.

SECTOR: Materials
BETA COEFFICIENT: 1.15
10-YEAR COMPOUND EARNINGS PER SHARE GROWTH: 5.5 percent
10-YEAR COMPOUND DIVIDENDS PER SHARE GROWTH: 1.5 percent

	2002	2003	2004	2005	2006	2007	2008	2009
Revenues (Mil)	1,980	2,049	3,156	3,622	4,041	4,499	5,027	4,586
Net income (Mil)	126	91	139	189	106	283	281	521
Earnings per share	2.45	2.04	2.48	2.36	2.62	4.05	4.09	7.55
Dividends per share	1.04	1.04	1.04	1.04	1.04	1.16	1.23	1.24
Cash flow per share	4.32	3.71	4.36	5.17	5.45	6.52	6.75	10.09
Price: high	36.4	34.4	37.4	44.5	50.8	69.9	61.4	97.8
low	26.2	26.5	29.4	35.2	38	48.8	23.6	68.9

Lubrizol Corporation
29400 Lakeland Boulevard
Wickliffe, OH 44092–2298
(440) 347-1206
Website: *www.lubrizol.com*

AGGRESSIVE GROWTH

Marathon Oil Corporation

Ticker symbol: MRO (NYSE) □ S&P rating: BBB+ □ Value Line financial strength rating: A+ □ Current yield: 3.3 percent

Company Profile

Marathon Oil is a vertically integrated producer, refiner and marketer of petroleum and natural gas products. It sells crude to other refiners, but its primary revenue stream is through the sale of its refined petroleum products to resellers and to end consumers via company-owned retail locations.

Marathon operates in four segments: Exploration and Production, Oil Sands Mining, Refining, Marketing, and Transportation, and Integrated Gas. E&P is a worldwide producer and marketer of liquid hydrocarbons and natural gas. OSM mines, extracts and transports bitumen from deposits in Alberta, Canada and upgrades it to produce synthetic crude. RM&T refines, markets and transports petroleum products throughout the Midwest and southeastern regions of the United States. Finally, IG transports liquefied natural gas and methanol worldwide.

The company has exploration rights/interests in the United States, Angola, Norway, Indonesia, Equatorial Guinea, Libya, Canada, and the U.K. The bulk of their activities are in the Gulf Coast of the United States.

Marathon, via acquisition, holds a 20 percent outside-operated interest in the Athabasca Oils Sands Project in Alberta, Canada. Oil sands mining bears no resemblance to any of Marathon's other oil production processes. Oil sands operations more closely resemble a coal surface mine. Output from these operations is on the order of 30,000 barrels of synthetic crude per day, with significantly higher than normal refining costs.

Financial Highlights, Fiscal Year 2009

FY2009 proved to be a rocky road for most vertically integrated refiners, Marathon included. Revenues fell 32 percent primarily due to the lower average selling price of gasoline through the RM&T segment. The year-to-year decline in RM&T revenue alone was nearly $19 billion. Further declines were seen in revenue from the E&P segment, which had sharply lower realizations for liquid hydrocarbons, leading to a drop of $4.2 billion compared to FY2008. Revenues from OSM and IG were off as well, but their relative contributions were rather small in comparison.

On the bright side, the company's Volund field in Norway brought in its first oil ahead of schedule, and additional discoveries were made adjacent to this field. In addition, the Droshky deepwater development in the Gulf of Mexico is on schedule and under budget. In the RM&T segment, the company's Speedway SuperAmerica retail outlets reported improved comps with regards to gasoline volumes and merchandise revenues.

The company also divested of several properties, including E&P operations in Ireland and interests in offshore Gabon and offshore Angola.

Reasons to Buy

The Garyville, Louisiana refinery expansion is nearly complete and is expected to add 180,000 barrels per day refining capacity, making Garyville the fourth-largest refinery in the country. Other refiners have put plant expansions on the back burner recently, but only after they realized that they couldn't get their new equipment online prior to Garyville. Being first, Marathon was also able to utilize post-Katrina tax-exempt recovery bonds and financed $1 billion of the project with low-interest, thirty-year fixed loans.

The recent stabilization of oil prices has done Marathon a lot of good. Revenues for 2010 are expected to rebound nicely to 2007 levels, and earnings are expected to double year-to-year.

The company continues to be successful with its recent exploratory wells, finding developable assets in 96 percent of its holes in 2009 and over 86 percent in the past three years.

The company has good fuel flexibility at the retail level, with the ability to blend e10 ethanol-blended fuels throughout its network. Should oil prices spike again, Marathon can reformulate quickly and take advantage of what may well be a glut of ethanol on the market.

The Norwegian offshore is growing as a core area, with Marathon operating eight licenses and holding interests in over 600,000 gross acres.

Reasons for Caution

Cap-and-trade legislation appears to be dead for the time being (as of mid-2010), but may be resurrected as a cap-and-dividend policy, where credits are sold purely at auction. This will still be an additional expense for refiners, but utilities will bear most of the implementation burden. Also, the OSM business will likely be on hiatus until crude prices rise enough to provide profitable operations here.

SECTOR: Energy
BETA COEFFICIENT: 1.30
10-YEAR COMPOUND EARNINGS PER SHARE GROWTH: 20.5 percent
10-YEAR COMPOUND DIVIDENDS PER SHARE GROWTH: 8.50 percent

	2002	2003	2004	2005	2006	2007	2008	2009
Revenues (Mil)	27,470	36,678	45,135	58,596	59,917	59,389	72,128	48,456
Net income (Mil)	563	1,012	1,314	3,051	4,636	3,755	3,528	1,184
Earnings per share	0.91	1.63	1.94	4.22	6.42	5.43	4.95	1.67
Dividends per share	0.46	0.48	0.52	0.61	0.77	0.92	0.96	0.96
Cash flow per share	2.85	3.52	3.65	6.01	8.85	7.56	8.08	5.38
Price: high	15.1	16.8	21.3	36.3	49.4	67	63.2	33.1
low	9.4	9.9	15	17.8	30.2	41.5	19.3	27.6

Marathon Oil Corporation
5555 San Felipe Road
Houston, TX 77056
(713) 629-6600
Website: *www.marathon.com*

McCormick & Company, Inc.

Ticker symbol: MKC (NYSE) □ S&P rating: A- □ Value Line financial strength rating: A+ □ Current yield: 2.7 percent

Company Profile

McCormick manufactures, markets and distributes spices, herbs, seasonings, and flavors to the global food industry. They are the largest such supplier in the world. Customers range from retail outlets and food manufacturers to foodservice businesses.

Industrial customers include foodservice, food-processing businesses and retail outlets. This industrial segment was responsible for 42 percent of sales and 19 percent of operating profits. A majority of the top 100 food companies are MKC's customers.

McCormick's U.S. Consumer business (58 percent of sales and 81 percent of operating profits), its oldest and largest, manufactures consumer spices, herbs, extracts, proprietary seasoning blends, sauces, and marinades. They are sold under such brand names as McCormick®, Schilling®, Produce Partners®, Golden Dipt®, Old Bay® and Mojave®.

Many of the spices and herbs purchased by the company, such as black pepper, vanilla beans, cinnamon, herbs and seeds must be imported from countries such as India, Indonesia, Malaysia, Brazil and the Malagasy Republic. Other ingredients such as paprika, dehydrated vegetables, onion and garlic, and food ingredients other than spices and herbs originate in the United States.

The company was founded in 1889 and has approximately 7,500 full-time employees in facilities located around the world. Major sales, distribution and production facilities are located in North America and Europe. Additional facilities are based in Mexico, Central America, Australia, China, Singapore, Thailand and South Africa. In 2009, 41.9 percent of sales were outside the United States.

Financial Highlights, Fiscal Year 2009

In 2009 revenues rose 5 percent to $3.2 billion, driven largely by higher unit volumes and a favorable product mix, with the Lawry's acquisition accounting for another 2 percent of revenue gain. Unfavorable foreign exchange rates had a negative impact to sales amounting to 5 percent for the year. Earnings were up 17.2 percent to $300 million due to favorable product mix and operating cost reductions.

Cash from operations reached a record $416 million, of which $252 million was used to pay down debt from the 2008 Lawry's purchase and another $125 million was used to fund additional dividends. Dividends were increased 9 percent to $0.96/share.

The company achieved $42 million in incremental cost reductions in the last year of its five-year restructuring program. This was some 40 percent above their target, increasing operating margin by 220 basis points to a record 18 percent.

In 2009, excluding restructuring charges, the consumer business contributed 60 percent of sales and 82 percent of operating income and the industrial business contributed 40 percent of sales and 18 percent of operating income.

The company reiterated its intent to grow revenue through acquisitions at a targeted rate of 2 percent per year.

Reasons to Buy

McCormick's is about as "pure" a play as there is in this book. They make seasonings (spices/herbs/flavorings), a few specialty foods, and nothing else. They sell into three distinct markets but not much other than the packaging changes. Their revenues were moderately affected by the recession, but earnings growth was solid.

They're the largest branded producer of seasonings in North America, and they're also the largest private-label producer of seasonings in North America, giving them a substantial level of price protection. McCormick is not just a producer/supplier, however—they also create new seasoning products. In fact, every year since 2005, between 13 percent and 18 percent of their industrial business sales have come from new products launched in the preceding three years. Keeping up with changing tastes requires McCormick to produce that new, hot flavor and to come up with new and interesting flavors and blends of existing seasonings.

The company expects to see earnings growth of 4 to 6 percent for the foreseeable future. Of that, 2 to 3 percent is organic growth, 1 to 2 percent is from new products, and 1 to 3 percent is from acquisitions. The company generates sufficient cash flow to fund new product initiatives and has easy access to the capital markets for acquisitions. Recently, these numbers have proven to be very conservative, as per-share earnings are up nearly 50 percent since 2005, and another 16 percent is targeted through 2011.

McCormick's sales have increased every year for the past fifty years, and the company has paid a dividend every year since 1925. In 2009 they raised the dividend for the twenty-fourth consecutive year.

Reasons for Caution

There are no real reasons for caution, except that MKC is likely to grow only modestly except by acquisition. That said, the company is a solid performer and a solid defensive play.

SECTOR: Consumer Staples

BETA COEFFICIENT: .60

10-YEAR COMPOUND EARNINGS PER SHARE GROWTH: 12 percent

10-YEAR COMPOUND DIVIDENDS PER SHARE GROWTH: 10.5 percent

	2002	2003	2004	2005	2006	2007	2008	2009
Revenues (Mil)	2,045	2,270	2,526	2,592	2,716	2,916	3,177	3,192
Net income (Mil)	180	199	214	215	202	230	282	311
Earnings per share	1.29	1.4	1.52	1.56	1.72	1.92	2.14	2.35
Dividends per share	0.42	0.46	0.56	0.64	0.72	0.8	0.88	0.96
Cash flow per share	1.76	1.93	2.1	2.24	2.45	2.64	2.83	3.08
Price: high	27.3	30.2	38.9	39.1	39.8	39.7	42.1	36.8
low	20.7	21.7	28.6	29	30.1	33.9	28.2	28.1

McCormick & Company, Inc.

18 Loveton Circle

P. O. Box 6000

Sparks, MD 21152–6000

(410) 771-7244

Website: *www.mccormick.com*

McDonald's Corporation

Ticker symbol: MCD (NYSE) □ S&P rating: A □ Value Line financial strength rating: A++ □ Current yield: 3.5 percent

Company Profile

The company operates and franchises McDonald's restaurants. At 2009 year-end there were approximately 32,478 restaurants in 118 countries, over 26,000 of which were operated by franchisees and 6,200 were operated by the company. Franchisees pay for and own the equipment, signs, and interior of the businesses, and are required to reinvest in same from time to time. The company owns the land and building or secures leases for both company-operated and franchised restaurant sites.

Revenues to the company come in the form of sales from company-owned stores and rents, fees, royalties and other revenue streams from the franchisees. The company is primarily as a franchisor and has recently begun to sell off more of its company-owned stores, in the process realizing benefits to cash flow, reduced operational costs, and reduced exposure to commodities prices.

McDonald's completely dominates the fast food hamburger restaurant market segment with a 35 percent market share. Burger King and Wendy's are the next largest

competitors at 4 percent market share each. In the overall fast food segment, McDonald's is still the single biggest player with a 19 percent market share by revenue, followed by Doctor's Associates, Inc. (Subway) with a 10 percent share. The company spent approximately $2 billion in 2009 to open 868 new restaurants and refurbish 1,850 locations.

The company generates about 64 percent of its revenue outside the United States. Revenue growth in 2009 was strongest in Europe (where the Quarter-Pounder's called a Royale with Cheese) with 5.2 percent growth. APMEA (Asia Pacific, Middle East, and Asia) was next with growth of 3.4 percent year/year, while the United States was trailing the pack with 2.6 percent growth year/year.

Financial Highlights, Fiscal Year 2009

McDonald's posted reduced revenues of $22.7 billion in 2009, off 3.2 percent versus 2008. Despite the decline, improved margins, strong comps and currency movements led to an 18 percent increase in earnings year-over-year. The company is continuing to refranchise existing locations, totaling 1,100 restaurants in 2008 and 2009. Rents and royalty incomes are a low cost and very stable revenue stream with low capital requirements, and we expect this refranchising trend to continue even as McDonald's opens new locations.

The company sold off its interests in Redbox, a movie-rental kiosk business. The company has also closed the books on all of its non-McDonald's restaurant businesses including (most recently) Pret-a-Manger and Boston Market.

Reasons to Buy

In the early part of the decade McDonald's had been adding mainly company-owned stores in an effort to boost revenues, but profitability suffered. In 2003, McDonald's initiated a new strategy that called for increasing sales at its existing stores by expanding menu options, expanding store hours and renovating stores. They also began franchising a higher percentage of its stores, driving revenue with reduced capital expense. The strategy has paid off handsomely—revenues have grown by 35 percent, which would be impressive on its own, but net margin is up 930 basis points and net income is up nearly 150 percent over the same period. As a result, share price is up 450 percent from its 2003 lows.

McDonald's is growing rapidly in China, where in 2008 they opened their 1,000th store. Local menus continue to evolve, and the convenience that fast food provides is highly valued.

McDonalds' menu additions are proving very popular, and consumers are welcoming the novelty of the newer menu items like McCafe, brewed teas, and expanded salad selections.

As the global economy regains momentum, higher levels of discretionary spending can be expected in emerging economies, where McDonald's is targeting high growth. Over the next three years, the company plans to open 600 new restaurants in China.

Reasons for Caution

Concerns over childhood obesity have drawn attention to dietary factors, and fast-food restaurants will likely be central to most conversations on the topic. Some states are requiring the posting of signs with caloric content next to item price, but it's not clear that this will lead to a decline in sales in the near term.

SECTOR: Restaurants
BETA COEFFICIENT: 0.65
10-YEAR COMPOUND EARNINGS PER SHARE GROWTH: 9.5 percent
10-YEAR COMPOUND DIVIDENDS PER SHARE GROWTH: 24.0 percent

	2002	2003	2004	2005	2006	2007	2008	2009
Revenues (Mil)	15,406	17,141	19,065	20,460	21,586	22,787	23,522	22,745
Net income (Mil)	1,692	1,831	2,358	2,509	2,873	3,522	4,201	4,451
Earnings per share	1.32	1.43	1.93	1.97	2.3	2.91	3.67	4.11
Dividends per share	0.24	0.4	0.55	0.67	1	1.5	1.63	2.05
Cash flow per share	2.16	2.36	2.88	2.98	3.43	4.06	4.85	5.2
Price: high	30.7	27	33	35.7	44.7	63.7	67	64.8
low	125	12.1	24.5	27.4	31.7	42.3	45.8	50.4

McDonald's Corporation
One McDonald's Plaza
Oak Brook, IL 60523
(630) 623-3000
Website: *www.mcdonalds.com*

Medtronic, Inc

Ticker symbol: MDT (NYSE) □ S&P rating: AA- □ Value Line financial strength rating: A++ □
Current yield: 2.1 percent

Company Profile

Medtronic is the world's largest manufacturer of implantable medical devices and is a leading medical technology company, providing lifelong solutions for people with chronic diseases. Key businesses include:

- Medtronic Cardiac Rhythm Management develops products that restore and regulate a patient's heart rhythm, as well as improve the heart's pumping function. MCRM markets implantable pacemakers, defibrillators, monitoring and diagnostic devices, and cardiac resynchronization devices, including the first implantable device for the treatment of heart failure.
- Medtronic Cardiac Surgery develops products that are used in both arrested and beating heart bypass surgery. MCS also markets the industry's broadest line of heart valve products for both replacement and repair, plus autotransfusion equipment and disposable devices for handling and monitoring blood during major surgery.

- Medtronic Vascular develops products and therapies that treat a wide range of vascular diseases and conditions. These products include coronary, peripheral and neuro-vascular stents, stent graph systems for diseases and conditions throughout the aorta, and distal protection systems.
- Medtronic Neurological and Diabetes offers therapies for movement disorders, chronic pain, and diabetes. It also offers diagnostics and therapeutics for urological and gastrointestinal conditions, including incontinence, benign prostatic hyperplasia (BPH), enlarged prostate and gastroesophageal reflux disease (GERD).
- Medtronic Spinal develops and manufactures products that treat a variety of disorders of the cranium and spine, including traumatically induced conditions, deformities, and tumors.

Financial Highlights, Fiscal Year 2010 (FY10 ends April 30, 2010)

Medtronic's revenues grew 8 percent year/year to $14.6 billion, while non-GAAP (our standard for this company) earnings rose 9 percent to $3.58 billion. Per-share earnings grew 10 percent.

Fourth quarter revenues broke $4 billion, a first for Medtronic. The final number, $4.2 billion, represents a 10 percent increase over 4Q2009 revenues. Earnings for the quarter were $986 million, up 8 percent over the prior year.

International revenue grew 15 percent for the year, representing 41 percent of the company's total revenue. International's fourth quarter revenue grew 20 percent over 4Q2009.

Dividends were increased 34 percent to $.85/share, and the company bought back 25 million shares of stock, or approximately 2.3 percent of the outstanding shares.

Reasons to Buy

Medtronic has a dominant market share in three of its seven core lines (ICD, Diabetes, and Neurological), and all seven core business grew revenue and earnings in 2010. Four of the seven turned in double-digit revenue growth. These results are comparable to those turned in last year—if the recession has affected Medtronic's top line at all it hasn't been enough to keep revenues, earnings, cash flow and margins from continuing to march up and to the right.

The company balance sheet strengthened considerably in FY2010, with cash, cash equivalents and short-term investments growing 125 percent to $3.78 billion, while cash flow from operations grew 6.5 percent to $4.13 billion. Medtronic requires significant capital for product development and acquisitions, and this money will not be sitting around for very long.

Medtronic is a pioneer in an emerging field of medicine: restoration of normal brain function and chemistry to millions of patients with central nervous system disorders. The company's DBS (Deep Brain Stimulation) systems treat disorders by modulating the nervous system with electrical stimulation, chemicals, and biological agents delivered in precise amounts to specific sites in the brain and spinal cord. This system has been used successfully to treat the most severe symptoms of conditions such as Parkinson's disease, and in March of 2010 Medtronic received FDA approval for techniques employing DBS devices for treatment of epilepsy.

Reasons for Caution

Medtronic hasn't traded over $60 per share in over eight years, despite consistently strong margins, improving EPS, and very healthy cash flow. The current CEO explains it by saying the company has simply had poor communication with Wall

Street, overpromising and under-delivering on results. As a result, some feel the current guidance from the company for 5 to 8 percent growth over the next few years may be a lowball figure.

SECTOR: **Health Care**
BETA COEFFICIENT: **.75**
10-YEAR COMPOUND EARNINGS PER SHARE GROWTH: **15.0 percent**
10-YEAR COMPOUND DIVIDENDS PER SHARE GROWTH: **16.5 percent**

	2003	2004	2005	2006	2007	2008	2009	2010
Revenues (Mil)	7,665	9,087	10,055	11,292	12,299	13,515	14,599	15,817
Net income (Mil)	1,600	1,959	2,270	2,687	2,798	2,984	3,282	3,577
Earnings per share	1.3	1.63	1.86	2.21	2.41	2.61	2.92	3.22
Dividends per share	0.25	0.28	0.31	0.36	0.41	0.47	0.63	0.85
Cash flow per share	1.75	2.02	2.26	2.8	2.96	3.22	3.45	3.85
Price: high	49.7	52.9	53.7	58.9	59.9	58	57	44.9
low	32.5	42.2	44	48.7	42.4	44.9	28.3	24.1

Medtronic, Inc
710 Medtronic Parkway N. E.
Minneapolis, MN 55432–5604
(763) 505-2692
Website: *www.medtronic.com*

Monsanto Company

Ticker symbol: MON (NYSE) □ S&P Rating: A+ □ Value Line financial strength rating: A □ Current yield: 1.4 percent

Company Profile

Monsanto was once a major chemical company with a broad pedigree ranging from saccharine to sulfuric acid to Agent Orange and DDT. Monsanto was absorbed into Pharmacia Upjohn in 2000, which kept its pharmaceutical products and spun off the agricultural products business into a "new" Monsanto in 2002. Today's Monsanto provides a set of leading-edge, technology-based agricultural products for use in farming in the United States and overseas. The company has two primary business segments: Seeds and Genomics and Agricultural Productivity.

The Seeds and Genomics segment produces seeds for a host of crops, most importantly corn and soybeans but also canola, cotton and a variety of vegetable and fruit seeds. Most of the seed products are bioengineered to provide greater yields and to be more resistant to insects and weeds. Familiar to many consumers, especially those who travel in the Midwest, is the DeKalb seed brand, but there are many others.

The Agricultural Productivity segment offers glyphosate-based herbicides, popularly known and sold under the Roundup brand, for agricultural, industrial, and residential lawn and garden applications. Beyond this market-leading product, the division also offers other selective herbicides for control of pre-emergent annual grass and small seeded broadleaf weeds in corn and other crops. The company owns many of the major brands in both seed and herbicide markets.

The company also partners with other agricultural and chemical companies like Cargill, BASF and Biotechnology, Inc. to develop other high-tech agricultural and food processing solutions.

Financial Highlights, Calendar Year 2009 (Fiscal Year ends August 31)

Weakening demand in many of its markets slowed Monsanto's pace somewhat during the global economic downturn. Still, the company saw modest increases in sales, from which it managed to generate an immodest 29.2 percent increase in earnings. It's good to be the king.

Cash flow generation continues to be very strong. Working capital was up 32 percent in 2009 versus 2008. Free cash flow totaled $1.5 billion, a 96 percent increase over 2008, which the company plans to use primarily for increased R&D spending and share repurchase.

Net sales of Roundup and other glyphosate-based products fell 14 percent in a dynamic herbicide market. The growth of generic products put both volume and pricing pressure on Monsanto's flagship product. The company has stated that for the foreseeable future the bulk of its earnings growth will come from the Seed and Genomics business.

Reasons to Buy

In 2005, court decisions in the United States and Canada confirmed Monsanto's claim to ownership of the genetic content of its seed products. Since then, Monsanto's profits are up 333 percent on a revenue increase of 86 percent. There have been further legal challenges in the meantime, but none have significantly eroded the protections afforded to what is essentially the company's intellectual property. With nearly a dozen more bioengineered product lines in the pipeline, Monsanto looks to be well positioned for continued earnings growth.

The company projects a CAGR in earnings of 17 to 19 percent through 2012, based mainly on increased revenues from seeds and

traits (genomic data licensed to other firms). As Value Line puts it, Monsanto ". . . appears to have engineered a 'recession-resistant' model." The company will fare well as bioengineered seed becomes more ubiquitous, particularly in the emerging international markets.

Financial performance, especially in the past four years, is rock solid. The share price, however, has remained essentially flat since the beginning of the global recession while earnings have soared, and the stock is trading at its lowest multiple in seven years. If there's any stock that's a bargain at $78/share, it might be Monsanto.

Reasons for Caution

The company has leadership and a strong lock on key markets, providing substantial pricing power and margin performance. But even the best-engineered companies can't grow forever. Patents have expired and competition for Roundup is starting to hit the market; the company is adjusting by offering new packaging and delivery methods for the products and by strengthening its offerings in the biotech and seed businesses. Still, the company's success has drawn some fire from the farming community for anti-competitive practices, and will certainly draw competition, which could cause performance to deteriorate.

SECTOR: **Industrials**
BETA COEFFICIENT: **1.10**
5-YEAR COMPOUND EARNINGS PER SHARE GROWTH: **30.0 percent**
5-YEAR COMPOUND DIVIDENDS PER SHARE GROWTH: **19 percent**

	2002	2003	2004	2005	2006	2007	2008	2009
Revenues (Mil)	4,673	4,936	5,457	6,294	7,344	8,563	11,365	11,724
Net income (Mil)	313	334	434	565.7	722.1	1.027	1,895	2,448
Earnings per share	0.6	0.64	0.61	1.05	1.31	1.98	3.39	4.41
Dividends per share	0.24	0.24	0.28	0.34	0.34	0.55	0.83	1.01
Cash flow per share	1.48	1.5	1.73	2.06	2.28	2.85	4.5	5.49
Price: high	17	14.5	28.2	39.9	53.5	116.3	145.8	93.4
low	6.6	6.8	14	25	37.9	49.1	63.5	66.6

Monsanto Company
800 North Lindbergh Boulevard
St Louis, MO 63167
Phone: (314) 694-1000
Website: *www.monsanto.com*

NetApp, Inc.

Ticker symbol: NTAP (NASDAQ) ❑ S&P rating: NR ❑ Value Line financial strength rating: B++ ❑
Current yield: nil

Company Profile

NetApp, Inc. provides storage and data management solutions designed to reduce the cost of managing and protecting data while at the same time increasing its availability. The company designs and produces systems, software and services that implement secure backup, archival, and online storage and retrieval of business-critical data across a number of platforms.

NetApp's products are designed for large, network-leveraged installations and, as such, the company works with key partners such as Cisco, IBM, Microsoft, SAP and VMware to develop integrated solutions that optimize final system performance for their applications and infrastructure.

The company's primary solutions are based on an ethernet network attached storage (NAS) technology that fits very well in mid-sized businesses, but most very large companies are invested in "enterprise-class" configurations that use an older technology, SAN (storage area networks), that connect using fiber channel, rather than ethernet. The SAN market is dominated by one of NetApp's competitors, EMC,

however, NetApp claims its software tools allow users to integrate NAS and SAN installations and manage them as one space.

The company was incorporated in 1992 and now has more than 8,300 employees in 130 locations around the world.

Financial Highlights, Fiscal Year 2010 (FY2010 ended April 30, 2010)

Revenues for FY2010 were $3.9 billion, up 15 percent, from FY2009. Improved revenue performance in fiscal 2010 was the result of improvements in product, software entitlements and maintenance and service revenues (revenues in fiscal 2009 were negatively impacted by a $128.7 million settlement with the General Services Administration).

Gross profit margins rose during fiscal 2010, due largely to reductions in product materials cost, partially offset by a decrease in the overall average selling prices of NetApp's products and disadvantageous product mix. Gross margin in FY2009 was also negatively impacted by the GSA settlement.

During FY2010, sales and marketing, research and development, and general and administrative expenses totaled $2.1 billion, up 10 percent from FY2009, reflecting the impact of an increase in incentive compensation and commissions expense related to the stronger sales and operating profit performance. During the year the company entered into a merger agreement with Data Domain, Inc., which was subsequently terminated. In accordance with the agreement, the company received a $57 million termination fee, which, after deducting $15.9 million of incremental costs incurred relating to the transaction, resulted in net proceeds of $41.1 million.

Earnings for FY2010 came in at $400 million, up 101 percent over FY2009 (excluding the effects of the GSA settlement), and up 32 percent over FY2008. Significant improvements in COGS accounts for the bulk of the increase.

Reasons to Buy

As the company has grown, its revenue stream has shifted toward higher-margin software licenses, maintenance, and services and away from the lower-margin system products, which include hardware. It's not clear that this trend is sustainable in the long term, but the company maintains healthy margins regardless of product mix.

The trend toward virtualization of data centers plays right into the strength of NetApp's product lineup, as most of their solutions rely on the integration of local and middle storage into an ethernet-based infrastructure. Their Data OnTap product is an operating system designed to scale storage platforms up to 14 petabytes (14 million gigabytes) and still treat them as one device.

In April 2010, NetApp announced the acquisition of Bycast, a private developer of object-based storage software that manages petabyte-scale, globally distributed repositories of images, video and records for enterprises. The company services about 250 enterprises worldwide. Its software is specialized for improving efficiency and reducing the administrative burden of moving and storing huge volumes across multiple geographies. This is a very nice fit into the top tier of NetApp's existing software product hierarchy, and employs technology that will be very helpful in a solution that would, for instance, store, archive and automate the retrieval of digitized patient medical records (where have we heard about that project?) or provide on-demand access for video content.

Reasons for Caution

NetApp is up against some very large, very clever competitors with enormous resources. HP, Dell, EMC, and others all play in and around this space and are capable at any time of deciding to become a far more significant presence.

SECTOR: Technology
BETA COEFFICIENT: 1.15
10-YEAR COMPOUND EARNINGS PER SHARE GROWTH: 24.0 percent
10-YEAR COMPOUND DIVIDENDS PER SHARE GROWTH: Nil

	2003	2004	2005	2006	2007	2008	2009	2010
Revenues (Mil)	892	1,170	1,598	2,067	2,804	3,303	3,406	3,850
Net income (Mil)	83.8	146	238	315	298	310	87	375
Earnings per share	0.24	0.40	0.62	0.81	0.77	0.86	0.26	1.05
Dividends per share	-	-	-	-	-	-	-	-
Cash flow per share	0.40	0.56	0.83	1.06	1.11	1.33	0.77	1.55
Price: high	28.0	26.7	35.0	35.0	41.6	40.9	27.5	35.0
low	5.2	9.3	15.9	22.5	25.8	22.5	10.4	12.4

NetApp, Inc.
495 E. Java Drive
Sunnyvale, CA 94089
(408) 822-6000
Website: *www.netapp.com*

NIKE, Inc.

Ticker symbol: NKE (NYSE) ❑ S&P rating: NR ❑ Value Line financial strength rating: A+ ❑ Current yield: 1.5 percent

Company Profile

NIKE's principal business activity is the design, development and worldwide marketing of footwear, apparel, equipment, and accessory products. NIKE is the largest seller of athletic footwear and athletic apparel in the world. Their products are sold to retail accounts, through NIKE-owned retail outlets, and through a mix of independent distributors and licensees in over 180 countries around the world.

NIKE does no manufacturing—virtually all of their footwear and apparel are manufactured by independent contractors outside the United States, while equipment products are produced both in the United States and abroad.

NIKE's shoes are designed primarily for athletic use, although a large percentage of these products are worn for casual or leisure purposes. Their shoes are designed for men, women and children for running, training, basketball, and soccer use, although they also carry brands for casual wear.

NIKE sells apparel and accessories for most of the sports addressed by their shoe lines, as well as athletic bags and accessory items. NIKE apparel and accessories are designed to complement their athletic footwear products, feature the same trademarks and are sold through the same marketing and distribution channels.

NIKE has a number of wholly owned subsidiaries, including Cole Haan, Converse, Hurley and Umbro, which variously design, distribute, and license dress, athletic and casual footwear, sports apparel, and accessories. In FY2009, these subsidiary brands, together with NIKE Golf accounted for approximately 43 percent of total revenues.

The company has more than 23,000 retail accounts in the United States. The company makes substantial use of a "futures" ordering program, which allows retailers to order five to six months in advance of delivery with the commitment that their orders will be delivered within a set time period at a fixed price. In FY2009, 87 percent of their U.S. wholesale footwear shipments of NIKE-branded products were made under the futures program.

Financial Highlights, Fiscal Year 2009

NIKE's sales grew just 3 percent in FY2009, with slightly decreased revenue across all product lines except NIKE brand footwear, which was up 6 percent. The highest volume regions, United States and Europe, the Middle East, and Asia, combined for flat earnings growth across all product lines. The Asia Pacific and Americas regions, however, grew revenues 15 percent and 10 percent, respectively, including a 9 percent negative impact due to unfavorable currency exchange rates in the Americas. Earnings growth for the two regions was even stronger, at 23 percent and 13 percent respectively.

Sales performance in mainland China remains encouraging, with 2009 showing a 22 percent revenue growth over an already strong 2008. Gross margins are improving year-to-year, and marketing expenses are growing at a lower rate than revenue.

Reasons to Buy

Why buy NIKE? In a word, margins. NIKE makes more from every unit of revenue than any of its competitors. With net profit averaging 9 percent over the last five years, NIKE earns at four times the rate of Adidas, its next closest competitor in terms of size, and twice the rate of its closest competitor in terms of profitability, Puma. They're the clear leader in their industry and extend their lead every year.

More impressive to us than NIKE's performance against its competition, though, was last year's performance against the worldwide economic trend. In what was probably the worst consumer discretionary spending environment in the last twenty years, NIKE continued to grow organic sales and held margins and earnings at their industry-leading levels. In last year's edition we warned against the possibility of a moderate downturn for NIKE's numbers, but they aligned their operations to the bottom line, took some restructuring charges and have come through the recession with a somewhat leaner organization and in even better shape against their competition.

Over the past two years, the AP and Americas regions have grown revenue 41 percent and 30 percent, respectively. Many of these are emerging markets (including mainland China) where margins are not quite as high, but the power of NIKE's brand marketing is clearly evident, and the numbers bode well for continued earnings growth and firmer margins.

We think we just talked ourselves into buying some shoes.

Reasons for Caution

NIKE's fiscal year ends on May 31, so we can expect to see some continued recessionary effects in the 2010 results. The first half of 2010, however, has been very strong in terms of earnings.

SECTOR: **Consumer Discretionary**
BETA COEFFICIENT: **0.85**
10-YEAR COMPOUND EARNINGS PER SHARE GROWTH: **12.5 percent**
10-YEAR COMPOUND DIVIDENDS PER SHARE GROWTH: **15 percent**

	2002	2003	2004	2005	2006	2007	2008	2009
Revenues (Mil)	9893	10697	12253	13740	14955	16326	18627	19,176
Net income (Mil)	668	749	945	1212	1392	1458	1734	1,727
Earnings per share	1.23	1.39	1.76	2.25	2.63	2.86	3.44	3.52
Dividends per share	0.24	0.27	0.37	0.48	0.59	0.71	0.88	0.98
Cash flow per share	1.78	1.9	2.37	2.64	3.2	3.43	4.15	4.25
Price: high	32.1	34.3	46.2	45.8	50.6	67.9	70.6	66.6
low	19.3	21.2	32.9	37.6	37.8	47.5	42.7	38.2

NIKE, Inc.
One Bowerman Drive
Beaverton, OR 97005
(503) 671-6453
Website: *www.nikebiz.com*

CONSERVATIVE GROWTH

Norfolk Southern

Ticker symbol: NSC (NYSE) ❑ S&P rating: BBB+ ❑ Value Line financial strength rating: B+ ❑
Current yield: 2.7 percent

Company Profile

Norfolk Southern Corp. was formed in 1982 as a holding company when the Norfolk & Western Railway merged with the Southern Railway. Including lines received in the split takeover (with CSX) of Conrail, the current railroad operates 21,000 route-miles of track in twenty-two eastern and southern states. They serve every major port on the east coast of the United States and have the most extensive intermodal network in the East.

Company business is about 29 percent coal, 19 percent intermodal, 12 percent agricultural and consumer products, 12 percent metals and construction, and 38 percent other. Within those categories, the railroad transports the usual mix of raw materials, intermediate products like parts, and manufactured goods. The company has been an innovator in the intermodal business, that is, combining trucking and rail services—the "Roadrailer," a train of coupled-together highway vans on special wheelsets is an example; at the terminal, a cab simply backs up to the van and drives it off.

The company provides a number of logistics services and has substantial traffic to and from ports and overseas destinations.

Financial Highlights, Fiscal Year 2008

Norfolk's 2009 was a tale of two halves, with the first half bringing a full load of bad news and ever-worsening prospects, but the second half providing some relief and signs that the worst had passed. Regardless, 2009 was the worst year for NSC in quite some time. NSC logged only 159 billion revenue ton-miles traveled, some 20 percent under the average of the prior five years. Revenue per ton-mile was off 8 percent compared to 2008, but was moderately higher than the four years prior. In the end, revenue was off 25 percent versus 2008 and earnings from operations fell 40 percent (36 percent from operations, 4 percent from reduction in fuel surcharges).

There were few bright spots, as volumes were down in all of the business groups. The domestic intermodal segment did "well," nearly equaling its 2008 results, but did far better than the conventional domestic trucking industry as a whole, where volumes were down some 18 percent over the same period. Ethanol revenues were flat overall on higher per-mile charges and reduced volumes.

NSC has announced a projected decline in 2009 revenues due to the weak economy and decreased fuel surcharges. What remains to be seen are how long this will last and whether costs can be controlled; lower fuel prices put at least some wind behind their back.

Reasons to Buy

NSC's results for the first quarter 2010 continue the momentum established in the second half of 2009—revenues and earnings each are up 45 percent against 1Q2009. In addition, first quarter volumes are up versus 4Q2009, which is a rare reversal in the seasonal nature of the rail business. Its operating ratio, generally highest in the first quarter, fell 510 basis points year-over-year to 75.2 percent. Volumes were up across the board in a very strong quarter. Year-over-year projections are for a 7 percent increase in revenues and a 20 percent increase in earnings.

NSC's 2009 operating ratio of 75.4 percent (the ratio of variable or operating costs to revenue, up some 4 percent over 2008), still

one of the best in the industry and better than the best-ever 76 percent posted by our second favorite rival Union Pacific. This railroad has done an excellent job containing costs and sizing its physical plant for its demand.

NSC has proven over the last thirty years that they can compete effectively for long-haul truck business with their intermodal offerings, and have some of the most competitive service and terminal structures in the business. They have gained market share from trucks. Additionally, NSC serves some of the more dynamic and up-and-coming manufacturing markets in the United States, namely, Asian and other foreign-owned manufacturing facilities found particularly in the Southeast. Toyota recently gave NSC its highest award for overall logistics excellence, its seventh such award since 1996.

Reasons for Caution

While domestic intermodal is doing well, international freight is still down and is likely to remain so for some time, as it depends heavily on shipments from mainland China, specifically consumer goods. Growth in this segment is likely to lag behind the rest of the company so long as unemployment and low consumer confidence hold spending down.

SECTOR: Transportation
BETA COEFFICIENT: 0.99
10-YEAR COMPOUND EARNINGS PER SHARE GROWTH: 10.0 percent
10-YEAR COMPOUND DIVIDENDS PER SHARE GROWTH: 4.0 percent

		2002	2003	2004	2005	2006	2007	2008	2009
Revenues (Mil)		6,270	6,468	7,312	8527	9407	9,432	10,661	8
Net income (Mil)		460	529	870	1,161	1,481	1,464	1,716	1,034
Earnings per share		1.18	1.35	2.18	2.82	3.58	3.68	4.52	2.76
Dividends per share		0.26	0.3	0.36	0.48	0.68	0.96	1.22	1.36
Cash flow per share		2.51	2.66	3.67	4.72	5.58	5.9	6.88	5.07
Price:	high	27	24.6	36.7	45.8	57.7	59.6	75.5	54.8
	low	17.3	20.4	29.6	39.1	45.4	41.4	26.7	46.2

Norfolk Southern
Three Commercial Place
Norfolk, VA 23510-2191
Phone: (757) 629-2680
Website: *www.nscorp.com*

Northern Trust Corporation

Ticker symbol: NTRS (NASDAQ) ❑ S&P rating: AA− ❑ Value Line financial strength rating: B++ ❑ Current yield: 2.0 percent

Company Profile

Northern Trust Corporation, founded in 1889, is a multi-bank holding company headquartered in Chicago that provides personal wealth management and financial services and corporate and institutional services through the corporation's principal subsidiary (The Northern Trust Company) and other bank subsidiaries. The corporation has seventy-nine offices located in eighteen of the more populous states. As of March 31, 2010, Northern Trust Corporation had approximately $76 billion in banking assets, more than $647 billion in assets under management and $3.7 trillion in assets under custody.

Global offices are situated in Amsterdam, Bangalore, Beijing, Dublin, Hong Kong, Limerick, London, Singapore, Tokyo, and Toronto. The corporation also owns two investment management subsidiaries, Northern Trust Investments, N.A. and Northern Trust Global Advisors, Inc.

Northern Trust Corporation organizes client services around two principal business units: Personal Financial Services (PFS) and Corporate and Institutional Services

(C&IS). Northern Trust Global Investments (NTGI) provides investment products and services to clients of both PFS and C&IS.

Personal Financial Services offers personal trust, estate administration, private banking, residential real estate mortgage lending, securities brokerage, and investment management services to individuals, families and small businesses. PFS operates through a network of eighty-four offices in the eighteen states where Northern Trust operates. Approximately 25 percent of the wealthiest American families employ NTRS for asset management or administration.

Corporate and Institutional Services is a leading provider of trust, global custody, investment, retirement, commercial banking, and treasury management services worldwide. They provide asset management services to large corporations and institutions such as foundations, public retirement funds, insurance companies, and endowments. Other services include benefit payments, portfolio analysis, and electronic funds transfer.

Northern Trust's institutional clients reside in over forty countries and include corporations, public retirement funds, foundations, endowments, governmental entities, and financial institutions.

Financial Highlights, Fiscal Year 2009

In FY2009, Northern Trust saw revenues decline 12 percent to $3.83 billion due mainly to continued low interest rates, reduced foreign exchange trading income, and narrow spreads. Net income grew 9 percent to $864 million, however, primarily as a result of the absence of 2008's client support charges. Per-share earnings fell $.47 from preferred stock dividends and discount accretion in connection with the NTRS's participation in the U.S. Treasury's Capital Purchase Program. This earnings decline was predicted in our cautions last year; its impact is limited to 2009, however.

The company raised additional capital with a stock issue that netted $334 million and another $500 million through the sale of senior notes.

Reasons to Buy

Northern Trust generates the majority of its revenues from fee-based services to its clients. Most fees are based on asset value, so as deposits go up, or as asset valuations increase, Northern Trust's revenue increases. NTRS is thus motivated to grow conservatively and protect capital investment at all costs.

NTRS's clients concerns, and thus NTRS asset management strategy, is focused on capital preservation. NTRS's investment strategy is very conservative and their leverage is the lowest among all their competitors. Their capital ratio of 13.4 percent is more than double the ratio required for the highest regulatory classification of "well capitalized." Given our banking system's recent experience with capitalization ratios, this is comforting.

NTRS is one of only two large banks that did not suspend or alter their dividend in 2009.

NTRS credit quality is one of the very best in the banking industry. Nonperforming assets represent less than 1.2 percent of their year-end loan portfolio, as compared to the 3.95 percent average of the top twenty U.S. banks. Also, over 90 percent of their balance sheet investment portfolio is made up of U.S. Treasuries, government-sponsored agency and triple-A rated securities. NTRS does not underwrite mortgage loans to subprime borrowers, nor do they lend directly to hedge funds. They are not in the investment banking or credit card business. Their conservative approach to asset management has allowed them to ride out the housing crisis, credit crunch, and general economic downturn relatively unscathed.

Reasons for Caution

It appears that interest rates will remain at historically low levels for the foreseeable future, which will continue to act as a drag on NTRS's Treasury-heavy portfolios.

SECTOR: **Financials**
BETA COEFFICIENT: **1.10**
10-YEAR COMPOUND EARNINGS PER SHARE GROWTH: **9.5 percent**
10-YEAR COMPOUND DIVIDENDS PER SHARE GROWTH: **10.5 percent**

		2002	2003	2004	2005	2006	2007	2008	2009
Assets (Mil)		39,478	41,450	45,277	53,414	60,712	67,611	82,054	77,324
Net income (Mil)		447	418	506	584	665	727	782	864
Earnings per share		1.97	1.95	2.33	2.64	3	3.24	3.47	3.16
Dividends per share		0.68	0.68	0.76	0.84	0.94	1.03	1.12	1.12
Loans ($Mil)		16,627	16,437	16,590	18,649	22,469	25,192	30,526	27,497
Price:	high	62.7	48.8	51.3	55	61.4	83.2	88.9	66.1
	low	30.4	27.6	38.4	41.6	49.1	56.5	33.9	43.3

Northern Trust Corporation
50 South La Salle Street
Chicago, IL 60675
(312) 444-4281
Website: *www.northerntrust.com*

Nucor Corporation

Ticker symbol: (NYSE) ❏ S&P rating: A ❏ Value Line financial strength rating: A+ ❏ Current yield: 3.3 percent

Company Profile

Nucor is the fourth-largest global steel producer (by market cap) and the largest U.S.-based producer. They are also the largest recycler in North America. Their production model is unique, based on numerous mini-mills and the exclusive use of scrap material as production input. Nucor operates scrap-based steel mills in twenty-two facilities, producing bar, sheet, structural and plate steel product. Production in 2008 totaled 20.4 million tons.

Nucor's steel mills are among the most modern and efficient in the United States. Recycled scrap steel and other metals are melted in electric arc furnaces and poured into continuous casting systems. Sophisticated rolling mills convert the various types of raw cast material into rebar and basic shapes such as angles, rounds, channels, flats, sheet, beams, plate, and other products.

The company operates in five primary segments:

1. Reinforcing Products—Harris Steel fabricates rebar for large infrastructure projects and the commercial construction markets.

2. Steel Mesh, Grating and Fastener—Nucor manufactures wire products, grating, and industrial bolts for construction, automotive, machine tools, agriculture, and military applications.

3. Vulcraft and Verco—The nation's largest producers of open-web steel joists, joist girders and steel deck, used primarily for non-residential building construction.

4. Buildings Group and Light Gauge Steel Framing—Nucor manufactures custom-engineered and standard metal buildings and components for the commercial, residential and institutional construction markets.

5. Cold Finish—Nucor is North America's largest producer of cosmetic cold finish products for a range of industrial markets, including the automotive, agricultural, appliance and motor industries.

Financial Highlights, Fiscal Year 2009

Ouch. In 2009, Nucor posted a net loss of $293.6 million ($0.94 per share), compared with record net earnings of $1.83 billion ($5.98 per share), in 2008. Net sales fell

53 percent to $11.2 billion from a record $23.7 billion in 2008. Cash flow from operations for 2009 fell 53 percent to $1.2 billion from a record $2.5 billion in 2008. Cash and short-term investments at the end of 2009 were $2.2 billion, compared with $2.4 billion at 2008 year end.

Most of the decline in revenues was due to volumes declines, as the recession cut deeply into orders across almost all of Nucor's product lines. The only segment with positive results was a 10 percent increase in orders for some concrete reinforcing rods used in large infrastructure projects. A factor in the earnings decline was Nucor's commitment to a large quantity of expensive pig iron as feedstock just before commodity prices tumbled late in 2008.

Reasons to Buy

As 2009 wore to a close and the world figured out that the bottom was in the rear-view mirror, Nucor's orders began to pick up significantly. Industry-wide, their customer's inventories were at their lowest levels in over twenty-five years. As a result, Nucor's 4Q2009 and 1Q2010 brought a 50 percent increase in revenues, earnings went positive, and for FY2010 the company should post revenues of $15 billion and earnings near to $1.80 per share. The company warns that a full recovery will be protracted, however.

Nucor is in better shape than most of its competitors. They've been very conservative with the business over the past five years of growth and have very low levels of debt. Their debt/equity ratio is half that of the industry average and their asset/liability ratio is approximately four times the average. Due to the cost of U.S.-based labor, they have a lower net margin than the industry average, but due to their very efficient business model they generate about 80 percent more revenue per employee than average.

Nucor is the lowest-cost producer in the world—their gross margin is 40 percent higher than the largest player in the industry. Their capital structure is solid and puts them in a better position than any of their competitors to buy up capacity should others fail to recover quickly. Their large rapid-start capacity positions them well to take advantage of the opportunity as demand turns around, and they're widely acknowledged to be one of the best run and most innovative players in the industry.

We like these guys. When business was going well in 2006 and 2007 and they ended up with some extra money, they declared a special dividend and returned an additional $1.50/share to stockholders. Sometimes it's nice to have a stock in your portfolio that you cheer for, and this one's ours.

Reasons for Caution

Nucor (and other domestic producers) still have to compete with what many claim are "dumping" practices from overseas producers, who (it is claimed) sell product in the United States below their cost in order to cripple their competition.

SECTOR: **Industrials**
BETA COEFFICIENT: **1.25**
10-YEAR COMPOUND EARNINGS PER SHARE GROWTH: **22 percent**
10-YEAR COMPOUND DIVIDENDS PER SHARE GROWTH: **36 percent**

		2002	2003	2004	2005	2006	2007	2008	2009
Revenues (Mil)		4,802	6,266	11,377	12,701	14,571	16,593	23,663	11,190
Net income (Mil)		162	63	1,122	1,310	1,758	1,472	1831	d294
Earnings per share		0.52	0.2	3.51	4.13	5.73	4.98	6.01	d0.94
Dividends per share		0.19	0.2	0.24	0.93	2.15	2.44	1.91	1.41
Cash flow per share		1.5	1.36	4.72	5.43	7.05	6.51	7.36	0.60
Price:	high	17.5	14.7	27.7	35.1	67.6	69.9	83.6	51.1
	low	9	8.8	13	22.8	33.2	41.6	25.3	29.8

Nucor Corporation
1915 Rexford Road
Charlotte, NC 28211
(704) 366-7000
Website: *www.nucor.com*

Oracle Corporation

Ticker symbol: ORCL (NASDAQ) ❑ S&P rating: A ❑ Value Line financial strength rating: A++ ❑ Current yield: 0.8%

Company Profile

Oracle Corporation supplies the world's most widely used information management software, the Oracle database. They are also the world's second largest independent software company. In addition to their namesake database, Oracle also develops, manufactures, markets, distributes and services middleware and applications software that help its customers manage their businesses.

Oracle is organized into three businesses: software, hardware systems, and services, which in the most recent quarter accounted for 78 percent, 7 percent, and 15 percent of revenues respectively. Foreign sales represented 56 percent of revenue and 52 percent of earnings in FY2009.

The company's new software licenses segment includes the licensing of database and middleware software, which consists of Oracle Database and Oracle Fusion Middleware, as well as applications software. New software license revenues represented 31 percent of the company's total revenues during fiscal 2009.

Oracle's database and middleware software provides a platform for running and managing business applications for mid-size businesses and large global enterprises. Designed for enterprise grid computing, the Oracle Database is available in four editions, scaled to the size of the intended application. Oracle Exadata is a family of storage software and hardware products designed to improve data warehouse query performance.

Oracle Consulting assists customers in deploying its applications and technology products. The company's consulting services include business/IT strategy alignment, business process simplification, solution integration, and product implementation, enhancements and upgrades. The company provides training to customers, partners and employees. Oracle offers thousands of courses covering all of its product offerings.

Financial Highlights, Fiscal Year 2010 (ended June 24, 2010)

Sales rose 15 percent versus 2009, including an 8 percent contribution from the sales of Sun hardware. Earnings grew only 11 percent, as operating margin fell 130 basis points reflecting a high level of integration costs. Disciplined cost management led to the generation of over $8 billion in free cash flow from fourth quarter 2009 through the third quarter 2010.

The company completed four notable acquisitions during the year: Relsys International in July 2009, Silver Creek Systems and Sun Microsystems in January 2010, and Phase Forward in April 2010. Relsys and Phase Forward will significantly strengthen Oracle's vertical applications for the pharmaceutical industry.

Reasons to Buy

The big question exiting the year is going to be "How is the Sun integration coming along?" We're happy to report that it seems to be going very well. Oracle has quickly taken a hard look at a couple of the cost drivers that it knows something about: supply chain and product line complexity. By significantly reducing the number of supported system configurations, Oracle has shaken out a fair amount of the cost of producing every system. Long story short, the company expects to see a far more profitable hardware segment beginning in mid-2011.

New software license revenues were up 13 percent in 3Q2010. New software licenses are a strong indicator of future revenue growth

in the maintenance and services business.

Oracle's Exadata product has been selling very well. Exadata is an integrated software/hardware product sold as a unit to run Oracle's database in an OLTP environment. It's designed to be easy to deploy and configure, and provide very high levels of performance due to its use of extremely low-latency storage. It's the fastest growing product in Oracle's history and is turning over $100 million per quarter only a year after being introduced. The product should do wonders for getting Sun's hardware business off to a solid start.

Oracle is still sitting on a mountain of cash (nearly $18 billion as of 3/1/2010). They are in a terrific position to build a suite of vertical applications on integrated hardware platforms for customers willing to pay for a pre-configured solution. Research facilities, such as those in the aforementioned pharmaceutical industry, are a perfect example.

The company recently started paying a modest dividend showing a greater orientation toward longer term shareholder value.

Reasons for Caution

There will be continued costs associated with the integration of Sun and the other recent acquisitions, which will depress margins somewhat through at least the end of 2011.

SECTOR: **Technology**
BETA COEFFICIENT: **0.9**
10-YEAR COMPOUND EARNINGS PER SHARE GROWTH: **22.0 percent**
10-YEAR COMPOUND DIVIDENDS PER SHARE GROWTH: **Nil**

	2003	2004	2005	2006	2007	2008	2009	2010
Revenues (Mil)	9,475	10,156	12,119	14,771	18,208	22,609	23,495	26,975
Net income (Mil)	2,307	2,681	3,541	4,246	5,295	6,799	7,393	8,220
Earnings per share	0.43	0.50	0.68	0.80	1.01	1.30	1.44	1.62
Dividends per share	-	-	-	-	-	-	0.05	.20
Cash flow per share	0.50	0.56	0.73	0.85	1.09	1.37	1.53	1.70
Price: high	14.0	15.5	14.5	19.8	23.3	23.6	25.1	26.6
low	10.6	9.8	11.3	12.1	16.0	15.0	13.8	22.2

Oracle Corporation
500 Oracle Parkway
Redwood City, CA 94065
(650) 506-7000
Website: *www.oracle.com*

Pall Corporation

Ticker symbol: PLL (NYSE) ❑ S&P rating: BBB ❑ Value Line financial strength rating: A ❑ Current yield: 1.7 percent

Company Profile

Okay, raise your hand if you've heard of Pall Corporation. Anyone? No? Well, neither had we, until we started looking around for quality industrial suppliers who were number one or two in their markets.

Pall supplies filtration, separation and purification technologies for the removal of solid, liquid and gaseous contaminants from a variety of liquids and gases. Their products are used in thousands of industrial and clinical settings: removal of contaminants from gas reagents in every semiconductor production facility in the world, removal of bacteria and virus spores from water in hospitals and other clinical settings, and detection of bacteria in blood samples. Their products range in scale from simple in-line filters sold 100 to the carton up to entire graywater treatment systems with capacities up to 150,000 gallons/day.

Pall's product and customers fall into two broad categories: Life Sciences and Industrial.

The company's Life Sciences technologies facilitate the process of drug discovery, development, regulatory validation and production.

They're used in the research laboratory, pharmaceutical and biotechnology industries, in blood centers and in hospitals at the point of patient care. The company's medical products improve the safety of the use of blood products in patient care and help control the spread of infections in hospitals. Pall's separation systems and disposable filtration and purification technologies are critical to the development and commercialization of chemically synthesized and biologically derived drugs and vaccines. The company provides a range of advanced filtration solutions for each critical stage of drug development through drug production. Its filtration systems and validation services assist drug manufacturers through the regulatory process and on to the market.

Pall provides process technologies throughout the industrial marketplace, including the aerospace, transportation, microelectronics, consumer electronics, municipal and industrial water, fuels, chemicals, energy, and food and beverage markets. Within the food and beverage market, filtration solutions are provided to the wine, beer, soft drink, bottled water and food ingredient markets. The company sells filtration and fluid monitoring equipment to the aerospace industry for use on commercial and military aircraft, ships and land-based military vehicles to help protect critical systems and components. Pall also sells filtration and purification technologies for the semiconductor, data storage, fiber optic, advanced display and materials markets.

Financial Highlights, Fiscal Year 2009

Pall recorded relatively small declines in both revenues and earnings in FY2009 of 9.5 percent and 10 percent, respectively. Compared to the results posted by many other industrial suppliers over the same period, 10 percent off the top is not at all bad. As an example of the value of Pall's diverse customer base, the sales declines in the Industrial segment were at least partially offset by gains in the Life Sciences segment.

Operating margin improved slightly, primarily reflecting product mix changes. EPS for FY2009 fell $.12, with unfavorable foreign currency exchanges accounting for $.16 of the decline and the acquisition of GeneSystems for another $.05.

Pall ended FY2009 with approximately $500 million in backlog, of which all but $100 million is expected to be shipped in FY2010.

Reasons to Buy

We like industrials with a diversified customer base. Pall's customers fall into five broad categories: Bio-Pharmaceuticals, Medical, Energy/Water/Process Technologies, Aerospace, and Microelectronics. The smallest segment represents 9 percent of their sales, the largest 38 percent (Energy/Water/Process). If we could select an ideal mix of mix of markets to sell into, it would look very much like that. Pall's customers are also geographically balanced, with Europe accounting for 41 percent of sales, the Western Hemisphere 33 percent, and Asia 26 percent.

Nearly 75 percent of Pall's revenues come from consumables, including industry standard product types and products specifically designed to be used in Pall-branded equipment.

We really like the sales model. A single industrial facility might have hundreds of filtration and purification applications. The facility might require various levels of treatment on its airflow, its water supply, its chemical stores, its monitoring equipment, and its wastewater and effluent.

The company is in the process of reducing costs further through factory rationalizations and improved leverage of raw materials sourcing.

Reasons for Caution

Pall's best prospect for growth that significantly outpaces the industrial economy is through acquisition in this fragmented market. Unfortunately, ready cash may be dear unless and until Pall can pump up the cash flow.

SECTOR: Industrials
BETA COEFFICIENT: **1.00**
10-YEAR COMPOUND EARNINGS PER SHARE GROWTH: **6.5 percent**
10-YEAR COMPOUND DIVIDENDS PER SHARE GROWTH: **-1.0 percent**

	2002	2003	2004	2005	2006	2007	2008	2009
Revenues (Mil)	1,291	1,614	1,771	1,902	2,017	2,250	2,572	2,392
Net income (Mil)	73.2	144	152	141	146	128	217	196
Earnings per share	0.59	1.16	1.20	1.12	1.16	1.02	1.76	1.64
Dividends per share	0.52	0.36	0.36	0.40	0.44	0.48	0.51	0.58
Cash flow per share	1.20	1.81	1.90	186.	1.97	1.81	2.60	2.44
Price: high	24.5	27.0	29.8	31.5	35.6	49.0	43.2	37.3
low	14.7	15.0	22.	25.2	25.3	33.2	21.6	18.2

Pall Corporation
2200 Northern Boulevard
East Hills, NY 11548
(516) 484-5400
Website: *www.pall.com*

Panera Bread Company

Ticker symbol: PNRA (NASDAQ) ❑ S&P rating: NR ❑ Value Line financial strength rating: A+ ❑
Current yield: nil

Company Profile

Panera Bread Company operates and franchises bakery-cafes (restaurants) in forty states and Canada. These restaurants sell deli-style foods in an upscale, comfortable setting in which the star attraction is the bread, which is baked on-site (the dough is prepared elsewhere). Specialties include soups, sandwiches, salads and, of course, artisan breads. Meals are prepared for both dining in and take-out, and bread items such as bagels, loaves, muffins, scones, and rolls are available for purchase any-time as separate items. Menus and all bread recipes are created by Panera, with "proprietary" ingredients supplied to the restaurants from Panera-approved vendors. Menu items are rotated from time to time, and special seasonal items are added as appropriate to create interest.

As of April 12, 2010, there were 1,380 restaurants in opera-tion; 585 company owned and 795 franchise-operated. The company also owns and operates twenty-one fresh dough facilities (an additional two fresh dough facilities are franchisee-owned).

The company reports revenue under three business segments: company-owned restaurant sales, franchise royalties and fees, and fresh dough sales to franchisees. In FY2009, approximately 85 percent of company revenue came from res-taurant food sales. Included in the food sales tally are revenues from Via Panera, a catering service avail-able at both company-owned res-taurants and at franchisees.

Financial Highlights, Fiscal Year 2009

Panera has been on a good run as of late, soldiering through the recession with consecutive years of revenue and earnings increases. FY2009 revenues were up 4 percent primarily on the contribution from sixty-nine new restaurants system-wide and, to a lesser extent, a 0.5 percent increase in comps, partially offset by the closure of fourteen restaurants system-wide. Earnings were up 30 percent primarily as a result of savings on the cost of sales of fresh dough to franchisees, due to reduction in the price of wheat and fuel.

First quarter 2010 results have been more encouraging, with comps up 9.5 percent and EPS up 44 percent year over year.

Reasons to Buy

Panera plans to open another eighty-five restaurants in 2010 and more still in 2011. The company has given guidance of $3.40-$3.44 per share in 2010, and turned in $0.82 per share in the first quarter. At least one analyst, Matthew Spencer at Value Line, feels that earnings of $3.95 are foreseeable in 2011.

The company is expected to introduce new menu items throughout 2010, creating incremental foot traffic. The catering business, down recently as its traditional small-office client base has been scaling back during the recession, is expected to rebound as business conditions improve.

The company has a strong balance sheet, with no debt and significant levels of cash. Whether the company will use this to accelerate growth or repurchase shares as part of the recently authorized buyback plan is not yet clear, however.

Reasons for Caution

The company's financial requirements for franchisee qualification are very high, and potential franchisees must commit to multiple locations in order (they say) to better leverage the dough manufacturing and distribution assets. Given that the franchisees must be supplied with fresh dough every day via truck, we wonder if a more cost effective dough-making scheme wouldn't also remove at least one of the barriers to accelerated growth.

SECTOR: Restaurants
BETA COEFFICIENT: 0.95
10-YEAR COMPOUND EARNINGS PER SHARE GROWTH: 58.0 percent
10-YEAR COMPOUND DIVIDENDS PER SHARE GROWTH: Nil

	2002	2003	2004	2005	2006	2007	2008	2009
Revenues (Mil)	278	356	479	640	829	1,0687	1,299	1,354
Net income (Mil)	21.8	30.6	38.6	52.2	59.9	58.5	67.2	86.1
Earnings per share	0.73	1.01	1.25	1.65	1.87	1.82	2.22	2.78
Dividends per share	-	-	-	-	-	-	-	-
Cash flow per share	1.22	1.67	2.10	2.73	3.28	3.70	4.37	4.85
Price: high	37.9	47.8	45.1	72.6	75.9	62.8	65.0	68.9
low	23.6	24.5	32.3	39.0	46.3	33.3	30.6	42.3

Panera Bread Company
6710 Clayton Road
Richmond Heights, MO 63117
(314) 633-7100
Website: www.panerabread.com

Patterson Companies, Inc.

Ticker symbol: PDCO (NASDAQ) ❑ S&P rating: A ❑ Value Line financial strength rating: A ❑ Current yield: 1.3 percent

Company Profile

Patterson Companies is a value-added distributor operating in three segments—Dental Supply, Veterinary Supply, and Rehabilitative Supply. Dental Supply (70 percent of sales) provides a complete range of consumable dental products, equipment, and software, turnkey digital solutions, and value-added services to dentists and dental laboratories for the North American market. Veterinary Supply is the nation's second-largest distributor of consumable veterinary supplies, equipment, diagnostic products, vaccines and pharmaceuticals to companion-pet veterinary clinics. Rehabilitative Supply distributes medical supplies and assistive products globally to hospitals, long-term care facilities, clinics, and dealers.

Patterson has one-third of the dental supply market. Their main competitor is HSIC, which also has about a one-third share, with the remaining third fragmented among a number of smaller players. As one of the lead dogs, Patterson has the clout to negotiate a number of exclusive distribution deals. They are sole distributor for the industry's most popular line of dental chairs,

and also have an exclusive on the CEREC 3D dental restorative system, an alternative to traditional dental crowns. Patterson is also the leading provider of digital radiography systems, which create instant images of dental work, superior to the images generated by traditional x-ray equipment.

Patterson's veterinary business, Webster Veterinary, is the second largest distributor of consumable veterinary supplies to companion-pet veterinary clinics. Their line also includes equipment and software, diagnostic products, and vaccines and pharmaceuticals.

Patterson's rehab business, Patterson Medical, is the world's leading distributor of rehabilitation supplies and patient assistive products. They sell into the global physical and occupational therapy markets, whose customers include hospitals, long-term care facilities, clinics and dealers.

Financial Highlights, Fiscal Year 2009

Patterson's top-line grew 7 percent to $3 billion, moderating their five-year sales CAGR of 13 percent. Earnings grew 8 percent to $225 million, while per-share earnings increased 12 percent due to the re-purchase of 18 million shares of stock (financed by debt).

The company continues to grow through acquisition. In 2009 they acquired Dolphin Imaging Systems and Dolphin Practice Management, which are the leading providers of 3D imaging and practice management software for specialized, high-end dental practitioners. They added major distributors in both their dental and veterinary businesses and opened several new branch offices both through acquisition and internal growth. And while debt grew substantially (to $655 million), they have managed to reduce their overall cost of capital by 100 basis points.

Sales in the smaller of the company's operations, Veterinary and Medical, outpaced the larger segment by a fair margin. While Dental grew at only 6 percent, Medical and Veterinary grew at 11 and 12 percent, respectively. Dental sales saw a shift away from consumables and toward high-ticket items, presumably as a result of fewer patient office visits during the economic downturn and the need for practitioners to accelerate their rates of return.

The company also committed to a cost reduction program, recognizing the opportunities presented by several recent acquisitions.

In early 2010 the company initiated its first-ever dividend with a $.10 per share quarterly payout, reflecting the company's confidence in its growth prospects and strong current cash flows.

Reasons to Buy

Patterson Dental uses their size market leadership position to offer services that its smaller competitors cannot, such as financing, local service and support, and software services. During the recent business downturn, the company supplied all its customers with its EagleSoft practice management software at no charge and revised their commission structures.

The aforementioned CEREC 3D is an imaging and milling system that allows the dentist to take an image of the area to be restored and in less than thirty minutes produce a crown, inlay, or other device that is then fitted to the patient's existing dental structure. It's a compelling proposition for high-volume offices where patient throughput is at a premium and the equipment can be fully utilized. Sales of this high-ticket item have been very good and generate ongoing supplies revenue. Patterson's exclusive license to this product is a powerful foot in the door for new accounts.

Patterson Medical is the only single-source supplier in their very fragmented market. They have a 10 percent share and are over three times as large as their nearest competitor. They own many of the leading brands in the market, and have distribution in the U.K. and France, as well as all of North America.

We like the company's moves into the companion-pet veterinary and rehabilitative markets, both of which are driven by a growing and profitable demographic.

Reasons for Caution

The company has issued a fair amount of debt in recent deals. Credit is still fairly cheap, but availability remains an issue. The company's cash flow is more than strong enough to service its current debt level, but new debt may be more difficult to obtain, possibly damping Patterson's acquisition strategy somewhat and slowing demand for the company's big-ticket items.

SECTOR: Health Care
BETA COEFFICIENT: .90
10-YEAR COMPOUND EARNINGS PER SHARE GROWTH: 18.0 percent
10-YEAR COMPOUND DIVIDENDS PER SHARE GROWTH: NA

	2002	2003	2004	2005	2006	2007	2008	2009
Revenues (Mil)	1,416	1,657	1,969	2,421	2,615	2,798	2,998	3.094
Net income (Mil)	95	116	150	184	198	208	225	200
Earnings per share	0.70	0.85	1.09	1.32	1.43	1.51	1.69	1.69
Dividends per share	0	0	0	0	0	0	0	0.4
Cash flow per share	0.95	1.23	1.53	1.60	1.68	2.05	1.88	2.00
Price: high	27.6	35.8	43.7	53.8	38.3	40.1	37.8	30.9
low	19.1	17.7	29.7	33.4	29.6	28.3	15.8	27.9

Patterson Companies, Inc.
1031 Mendota Heights Road
St. Paul, MN 55120–1419
(651) 686-1775
Website: *www.pattersondental.com*

AGGRESSIVE GROWTH

Paychex, Inc.

Ticker symbol: PAYX (NASDAQ) ☐ S&P rating: NR ☐ Value Line financial strength rating: A ☐
Current yield: 4.3 percent

Company Profile

Paychex, Inc. provides payroll, human resource, and benefits outsourcing solutions for small- to medium-sized businesses. Founded in 1971, the company has more than 100 offices and serves over 550,000 clients in the United States and an additional 1,400 clients in Germany. The company has two sources of revenue: service revenue, paid by clients for services, and interest income on the funds held by Paychex for clients.

Paychex offers a portfolio of services and products, which includes:

- payroll processing
- payroll tax administration services
- employee payment services
- regulatory compliance services (new-hire reporting and garnishment processing)
- comprehensive human resource outsourcing services
- retirement services administration
- workers' compensation insurance services
- health and benefits services

- time and attendance solutions
- medical deduction, state unemployment, and other HR services and products

The company's products are marketed primarily through their direct sales force, the bulk of which is focused on payroll products. In addition to the direct sales force, the company utilizes their relationships with existing clients, CPAs, and banks for new client referrals. Approximately two-thirds of their new clients come via these referral sources.

The company also sells a Major Market Services product for its larger clients. The MMS product is a license that allows the client to run the Paychex software on the client's own servers and administer the payroll function with its own personnel.

In addition, Advantage Payroll Services Inc. (Advantage), a wholly owned subsidiary of Paychex, Inc., has license agreements with independently owned associate offices (Associates), which are responsible for selling and marketing Advantage payroll services and performing certain operational functions, while Paychex, Inc. and Advantage provide the centralized back-office payroll processing and payroll tax administration services. The marketing and selling by the Associates is conducted under their own brands and logos.

Financial Highlights, Fiscal Year 2009 (ended May 31, 2009)

Paychex experienced its first-ever decline in client base in FY2009, and that was the good news. The bad news was what came later, but we'll get to that. In addition to the 3 percent drop in client base, Paychex had a 43 percent decline in interest on funds held for clients. In 2008, that interest represented about 6.5 percent of total revenue. In 2009, that dropped to 3.5 percent as the interest rate paid on the very conservative investments Paychex typically employs for this use fell nearly to zero. Net income declined 7 percent on the year.

The bad news is the results for FY2010 have so far been less than stellar. The company's revenue is tied to their number of clients and the number of employees at each client. With unemployment still very high in the United States, Paychex' revenue has suffered. For the year, FY2010 revenue is projected to fall 2 to 5 percent and earnings will decline 10 to 12 percent.

Reasons to Buy

Paychex's primary market is firms with fewer than 100 employees. This is one of the primary reasons that Paychex has lost clients—many small businesses are undercapitalized and simply went out of business during the recession. On the other hand, as the economy turns around, smaller firms are the first place that new jobs will appear.

The company is very conservatively run and is well financed. They carry no debt and will have no difficulty funding the generous dividend, even at its current payout level of 84 percent.

Fragmentation in the market and Paychex's extremely strong financial position would allow the company to grow market share through acquisition should they decide to do so.

Outsourcing of non-value-added functions is a trend that makes a great deal of sense for the majority of businesses in the United States, and Paychex is aggressively exploring the boundaries of the concept. They administer 10 percent of the 401(k) plans in the country, and they now offer health insurance and experienced 93 percent growth in that segment year/year. In 2009 this growth remained high (70 percent) and the company projects growth in this area to remain above 50 percent at least over the next two years.

Reasons for Caution

Paychex typically has around $4 billion in cash at any one time, and transfers between $1 to 2 billion per day. In FY2009 they moved half a trillion dollars on behalf of their clients. As long as interest rates remain at the current historically low levels, the float that used to generate an important fraction of Paychex's revenue will be forgone.

SECTOR: **Information Technology**
BETA COEFFICIENT: **.85**
10-YEAR COMPOUND EARNINGS PER SHARE GROWTH: **18.0 percent**
10-YEAR COMPOUND DIVIDENDS PER SHARE GROWTH: **26.5 percent**

	2002	2003	2004	2005	2006	2007	2008	2009
Revenues (Mil)	955	1,099	1,294	1,445	1,675	1,887	2,066	2,083
Net income (Mil)	274	294	303	369	465	515	576	534
Earnings per share	0.73	0.78	0.8	0.97	1.22	1.35	1.56	1.48
Dividends per share	0.42	0.44	0.47	0.51	0.61	0.79	1.20	1.24
Cash flow per share	0.81	0.89	0.95	1.14	1.4	1.54	1.82	1.72
Price: high	42.2	40.5	39.1	43.4	42.4	47.1	37.5	32.9
low	20.4	23.8	28.8	28.8	33	36.1	23.2	20.3

Paychex, Inc.
911 Panorama Trail South
Rochester, NY 14625-0397
(585) 383-3406
Website: *www.paychex.com*

AGGRESSIVE GROWTH

Peet's Coffee and Tea

Ticker symbol: PEET (NASDAQ) □ S&P rating: BBB □ Value Line financial strength rating: B++ □ Current yield: nil

Company Profile

Peet's Coffee & Tea is a specialty coffee roaster and marketer of fresh roasted whole bean coffee and tea. They sell coffee through multiple channels of distribution, including grocery stores, home delivery, office, restaurant and foodservice accounts and company-owned retail outlets. As of January 2010 they operated 192 retail stores in six (mainly western) states. These stores account for approximately two-thirds of their net revenues.

The company was founded in 1966 and is widely considered to be the first ultra-premium coffee retailer in the United States and an inspiration for Starbucks and others. The company was purchased by two of the founders of Starbucks after they sold that firm in 1987 to Howard Schultz and other investors.

The business is operated through two reportable segments: retail and specialty sales.

Their stores are designed to facilitate the sale of fresh whole bean coffee and to encourage customer trial of coffee through coffee beverages. Like Starbucks, Peet's stores have attractive environments and are effective gathering places for all walks of urban and suburban life.

In addition to sales through retail stores, the company sells products through a network of nearly 8,500 grocery stores, including Safeway, Albertson's, Ralph's, Kroger, Publix and Whole Foods Market. To support these sales, reps deliver directly to their stores anywhere between one to three times per week, properly shelve the product, rotate to ensure freshness, sell and erect free-standing displays and forge store-level selling relationships.

Financial Highlights, Fiscal Year 2009

The recession took some of the edge off of Peet's recent momentum, as revenues grew only 9.3 percent (versus 14.2 percent in FY2008). They missed their internal revenue goals by about $10 million, but managed to exceed their earnings target by a few percents as a result of enhanced cost controls and some positive returns from an unsuccessful purchase bid for Diedrich's Coffee. Bottom line, net margins were up 230 basis points, or 2.3 percent, although up only 50 points from ongoing operations. The first half of 2010 looks strong and the company projects 2010 revenues to gain 11 percent and per-share earnings to grow nearly 20 percent.

Peet's remains debt-free and has actually shrunk its share base over the last five years while sales have doubled.

The company also announced a partnership with Godiva Chocolates to sell and distribute a number of Godiva-branded coffees in supermarkets, mass-merchandisers and related channels. The Godiva products will not be available through Peet's retail outlets.

Reasons to Buy

As size provides a measure of safety, there aren't too many small-cap companies profiled in this book. However, Peet's is a company that delivers a sought-after product, a quality customer experience, and a sound, conservative business plan that offers significant long-term growth potential. "Small-cap value" is a good place to be with at least a portion of your portfolio.

In keeping with their policy of careful, controlled growth, the company opened only eight stores in FY2009 and closed four others, compared to net openings of twenty-two and thirty stores the prior two years. The company continues to emphasize their grocery and direct-to-consumer businesses as their growth engine, as this segment has four times the margins of its retail business. Why open a lot of stores if it's not the profitable part of your business?

In contrast, the company signed up twenty-five new licensed partner locations and 144 new "We Proudly Brew" accounts that serve Peet's coffee in their own branded locations. We feel this is a logical approach to growing a coffee brand in the post-Starbucks era. Coffee brands are not going to experience the explosive growth that was seen in the nineties, and the costs of retail outlets, if they serve mainly only to promote the brand, can quickly become burdensome. Peet's is more profitable in the part of the business that scales more quickly and economically, and we think that's a good thing.

It's emphasized in all the company literature and bears repeating here—Peet's is a large-scale roaster of coffees first and a coffeehouse second. Their partnership with Godiva is recognition of the real value of Peet's DSD retail-support model.

Reasons for Caution

Peet's growth will require the expansion of its transportation infrastructure at a time when transportation costs continue to be volatile, and the cost of raw materials and the delivered cost of the final product both have a large transportation component. Growth will also require large investments in new roasting capacity. Finally, the stock continues to trade at fairly high multiples (low 30s at the time of this writing).

SECTOR: **Restaurant**
BETA COEFFICIENT: **0.75**
10-YEAR COMPOUND EARNINGS PER SHARE GROWTH: **17.5**
10-YEAR COMPOUND DIVIDENDS PER SHARE GROWTH: **Nil**

	2002	2003	2004	2005	2006	2007	2008	2009
Revenues (Mil)	104	120	146	175	211	250	285	311
Net income (Mil)	4.7	5.2	8.8	10.7	8.9	9.2	11.2	17
Earnings per share	0.4	0.39	0.63	0.74	0.63	0.65	0.8	1.04
Dividends per share	-	-	-	-	-	-	-	-
Cash flow per share	0.82	0.85	1.16	1.39	1.32	1.58	1.99	2.38
Price: high	19.1	23.5	27.4	37.3	32.8	30.4	29.8	42.2
low	10.6	12.6	16.1	23	24.3	23	17.8	19.3

Peet's Coffee and Tea
1400 Park Avenue
Emeryville, CA 94608-3520
(510) 594-2100
Website: *www.peets.com*

PepsiCo, Inc.

Ticker symbol: PEP (NYSE) □ S&P rating: A □ Value Line financial strength rating: A++ □ Current yield: 2.9 percent

Company Profile

PepsiCo is a global beverage, snack and food company. They manufacture, market and sell a variety of salty, convenient, sweet and grain-based snacks, carbonated and non-carbonated beverages and foods in approximately 200 countries, with their largest operations in North America (United States and Canada), Mexico and the United Kingdom.

PepsiCo is organized into three business units and five reportable segments, as follows:

- PepsiCo Americas Foods, which includes Frito-Lay North America, Quaker Foods North America and all of the Latin American food and snack businesses, including the Sabritas and Gamesa businesses in Mexico;
- PepsiCo Americas Beverages, which includes PepsiCo Beverages North America and all of the Latin American beverage businesses; and
- PepsiCo International, which includes all PepsiCo businesses in the United Kingdom, Europe, Asia, Middle East and Africa.

The remaining two segments are the United Kingdom and Europe; and the Middle East, Africa, and Asia.

Many of PepsiCo's brand names are over 100 years old, but the corporation is relatively young. PepsiCo was founded in 1965 through the merger of Pepsi-Cola and Frito-Lay. PepsiCo now has at least eighteen brands that generate over $1 billion in retail sales. The top two brands are Pepsi-Cola and Mountain Dew, but beverages constitute less than half of Pepsi's sales. They are primarily a snack company, with beverages coming in second. Frito-Lay brands alone account for more than half of the U.S. snack chip industry.

PepsiCo began its international snack food operations in 1966. Today, with operations in more than forty countries, it's the leading multinational snack chip company, with more than a 25 percent market share of international retail snack chip sales. Brand Pepsi and other Pepsi-Cola products—including Diet Pepsi, Pepsi-One, Mountain Dew, Slice, Sierra Mist, and Mug brands—account for nearly one-third of total soft drink sales in the United States, a consumer market totaling about $60 billion. Pepsi-Cola also offers a variety of non-carbonated beverages, including Aquafina bottled water, Lipton ready-to-drink tea, and Frappuccino ready-to-drink coffee through a partnership with Starbucks.

PepsiCo acquired Tropicana, including the Dole juice business, in August 1998 and now markets these products in sixty-three countries. Tropicana Pure Premium is the third largest brand of all food products sold in grocery stores in the United States. Gatorade, acquired as part of the Quaker Oats Company merger in 2001, is the world's leading sports drink.

Financial Highlights, Fiscal Year 2009

Sales through the recession were basically flat year to year, tracking the performance of the snack food and soft beverage markets overall. Strong cost controls and reduced selling expenses led to an earnings increase of 17 percent, however, as operating margin grew nearly 300 basis points and net margin nearly 200 points.

The first three quarters saw volume growth averaging 5 percent, but the strengthening dollar versus the euro during the period effectively negated any effect on the bottom line. On a constant-currency basis, revenue and earnings grew 5 and 6 percent, respectively.

In early 2010 the company completed the $8.2 billion acquisition of its two largest bottlers, Pepsi Bottling Group and PepsiAmericas.

Reasons to Buy

While the acquisition of the two bottlers will create some integration expenses in 2010, the longer-term cost reductions are expected to generate savings of $150 million in 2010 and $400 million by 2012 through the elimination of manufacturing redundancies and the streamlining of distribution. The plan makes a great deal of sense for PepsiCo, and not long after they announced their intention to do so, Coca-Cola announced their own plan to acquire their largest bottler as well.

In the first quarter of 2010, PepsiCo's revenues increased 13.4 perecent versus 1Q2009, while earnings grew 26 percent to $1.4 billion.

The company is taking an aggressive approach to geographical expansion, with good results so far. Their Russian business is expected to grow at double-digit rates over 2009's $2 billion in revenue, and PepsiCo plans to invest more than $2.5 billion in manufacturing and distribution in China over the next three years.

Prices of key commodities, such as sugar, corn, rice, and wheat have been trending significantly downward in early-mid 2010. Whether the effect of these reduced prices will be reflected in Pepsi's bottom line will depend on the effectiveness of their hedging strategies, but it bodes well for the longer-term view.

Reasons for Caution

PepsiCo will need to move quickly to retain the health-conscious market. They have many new and reformulated products in the works that use healthier ingredients and reduced levels of sodium and transfats, but the competition for this segment is intense. On the plus side, there's no clear leader in this emerging segment, and there's no better distributor for new products than Frito-Lay.

SECTOR: Consumer Staples
BETA COEFFICIENT: .60
10-YEAR COMPOUND EARNINGS PER SHARE GROWTH: 11.5 percent
10-YEAR COMPOUND DIVIDENDS PER SHARE GROWTH: 12.0 percent

	2002	2003	2004	2005	2006	2007	2008	2009
Revenues (Mil)	25,112	26,971	29,261	32,562	35,137	39,474	43,251	43,232
Net income (Mil)	3,313	3,494	4,174	4,078	5,065	5,543	5,142	5,946
Earnings per share	1.85	2.01	2.44	2.39	3.00	3.34	3.21	3.77
Dividends per share	0.60	0.63	0.85	1.01	1.16	1.43	1.60	1.75
Cash flow per share	2.68	2.81	3.14	3.65	3.95	4.38	4.30	4.84
Price: high	53.5	48.9	55.7	60.3	66	79	79.8	64.5
low	34	36.2	45.3	51.3	56	61.9	49.7	43.8

PepsiCo, Inc.
700 Anderson Hill Road
Purchase, NY 10577–1444
(914) 253-3055
Website: www.pepsico.com

Perrigo Company

Ticker symbol: PRGO (NASDAQ) ❏ S&P rating: NA ❏ Value Line financial strength rating: B++ ❏
Current yield: 0.4 percent

Company Profile

Perrigo is the world's largest manufacturer of over-the-counter pharmaceutical products for the store brand market. They also manufacture generic prescription pharmaceuticals, nutritional products, and active pharmaceutical ingredients.

The company operates in three segments: Consumer Healthcare makes private-label OTC drugs and nutritional products, Rx produces generic prescription drugs, and API makes chemicals and pharmaceutical products under contract. The company has other miscellaneous businesses that together constitute about 10 percent of revenues. Consumer Healthcare is by far the largest segment, generating about 75 percent of Perrigo's revenue in 2008.

The company's success depends upon its ability to manufacture and quickly market generic equivalents to branded products. They employ internal R&D resources to develop product formulations and also manufacture in quantity for their customers. They also develop retail packaging specific to the customer's needs.

The company produces and markets over 1,100 store brand products to approximately 100 customers, including Wal-Mart, CVS, Walgreens, Kroger, Safeway, Costco and other national and regional drugstores, supermarkets, and mass merchandisers. Wal-Mart is their single largest customer and accounts for 20 percent of Perrigo's net sales in 2008. The retail market for the branded equivalents of Perrigo's most widely used products is over $12 billion.

The company's products are manufactured in nine separate facilities around the world. Its major markets are in North America, Mexico, the U.K., and China. Their main Consumer Healthcare customers include food, drug, and mass merchandise retailers, club stores, dollar stores, and wholesalers. Their main Pharmaceuticals customers include wholesalers, food, drug and mass merchandise retailers, drug distributors, governments, and group purchasers.

Financial Highlights, Fiscal Year 2009

Perrigo's FY2009 results, while not as strong as the blockbuster 2008, were still impressive given the larger market trends. Revenues were up

16 percent to just over $2 billion, driven by record sales in the Consumer Healthcare segment of $259 million (up 23 percent). Earnings rose a more modest 6 percent to $144 million.

The company had a number of significant approvals in 2008, including generic forms of Miralax®, Nasacort® AQ, and Klaron® lotion. New FDA filings included Duac® gel and Minoxidil topical aerosol foam, a generic form of Men's Rogaine® Foam.

Reasons to Buy

Perrigo expects that over the next four years, prescription drugs worth $9 billion in sales will be approved for OTC use. Prescription-to-OTC transitions are one of Perrigo's main revenue drivers. Similarly, Perrigo sees an addition $2.6 billion in sales of branded Rx products with potential for generic equivalent product introductions. With its 70 percent market share of the private-label OTC market, Perrigo is in a position to capture the larger share of those new opportunities.

Perrigo is consolidating its API production and is closing its higher-cost API production facility in Germany. The company has purchased a large stake in an API manufacturing facility in India, which it plans

to expand and use as a production center for higher-volume API products as well as Rx and Rx-to-OTC candidates.

Cash flow has improved dramatically over the last three years and the company is well funded for growth through acquisition. In FY2009 the company made four significant acquisitions, two of which expanded their geographic coverage and two of which were category expansions. The acquisitions are expected to add $130 million to annual revenues. In early 2010 the company paid $808 million cash for PBM holdings, a store-brand infant formula manufacturer and also acquired a leading OTC pharmaceutical supplier in Australia and New Zealand.

Early FY 2010 results indicate strong growth in earnings, with indications of a 40 percent increase in share net on perhaps a 10 percent growth in revenues.

Reasons for Caution

Starting in 2011, U.S. citizens will no longer be able to use pretax HSA funds to pay for over-the-counter medications. The full impact of this policy change is not yet known, but it seems clear the net effect on Perrigo's OTC sales will be negative.

SECTOR: Health Care
BETA COEFFICIENT: 0.70
10-YEAR COMPOUND EARNINGS PER SHARE GROWTH: 14.5 percent
10-YEAR COMPOUND DIVIDENDS PER SHARE GROWTH: NA

	2002	2003	2004	2005	2006	2007	2008	2009
Revenues (Mil)	826	826	898	1,024	1,366	1,447	1,822	2,007
Net income (Mil)	44.5	51.9	67.5	37.9	74.1	78.6	150	176
Earnings per share	0.59	0.73	0.93	0.49	0.79	0.84	1.58	1.87
Dividends per share		0.05	0.13	0.16	0.17	0.18	0.21	0.22
Cash flow per share	0.97	1.11	1.35	0.77	1.41	1.46	2.35	2.67
Price: high	14.8	16.7	25	19.9	18.7	36.9	43.1	61.4
low	9.3	10.5	15.6	12.8	14.4	16.1	27.7	37.5

Perrigo Company
515 Eastern Avenue
Allegan, MI 49010
(269) 673-8451
Website: *www.perrigo.com*

Praxair, Inc.

Ticker symbol: PX (NYSE) ❑ S&P rating: A ❑ Value Line financial strength rating: A ❑ Current yield: 2.4 percent

Company Profile

Praxair, Inc. is the largest pro-ducer of industrial gases in North and South America and the sec-ond-largest supplier of industrial gases in the world. The company, which was spun off to Union Car-bide shareholders in June 1992, supplies atmospheric, process and specialty gases, high-performance coatings, and related services and technologies.

Praxair's primary products are atmospheric gases—oxygen, nitro-gen, argon, and rare gases (pro-duced when atmospheric air is purified, compressed, cooled, dis-tilled and condensed), and process and specialty gases—carbon diox-ide, helium, hydrogen, and acety-lene (produced as by-products of chemical production or recovered from natural gas).

The gas products are sold into the packaged-gas market and the merchant market. In the packaged-gas market, bulk gases are packaged into high-pressure cylinders and either delivered to the customer or to distributors. In the merchant market, bulk gases are liquefied and transported by truck to the custom-er's facility.

The company also designs, engineers and constructs cryogenic and non-cryogenic gas supply sys-tems for customers who choose to produce their own atmospheric gases on-site. This is obviously a capital-intensive delivery solution for Praxair, but results in lower delivered cost to the customer and higher returns for Praxair, as all operational costs are paid by the customer. Contracts for these instal-lations can run to twenty years.

Praxair Surface Technologies is a subsidiary that applies metallic and ceramic coatings and powders to metal surfaces in order to resist wear, high temperatures and corro-sion. Aircraft engines are its primary market, but it serves others, includ-ing the printing, textile, chemical and primary metals markets, and provides aircraft engine and air-frame component overhaul services.

Financial Highlights, Fiscal Year 2009

Praxair's FY2009 turned out much like many of our other industrial suppliers: revenues and earnings are down significantly, cash flow is up due to cost-cutting measures, and the second half looks far better than the first. After the roller coaster that was 2009, nothing has fundamentally changed in Praxair's business model, except that now it can move forward with more favorable debt loads—they issued over $1 billion in new debt last year and retired older paper.

First quarter 2010 results are very encouraging, with sales and operating margin both up 14 percent, with the sales increase split between volume and pricing gains.

Reasons to Buy

Praxair entered 2010 with a backlog of over $2 billion in new facilities projects under contract. On-site delivery programs represent 25 percent of Praxair's revenue but account for 50 percent of its operating profit. These facilities generate a contracted return (with some variability) for five to twenty years, depending on the product, and Praxair's standard contracts include energy surcharge pass-through and take-or-pay provisions.

Praxair is the largest gas provider in the emerging markets of China, India, Brazil, and Mexico. Praxair China now has fifteen wholly owned subsidiaries and at least ten joint ventures. Asian markets account for 8 percent of Praxair's sales.

The petroleum industry is recovering heavier and heavier crude oil sources, such as the tar sands in Alberta. To refine these sources at existing facilities requires the input of greater and greater volumes of hydrogen. The largest of Praxair's forty-two current major projects are hydrogen production facilities in North America serving refineries, and hydrogen for refining is now Praxair's largest growth market. Exxon's recent purchase of XTO for its oil shale holdings and fracturing technology is a strong indicator of future growth in heavy crude refining.

Praxair is moving quickly on a solution for carbon sequestration at coal-fired facilities (primarily power plants) that may be funded soon by the DOE and, if successful, could generate revenues on the order of $150 million per installation.

Four large players control 75 percent of the world's industrial gas supply. Since the end products are essentially identical, simple transportation costs tend to drive regionalization of the markets. Praxair, with its many plants and pipelines, has created substantial barriers to entry in many of its established and emerging markets.

Reasons for Caution

There appear to be no major downsides, short of continued deep recession and weakness in global industrial production. Consolidation of smaller players by Praxair's competitors (Air Liquide, Linde, and Air Products) may force Praxair to follow suit at some point.

SECTOR: **Materials**
BETA COEFFICIENT: **1.0**
10-YEAR COMPOUND EARNINGS PER SHARE GROWTH: **11.5 percent**
10-YEAR COMPOUND DIVIDENDS PER SHARE GROWTH: **19.0 percent**

	2002	2003	2004	2005	2006	2007	2008	2009
Revenues (Mil)	5,128	5,613	6,594	7,656	8,324	9,402	10,796	8,956
Net income (Mil)	548	585	607	726	988	1,177	1,335	1,254
Earnings per share	1.66	1.77	2.10	2.20	3.00	3.62	4.19	4.01
Dividends per share	0.38	0.46	0.6	0.72	1.00	1.20	1.50	1.60
Cash flow per share	3.18	3.36	3.94	4.61	5.25	6.18	8.63	6.85
Price: high	30.6	38.3	46.2	54.3	63.7	92.1	77.6	86.1
low	22.4	25	34.5	41.1	50.4	58	53.3	53.3

Praxair, Inc.
39 Old Ridgebury Road
Danbury, CT 06810–5113
(203) 837-2354
Website: *www.praxair.com*

The Procter & Gamble Company

Ticker symbol: PG (NYSE) ❏ S&P rating: AA- ❏ Value Line financial strength rating: A++ ❏ Current yield: 2.7 percent

Company Profile

Procter & Gamble dates back to 1837, when William Procter and James Gamble began making soap and candles in Cincinnati, Ohio. The company's first major product introduction took place in 1879 when it launched Ivory soap. Since then, P&G has continually created a host of blockbuster products and currently has twenty-four billion-dollar brands.

P&G is a uniquely diversified consumer products company with a strong global presence. P&G markets its broad line of products to nearly 5 billion consumers in more than 180 countries.

The company is a recognized leader in the development, manufacturing and marketing of quality laundry, cleaning, paper, personal care, food, beverage, and health care products, including prescription pharmaceuticals. Among the company's nearly 300 brands are Gillette, Tide, Always, Whisper, Pro-V, Oil of Olay, Pringles, Duracell, Ariel, Crest, Pampers, Pantene, Vicks, Bold, Dawn, Head & Shoulders, Cascade, Iams, Zest, Bounty, Braun, Comet, Scope, Old Spice, Charmin, Tampax, Downy, Cheer and Prell.

Total 2009 sales exceeded $79 billion and the company has nearly 135,000 employees working in more than eighty countries.

Financial Highlights, Fiscal Year 2009

P&G's revenues in 2009 tapered 5 percent as consumers were hit with tightening credit, reduced wages, employment uncertainty, and in many cases, unemployment. Earnings fell as well, down 5.5 percent. P&G's "core," their top forty-three brands with revenues of $500 million or more, experienced EPS growth of 8 percent in 2009. These core products represent 85 percent of P&G's revenues and 90 percent of their earnings. Newer, less well-established brands did not perform as well—recessions may be an unfortunate time to introduce new consumer products.

Reasons to Buy

Regardless of developments in the world economy, people will continue to shave, bathe, do laundry and care for their babies, and P&G is the global leader in Baby Care, Feminine Care, Fabric Care, and Shaving Products. Everyone should consider at least one defensive play in their portfolio, and P&G deserves to be at the top of the list.

P&G is a market leader in Consumer Health Care, a $240 billion market, with just a 5 percent share. Similarly, Beauty and Grooming is a $300 billion market, and P&G is the market leader with just a 13 percent share. P&G plans to grow their core businesses over the next several years and even small changes in market share in markets this size generate large returns.

P&G is extending its reach to capture share in channels and markets that are currently underserved. Developing markets are a huge opportunity, representing 86 percent of the world's population, and P&G feels they can be a leader in many product categories. Emerging markets already represent 32 percent of their revenue, up from 20 percent in 2002. They're also broadening their distribution channels to pursue opportunities in drug and pharmacy outlets, "convenience" stores, export operations and even e-commerce. P&G does less than $1 billion in online sales at this time, and the company feels they can increase that substantially.

P&G's recent concentration on the Beauty and Health Care segments has paid benefits, and the company plans to focus on expanding its product offerings in these segments. Health Care, for example,

represented 17 percent of 2009 net sales, but accounted for 21 percent of earnings.

According to a company spokesperson, "More than 70 percent of the company's growth, or roughly $20 billion in net sales, has come from organic growth and strategic acquisitions in these businesses. Well over half of P&G sales now come from these faster-growing higher-margin businesses."

P&G regards innovation as one of their key differentiators and aggressively pursues new market opportunities, both in the U.S. market and globally. Over the next five years, the company is building twenty new manufacturing facilities, most of them in developing markets and capable of producing multiple product lines.

Reasons for Caution

In a slow economy, consumers will be motivated to save wherever possible. Among Procter & Gamble's chief competitors for shelf space are low-cost store brands and generics. A change in consumer preference may dilute market share for P&G, but since they have either the number one or number two retail positions in the majority of their key global categories, P&G feels that any shift in purchasing patterns will damage their traditional competitors more than it will themselves.

SECTOR: **Consumer Staples**
BETA COEFFICIENT: **.60**
10-YEAR COMPOUND EARNINGS PER SHARE GROWTH: **10.5 percent**
10-YEAR COMPOUND DIVIDENDS PER SHARE GROWTH: **11 percent**

	2002	2003	2004	2005	2006	2007	2008	2009
Revenues (Mil)	40,238	43,377	51,407	56,741	68,222	76,476	83,503	79,029
Net income (Mil)	4,352	5,186	6,481	7,257	8,684	10,340	12.075	11,293
Earnings per share	1.54	1.85	2.32	2.53	2.64	3.04	3.64	3.58
Dividends per share	0.76	0.82	0.93	1.03	1.15	1.28	1.45	1.64
Cash flow per share	2.55	2.82	3.18	3.51	3.51	4.25	4.97	4.65
Price: high	47.4	50	57.4	59.7	64.2	75.2	73.8	63.5
low	37.1	39.8	48.9	51.2	52.8	60.4	54.9	43.9

The Procter & Gamble Company
1 Procter & Gamble Plaza
Cincinnati, OH 45202
(513) 983-1100
Website: *www.pg.com*

Ross Stores, Inc.

Ticker symbol: ROST (NASDAQ) ❑ S&P rating: BBB ❑ Value Line financial strength rating: A ❑
Current yield: 1.2 percent

Company Profile

Ross Stores is the second-largest off-price retailer in the United States. Ross and its subsidiaries operate two chains of apparel and home accessories stores. They ended FY2009 with a total of 1,005 stores, of which 953 were Ross Dress for Less® locations in twenty-seven states and Guam and fifty-two were dd's DISCOUNTS® stores in four states. Just over half the company's stores are located in three states—California, Florida, and Texas.

Both chains target value-conscious women and men between the ages of eighteen and fifty-four. Ross's target customers are primarily from middle income households, while the dd's DISCOUNTS target customers are typically from more moderate income households. Merchandising, purchasing, pricing and the locations of the stores are all aimed at these customer bases. Ross and dd's DISCOUNTS both offer first-quality, in-season, name brand and designer apparel, accessories and footwear for the family at savings of either 20 to 60 percent off department store prices (at Ross) or 20 to 70 percent off (at dd's DISCOUNTS). Both stores also offer discounted home furnishings as well.

Ross believes they derive a competitive advantage by offering a wide assortment of products within each of their merchandise categories in well-organized and easy-to-shop store environments. Their strategy is to offer competitive values to target customers by focusing on the following key objectives:

- Maintain an appropriate level of recognizable brands, labels and fashions at strong discounts throughout the store
- Meet customer needs on a more local basis
- Deliver an in-store shopping experience that reflects the expectations of the off-price customer
- Manage real estate growth to compete effectively across all markets

Financial Highlights, Fiscal Year 2009

Ross knocked the ball out of the park in 2009. Sales increased 11 percent to a record $7.2 billion on the strength of a 6 percent rise in comps. Dresses, Shoes, and Home were the biggest category gainers, while the Mid-Atlantic and Southeast had the largest same store sales gains.

Net earnings for the year grew 45 percent to a record $443 million, up from $305 million in 2008. Per share net rose 52 percent to $3.54, on top of a 23 percent gain in 2008.

Reasons to Buy

Driving the increased profitability in 2009 were strong inventory management and infrastructure changes that we discussed in last year's edition: "Ross is improving their infrastructure, implementing information system enhancements and process changes to improve merchandising capabilities (micro-merchandising). The new tools are designed to strengthen their ability to plan, buy and allocate at a more local versus regional level." These changes allowed Ross to drive inventory levels 11 percent lower even as sales volume was accelerating. The reduced inventory levels meant an increased number of turns, and fresher inventory leading to fewer markdowns as a result.

The good news is that Ross feels there are yet more opportunities for inventory reduction, so we can expect to see more of the same with regards to better inventory management and improved profitability through 2010, with

the full effect visible starting in 2011. The company says that average store inventories in 2010 will be down an additional mid-to-high single digit percentage compared to 2009's reduced levels.

As an indication of what may be coming down the road, first quarter 2010 results are exceptionally strong, with EPS coming in at $1.16, up 61 percent from the already good prior year. Operating margin was up 320 basis points (3.2 percent) to a record 12.1 percent. Net sales rose 14 percent over the same period, with a 10 percent increase in comparable store sales.

The company is planning for 4 to 5 percent total store count growth in 2010 and as much as 7 percent unit growth in 2011. Management feels they can double their current 1,000 store count before approaching saturation.

The company is in the midst of a two-year, $750 million stock repurchase program that will reduce outstanding shares by nearly 11 percent.

Reasons for Caution

The stock is trading at an all-time high, and there are questions about Ross's ability to acquire the same quantity and quality of merchandise as the economy picks up and full-price retailers begin to see higher levels of foot traffic.

SECTOR: Retail
BETA COEFFICIENT: 0.80
10-YEAR COMPOUND EARNINGS PER SHARE GROWTH: 14.0 percent
10-YEAR COMPOUND DIVIDENDS PER SHARE GROWTH: 21.5 percent

	2002	2003	2004	2005	2006	2007	2008	2009
Revenues (Mil)	3,531	3,921	4,240	4,944	5,570	5,975	6,486	7,184
Net income (Mil)	201	228	180	200	241	261	305	443
Earnings per share	1.26	1.47	1.19	1.36	1.70	1.90	2.33	3.54
Dividends per share	0.10	0.13	0.18	0.22	0.26	0.32	0.40	0.49
Cash flow per share	1.73	2.02	1.87	2.15	2.51	2.85	3.51	4.90
Price: high	23.6	28.1	32.9	31.4	31.8	35.2	41.6	50.5
low	15.9	16.3	21.0	22.3	22.1	24.4	21.2	28.1

Ross Stores, Inc.
4440 Rosewood Dr.
Bldg 4
Pleasanton, CA 94588-3050
(925) 965-4400
Website: *www.rossstores.com*

Schlumberger Limited

Ticker symbol: SLB (NYSE) ❏ S&P rating: A+ ❏ Value Line financial strength rating: A+ ❏ Current yield: 1.3 percent

Company Profile

Schlumberger Limited is the world's leading oilfield services company. It provides technology, information solutions and integrated project management services with the goal of optimizing reservoir performance for its customers in the oil and gas industry. Founded in 1926, today the company employs more than 76,000 people in eighty countries.

The company operates in two business segments:

Schlumberger Oilfield Services supplies a wide range of products and services including oilfield services such as formation evaluation, directional drilling, well cementing/stimulation, well completions and productivity. Consulting services provided include consulting, software, information management and IT infrastructure services that support core industry operational processes. WesternGeco, which accounted for 10 percent of the company's revenue, provides reservoir imaging, monitoring, and development services to land, marine, and shallow-water well projects.

Schlumberger manages its business through twenty-eight "GeoMarket" regions, which are grouped into four geographic areas: North America, Latin America, Europe, Commonwealth of Independent States and Africa, and Middle East and Asia. The GeoMarket structure provides a single point of contact at the local level for field operations and brings together geographically focused teams to meet local needs and deliver customized solutions.

Financial Highlights, Fiscal Year 2009

Schlumberger's 2009 results reflect the fortunes of most of our oil-related stocks. The large drop in oil demand in 2009 that resulted from the global economic recession, together with increased production capacity, led to spare oil production capacity reaching its highest level in nearly two decades. During 2009, the worldwide demand forecasts of 84.4 million barrels of oil per day represented the second consecutive year-on-year drop in oil demand for the first time in twenty-five years. Within the United States, natural gas wellhead prices reached their lowest levels since 2002.

Within this market, Oilfield Services revenue in 2009 declined

16 percent versus 2008, falling to $20.52 billion. Lower natural gas prices and unfavorable market fundamentals led to a 37 percent decline in North American revenue, primarily in the U.S. Land and Canada GeoMarkets.

Full-year 2009 revenue of WesternGeco was, at $2.12 billion, 25 percent lower than 2008. Revenue decreased across all product lines, with the largest declines seen in the Marine and Multiclient activity. Marine revenue fell on lower activity combined with reduced pricing as a result of weak market conditions. Multiclient revenue decreased primarily in North America, as customers continued to reduce discretionary spending.

In February 2010 Schlumberger announced the acquisition of Smith International for $11.3 billion in an all-stock deal. Smith is a Houston-based oilfield services company whose expertise in downhole and drilling operations should complement Schlumberger's expertise in measurement and steering technology. This is Schlumberger's largest acquisition to date. The deal's price represents a 37 percent premium to the stock price at the time of the announcement.

Also in February 2010, Schlumberger announced plans to acquire Geoservices, a French-based company specializing in energy services in a deal valued at $1.1 billion,

including debt. Schlumberger paid two times Geoservice's 2009 revenue for the company, which specializes in well logging and intervention.

Reasons to Buy

The first page of Schlumberger's annual report begins with: "The age of easy oil is over." Written many months before the explosion of BP's deepwater platform in the Gulf of Mexico and the ensuing spill, the sentence seems prescient and is perhaps the most succinct statement of Schlumberger's advantages in the E&P business. Their expertise is most valuable in the most technically challenging projects, such as the several recent sub-salt offshore finds in Brazil, West Africa, and the Gulf of Mexico.

Schlumberger has been quick to develop local technical resources to support E&P activity. In 2009 the company opened research centers in Saudi Arabia, Norway, and Russia. They have also announced plans to build an 85,000-square-foot research facility in Brazil in conjunction with the Federal University of Rio de Janeiro. Local presence is often vital to many development programs.

Unlike a lot of players in the oil business, they've been prudent with their money. Income from the boom years has been used to fund selected acquisitions of companies that operate only in their core business segment. They've also plowed money back into the company in the form of increased spending on R&D, returned it to the shareholders in increased dividends (up over 110 percent since 2004), set it aside for share repurchase ($8 billion approved through 2011), and retained it as cash (Schlumberger exited 2009 with $4.6 billion on-hand). Schlumberger invests more each year in R&D than all other oilfield services companies combined.

Reasons for Caution

Natural gas markets continue to be oversupplied. Oil projects may well pick up in the second half of 2010, but it will be some time before there is any acceleration in E&P activity in the natural gas sector.

SECTOR: Energy
BETA COEFFICIENT: 1.20
10-YEAR COMPOUND EARNINGS PER SHARE GROWTH: 13 percent
10-YEAR COMPOUND DIVIDENDS PER SHARE GROWTH: 6 percent

	2002	2003	2004	2005	2006	2007	2008	2009
Revenues (Mil)	13,474	13,893	11,480	14,309	19,230	23,277	27,163	22,702
Net income (Mil)	694	911	1,236	2,022	3,747	5,177	5,397	3,142
Earnings per share	0.6	0.78	1.03	1.67	3.04	4.18	4.42	2.61
Dividends per share	0.38	0.38	0.38	0.41	0.48	0.7	0.81	0.84
Cash flow per share	1.92	2.12	2.16	2.86	4.51	5.94	6.42	4.70
Price: high	31.2	28.1	34.9	51.5	74.8	114.8	112	71.1
low	16.7	17.8	26.3	31.6	47.9	56.3	37.1	35.1

Schlumberger Limited
5599 San Felipe, 17th Floor
Houston, TX 77056
(713) 375-3535
Website: *www.slb.com*

Sigma–Aldrich Corporation

Ticker symbol: SIAL (NASDAQ) ❑ S&P rating: A ❑ Value Line financial strength rating: A ❑ Current yield: 1.2 percent

Company Profile

Sigma-Aldrich is a manufacturer and reseller of chemicals and laboratory equipment used in research and large-scale manufacturing activities. The company sells over 130,000 chemicals, over one-third of which it manufactures internally. They also stock over 40,000 laboratory equipment items. Most of the company's 92,000 customer accounts are research institutions that use basic laboratory essentials like solvents, reagents, and other supplies. The company also sells chemicals in large quantities to pharmaceutical companies, but no single account provided more than 2 percent of Sigma-Aldrich's total sales in 2009. Sigma-Aldrich's business model is to provide their generic and specialized products with expedited (in most cases, next day) delivery.

Sigma-Aldrich operates four business units, each catering to a separate class of customer and product. Research Essentials sells common lab chemicals and supplies such as biological buffers, cell culture reagents, biochemicals, solvents, reagents and other lab kits to customers in all sectors. Research Specialties sells organic chemicals, biochemicals, analytical reagents, chromatography consumables, reference materials and high-purity products. Research Biochemicals provides "first to market products" to high end biotech labs, selling immunochemical, molecular biology, cell signaling and neuroscience biochemicals. Fine Chemicals fills large-scale orders of organic chemicals and biochemicals used for production in the pharmaceutical, biotechnology, and the high-tech electronics industry.

The company's biochemical and organic chemical products and kits are used in scientific and genomic research, biotechnology, pharmaceutical development, the diagnosis of disease, and as key components in pharmaceutical and other high technology manufacturing. Sigma-Aldrich has customers in life science companies, university and government institutions, hospitals, and industry. The company operates in thirty-six countries and has over 7,900 employees providing service in 165 countries worldwide. Nearly half their sales were to U.S. customers, one-third to Canada, Asia Pacific and Latin America, and the rest to Europe.

Financial Highlights, Fiscal Year 2009

Sales for FY2009 declined 2.5 percent to $2.15 billion, though earnings grew to a record $347 million. Share net grew 5.7 percent to $2.80. All four business segments turned in positive results, but none had top-line growth greater than 2 percent. Sales growth improved in Canada, Asia Pacific and Latin America, while growth in the focus markets of India, China and Brazil was an impressive 18 percent on a constant currency basis.

Operating margins grew 40 basis points in spite of the strong currency headwinds. The company's global supply chain initiatives, begun in 2007, generated $22 million in savings and contributed to the improved margins. The nearly $400 million in free cash flow set a new record for the company and enabled an increase in the dividend for the thirty-fifth consecutive year and funded another $67 million in share repurchase.

The company invested in a number of new facilities in 2009, including new manufacturing facilities in Israel, two in the United States, and a new warehousing and distribution center in Shanghai. The company also introduced 40,000 new products in 2009, including 15,000 new antibodies used in disease research.

The company continues to grow its e-commerce capability and (via acquisition of a software company) now has the industry's largest searchable database of over 60 million different chemical compounds.

Reasons to Buy

The company expects FY2010 organic sales growth in the 5 to 6 percent range. With the anticipated improvement in operating margin, this should yield EPS growth of 10 percent to $3.10. In fact, the company's first quarter results exceeded expectations, with $572 million in sales (10.2 percent total growth, 4.4 percent organic) generating a record $100 million in earnings. The earnings growth was a healthy 19 percent (10 percent on a constant-currency basis). Nearly all of the sales growth was volume-driven, as pricing grew less than 1 percent. The company took the opportunity to raise its divided a nominal 10 percent.

S-A's strong balance sheet should permit it to fund growth in its target markets of India, China, and Brazil, both organically and through acquisition. The company's broad product and geographic reach, as well as its sterling reputation among researchers, opens a lot of doors in markets where competition may be nascent.

Reasons for Caution

The company's growth is tied to the state of research in the chemical and bio/pharmaceutical industries. As

cash flow improves after the recession, product development funding
will improve and S-A's top line will

grow. Getting this stock now at 20
percent under its 2008 high should
not disappoint.

SECTOR: **Industrials**
BETA COEFFICIENT: **.95**
10-YEAR COMPOUND EARNINGS PER SHARE GROWTH: **12.5 percent**
10-YEAR COMPOUND DIVIDENDS PER SHARE GROWTH: **14 percent**

	2002	**2003**	**2004**	**2005**	**2006**	**2007**	**2008**	**2009**
Revenues (Mil)	1,207	1,298	1,409	1,667	1,798	2,039	2,201	2,148
Net income (Mil)	131	193	233	258	276	311	342	347
Earnings per share	0.89	1.34	1.67	1.88	2.05	2.34	2.65	2.80
Dividends per share	0.17	0.21	0.26	0.38	0.42	0.46	0.52	0.58
Cash flow per share	1.39	1.84	2.23	2.55	2.74	3.09	3.6	3.61
Price: high	26.4	29	30.8	33.6	39.7	56.6	63	56.3
low	19.1	20.5	26.6	27.7	31.3	37.4	34.3	31.5

Sigma–Aldrich Corporation
3050 Spruce Street
St. Louis, MO 63103
(314) 771–5765
Website: *www.Sigma-Aldrich.com*

J.M. Smucker Company

Ticker symbol: SJM (NYSE) ❑ S&P rating: NR ❑ Value Line financial strength rating: A+ ❑ Current yield: 2.2 percent

Company Profile

If you happened to think of a nice jar of refreshing purple grape jam when you heard the name "Smucker" you were on the right track. This eastern Ohio-based firm has been a leading manufacturer of jams, jellies and other processed foods for years, and thanks in large part to divestures from the Procter & Gamble food division and from other companies, has grown itself into a premier player in the packaged food industry.

Smucker manufactures and markets products under its own name but also under a number of other household names like Crisco, Folgers, Jif, Laura Scudder's, Hungry Jack, Eagle, and Pillsbury among others. The company also produces cooking oils, toppings, juices and baking ingredients. The company has had good success in revitalizing such brands as Folgers and Jif through improved marketing, channel relationships, and better overall focus on the success of these brands. Overall, the company aims to sell the "number one" brand in the various markets it serves. Operations are centered in the United States, Canada and Europe.

Even as a $4.5 billion a year enterprise, the company still retains the feel of a family business, with brothers Tim and Richard Smucker sharing the CEO responsibilities as chairman and president respectively.

Financial Highlights, Fiscal Year 2009

In June 2010 the company announced better-than-expected results for the fiscal year ended April 30, a surprise to many investors who were expecting a relatively tough year with competition and increased prices for certain commodities. Top-line revenues actually grew, while many analysts had expected a modest decline as consumers pulled back from buying premium brands. Performance in the relatively new coffee businesses exceeded expectations, and lower prices for certain commodities actually helped. The company was able to increase cash flow and increase the dividend some 14 percent, and continues to focus on delivering cash value to shareholders in the future.

Reasons to Buy

In fact, Smucker has raised dividends every year since 2002, and seems on track to do so in the future. This is a very well managed company with an excellent reputation in its markets. In recent years, it has a proven track record in buying and revitalizing key brands, the most prominent being former Procter & Gamble food brands and International Multifoods brands. We expect this trend to continue. Additionally, the company is trying out new initiatives for packaging and delivering foods, including "jar-free" peanut butter and healthier fare in certain categories, which should add to its competitive lead and to margins.

Finally, the company is in a very steady and safe business, and will enjoy a dominant marketing position and opportunities to improve margins in most of its businesses.

Reasons for Caution

In the food business one must always keep an eye on raw commodity costs, as we learned with regard to corn, wheat and other commodities in 2008. While the brands are strong, companies like Smucker must always worry about generic competition and the increased buying power of mega-channel players like Wal-Mart.

SECTOR: Consumer Staples
BETA COEFFICIENT: 0.7
10-YEAR COMPOUND EARNINGS PER SHARE GROWTH: 10.5 percent
10-YEAR COMPOUND DIVIDENDS PER SHARE GROWTH: 8.5 percent

		2002	2003	2004	2005	2006	2007	2008	2009
Revenues (Mil)		1311.7	1417.0	2043.9	2154.7	2148.0	2524.8	3757.9	4605
Net income (Mil)		10.4.4	120.9	150.1	155.1	164.6	178.9	321.4	494
Earnings per share		2.19	2.40	2.60	2.65	2.89	3.15	3.77	4.15
Dividends per share		.83	.92	1.02	1.08	1.14	1.22	1.31	1.40
Cash flow per share		2.86	3.20	3.52	3.97	3.94	4.42	3.73	5.60
Price:	high	40.4	46.8	53.5	51.7	50.0	64.3	56.7	62.7
	low	28.7	33.0	40.8	43.6	37.2	46.6	37.2	34.1

The J.M. Smucker Company
One Strawberry Lane
Orrville, OH, 44667
(330) 682-3000
Website: www.smuckers.com

GROWTH AND INCOME

Southern Company

Ticker symbol: SO (NYSE) ❑ S&P Rating: A ❑ Value Line financial strength rating: A ❑ Current yield: 5.6 percent

Company Profile

Through its four primary operating subsidiaries, Georgia Power, Alabama Power, Mississippi Power and Gulf Power, Southern Company serves some 4.4 million customers in a large area of Georgia, Alabama, Mississippi, northern Florida and parts of the Carolinas. The company also wholesales power to other utilities in a wider area.

The revenue mix is balanced: 33 percent residential, 31 percent commercial, 19 percent industrial, and 15 percent other. The service area includes the Atlanta metropolitan area and a large base of modern manufacturing facilities like the many Asian-owned manufacturing facilities in the region. The fuel mix is more diverse and less vulnerable to price fluctuations than some, with 57 percent coal, 23 percent oil and gas, 16 percent nuclear and 4 percent hydroelectric. That said, with its high percentage of coal-fired plants, SO must work to stay up with environmental regulations and pay close attention to transportation costs.

The company also has engaged in telecommunications services, operating as a regional wireless carrier in Alabama, Georgia, southeastern Mississippi, and northwest Florida and operating some fiber optic networks collocated on company rights of way. The company also provides consulting services to other utilities.

Financial Highlights, Fiscal Year 2009

Another rocky year in the capital markets, another year of steady earnings from Southern Company. Ho hum. Although many of its industrial customers scaled their energy usage back considerably, Southern still posted reasonable returns in the face of declining revenues. Income was up 6 percent to $1.9 billion, while revenues were off 8 percent to $15.7 billion. Per-share earnings were only up 3 percent, as the company issued 43 million new shares during the year.

Residential and commercial usage fell 1 to 2 percent each, while industrial customers scaled back nearly 12 percent. The total decline in usage of 4.8 percent was the largest year-over-year decline in the history of the company. During the year, the company shifted nearly 7 percent of its total electrical output from coal to oil/gas due to the over-supply conditions on the natural gas market.

Reasons to Buy

The recovery hoped for in 2010 appears to be under way, as first quarter results are very encouraging. The company earned $.60 per share in the first quarter on revenues that were up 13.4 percent year-over-year. Total electrical usage was up 10.3 percent in the first quarter, compared with the first quarter of 2009. Residential electricity sales increased 20.6 percent. Electricity sales to commercial customers increased 3.4 percent, and industrial sales increased 6.7 percent.

The appeal of this stock lies almost entirely in its dividend, which the company recently raised (yet again) to $1.82 per share. This puts the dividend just below a 6 percent rate. This sort of return won't put you into a yacht, but if you've already got one it will certainly help you keep it. At a fairly high payout rate of 75 percent, this dividend would put 2010 earnings in the $2.45 range, on the low end of most of the current estimates.

Utilities have the reputation of being a retiree's stock, something that's only a little bit better than a bond. This may have been true years ago, but if you've been following the bond market lately you know that 6 percent is quite a bit better than what you're getting out of the bond market. The prospect of a share price increase when you sell it to someone who really wants the dividend just sweetens the deal.

Southern serves a growing, diverse and economically stable customer base. This is not Detroit Edison; they aren't dependent on any one dominant industry and rate requests are generally treated favorably due to the low overall tax rate in the area. Finally, the company is in the intermediate stages of getting licensed to build new nuclear power facilities; in today's environment, while that does add some risk, we feel this is a good economic move for the future.

Reasons for Caution

Electric utilities are always subject to rate and other forms of regulation, and one never knows what will happen in that arena. Additionally, utilities are always vulnerable to capital costs and the attractiveness of alternative fixed income investments, and are sensitive to rising interest rates, especially if they rise quickly. Finally, all electric utilities are exposed to new environmental regulations and the need to replace aging infrastructure.

SECTOR: Utilities
BETA COEFFICIENT: 0.55
10-YEAR COMPOUND EARNINGS PER SHARE GROWTH: 3.0 percent
10-YEAR COMPOUND DIVIDENDS PER SHARE GROWTH: 2.0 percent

	2002	2003	2004	2005	2006	2007	2008	2009
Revenues (Mil)	10.549	11,251	11,902	13,554	14,356	15,353	17,127	15,743
Net income (Mil)	1,510	1,602	1,589	1,621	1,608	1,782	1,807	1,912
Earnings per share	1.85	1.97	2.06	2.13	2.1	2.28	2.25	2.32
Dividends per share	1.36	1.39	1.42	1.48	1.54	1.6	1.66	1.73
Cash flow per share	3.46	3.53	3.65	4.03	4.01	4.22	4.43	4.25
Price: high	31.1	32	34	36.5	37.4	39.3	40.6	33.8
low	23.2	27	27.4	31.1	30.5	33.2	29.8	30.8

Southern Company
30 Ivan Allen Jr. Boulevard NW
Atlanta, GA 30308
Phone: (404) 506-5000
Website: *www.southernco.com*

St. Jude Medical, Inc.

Ticker symbol: STJ (NYSE) ❑ S&P rating: B+ ❑ Value Line financial strength rating: A ❑ Current yield: nil

Company Profile

St. Jude Medical, Inc. designs, manufactures, and distributes cardiovascular medical devices including pacemakers, implantable cardioverter defibrillators (ICDs), vascular closure devices, catheters, and heart valves. The company has four main business segments:

Their Cardiac Rhythm Management portfolio (responsible for 60 percent of St. Jude's FY2009 revenue) includes products for treating heart rhythm disorders as well as heart failure. Its products include ICDs, pacemaker systems, and a variety of diagnostic and therapeutic electrophysiology catheters. The company also develops catheter technologies for the Cardiology/Vascular Access therapy area. Those products include hemostasis introducers, catheters, and a market-leader vascular closure device.

The Cardiovascular segment has been the leader in mechanical heart valve technology for more than twenty-five years. St. Jude Medical also develops a line of tissue valves, vascular closures and valve-repair products. The company will enter the pericardial stented tissue valve and coronary guide wire markets with new product introductions in the second half of 2010.

The company's Neuromodulation segment produces neurostimulation products, which are implantable devices for use primarily in chronic pain management and in treatment for certain symptoms of Parkinson's Disease and epilepsy.

The Atrial Fibrillation business produces a 3D heart mapping system. This tool is used by cardiologists to diagnose and treat irregular heart rhythms, among other uses. The AF unit also produces specialized catheters and other devices used in the treatment of atrial fibrillation.

St. Jude Medical products are sold in more than 100 countries. The company has twenty principal operations and manufacturing facilities around the world.

Financial Highlights, Fiscal Year 2009

Shrugging off the recession, St. Jude's continued their run of yearly revenue and earnings growth. Net sales were up 7.3 percent, driven by volume growth across all segments. Growth in AF and Neuromodulation were particularly stimulating, at 15 and 30 percent respectively.

Earnings rose 4 percent on volume, as net margin fell 60 basis points (0.4 percent). The company grew R&D spending 5 percent and repurchased 6 percent of its outstanding shares.

The company completed its acquisition of Radi Medical Systems for $250 million in cash. Radi, based in Sweden, makes products that assist in the diagnosis and treatment of heart lesions. The business is expected to generate $80 million in sales the first year and integrates well in the Cardiovascular segment.

Reasons to Buy

Over the past two years, both the Neuromodulation and Atrial Fibrillation segments have seen net revenues grow more than 50 percent. The techniques employed in neuromodulation are growing quickly in the field as a preferred treatment for long-term pain management. St. Jude (and others) see this as a disruptive technology, potentially replacing drug and physical therapy regimens and offering improved lifestyle at a reduced cost.

Medical equipment shares are out of favor at the moment due to the inclusion in the most recent health care legislation of a 2.3 percent excise tax on gross sales of medical devices, due to take effect in 2013. We're not sure why this should have any effect at all on the bottom line of companies like St. Jude medical, as nearly all of their devices are paid for by insurers, giving device makers a fair amount of price flexibility. Further, the tax is a write-down against earnings. We'd be surprised at any significant impact to earnings in the year following the initiation of the tax.

Early in 2010 Boston Scientific halted shipment and had to recall all of its ICDs from the market. They had modified their manufacturing process and had failed to get approval for the changes from the FDA. This leaves the ICD market to St. Jude and Medtronic for at least a year as Boston tries to recover. Assuming St. Jude and Medtronic split the Boston share 50/50, St, Jude's earnings should get a boost of around $.03/share per month through the end of 2010.

Reasons for Caution

The MediGuide acquisition may have been a bit of a reach. St Jude essentially took an impairment in the current year of over $300 million due to the fact that the technology acquired was not ready for market and may not be for another two to three years, if ever.

SECTOR: Health Care
BETA COEFFICIENT: .80
10-YEAR COMPOUND EARNINGS PER SHARE GROWTH: 20.0 percent
10-YEAR COMPOUND DIVIDENDS PER SHARE GROWTH: no dividend

	2002	2003	2004	2005	2006	2007	2008	2009
Revenues (Mil)	1,590	1,932	2,294	2,915	3,302	3,779	4,363	4,681
Net income (Mil)	276	339	410	394	548	652	807	838
Earnings per share	0.76	0.92	1.1	1.04	1.47	1.85	2.31	2.43
Dividends per share	-	-	-	-	-	-	-	-
Cash flow per share	0.99	1.2	1.38	1.42	2.05	2.48	2.92	3.24
Price: high	21.6	32	42.9	52.8	54.8	48.1	48.5	42
low	15.3	19.4	29.9	34.5	31.2	34.9	25	28.9

St. Jude Medical, Inc.
One Lillehei Plaza
St. Paul, MN 55117
(651) 766–3029
Website: *www.sjm.com*

AGGRESSIVE GROWTH

Staples, Inc.

Ticker symbol: SPLS (NASDAQ) □ S&P rating: BBB □ Value Line financial strength rating: A+ □ Current yield: 1.5 percent

Company Profile

Staples, Inc. launched the office supplies superstore industry with the opening of its first store in Brighton (near Boston), Massachusetts, in May 1986. Its goal was to provide small business owners the same prices on office supplies previously available only to large corporations. Staples is now a $16 billion retailer of office supplies, business services, furniture and technology to consumers and businesses in twenty-seven countries throughout North and South America, Europe, Asia and Australia. Staples is the largest operator of office stores in the world, with 2,243 stores of all type.

The company operates three business segments: North American Retail, North American Delivery, and International Operations. The company's North American Retail segment consists of the company's United States and Canadian business units that sell office products, supplies, and services.

The North American Delivery segment consists of the company's U.S. and Canadian contract, catalog and Internet business units that sell and deliver office products, supplies, and services directly to customers. Included in this segment is Quill (acquired in 1998), a direct mail catalog business serving over a million medium-sized businesses in the United States.

International Operations has nearly 400 retail stores in the U.K., Germany, the Netherlands, Portugal and Belgium. It also sells and delivers office products and supplies directly to businesses throughout most of Europe via its catalog business, the contract stationer business and the Internet e-commerce business. Staples also has a growing retail presence in Asia and South America.

Financial Highlights, Fiscal Year 2009

Staples' 2009 results were dominated by the downturn in the business environment. Two years ago the company would have been looking forward to 2009 and its first full-year results following the acquisition of Corporate Express, but now the company is looking at a rather modest 5 percent year-to-year increase in revenues and 14 percent decline in earnings.

The big hit was to North American Retail, where sales fell 1.3

percent with a 2 percent decline in comparable same-store sales. Durables fell significantly, with consumables picking up some of the slack. Earnings for the business unit grew 20 basis points on marketing and supply chain improvements.

North American Delivery and International Operations both recorded sales increases (8 and 13 percent, respectively), but these increases were attributable primarily to the CE acquisition. Retail comps in International fell 9 percent. Earnings in North American Delivery fell 80 basis points largely due to the inclusion of Corporate Express, where margins were lower than the existing business. Earnings in International fell 100 basis points due to losses in China and in the printing business.

Reasons to Buy

We give Staples high marks for bold moves. The purchase of Corporate Express was the right way to grow the business. It offered terrific leverage in supply chain and customer base, increased the company's geographic base, and it delivered a model for future growth not bound to retail. The two problems with the deal were the price, which could have been better, and the timing, which couldn't have been much worse.

In the opinion of most analysts, Staples paid top dollar for

CE, which wasn't necessarily a bad thing as it was also able to persuade most of the CE management to remain in place. However, buying an office-supply delivery retailer at the onset of an enormous downturn in the worldwide economy is going to leave a mark. Staples had hoped the improved volumes would more than pay for transition costs, but it hasn't worked out that way.

So why buy? Well, in early 2010 much of the market is short on Staples (and maybe staples, if their revenue numbers are any indication). Call it a simple case of unmet expectations—that's fine with us. For 2011 the stock looks like a much more attractive buying proposition. The share should have bottomed out by then, the business environment will have turned around, and the company's sales should start improving. Staples is still in better financial shape than its competition and has a more robust business model than either OfficeMax or Office Depot.

Reasons for Caution

Consumer (and corporate) spending remains soft in 2010. Whether this is part of a longer over-arching trend or simply a recessionary hangover is still unclear. Saturation in North America is also a risk, as many existing cities and suburbs have all the office supply superstore coverage they need.

SECTOR: Retail
BETA COEFFICIENT: 1.05
10-YEAR COMPOUND EARNINGS PER SHARE GROWTH: 13.5 percent
10-YEAR COMPOUND DIVIDENDS PER SHARE GROWTH: NA

	2002	2003	2004	2005	2006	2007	2008	2009
Revenues (Mil)	11,596	13,181	14,448	16,079	18,161	19,373	23,084	23,275
Net income (Mil)	417	552	708	834	974	996	924	794
Earnings per share	0.63	0.75	0.93	1.04	1.32	1.38	1.29	1.1
Dividends per share				0.13	0.17	0.29	0.33	0.33
Cash flow per share	0.96	1.11	1.33	1.56	1.79	1.98	2.06	1.85
Price: high	15	18.6	22.5	24.1	28	27.7	26.6	25.1
low	7.8	10.5	15.8	18.6	21.1	19.7	13.6	14.4

Staples, Inc.
500 Staples Drive
Framingham, MA 01702
(800) 468-7751
Website: www.staples.com

Starbucks Corporation

Ticker symbol: SBUX (NASDAQ) □ S&P rating: BBB □ Value Line financial strength rating: A □
Current yield: nil

Company Profile

Starbucks Corporation, formed in 1985, is the leading retailer, roaster, and brand of specialty coffee in the world. The company sells whole bean coffees through its specialty sales group, mail-order business, supermarkets, and online. The company has 6,769 company-owned stores in the United States and 2,081 in international markets, in addition to 7,856 licensed stores worldwide. Retail sales constitute the bulk of its revenue.

They also have joint ventures with Pepsi-Cola and Dreyer's to develop bottled coffee drinks and ice creams, and a partnership with Kraft Foods to distribute coffee in grocery stores. All channels outside the company-operated retail stores are collectively known as specialty operations.

The company's retail goal is to become the leading retailer and brand of coffee in each of its target markets through product quality and by providing a unique Starbucks Experience, which the company defines as a third place beyond home and work. The "experience" is built upon superior customer service and a clean,

well-maintained retail store that reflects the personality of the community in which it operates, thereby building a high degree of customer loyalty.

The company's specialty operations strive to develop the Starbucks brand outside the company-operated retail store environment through a number of channels, with a strategy to reach customers where they work, travel, shop and dine. The strategy employs various models, including licensing arrangements, foodservice accounts and other initiatives related to the company's core businesses.

In its licensed retail store operations, the company leverages the expertise of its local partners and shares Starbucks operating and store development experience. As part of these arrangements, Starbucks receives license fees and royalties and sells coffee, tea and related products for resale in licensed locations.

Financial Highlights, Fiscal Year 2008

During fiscal 2009, a net 474 company-owned retail stores were closed in the United States as a result of the restructuring begun in 2008. The strategy of closing underperforming stores appears to be bearing fruit, as cash flow and return on capital have both improved.

For 2009, Starbucks posted a revenue decline of 6 percent and an increase in earnings of 14 percent. The company claims that it no longer has to rely on high revenue growth to drive profitability, and these numbers would seem to confirm that (although 5 percent of the earnings increase was due to favorable currency exchange).

Starbucks say that they have removed $580 million in structural costs from 2009's results alone, with more cost reductions in the works for 2010. The effects have certainly been felt, as gross margins (18 percent), operating margins (13.4 percent), and net margin (6.1 percent) have all made a u-turn from 2008's results.

The company introduced its VIA line of instant coffee, which has so far been well accepted by customers. The company plans to release the product to select retail distributors later in 2010.

Reasons to Buy
The restructuring undertaken in 2008 has addressed the major structural problems in the business, and financial measures are turning around even in the face of a strong recessionary business environment. The FY2009 numbers are much

improved, and early projections for FY2010 results are even better—sales of $10.9 billion, operating margin in the 16 percent range, and EPS around $1.25.

The company has a steadily (and profitably) growing presence in Europe and China. The company plans to target the majority of its near-term growth outside the U.S. market, which may be approaching saturation.

Starbucks is a solid product concept. It has many imitators, but its brand loyalty runs deep and the company appears to be well on the way to recovery from a simple case of growth-itis. We still like its long-term growth potential, as long as it is carefully measured. We're particularly excited about the prospects for the VIA product, as we feel it could be an earnings star, and we look forward to seeing what happens with the European expansion over the next two years.

Reasons for Caution
It's not completely clear that consumer tastes have not been permanently affected by the recent recession. It may well be that coffee drinkers have learned to get along without the $5 latte and are now just $1.50 drippers. Spending per visit is a stat that will bear watching as the economy starts to turn around—revenues may have a lid on them now.

SECTOR: **Restaurant**
BETA COEFFICIENT: **1.15**
10-YEAR COMPOUND EARNINGS PER SHARE GROWTH: **21.5 percent**
10-YEAR COMPOUND DIVIDENDS PER SHARE GROWTH: **Nil**

	2002	2003	2004	2005	2006	2007	2008	2009
Revenues (Mil)	3,289	4,076	5,294	6,369	7,787	9,412	10,383	9,774
Net income (Mil)	218	268	392	495	519	673	525	598
Earnings per share	0.28	0.34	0.48	0.61	0.73	0.87	0.71	0.8
Dividends per share	0	0	0	0	0	0	0	0
Cash flow per share	0.55	0.64	0.85	1.09	1.28	1.54	1.46	1.53
Price: high	12.9	16.7	32.1	32.5	40	36.6	21	24.5
low	9.2	9.8	16.5	22.3	28.7	19.9	7.1	21.3

Starbucks Corporation
2401 Utah Avenue South
Seattle, WA 98134
(206) 447-1575
Website: *www.starbucks.com*

AGGRESSIVE GROWTH

Stryker Corporation

Ticker symbol: SYK (NYSE) ❑ S&P rating: A+ ❑ Value Line financial strength rating: A++ ❑ Current yield: 1.1 percent

Company Profile

Stryker Corporation was founded in 1941 by Dr. Homer H. Stryker, a leading orthopedic surgeon and the inventor of several orthopedic products. The company now ranks as a dominant player in a $12 billion global orthopedics industry. SYK has a significant market share in such sectors as artificial hips, prosthetic knees and trauma products.

Stryker develops, manufactures and markets worldwide products such as orthopedic implants, trauma systems, powered surgical instruments, endoscopic systems, and patient care and handling equipment.

Stryker's Physiotherapy Associates division provides physical, occupational and speech therapy to orthopedic and neurology patients in over 400 clinics worldwide. The physical therapy business represents a solid complementary business for Stryker, in view of the high number of its surgeon customers who prescribe physical therapy following orthopedic surgery.

Stryker's revenue is split roughly 60/40 between Implants and Equipment and 64/36 domestic and international.

Financial Highlights, Fiscal Year 2009

The company reported sales of $6.72 billion for 2009, essentially flat versus 2008. Sales of spinal implant systems and craniomaxillofacial implant systems were quite positive, posting gains of 10 and 8 percent respectively.

Fully diluted net earnings were $1.11 billion, a 4 percent decline, due largely to changes in product mix and a higher level of unfavorable currency exchanges.

The company raised the dividend 50 percent to $.50 per share.

Two acquisitions were notable in 2009. The company paid $525 million in cash for Ascent Healthcare Solutions, the U.S. market leader in the growing field of reprocessing and remanufacturing of medical devices. They also acquired OtisMed, whose software technology may complement Stryker's Triathlon Knee System.

The company recently offered $1 billion in senior unsecured notes, the proceeds from which will likely be used to fund acquisitions. Stryker has been successful in acquiring companies with complementary products, and we expect them to continue this strategy.

Reasons to Buy

Stryker's top-line is driven largely by elective surgeries, and 2009 turned out to be the year for delaying whatever medical procedures could be delayed. Many consumers decided to wait and see how the medical care legislation would turn out, and some were simply deciding to hold on to their cash until economic conditions improved. The good news for Stryker is twofold: medical care reform did not significantly increase the cost to consumers of implant surgeries, and those dodgy hips aren't getting any better and eventually will need to be replaced. In fact, joint-replacement surgeries started to rebound in late 2009 and have continued the pace in early 2010.

Hospitals and other institutions were under many of the same economic pressures as consumers and simply delayed many of the big-ticket purchases that had been planned for 2009. Stryker's Medical/Surgical equipment sales were off 5 percent in 2009, but we expect the medical equipment market to turn around significantly in late 2010 and Stryker should benefit.

The market leader in replacement hip devices, Zimmer, stumbled in 2009 and had to suspend its leading product, allowing Stryker (and others) to gain appreciable market share.

Stryker is the tenth largest supplier of medical technology in the world and are number one in sales in the $35.6 billion orthopedic market. They are also number one (by a 3:1 margin) in the $3.3 billion worldwide operating room equipment market, and a strong number two in the $1.9 billion patient handling market. Although they have strong presence in all of their orthopedics markets, they do not lead in any of them and have significant opportunity for the capture of additional market share.

Reasons for Caution

Stryker Biotech, its former president and three of its current sales managers were indicted in federal court in October 2009 by the FDA for participating in a fraudulent marketing scheme, specifically for recommending a particular medical procedure that had not been approved by the FDA in all applications. Conviction of these charges could result in significant monetary fines and Stryker Biotech's exclusion from participating in federal and state health care programs, which could have a material effect on Stryker Biotech's business.

SECTOR: Health Care
BETA COEFFICIENT: .80
10-YEAR COMPOUND EARNINGS PER SHARE GROWTH: 22.5 percent
10-YEAR COMPOUND DIVIDENDS PER SHARE GROWTH: 23 percent

	2002	2003	2004	2005	2006	2007	2008	2009
Revenues (Mil)	3,012	3,625	4,262	4,872	5,406	6,001	6,718	6,722
Net income (Mil)	346	454	586	644	778	1,017	1,148	1,107
Earnings per share	0.88	1.12	1.43	1.57	1.89	2.44	2.78	2.77
Dividends per share	0.05	0.07	0.09	0.11	0.11	0.22	0.33	0.5
Cash flow per share	1.37	1.71	2.08	2.49	2.85	3.33	3.87	3.75
Price: high	33.8	42.7	57.7	56.3	55.9	76.9	74.9	52.7
low	21.9	29.9	40.3	39.7	39.8	54.9	35.4	30.8

Stryker Corporation
P. O. Box 4085
Kalamazoo, MI 49003–4085
(616) 385-2600
Website: *www.strykercorp.com*

Suburban Propane Partners, L.P.

Ticker symbol: SPH (NYSE) ❑ S&P rating: BB ❑ Value Line financial strength rating: B+ ❑ Current yield: 7.4 percent

Company Profile

You probably know this company best for its propane distribution business and the white sausage-shaped tanks dotting the landscape especially in rural areas, and for the trucks serving them. Suburban Propane Partners, L.P., through its subsidiaries, engages in the retail marketing and distribution of propane, fuel oil, and refined fuels, and to a lesser extent in the marketing of natural gas and electricity in the United States.

The Propane segment is the largest segment, and engages in the retail distribution of propane to residential, commercial, industrial, and agricultural customers, as well as wholesale distribution to large industrial end users. The Fuel Oil and Refined Fuels segment engages in the retail distribution of fuel oil, diesel, kerosene, and gasoline to residential and commercial customers for use primarily as a source of heat in homes and buildings primarily in the East, while the Natural Gas and Electricity segment markets those commodities to to residential and commercial customers in the deregulated energy markets of New York and Pennsylvania.

Suburban Propane Partners, L.P. is also involved in selling and

servicing heating, ventilation and air conditioning (HVAC) units that consume its fuels. As of September 2009, the company served approximately 850,000 residential, commercial, industrial, and agricultural customers through approximately 300 locations in thirty states, concentrated in the east and west coast regions of the United States, including Alaska.

Financial Highlights, Fiscal Year 2009

Despite the visibility of the white tanks in the residential segment, Suburban's business is more concentrated in non-residential customers, accounting for some 63 percent of its customer base, and these customers have been hurt by the recession. As a result of this and price declines from 2008, revenues declined sharply from $1.57 billion in 2008 to $1.14 billion in 2009. The company has reacted well to the downturn by cutting costs and lowering interest costs (some 30 percent from the previous year), but there are lingering concerns that many of the small businesses the company has served are either gone or merged with other companies.

In the second fiscal quarter ending in March 2010 the business continued to soften, with a 7.4 percent decrease in the total gallons of propane sold at retail. Net income per unit dropped to an adjusted $3.10 from $3.79 the year before in this typically seasonally strong quarter. Sales in the smaller but more sensitive heating oil segment showed a sharper drop with favorable weather conditions (3 percent warmer than normal in the Northeast, 6 percent warmer in the Southeast) and customer conservation efforts. These numbers do not sound very positive, but the company remains confident that with moderation of wholesale propane prices and an economic recovery, the future looks solid.

Reasons to Buy

The main draw with companies like Suburban Propane is the high and steady dividend. SPH pays out between 70 and 95 percent of its earnings each year as dividends, making its shareholders feel like true company owners. Although demand has fluctuated recently with the recession, the business looks relatively stable long term and has taken steps to strengthen the balance sheet and secure the payout. Customers who use propane are likely to continue doing so, and propane commodity prices appear to be steady and predictable.

Reasons for Caution

As mentioned above, the recession has hit small businesses hard, and many of these users may be gone for good. There don't appear to be any substantial growth drivers in the form of new propane users on the horizon, although the company has made a few "bolt on" acquisitions in key markets to leverage its operating platform. Suburban should be looked at like a utility, with a relatively steady customer base and a high payout from earnings. This issue should be bought for income, not for price appreciation.

SECTOR: Energy
BETA COEFFICIENT: 0.75
10-YEAR COMPOUND EARNINGS PER SHARE GROWTH: 16.5 percent
10-YEAR COMPOUND DIVIDENDS PER SHARE GROWTH: 7.0 percent

	2002	2003	2004	2005	2006	2007	2008	2009
Revenues (Mil)	665.1	771.7	1307.3	1620.2	1661.6	1439.6	1574.2	1143.2
Net income (Mil)	49.1	46.2	28.9	(9.1)	90.7	123.3	111.2	165.2
Earnings per share	1.94	1.76	.96	(.29)	2.84	3.79	3.39	4.99
Dividends per share	2.28	2.33	2.41	2.45	2.50	2.69	3.14	3.28
Cash flow per share	3.15	3.70	2.17	.92	4.09	4.66	4.26	5.55
Price: high	28.5	32.5	35.7	37.4	39.2	49.6	42.6	47.7
low	20.0	26.9	27.6	23.5	26.0	35.1	20.4	31.0

Suburban Propane Partners, L.P.
240 Route 10 West
Whippany, NJ 07981
(973) 887-5300
Website: *www.suburbanpropane.com*

Sysco Corporation

Ticker symbol: SYY (NYSE) ❑ S&P rating: AA- ❑ Value Line financial strength rating: A++ ❑ Current yield: 3.3 percent

Company Profile

Sysco was founded in 1969 with the goal of becoming a national foodservice network. By 1977, the company had become the largest foodservice supplier in North America, a position they have retained for over thirty years. They conduct business in over 100 countries.

Sysco operates 186 distribution facilities across the United States, Canada and Ireland. Their ninety-nine Broadline facilities supply independent and chain restaurants and other food preparation facilities with a wide variety of food and non-food products. They have seventeen hotel supply locations, sixteen specialty produce facilities, twenty SYGMA distribution centers (specialized, high-volume centers supplying to chain restaurants), twelve custom-cutting meat locations, and two distributors specializing in the niche Asian foodservice market.

The company also supplies the hotel industry with guest amenities, equipment, housekeeping supplies, room accessories and textiles.

Most people are unaware of just how many times during the day they cross paths with Sysco's

products and services. Sysco's distribution facilities provide over 400,000 different food and related products (including 40,000 with Sysco brands) to over 400,000 restaurants, hotels, schools, hospitals, retirement homes, hotels and other locations where food is prepared.

Sysco is by far the largest company in the foodservice distribution industry. The company estimates that they serve about 16 percent of a $231 billion annual market. Sysco's sales dwarfs those of its two chief competitors, U.S. Foodservice and Performance Food Group.

Financial Highlights, Fiscal Year 2009

Sales declined 1.8 percent primarily due to deteriorating economic conditions and the impact that had on consumer spending. Volatile fuel prices and food costs adversely affected earnings through the first half, but stabilized significantly in the second half of the year. Overall product cost increases for the year accounted for 4.7 percent of revenue.

Operating income was nearly flat year-over-year as a percentage of sales as the company found ways to do more with less. Net earnings declined 4.5 percent due to reduced sales volume, higher fuel costs, increased losses on receivables, and losses on the surrender value of corporate-owned life insurance policies. Diluted EPS fell 2.2 percent.

The company repurchased nearly 11 million shares of stock and raised the dividend an additional 13 percent to $.93/share.

Reasons to Buy

Sysco keeps margins high by selling products under its own label, a strategy it began a year after its founding. Its private-label business carries an estimated 24 percent gross margin, or 10 percent more than it earns on national brands. This is a very healthy figure in the food industry.

The company is finding opportunities in the recession, acquiring its first broadline distribution business located outside North America. In May 2009 they acquired Pallas Foods, the leading food distributor in Ireland. Pallas' revenue in the year prior was approximately $200 million. The Irish operations will continue to be run by Pallas management.

Sysco's recent investments in technology continue to bear fruit.

Improvements in routing and inventory management have allowed the company to increase it shipment frequency by 10 percent with 4 percent fewer people, all while using 10 percent less fuel. Shipments per man-hour are up 15 percent, cases per trip are up 2 percent and errors are down 3 percent, according to the company.

The foodservice business is highly fragmented. Sysco is the largest player with approximately 17 percent market share, and over half the market is split among companies holding less than 1 percent each. This would be a good time to grow market share through acquisition, and Sysco's balance sheet is solid. Of interest is the fact that in the past two years Sysco's two largest competitors were bought and taken private by equity firms.

Reasons for Caution

Although the trend is slowing, the recession still has folks eating out less often and restaurants and hotels are buying fewer supplies and equipment. Last year was the first full-year decline in sales and earnings in Sysco's history, and 2010's organic growth will likely show only marginal volume gains.

SECTOR: Consumer Staples
BETA COEFFICIENT: .70
10-YEAR COMPOUND EARNINGS PER SHARE GROWTH: 13.5 percent
10-YEAR COMPOUND DIVIDENDS PER SHARE GROWTH: 17.5 percent

		2002	2003	2004	2005	2006	2007	2008	2009
Revenues (Mil)		23,351	26,140	29,335	30,282	32,628	35,042	37,522	36,853
Net income (Mil)		680	778	907	961	855	1,001	1,106	1,056
Earnings per share		1.01	1.18	1.37	1.47	1.35	1.6	1.81	1.77
Dividends per share		0.36	0.4	0.48	0.58	0.66	0.72	0.82	0.93
Cash flow per share		1.47	1.63	1.87	2.03	1.92	2.23	2.46	2.44
Price:	high	32.6	37.6	41.3	38.4	37	36.7	35	29.5
	low	21.2	22.9	29.5	30	26.5	29.9	20.7	19.4

Sysco Corporation
1390 Enclave Parkway
Houston, TX 77077–2099
(281) 584-1458
Website: *www.sysco.com*

Target Corporation

Ticker symbol: TGT (NYSE) ❑ S&P rating: A+ ❑ Value Line financial strength rating: A ❑ Current yield: 1.3 percent

Company Profile

Target Corporation (formerly Dayton Hudson Corporation) was formed in 1969 through the merger of two old-line department store companies, Dayton Corporation and J. L. Hudson Company. In 1990, TGT acquired another venerable retailer, Marshall Field & Company. The Dayton's and Hudson's stores (once run separately, but combined later under the Marshall Field umbrella) were sold to Federated Department Stores in late 2004. Target now operates nearly 1,740 stores, including 251 "Super-Targets," which also carry groceries.

Target is the nation's second-largest general merchandise retailer, specializing in large-store formats, including discount stores, moderate-priced promotional stores, and traditional department stores. Target stores are situated largely in California, Texas, Florida, and the upper Midwest. Current retail space is about 232 million square feet.

In 2000, the company formed "target.direct," the direct merchandising and electronic retailing organization. The business combines the e-commerce team of Target with its direct merchandising unit into one integrated organization. The target.direct organization operates seven websites, which support the store and catalog brands in an online environment and produces six retail catalogs.

Target positions itself against its main competitor, Wal-Mart, as a more upscale and trend-conscious "cheap chic" alternative. The typical Target customer has a higher level of disposable income, which the company courts through its offerings of proprietary goods from a number of high-end designers. By and large, however, there is a great deal of commonality between the company's branded offerings.

The company's revenues come from retail sales and credit card operations. Target is one of the few retailers that still finance their in-house credit operations.

Financial Highlights, Fiscal Year 2009

Target saw revenues increase only 0.9 percent in 2009, although earnings were up 15.2 percent for the year and 53 percent in the fourth quarter. Comps were also negative for the year but positive in the fourth quarter. Retailers are starting to see signs of life from consumers.

The company has begun to clean up its credit card operation, which in 2008 performed miserably, with a return on invested capital of 3.7 percent. In 2009 the ROIC rose to 7 percent, largely due to reduced expenses and a smaller pool of receivables.

Reasons to Buy

Although 2009 didn't look like much of a turnaround year, the fourth quarter numbers were impressive and should provide some momentum for TGT. It's been a dismal six quarters for retailers, and to see Target's earnings recover so quickly as the economy starts to turn around is very encouraging. Also, Target's credit card operation looks to have put most of its troubles behind it for now and cash flow remains strong.

Target has some of the highest customer satisfaction numbers in the industry, and though comps dropped year to year, store visits and unit volume were up in the fourth quarter. Price increases have carried Target through a tight economy, and they plan to leverage this with an increased percentage of store brands. They also plan to increase customer visits by expanding their grocery offerings.

Target is also introducing a new store format called PFresh, which is very much like their Super Target in terms of items, but in a smaller format. They will carry 90 percent of the grocery items that a Super Target carries, but the space devoted to the grocery area will be about 40 percent smaller. Grocery traffic may not require the amount of space that has been allocated in the Super Targets, and a "deli" atmosphere may in fact be more conducive to impulse sales.

Improved economic conditions should improve Target's market share. Trend data indicates that Target performs better than its competitors during periods of economic growth. As consumer confidence improves through late 2010, we expect Target to get the larger share of consumer spending growth.

Reasons for Caution

Target is up against some very tough competitors in Wal-Mart and, to a lesser extent (due to a different product mix), Costco. Also, these two competitors are growing their international presence, while Target has none and has no plans for growth outside the United States. Target is tied more closely to the domestic consumer market, consumer confidence, and access to credit than is either of its major competitors.

SECTOR: **Retail**
BETA COEFFICIENT: **1.05**
10-YEAR COMPOUND EARNINGS PER SHARE GROWTH: **14.5 percent**
10-YEAR COMPOUND DIVIDENDS PER SHARE GROWTH: **12.0 percent**

	2002	2003	2004	2005	2006	2007	2008	2009
Revenues (Mil)	43,917	48,163	46,839	52,620	59,490	63,367	64,948	63,435
Net income (Mil)	1,654	1,841	1,885	2,408	2,787	2,849	2214	2488
Earnings per share	1.81	2.01	2.07	2.71	3.21	3.33	2.86	3.3
Dividends per share	0.24	0.26	0.3	0.38	0.42	0.56	0.6	0.66
Cash flow per share	3.15	3.47	3.53	4.37	4.98	5.51	5.37	5.9
Price: high	46.2	41.8	54.1	60	60.3	70.8	59.6	51.8
low	24.9	25.6	36.6	45.6	44.7	48.8	25.6	25

Target Corporation
1000 Nicollet Mall
Minneapolis, MN 55403
(612) 370-6735
Website: *www.target.com*

AGGRESSIVE GROWTH

Teva Pharmaceutical Industries, Ltd.

Ticker symbol: TEVA (NASDAQ) ▫ S&P rating: A- ▫ Value Line financial strength rating: A ▫
Current yield: 1.2 percent

Company Profile

Teva was founded in Jerusalem in 1901 as Salomon, Levin and Elstein, Ltd., a small wholesale drug business that imported medicines, loaded them onto the backs of camels and donkeys, and distributed them to customers throughout the area. Teva is now among the top fifteen pharmaceutical companies in the world and is the largest generic pharmaceutical company.

The company develops, manufactures and markets generic and proprietary pharmaceuticals and active pharmaceutical ingredients. Its generic portfolio is extensive—in the United States. Teva USA markets nearly 400 generic pharmaceuticals. Its innovative drug line is far smaller, but includes some widely prescribed and very profitable medications, including Copaxone® (for the treatment of multiple sclerosis) and Azilect® (Parkinson's disease).

The company has over sixty manufacturing and marketing facilities worldwide, with the bulk of its operations located in Europe, the United States, and Israel. Over 80 percent of Teva's sales are in North America and Western Europe.

Financial Highlights, Fiscal Year 2009

Teva turned in yet another record year in 2009, with net sales up 25 percent to $13.9 billion and earnings up 28 percent to $3 billion. The company generated record annual cash flow from operations of $3.4 billion. Sales were up significantly across all product lines and geographies.

North American sales, representing 61 percent of total sales, grew 34 percent versus 2008, driven primarily by strong generic sales and increased sales of Copaxone® and ProAir™. The gain in sales also reflects the launch of a number of generics in 2009, including Prevacid® Delayed-Release, Allegra-D®, and Adderall XR®.

European sales increased 10 percent (22 percent in local currencies) compared to 2008, reaching $3.3 billion. The increased sales resulted from strong generic sales mainly in Germany, Spain, Poland and France, as well as increased sales of Copaxone® and Azilect®.

Reasons to Buy

Teva is the largest player in the volume-driven generic drug industry. Teva estimates that it supplies 16 percent of all prescriptions written in the United States, nearly twice as many as its next closest competitor (Mylan Labs).

As of February 5, 2010, Teva had 216 product applications awaiting final FDA approval, including forty-three tentative approvals. Collectively, the brand products covered by these applications had annual U.S. sales of over $113 billion.

In March 2010 Teva announced that it has won in bidding for Ratiopharm, the world's fourth-largest generic company in sales. The price, $5 billion, was $900 million higher than Pfizer's best offer and represents about four quarters of Teva's current cash flow, equivalent to two times Ratiopharm's current revenue. The purchase makes Teva the market leader in Europe, an area where it had lagged. Teva sees the worldwide generic drug market growing to $120 billion in 2012, and capturing market share any way it can is a priority for Teva.

The U.S. medical care reform bill included at least two provisions that should keep Teva shareholders happy. First was the decision not to allow imported prescription drugs into the United States. This will assure drug marketers of continued high margins for U.S.-based sales, and the United States accounts for the majority of Teva's sales. The second was a provision that left intact the negotiation process whereby pharmaceutical patent holders could pay generic manufacturers not to develop competing products for a set period of time. We'd like to get in on that—we tried not growing corn but we failed.

Over the past five years, the company's sales and earnings have tripled. The company is in outstanding financial shape, with ample cash flow and credit for future acquisitions and funding of internal R&D.

Reasons for Caution

Teva's success is greatly affected by their ability to prevail in so-called "Paragraph IV" patent challenges— challenges to the exclusivity rights granted to the patent holder by the FDA. As of March 2010, 133 of Teva's nearly 210 product applications to the FDA were Paragraph IV applications.

In May 2010, a jury in Nevada awarded a single plaintiff $356 million in a case in which a patient acquired hepatitis after being treated with Teva's Propofol. Teva, not surprisingly, plans to appeal.

SECTOR: Health Care
BETA COEFFICIENT: .55
5-YEAR COMPOUND EARNINGS PER SHARE GROWTH: 26.0 percent
5-YEAR COMPOUND DIVIDENDS PER SHARE GROWTH: 29.0 percent

	2002	2003	2004	2005	2006	2007	2008	2009
Revenues (Mil)	2,519	3,276	4,799	5,250	8,400	9,408	11,085	13,899
Net income (Mil)	410	691	965	1,072	1,867	1,952	2,374	3,029
Earnings per share	0.76	1.04	1.42	1.59	2.3	2.38	2.86	3.37
Dividends per share	0.09	0.14	0.16	0.27	0.3	0.39	0.49	0.60
Cash flow per share	0.96	1.36	1.94	2.13	3.03	3.22	3.37	4.45
Price: high	20.1	31.2	34.7	45.9	44.7	47.1	50	56.9
low	12.9	17.3	22.8	26.8	29.2	30.8	35.9	41.1

Teva Pharmaceutical Industries, Ltd.
5 Basel Street
P.O. Box 3190
Petach Tikva
Israel 49131
(215) 591-8912
Website: *www.tevapharm.com*

AGGRESSIVE GROWTH

The TJX Companies, Inc.

Ticker symbol: TJX (NYSE) □ S&P rating: A □ Value Line financial strength rating: A+ □ Current yield: 1.3 percent

Company Profile

The TJX Companies, Inc. is the leading off-price apparel and home fashions retailer in the United States and worldwide, with $20 billion in revenues in 2009, eight reporting businesses, and more than 2,700 stores. The company sells a variety of brand name merchandise at prices discounted 20 to 60 percent compared to department and specialty store prices. Its target customers are middle- to upper-middle income fashion and value conscious shoppers who fit the same general profile as a department store shopper.

T.J. Maxx, founded in 1976, is the largest off-price retailer of apparel and home fashions in the United States. T.J. Maxx offers brand name family apparel, giftware, home fashions, women's shoes and lingerie, and emphasizes accessories and fine jewelry at discount prices.

Marshalls is the second largest off-price retailer in the United States and was acquired by TJX in 1995. Marshalls and T.J Maxx address similar markets with a slightly different mix of goods. Marshalls and T.J. Maxx together have 1,700 stores and both have growth opportunities in the U.S. market.

HomeGoods, a chain of off-price home fashions stores, operates 289 stores in the United States. This chain operates in a stand-alone and superstore format, which couple HomeGoods with a T.J. Maxx or Marshalls. Ultimately, the company believes that the U.S. market could support 650 HomeGoods stores.

Winners operates 211 stores in Canada and has grown into the leading off-price family apparel retailer in that country since it was acquired by TJX in 1990. Patterned after T.J. Maxx, Winners offers brand name family apparel, giftware, fine jewelry, home fashions, accessories, lingerie, and family footwear.

With its launch in 2001, HomeSense introduced the home fashions off-price concept to Canada. Similar to HomeGoods in the United States, at year-end 2009 HomeSense operated seventy-nine stores with a typical store size of 24,000 square feet.

T.K. Maxx, a T.J. Maxx-like off-price apparel and home fashions concept, operates 263 stores in the United Kingdom, Ireland, Germany and Poland. T.K. Maxx has been very well received since its launch in 1994, and management sees the United Kingdom and Ireland supporting 300 stores in the long term.

A.J. Wright, launched in 1998, operates similarly to the company's other off-price concepts, but targets the moderate-income customer. A.J. Wright operates 150 stores in the United States, with an average size of 26,000 square feet. TJX believes 1,000 stores is a reasonable long-term target.

Financial Highlights, Fiscal Year 2010 (FY2010 ended January 31, 2010)

Net sales for FY2010 were up 7 percent to $20.3 billion on a 6 percent increase in comps and 4 percent bump from new stores. Store count and retail square footage increased 3 percent in 2010. Customer traffic was up significantly, more than offsetting a decline in the value of the average transaction. Cost of sales fell 210 basis points, or 2.1 percent, on improved merchandise margins, which was driven by the company's decision to run leaner inventory levels through the recession. Earnings for the year were up a very healthy 33 percent to $1.2 billion.

The company added ninety-one stores (forty-nine in Canada/Europe), representing an increase of 3.2 percent of selling space (9

percent increase in Canada/Europe). The company also completed its sale of the underperforming Bob's franchise to Versa Capital Management, for $23 million.

Reasons to Buy

TJX came through the recession far better than most, with solid organic growth, many new stores, and an inventory management plan that left them entering the new year with record levels of cash, record profits, and record margins. What's not to like? Not much, apparently, as the stock has been bid up to $45/share (June 2010). This is nearly 30 percent higher than its previous all-time high, making this very uncharted territory.

So—is TJX still a bargain or should you shop elsewhere? Well, consider that over the past year, which has been as bumpy a ride as we may see in a long time, TJX only increased their gross margin by 200 basis points, their net margin by 130 basis points, their cash flow by 30 percent, and per-share earnings by 40 percent—all on sales growth of 7 percent. They seem to have figured a few things out.

The company is on plan to open approximately 300 stores over the next two years, but we feel that's fairly conservative given their strong balance sheet. Not only that, but they've been getting much better than average margins at their European stores, and a high percentage of their growth plan is focused there.

Reasons for Caution

A.J. Wright's continues to run on very thin margins (1.6 percent net), even as sales have risen 24 percent over the past two years. Given the performance of the rest of the segments, one can't help but wonder about the viability of the model. Store growth is targeted for an additional 6 percent of square footage next year.

SECTOR: Retail
BETA COEFFICIENT: .80
10-YEAR COMPOUND EARNINGS PER SHARE GROWTH: 15 percent
10-YEAR COMPOUND DIVIDENDS PER SHARE GROWTH: 22 percent

	2003	2004	2005	2006	2007	2008	2009	2010
Revenues (Mil)	11,981	13,328	14,913	16,058	17,405	18,647	19,000	20,288
Net income (Mil)	578.4	658.4	683.4	690.4	7388	777.8	884	1,214
Earnings per share	1.08	1.28	1.34	1.29	1.63	1.66	2.01	2.84
Dividends per share	0.12	0.14	0.18	0.24	0.28	0.36	0.44	0.48
Cash flow per share	1.51	1.80	2.00	2.06	2.49	2.95	3.11	4.03
Price: high	22.5	23.7	26.8	26	29.8	32.5	37.5	40.6
low	15.3	15.5	20.6	20	22.2	25.7	17.8	19.2

The TJX Companies, Inc.
770 Cochituate Road
Framingham, MA 01701
(508) 390-2323
Website: *www.tjx.com*

Tractor Supply Company

Ticker symbol: TSCO (NASDAQ) ❑ S&P rating: not rated ❑ Value Line financial strength rating: A+ ❑ Current yield: 1.0 percent

Company Profile

Tractor Supply Company is the largest operator of retail farm and ranch stores in the United States. Their focus is the needs of recreational farmers and ranchers and those who enjoy the rural lifestyle, as well as tradesmen and small businesses. They operate retail stores, many in a "big box" format, under the names Tractor Supply Company and Del's Farm Supply. Their stores are located in towns outside major metropolitan markets and in rural communities. Representative merchandise includes supplies for horses, pets, and other farm animals, equipment maintenance products, hardware and tools, lawn and garden equipment, and work and recreational clothing and footwear.

Tractor Supply stores typically range in size from 15,500 square feet to 18,500 square feet of inside selling space and additional outside selling space. As of December 27, 2008, they operated 903 retail farm and ranch stores in forty-four states.

Del's Farm Supply operates twenty-seven stores primarily in the Pacific Northwest, offering a wide selection of products (primarily in the horse, pet and animal category)

targeted at those who enjoy the rural lifestyle. The company does not plan to grow Del's significantly beyond its current size.

They operate their own distribution network for supplying stores and in fiscal 2009, stores received approximately two-thirds of their merchandise through this network. The six distribution centers are located in Indiana, Georgia, Maryland, Texas, Nebraska, and Washington, representing total warehousing capacity of 2.9 million square feet. No warehousing expansions are needed or planned for 2010.

Tractor Supply Company also sells a subset of its store goods online.

Financial Highlights, Fiscal Year 2009

Tractor Supply stumbled a bit in 2008 but delivered remarkable earnings in 2009, with sales up 6.7 percent and diluted per-share earnings up a stellar 44 percent. The increase in sales was due mainly to new store openings, as comps were down 1.1 percent. The same-store daily transaction rate was up over 5 percent, but the average sale was off 6 percent as the number of "big ticket" purchases fell significantly.

Gross margin increased 200 basis points to 32.3 percent, due primarily to a decrease in the LIFO provision. Net margin was up 90 basis points to 3.6 percent. Both of these results are reversals of last year's results. Operating margin increased 130 basis points as a result of improved cost controls and supplier management.

TSCO opened seventy-five new stores in 2009 and closed none. Since 2004 they have closed only four stores.

Reasons to Buy

TSCO serves a growing, specialized niche in geographies often ignored by other retailers. They carry a specialized mix of merchandise that occupies a broad space— part big-box hardware, part garden shop, and part feed store. Their unique target market nonetheless has broad geographic distribution, giving TSCO room for growth, and they plan to grow more than 10 percent a year, with a target of 1,800 units.

The company has a solid balance sheet. In 2009 they eliminated their long-term debt, initiated their first-ever dividend, and continued their share repurchase program. Their working capital is now funded by their substantial cash flow, which increased 25 percent in 2009. There's nothing here to hold back TSCO's expansion plans. The company, in fact, opened nineteen new stores in the first quarter of 2010.

TSCO carries a higher percentage of house brands than you would find at a typical hardware retailer. They earn higher gross margins on these products and build rebuy loyalty in the process.

TSCO's 1Q2010 results have come in well ahead of 2009's pace, and although the heavy seasonality makes it difficult to draw solid comparisons, 2010 is clearly off to a very good start. Sales are up 10 percent and net margin is up over 120 basis points.

Pet and livestock feed have grown nearly 4 percent as a constituent of TSCO's total sales. This is a good trend for a retailer, as buyers are reluctant to change feed or vendors once an animal has accepted a particular brand.

Reasons for Caution

There's not a lot holding them back at this point. TSCO's growth is bound to attract competition. The sooner they can build out to their target size, the better they will be able to protect margins.

SECTOR: Retail
BETA COEFFICIENT: 0.9
10-YEAR COMPOUND EARNINGS PER SHARE GROWTH: 20.0 percent
10-YEAR COMPOUND DIVIDENDS PER SHARE GROWTH: NA

	2002	2003	2004	2005	2006	2007	2008	2009
Revenues (Mil)	1,210	1,473	1,739	2,068	2,370	2,703	3,008	3,207
Net income (Mil)	38.8	58.4	64.1	85.7	91	96.2	81.9	115.5
Earnings per share	0.99	1.45	1.57	2.09	2.22	2.4	2.19	3.15
Dividends per share	-	-	-	-	-	-		-
Cash flow per share	1.51	2.09	2.38	3.04	3.31	3.93	3.96	5.04
Price: high	22.8	44.9	45.8	58.6	67.6	57.7	47.5	54.5
low	8.4	14.7	30.2	33.2	38.8	35.1	26.7	28.7

Tractor Supply Company
200 Powell Place
Brentwood, TN 37027
(615) 440-4000
Website: *www.tractorsupply.com*

UnitedHealth Group

Ticker symbol: UNH (NYSE) ❑ S&P rating: A- ❑ Value Line financial strength rating: A+ ❑ Current yield: 1.6 percent

Company Profile

UnitedHealth Group is the parent company of a number of health insurers and service organizations. They are the second-largest publicly traded health insurance company in the United States, with over $81 billion in revenue reported in 2008.

The company operates in four business units: Health Benefits, which includes UnitedHealthcare, Ovations and AmeriChoice; OptumHealth; Ingenix and Prescription Solutions.

United Health Care sells health insurance plans to companies and individuals, Ovations provides Medicare benefits, and Ameri-Choice provides benefits to Medicaid clients.

Taken together, these operations generated $81.3 billion in revenue in 2009, or approximately 92 percent of UNH's overall revenue. As of January 1, 2010, UNC provided services to over 24,000 employer-sponsored health care plans.

The remainder of the company's revenue comes from their health services businesses, which consists of OptumHealth, Ingenix and Prescription Solutions.

OptumHealth is a comprehensive care management and services company targeted at end consumers. Ingenix provides clinical health care data, analytics, research and consulting services to other health care providers. Prescription Solutions is a pharmacy benefit management program.

Financial Highlights, Fiscal Year 2009

UNH's revenues grew 8 percent year over year to $87.1 billion due primarily to growth in the client base at both Ovations and AmeriChoice and premium rate increases at Ovations. The increase at AmeriChoice was particularly strong—it experienced organic growth of 24 percent, or 565,000 individual members. These increases led to revenue growth at Ovations and AmeriChoice of 15 and 40 percent respectively.

Prescription Solutions also turned in strong growth of 15 percent, netting $1.9 billion on increases in the customer base for Medicare Part D prescription drug plans. Prescription Solutions was the only segment to improve its operating margin year over year. The company as a whole gained 80 basis points of operating margin and saw diluted EPS rise nearly 35 percent.

Reasons to Buy

The company got off to a great start in 2010, turning in first quarter results that exceeded expectations by far. Improvements in the non-farm unemployment numbers has led to expectations of a modest gain in earnings, but per share net came in at a 27 percent year-over-year increase. These were solid numbers, based on volume and pricing gains, and are very encouraging for the year forward.

UNH provides insurance for some 80 million Americans. The scale of UNH's operation gives it tremendous leverage when negotiating for the services of health care providers. Hospitals are strongly motivated to join UNH's network as doing so will provide assurance of steady referrals.

The national unemployment rate appears to be turning to the good. After more than a year in the neighborhood of 10 percent, mid-2010 unemployment rates are in the low 9 percent range. As more people return to work, more employer-based insurance programs will require servicing.

The company recently raised the dividend from $.03 to $.50 and is changing from a yearly to a quarterly dividend cycle. This represents a large shift in approach to shareholder value, as the previous dividend was little more than ceremonial. The company also plans to shore up share prices with a stock repurchase. In 2009 they repurchased 4.5 percent of their outstanding shares and plan to buy back another 7 percent in 2010. For the period 2006–2010, they will have reduced their share base by 25 percent.

Reasons for Caution

Since 2007 the company has paid over $3 billion in fines, legal costs, and settlements pertaining to legal actions brought against them by various private and public agencies. The company is still legally exposed as a result of some actions taken by previous management with regard to Medicare payment rates. Current management appears to be serious about cleaning up the messes left behind, but the investor should be aware of this risk of additional litigation.

In addition, public sector sentiment toward the health insurance industry is hardly favorable these days; additional regulation beyond that already built into the recent health care legislation seems likely. These companies will have to be on their best behavior to prosper.

SECTOR: **Health Care**
BETA COEFFICIENT: **1.0**
10-YEAR COMPOUND EARNINGS PER SHARE GROWTH: **25.5 percent**
10-YEAR COMPOUND DIVIDENDS PER SHARE GROWTH: **23.0 percent**

	2002	**2003**	**2004**	**2005**	**2006**	**2007**	**2008**	**2009**
Revenues (Mil)	25,020	28,823	37,218	45,365	71,542	75,431	81,186	87,138
Net income (Mil)	1,352	1,825	2,587	3,300	4,159	4,654	3,660	3,822
Earnings per share	1.06	1.48	1.97	2.48	2.97	3.42	2.95	3.24
Dividends per share	0.01	0.01	0.02	0.03	0.03	0.03	0.03	0.03
Cash flow per share	1.34	1.82	2.30	2.76	3.59	4.35	3.86	4.20
Price: high	25.3	29.3	44.4	64.6	62.9	59.5	57.9	33.3
low	17	19.6	27.7	42.6	41.4	45.8	14.5	16.2

UnitedHealth Group
9900 Bren Street
Minnetonka, MN 55343
(952) 936-1300
Website: *www.unitedhealthgroup.com*

United Technologies Corporation

Ticker symbol: UTX (NYSE) ▫ S&P rating: A+ ▫ Value Line Financial Strength: A++ ▫ Current yield: 2.3 percent

Company Profile

United Technologies provides high-technology products to the aerospace and building systems industries throughout the world. Its subsidiary companies are industry leaders and include:

- **Pratt & Whitney**—Large and small commercial and military jet engines, spare parts and product support, specialized engine maintenance and overhaul and repair services for airlines, air forces, and corporate fleets; rocket engines and space propulsion systems; and industrial gas turbines.
- **UTC Fire and Security**— Security and fire protection systems, integration, installation and servicing of intruder alarms, access control and video surveillance, and monitoring, response and security personnel services; installation, and servicing of fire detection and suppression systems.
- **Hamilton Sundstrand**— Aircraft electrical power generation and distribution systems; engine and flight controls; propulsion systems;

environmental controls for aircraft, spacecraft and submarines; auxiliary power units; product support, maintenance and repair services; space life support systems; industrial products including mechanical power transmissions, compressors, metering devices, and fluid handling equipment.

- **Sikorsky**—Design and manufacture of military and commercial helicopters; fixed-wing reconnaissance aircraft; spare parts and maintenance services for helicopters and fixed-wing aircraft; and civil helicopter operations.
- **UTC Power**—Combined heat, cooling and power systems for commercial and industrial applications and fuel cell systems made by UTC Fuel Cells for commercial, transportation and space applications, including the U.S. space shuttle program.
- **Carrier**—Heating, ventilating and air conditioning (HVAC) equipment for commercial, industrial and residential buildings; HVAC replacement parts and services; building

controls; commercial, industrial, and transport refrigeration equipment.

- **Otis**—Design and manufacture of elevators; escalators, moving walks and shuttle systems, and related installation, maintenance and repair services; modernization products and service for elevators and escalators.

P&W, Otis, and Carrier together accounted for two-thirds of FY2009 revenues. In FY2009, 60 percent of UTC's revenue came from international customers, while U.S. government contracts accounted for 17 percent of revenues.

Financial Highlights, Fiscal Year 2009

Earnings per share in 2009 fell 16 percent to $4.12 behind a revenue decline of 10 percent. Continued difficulty in UTX's primary markets (aerospace, construction) led to depressed revenues in those segments, which are also the higher-margin segments of UTX's business. To address its cost structure, the company took $830 million (18 percent of current cash flow) in restructuring charges in FY2009.

The company raised the dividend 14 percent, making 2009 the seventh straight year of double-digit percentage increases. The dividend has tripled since 2002 and is expected to grow another 20 percent through FY2011.

The company issued $2.25 billion in debt to finance the purchase of General Electric's GE Security business. The purchase price, agreed to in November 2009, was $1.8 billion but, like most of us, UTX likes a little extra for walking-around money. The deal will bolster United's strategy of locking in revenue streams by offering multi-year service contracts for equipment and systems in commercial buildings.

Reasons to Buy

In spite of the tough economic conditions prevalent in 2009 the company managed to perform well in a number of key areas: achievement toward their cost goals resulted in healthy cash flow, which exceeded net income; the company shored up the pension fund, contributing $1.3 billion; total shareholder return ended up in the top third of the Dow and in the top half of the S&P 500. Okay, so it's not exactly time to retire to Paris, but it was a tough year all over. The company made good progress during 2009 in reducing its cost structure, and the numbers for early 2010 have taken a decidedly upward swing.

Unlike many of its competitors, United Technologies maintains a global presence, and UTX will be ready wherever the construction market begins to turn around first.

The company's brands, particularly Otis, are well known and very well supported worldwide. And like Honeywell, UTX has a broad portfolio of products geared toward improving energy efficiency, which will be a significant growth market for several years to come.

The company expects flat organic revenue growth throughout 2010 but expects improved earnings growth throughout the year. Earnings in early 2010 have indeed been ahead of 2009 (and ahead of estimates) on slightly reduced revenues. The company also expects that earnings contributions from its recent acquisitions will become significant in 2011.

The board of directors has authorized a share buy-back program for up to 60 million shares of the company, worth approximately $4.3 billion at current prices. The new authorization supersedes a previous program, approved in June 2008, which is nearing completion. The company repurchased $1.1 billion of its shares during 2009 and expects 2010 repurchases to total $1.5 billion.

Reasons for Caution

About 25 percent of UTC's revenues are generated through residential housing. The housing market in early 2010 shows some signs of life, but the year looks to be another weak one for the Carrier brand.

SECTOR: **Industrials**
BETA COEFFICIENT: **0.95**
10-YEAR COMPOUND EARNINGS PER SHARE GROWTH: **15.5 percent**
10-YEAR COMPOUND DIVIDENDS PER SHARE GROWTH: **14.5 percent**

	2002	2003	2004	2005	2006	2007	2008	2009
Revenues (Mil)	28,212	31,034	37,445	42,725	47,740	54,759	58,681	52,920
Net income (Mil)	2,236	2,361	2,788	3,069	3,732	4,224	4,689	3,829
Earnings per share	2.21	2.35	2.76	3.03	3.71	4.27	4.9	4.12
Dividends per share	0.49	0.57	0.7	0.88	1.02	1.28	1.55	1.54
Cash flow per share	3.15	3.07	3.68	4.09	4.79	5.5	6.38	5.43
Price: high	38.9	48.4	53	58.9	67.5	82.5	77.1	70.9
low	24.4	26.8	40.4	48.4	54.2	61.8	41.8	37.4

United Technologies Corporation
One Financial Plaza
Hartford, CT 06103
(860) 728-7912
Website: *www.utc.com*

Valmont Industries

Ticker symbol: VMI (NYSE) □ S&P rating: BBB- □ Value Line financial strength rating: B++ □
Current yield: 0.9 percent

Company Profile

Valmont Industries was founded in 1946 as a supplier of irrigation products and became one of the classic post-war industrial success stories, growing along with the need for increased farm output. They were early pioneers of the center-pivot irrigation systems that enabled much of that growth and which now dominate the high-yield agricultural business. These machines remain a mainstay of their product line, which includes:

Engineered Support Structures—poles, towers, and other metal structures used in lighting, communications, traffic management and international utilities. Products are available as standard designs and engineered for custom applications as needed for industrial, commercial, and residential applications. If you've ever sat at a stop light and wondered how a single cantilevered arm could support four 400-lb traffic signals, these are the folks to ask.

■ Irrigation—Valmont produces a wide range of equipment, including gravity and drip products, as well as their center-pivot designs which can service up to 500 acres from a single machine. Valmont also sells their irrigation controllers to other manufacturers.

■ Coatings—Developed as an adjunct to their other metals product businesses, the coatings business now provides services such as galvanizing, electroplating, powder coating and anodizing to industrial customers throughout the company's operating areas.

■ Utility Support Structures—This segment produces the very large concrete and steel substations and electric transmission support towers used by electric utilities. This has been Valmont's most profitable operation over the last few years, due mainly to increased volumes in a period of declining costs.

Financial Highlights, Fiscal Year 2009

As bad as the second half of calendar 2008 was for big infrastructure players like Valmont, the 2009 bounce showed Valmont in a far more favorable light. Although revenues were down some 5 percent, earnings increased 18 percent and net margins rose 22 percent. The company cut its (already low) long-term debt in half and return on capital reached a record high. The improved margins were mainly due to the reduced cost of raw materials, particularly in steel.

Sales for the fourth quarter tapered off a bit due to a flat utilities infrastructure market, but the company posted better-than expected earnings for the quarter and the year.

The reduced revenues were due to lower sales volume in all segments other than Utility Support Structures, where sales revenues were up 37 percent. This increase was due in large part to the very high existing backlog entering 2009, which was not the case entering 2010, as most of that backlog had been worked off.

Reasons to Buy

Although the turmoil in the financial markets has depressed somewhat the sale of big-ticket farm equipment over the past eighteen months, Valmont has retained market share and remains the leader among the four dominant U.S.-based players in the large-scale irrigation market. The company's continued emphasis on growth into new geographies should pay dividends as India and China begin to adopt more modern agricultural methods, which so far

have had very little penetration in those two countries.

Valmont has announced its intent to purchase Delta Plc in an all-cash deal for $430 million, including $350 million in Delta debt. Delta is a U.K.-based manufacturer of support structures for the lighting, wireless and utility industry, industrial access systems and road safety systems in the U.K. The company has operations in Australia, New Zealand, the United States, China, South Africa and throughout Southeast Asia. Delta's engineered support structures business and galvanizing facilities will add size and geographic coverage to Valmont's current businesses.

The Delta purchase is the sort of deal that we had hoped to see when we picked Valmont as one of our "100 Best" a year ago. Their strong cash position and solid fiscal management put this deal on their plate, and it's exactly the right kind of deal for Valmont, at the right time. At the end of 2009, about 25 percent of Valmont's revenues were generated by sales to customers outside the United States or by products produced outside of the United States, a figure that the company wants to increase significantly over the next two years. If they are able to do so, they will be well on their way to positioning themselves as a preferred, low-cost supplier to the developing markets.

Reasons for Caution

The Irrigation business' income was off some 60 percent in 2009, and agricultural spending is likely to remain depressed though the first half of 2010, slowing the recovery of the irrigation sector. The absence of a "concrete" transportation infrastructure policy from the government casts some shadows on Valmont's lighting business prospects.

SECTOR: Industrials
BETA COEFFICIENT: 1.35
10-YEAR COMPOUND EARNINGS PER SHARE GROWTH: 12.5 percent
10-YEAR COMPOUND DIVIDENDS PER SHARE GROWTH: 7.0 percent

		2002	2003	2004	2005	2006	2007	2008	2009
Revenues (Mil)		855	837	1,031	1,108	1,281	1,500	1,907	1,815
Net income (Mil)		33.6	25.9	26.9	40.2	61.5	94.7	132.4	155
Earnings per share		1.37	1.06	1.10	1.58	2.38	3.63	5.04	5.70
Dividends per share		0.28	0.31	0.32	0.34	0.37	0.41	0.50	0.58
Price:	high	25.5	24.3	28.0	35.3	61.2	99.0	120.5	89.3
	low	14.1	17.7	19.3	21.3	32.8	50.9	37.5	37.5

Valmont Industries
100 Abbott Park Road
Abbott Park, IL 60064–6400
(847) 937-3923
Website: *www.abbott.com*

Verizon Communications, Inc.

Ticker symbol: VZ (NYSE) ❏ S&P rating: A ❏ Value Line financial strength rating: A+ ❏ Current yield: 6.3 percent

Company Profile

Verizon operates two telecommunications businesses: Domestic Wireless, which provides wireless voice and data services, and Wireline, which provides voice, broadband data and video, Internet access, long-distance and other services, and which also owns and operates a very large global Internet Protocol network.

The Wireline segment also supplies Verizon's Fiber-to-the-Home (FiOS) broadband data infrastructure. One of Verizon's largest investments, FiOS provides a very high bandwidth link to the Internet, easily surpassing DSL and even cable. Over this network, Verizon can provide hundreds of HD video stream, high-speed data, and voice all simultaneously.

The Domestic Wireless segment is served by Verizon Wireless, which is a joint venture between Verizon Communications, Inc. and Vodafone. Verizon Communications owns a 55 percent share in the business, and Vodafone 45 percent. Verizon wireless is now the largest wireless carrier in the United States.

Financial Highlights, Fiscal Year 2009

Verizon's revenues grew 10.7 percent to $107.8 billion primarily due to the acquisition of Alltel and the inclusion of its revenues in the Wireless segment. Other sources of increased revenue were the 5.9 million new customers from sources other than acquisitions, and increased usage of existing network bandwidth.

Wireline revenues decreased 4.4 percent primarily due to lower demand for and use of basic local and long-distance services, offset somewhat by continued growth in FiOS services and customer base. The current wireline organization was restructured in preparation for its eventual sale (minus the FiOS business) later in 2010 to Frontier Communications. This sale is expected to generate $8.6 billion for Verizon.

In 2009 the company added nearly 1 million new FiOS subscribers, and total broadband and video revenues exceeded $6 billion. The total number of broadband customers now exceeds 15.4 million.

Overall, Verizon's earnings fell 6 percent to $6.93 billion. The decline was due in large part to the costs of integrating Alltel's hardware and customer base into Verizon's current network and the cost of maintaining duplicate network hardware where necessary. The company expects that these costs will diminish as the networks adopt compatible standards. No word from Verizon on when that might be. Sooner would be better than later.

Dividends rose 3.3 percent, and the company repurchased 30 million shares, or 1.1 percent of its outstanding stock.

On January 8, 2009, the company announced that it had completed its acquisition of Alltel from Atlantic Holdings for $28.1 billion. The acquisition makes Verizon wireless the largest wireless carrier in the United States, in terms of subscriber count, which at the time was 83.7 million customers. The company said the purchase would expand its wireless network coverage to nearly the entire U.S. population.

Reasons to Buy

Verizon's partial divestiture of its rural, low-speed wireline services is a good thing. Copper wireline's operating expenses are high, its pricing structures are often regulated (depending on the state), and it doesn't fit at all into Verizon's longer-term plans, which include fiber-optic broadband (FiOS) delivered to the home. The FiOS rollout is very capital intensive, and money that could be spent deploying a pipe that delivers as much as $150 per month in revenue per address to Verizon is instead being used to maintain hundreds of miles of copper that brings in as little as $10 per month. Easy math, and expect continued divestiture announcements from Verizon as credit markets firm up.

Verizon's win at the 700MHz spectrum auction last March gives them additional bandwidth for their current network and positioning it for the roll-out of the next generation of very high-speed wireless infrastructure (LTE). They spent $9.6 billion for this spectrum, and with their lead in subscriber base they should be in a position to capitalize handsomely when LTE begins to roll out later in 2010.

Verizon's shares are currently priced at a seven-year low. This would be a good entry point for shares of the largest wireless provider in the United States. The 6 percent dividend yield is a big plus.

Reasons for Caution

Integration costs of the Alltel network are far higher than anticipated and earnings from the purchase will be lower than anticipated at least through 2010.

SECTOR: Telecommunications Services
BETA COEFFICIENT: 0.7
10-YEAR COMPOUND EARNINGS PER SHARE GROWTH: 0.5 percent
10-YEAR COMPOUND DIVIDENDS PER SHARE GROWTH: 1.5 percent

	2002	2003	2004	2005	2006	2007	2008	2009
Revenues (Mil)	67,625	67,752	71,283	74,910	88,144	93,469	97,354	107,808
Net income (Mil)	8,361	7,282	7,261	7,151	6,021	6,854	7,235	6930
Earnings per share	3.05	2.62	2.59	2.56	2.54	2.36	2.54	2.4
Dividends per share	1.54	1.54	1.54	1.62	1.62	1.65	1.78	1.87
Cash flow per share	7.93	7.55	7.64	7.24	7.07	7.4	7.65	7.7
Price: high	51.1	44.3	42.3	41.1	38.9	46.2	44.3	34.8
low	26	31.1	34.1	29.1	30	35.6	23.1	26.1

Verizon Communications, Inc.
140 West Street
New York, NY 10007
(212) 395-1000
Website: *www.verizon.com*

Walgreen Company

Ticker symbol: WAG (NYSE) □ S&P rating: A+ □ Value Line financial strength rating: A+ □ Current yield: 1.6 percent

Company Profile

Walgreen Company is the nation's second largest drugstore operator. As of February 20, 2010, they operate 7,680 locations in fifty states, Guam, and Puerto Rico, as well as an additional 358 health care facilities (worksite/home care facilities, specialty pharmacies) operated by its Take Care Health Systems subsidiary. They lead the chain drugstore industry in sales and profits.

Founded in 1901, Walgreens today has 237,000 employees. The company's drugstores serve more than 4.4 million customers daily and average $8.3 million in annual sales per unit. That's $747 per square foot, among the highest in the industry. Walgreens has paid dividends in every quarter since 1933 and has raised the dividend in each of the past twenty-six years.

Competition from the supermarkets has convinced Walgreens that the best strategy is to build stand-alone stores. With the rise of managed care, many pharmacy customers now make only minimal co-payments for prescriptions, removing price as the major differentiator among drug outlets. That leaves convenience as the major

factor in choosing a pharmacy. The free-standing format makes room for drive-thru windows, which provide a quick way for drugstore customers to pick up or drop off prescriptions.

On the other hand, the company's stand-alone strategy is more expensive. Walgreen insists on building its units on corner lots near an intersection with a traffic light. Such leases normally cost more than a site in a strip mall.

Home meal replacement has become a $100-billion business industry-wide. In the company's food section, Walgreen's carries staples as well as frozen dinners, desserts, and pizzas. In some stores, expanded food sections carry such items as fruit and ready-to-eat salads.

Financial Highlights, Fiscal Year 2009

Walgreen reported its thirty-fifth consecutive year of record sales, but earnings, which had also grown for thirty-four consecutive years, fell 7 percent in FY2009. The bulk of the earnings decline can be attributed to the recognition of over $250 million in restructuring charges (13 percent of earnings) in 2009.

Pricing pressures also contributed to the decline, partially offset by increased volumes.

The company maintains its strong pharmacy orientation, with prescription drugs in 2009 accounting for 65 percent of sales. Non-prescription drugs added another 10 percent, while "front end" (general merchandise) sales accounted for 25 percent. Dividends were increased another 20 percent to $0.48/share. The company increased its outlet count by 600 in 2009.

In February 2010 the company agreed to buy Duane Reade Holdings, a New York based drugstore chain for $1.08 billion, including debt. Walgreen expects the acquisition will be dilutive to EPS for four quarters and accretive after that period. The acquisition should add approximately $125 million to the bottom line within three years.

Reasons to Buy

Walgreen has grown steadily and profitably through a combination of organic growth and opportunistic acquisitions. In the past few years this growth has quickened considerably—at one point they were opening a new location every sixteen hours. In 2009, the company decided to moderate this level of expansion and concentrate on cost-cutting and improved profitability. This decision took a bigger bite out of earnings in 2009 than

was anticipated. Comparable store sales in 2009 grew only 2 percent, as compared to 4 percent in 2008 and 8 percent in 2007. Tapering the growth in new stores and taking restructuring charges in 2009 (and 2010) will save money over time, but the downturn in the economy left Walgreen somewhat exposed during the restructuring.

Recent store data indicates that 35 percent of the average store's SKUs account for only one percent of sales volume. Consequently, the company plans to significantly reduce the number of SKUs as part of a broader physical redesign of its existing layout. Other cost-cutting measures focus on more efficient prescription fulfillment and delivery methods. In total, the company expects to net $1 billion in cost reductions with improved profitability by the end of 2010.

Although the decline in gross margin, operating margin, and net margin are in opposition to the company's stated goals for the year (reduce rate of growth, improve financial fundamentals, reduce costs), the bad news seems to be in the rear-view mirror as margins have improved in the first half of 2010.

Reasons for Caution

Walgreen and CVS Caremark have recently begun a fish-slapping contest, which has so far led to each withdrawing from the other's pharmacy network. This is clearly a lose/lose proposition, as customers will now likely find a third party's pharmacy to service their prescription. These two need to get together and work out their differences (for one, Walgreen claims CVS's policies encourage steering customers to CVS permanently). C'mon guys, it's a good time to kiss and make up—there's a big sale on lipstick on aisle two.

SECTOR: **Consumer Staples**
BETA COEFFICIENT: **.75**
10-YEAR COMPOUND EARNINGS PER SHARE GROWTH: **15.0 percent**
10-YEAR COMPOUND DIVIDENDS PER SHARE GROWTH: **12.5 percent**

		2002	2003	2004	2005	2006	2007	2008	2009
Revenues (Mil)		28,681	32,505	37,502	42,202	47,409	53,762	59,034	63,335
Net income (Mil)		1,019	1,176	1,360	1,478	1,751	2,041	2,157	2,006
Earnings per share		0.99	1.14	1.32	1.52	1.72	2.03	2.17	2.02
Dividends per share		0.15	0.15	0.18	0.22	0.27	0.33	0.4	0.48
Cash flow per share		1.29	1.47	1.72	1.99	2.3	2.74	3.03	3.02
Price:	high	40.7	37.4	39.5	49	51.6	49.1	39	40.7
	low	27.7	26.9	32	38.4	39.6	35.8	21.3	21.4

Walgreen Company
200 Wilmot Road
Mail Stop 2261
Deerfield, IL 60015
(847) 914-2972
Website: *www.walgreens.com*

Wells Fargo & Company

Ticker symbol: WFC (NYSE) ❑ S&P rating: AA- ❑ Value Line financial strength rating: A ❑ Current yield: 0.7 percent

Company Profile

Wells Fargo & Company is a diversified financial services company, providing banking, insurance, investments, mortgages, and consumer finance from more than 11,000 offices and other distribution channels across North America.

As of December 31, 2009, Wells Fargo had $1.2 trillion in assets, loans of $782 billion, deposits of $781 billion, and a market cap of $140 billion. Based on assets, they are the fourth largest bank holding company in the United States. They have 281,000 employees, or "team members," as they prefer to call them.

With the addition of Wachovia, Wells' profile in the industry has changed considerably. Here are some of the revised industry rankings for Wells Fargo as of December 31, 2009:

■ #1 in U.S. banking stores
■ #1 in small business lending
■ #1 in mortgage originations
■ #1 in middle market commercial lending
■ #1 in agriculture lending
■ #1 in Internet banking

■ #1 in commercial real estate brokerage
■ #1 in bank-owned insurance brokerage
■ #1 in retail banking deposits in United States
■ #2 in debit cards
■ #2 in student lending
■ #3 in auto financing

Financial Highlights, Fiscal Year 2009

Wells' FY2009 was supposed to be the start of the rebound, but it has turned out to be better than most of us expected. The company turned in some very gratifying numbers: revenues up 112 percent, net income up 362 percent, diluted EPS up 150 percent. Obviously, the Wachovia purchase had a great deal to do with the bounce, but the results are gratifying anyway.

On the downside, loan loss provision ended the year at $21.7 billion, almost ten times what it was in 2006 with only twice the loan value outstanding. To raise the needed levels of capital, the company sold three separate stock issues totaling 500 million shares.

Finally, the company estimated the cost of the merger at $5 billion,

$2.5 billion less than expected. And first year cost savings, beginning in 2011, are estimated to be . . . wait for it . . . $5 billion.

Reasons to Buy

Last year we recognized Wells for their (relatively) conservative positions and cautious behaviors during the mortgage free-for-all. They had less exposure overall than most and were able to spot the trouble earlier than many others. As a result, we're looking at a bank that today is in far better shape than many of its peers. Is it perfect? Certainly not; the ROA is less than half of what it ought to be, profits are where they were when the bank was less than half the size it is now, and bad loans still have a grip on a quarter of the earnings.

What's important to note, though, is the company has been able to do what all good companies want to do in these situations. By and large, they've been able to put the bad news behind them. It hasn't been easy, but the fact that they were able to do it at all in the space of a year speaks to the overall health of the bank. As it is, by the start of 2011, Wells will have completed the bulk of the largest bank merger in U.S. history and will have cleared a path through an economic environment that has put thousands of

other banks, large and small, out of business.

Despite the unprecedented contraction in the credit markets, Wells continues to lend to worthy customers. Wells made $711 billion in new loan commitments during 2009 to consumer, small business and commercial customers and refinanced 1.2 million home loans. Their mortgage default rate is one-third of the industry average, and 92 percent of their mortgages are current. And the company generated nearly $87 billion in revenue for the year. We're looking forward to seeing what the company can do with the capital now tucked away in extraordinary reserves.

Reasons for Caution

Wells' recovery is very encouraging. But are we really past all the bad news? When the calendar flipped from 2008 to 2009, did all of those suspect loans in Wachovia's portfolio suddenly reveal themselves? Are all of those $1.2 trillion worth of assets properly valued?

Or are we due for some more surprises on the downside? Wells took $0.48 per share out of 2009 earnings to increase its reserves against defaults so there's clearly more bad news to come, but it may already be paid for.

SECTOR: Financials
BETA COEFFICIENT: 1.35
10-YEAR COMPOUND EARNINGS PER SHARE GROWTH: 8.5 percent
10-YEAR COMPOUND DIVIDENDS PER SHARE GROWTH: 15.0 percent

	2002	2003	2004	2005	2006	2007	2008	2009
Loans (Bil)	192.8	249.2	269.6	296.1	306.9	344.8	843.8	758
Net income (Mil)	5,710	6,202	7,014	7,670	8,480	8,060	2,655	7,990
Earnings per share	1.66	1.83	2.05	2.25	2.49	2.38	0.7	1.75
Dividends per share	0.55	0.75	0.93	1	1.12	1.18	1.3	0.49
Revenues (Bil)	24.4	28.3	30.1	32.9	35.7	39.4	41.9	86.7
Price: high	27.4	29.6	32	32.4	37	38	30.5	31.5
low	19.1	21.7	27.2	28.8	30.3	29.3	7.8	7.8

Wells Fargo & Company
420 Montgomery Street
San Francisco, CA 94163
(415) 396-0523
Website: *www.wellsfargo.com*

CHANGE IN PRICE, 1/1/2007 THROUGH 3/9/2009

Company	Symbol	Price, 10/1/07	Price, 3/1/09	$Gain/ Loss	% Gain/ Loss
3M Company	MMM	$93.58	$45.46	(48.12)	−51.42
Abbott Laboratories	ABT	51.37	47.34	(4.03)	−7.85
Air Products & Chemicals	APD	98.85	46.25	(52.60)	−53.21
Alexander & Baldwin	ALEX	43.67	17.96	(25.71)	−58.87
Apache Corp	APA	91.96	53.46	(38.50)	−41.87
Apple	AAPL	156.34	89.31	(67.03)	−42.87
Archer Daniels Midland Co.	ADM	31.73	26.66	(5.07)	−15.98
AT&T	T	42.53	23.77	(18.76)	−44.11
Baxter International	BAX	56.63	50.91	(5.72)	−10.10
Becton, Dickinson and Co.	BDX	83.31	61.89	(21.42)	−25.71
C.R. Bard	BCR	88.99	72.38	(16.61)	−18.67
Campbell Soup	CPB	34.39	26.77	(7.62)	−22.16
CarMax	KMX	20.33	9.43	(10.90)	−53.62
Caterpillar	CAT	78.43	24.61	(53.82)	−68.62
Chevron Corp.	CVX	93.58	60.71	(32.87)	−35.13
Cintas Corp.	CTAS	37.10	20.29	(16.81)	−45.31
Colgate-Palmolive	CL	71.32	60.18	(11.14)	−15.62
Conoco-Phillips	COP	87.77	37.35	(50.42)	−57.45
Costco Wholesale Corp.	COST	61.37	42.34	(19.03)	−31.01
CVS Caremark Corp.	CVS	39.63	25.74	(13.89)	−35.05
Deere & Co.	DE	74.21	27.49	(46.72)	−62.96
Dentsply Intl.	XRAY	41.64	23.12	(18.52)	−44.48
Diebold Inc.	DBD	45.42	22.12	(23.30)	−51.30
Dominion Resources	D	42.15	30.18	(11.97)	−28.40
Dover Corp.	DOV	50.95	24.94	(26.01)	−51.05
E.I. du Pont de Nemours	DD	49.56	18.76	(30.80)	−62.15
eBay	EBAY	39.82	10.87	(28.95)	−72.70
Ecolab, Inc.	ECL	47.20	31.78	(15.42)	−32.67
EnCana Corp.	ECA	61.85	39.37	(22.48)	−36.35
Energen Corp.	EGN	57.12	26.80	(30.32)	−53.08
Entergy Corp.	ETR	10.8.29	67.39	(40.90)	−37.77
Exxon Mobil Corp.	XOM	92.56	67.90	(24.66)	−26.64
Fair Isaac Corp.	FICO	37.05	10.95	(26.10)	−70.45
FedEx Corp.	FDX	104.75	35.76	(68.99)	−65.86
Fluor Corp.	FLR	71.99	33.25	(38.74)	−58.81
FMC Corp.	FMC	52.02	35.93	(16.09)	−30.93
FPL Group, Inc.	FPL	60.88	45.33	(15.55)	−25.54
General Dynamics	GD	84.47	36.49	(47.98)	−56.80
General Mills	GIS	58.01	52.48	(5.43)	−9.53
Goodrich Corp.	GR	68.23	33.14	(35.09)	−51.43
Google	GOOG	567.27	337.99	(229.28)	−40.42
H.J. Heinz Co.	HNZ	46.20	32.67	(13.53)	−29.29
Harris Corp.	HRS	57.79	31.41	(26.38)	−45.65

CHANGE IN PRICE, 1/1/2007 THROUGH 3/9/2009

Company	Symbol	Price, 10/1/07	Price, 3/1/09	$Gain/ Loss	% Gain/ Loss
Hewlett-Packard	HPQ	49.79	20.03	(20.76)	−41.70
Honeywell Intl.	HON	59.47	26.83	(32.64)	−54.88
Hormel Foods	HRL	35.78	31.83	(3.95)	−11.04
Illinois Tool Works	ITW	59.64	27.80	(31.84)	−53.39
Intl. Business Machines	IBM	117.80	92.03	(25.77)	−21.88
Intl. Paper Company	IP	35.87	5.69	(30.18)	−84.14
Iron Mountain Inc.	IRM	30.48	18.58	(11.90)	−39.04
Johnson & Johnson	JNJ	65.70	50.00	(15.70)	−23.90
Johnson Controls Inc.	JCI	39.33	11.38	(27.95)	−71.07
Kellogg Company	K	56.00	38.92	(17.08)	−30.50
Kraft Food Inc.	KFT	34.51	22.78	(11.73)	−33.99
Lowe's	LOW	28.02	15.84	(12.18)	−43.47
Lubrizol Corp.	LZ	65.06	27.49	(37.57)	−57.75
Marathon Oil	MRO	30.61	23.27	(7.34)	−23.98
McCormick & Co.	MKC	35.97	31.35	(4.62)	−12.84
McDonalds Corp.	MCD	54.47	52.25	(2.22)	−4.08
Medtronic Inc.	MDT	56.41	24.92	(31.49)	−55.82
Monsanto	MON	85.74	76.27	(9.47)	−11.05
NIKE	NKE	58.66	41.53	(17.13)	−29.20
Norfolk Southern Corp.	NSC	51.91	27.41	(24.50)	−47.20
Northern Trust Corp.	NTRS	66.27	47.38	(18.89)	−28.50
Nucor	NEU	59.47	33.65	(25.82)	−43.42
Patterson Companies	PDCO	38.61	18.07	(20.54)	−53.20
Paychex Inc.	PAYX	41.00	22.06	(18.94)	−46.20
Peet's Coffee & Tea	PEET	27.91	21.55	(6.36)	−22.79
PepsiCo	PEP	73.26	48.14	(25.12)	−34.29
Perrigo Co.	PRGO	21.35	20.09	(1.26)	−5.90
Piedmont Natural Gas	PNY	25.09	24.14	(0.95)	−3.79
Praxair Inc.	PX	83.76	56.75	(27.01)	−32.25
Raytheon	RTN	63.82	39.97	(23.85)	−37.37
Ross Stores	ROST	25.64	29.52	3.88	15.13
Schlumberger	SLB	105.00	38.06	(66.94)	−63.75
Sigma-Aldrich	SIAL	48.74	35.70	(13.04)	−26.75
St. Jude Medical	STJ	44.07	33.16	(10.91)	−24.76
Staples Inc.	SPLS	21.49	15.95	(5.54)	−25.78
Starbucks	SBUX	26.20	9.15	(17.05)	−65.08
Stryker Corp.	SYK	68.76	33.67	(35.09)	-51.03
SYSCO Corp.	SYY	35.59	21.50	(14.09)	−39.59
Target Corp.	TGT	63.57	28.31	(35.26)	−55.47
Teva Pharmaceutical	TEVA	44.47	44.58	0.11	0.25
The Boeing Company	BA	106.65	31.44	(75.21)	−70.52
The Clorox Company	CLX	60.99	48.60	(12.39)	−20.31
The Coca-Cola Company	KO	57.47	40.85	(16.62)	−28.92

▼ Appendix A: Down Cycle Performance (continued)

Company	Symbol	Price, 10/1/07	Price, 3/1/09	$Gain/ Loss	% Gain/ Loss
Procter & Gamble	PG	70.34	48.17	(22.17)	−31.52
The Southern Company	SO	36.28	30.31	(5.97)	−16.46
TJX Companies Inc.	TJX	30.84	22.27	(8.57)	−27.79
Tractor Supply Co.	TSCO	46.09	31.24	(14.85)	−32.22
United Parcel Service	UPS	75.10	41.18	(33.92)	−45.17
United Technologies	UTX	80.48	40.83	(39.65)	−49.27
UnitedHealth Group	UNH	48.43	19.65	(28.78)	−59.43
Valmont	VMI	84.85	43.56	(41.29)	−48.66
Varian Medical	VAR	41.89	30.51	(11.38)	−27.17
Verizon	VZ	44.28	28.53	(15.75)	−35.57
Vulcan Materials	VMC	45.09	41.41	(3.68)	−8.16
W.W. Grainger	GWW	91.19	61.45	(29.74)	−32.61
Walgreen Co.	WAG	47.24	23.86	(23.38)	−49.49
Wells Fargo	WFC	47.24	12.10	(35.14)	−74.39

▼ Appendix B: Up Cycle Performance

CHANGE IN PRICE 3/1/2009 THROUGH 3/10/2010

Company	Symbol	Price 3/1/09	Shares	Invested 3/1/09	Price	Mkt Value 3/10/10	$ Gain	% Gain
3M Company	MMM	$45.45	22.00	$1,000	81.56	$1,794.10	$794.10	79.4%
Abbott Laboratories	ABT	47.35	21.12	$1,000	55.03	1,162.44	162.44	16.2
Air Products & Chemicals	APD	46.25	21.62	$1,000	74.40	1,608.65	608.65	60.9
Alexander & Baldwin	ALEX	17.96	55.68	$1,000	34.44	1,917.59	917.59	91.8
Apache Corp.	APA	53.45	18.71	$1,000	106.59	1,993.83	993.83	99.4
Apple	AAPL	89.29	11.20	$1,000	224.84	2,517.52	1,517.52	151.8
Archer Daniels Midland Co.	ADM	26.66	37.51	$1,000	30.24	1,134.28	134.28	13.4
AT&T	T	23.77	42.07	$1,000	25.52	1,073.62	73.62	7.4
Baxter Intl.	BAX	50.92	19.64	$1,000	58.48	1,148.69	148.69	14.9
Becton, Dickinson and Co.	BDX	61.88	16.16	$1,000	78.92	1,275.17	275.17	27.5
C.R. Bard	BCR	72.36	13.82	$1,000	83.23	1,149.90	149.90	15.0
Campbell Soup	CPB	26.77	37.36	$1,000	33.88	1,265.60	265.60	26.6
CarMax	KMX	9.43	106.04	$1,000	23.29	2,469.78	1,469.78	147.0
Caterpillar	CAT	24.61	40.63	$1,000	58.78	2,388.46	1,388.46	138.9
Chevron Corp.	CVX	60.72	16.47	$1,000	73.96	1,218.25	218.25	21.8
Cintas	CTAS	20.29	49.29	$1,000	26.42	1,302.12	302.12	30.2
Colgate-Palmolive	CL	60.17	16.62	$1,000	83.58	1,388.53	388.53	38.9

CHANGE IN PRICE 3/1/2009 THROUGH 3/10/2010

Company	Symbol	Price 3/1/09	Shares	Invested 3/1/09	Price	Mkt Value 3/10/10	$ Gain	% Gain
Conoco-Phillips	COP	37.36	26.77	$1,000	51.47	1,378.05	378.05	37.8
Costco Whole-sale Corp.	COST	42.34	23.62	$1,000	59.84	1,413.32	413.32	41.3
CVS Caremark	CVS	25.74	38.85	$1,000	34.85	1,353.92	353.92	35.4
Deere & Co.	DE	27.49	36.38	$1,000	58.49	2,127.68	1,127.68	112.8
Dentsply Intl.	XRAY	22.45	44.54	$1,000	34.67	1,544.32	544.32	54.4
Diebold Inc.	DBD	22.12	45.21	$1,000	31.10	1,405.97	405.97	40.6
Dominion Resources	D	30.18	33.13	$1,000	39.38	1,304.84	304.84	30.5
Dover Corp.	DOV	24.94	40.10	$1,000	46.33	1,857.66	857.66	85.8
E.I. du Pont de Nemours	DD	18.76	53.30	$1,000	35.20	1,876.33	876.33	87.6
EBay	EBAY	10.87	92.00	$1,000	25.56	2,351.43	1,351.43	135.1
Ecolab	ECL	31.78	31.47	$1,000	42.58	1,229.84	229.84	34.0
EnCana Corp.	ECA	39.37	25.40	$1,000	34.24	869.70	(130.30)	−13.0
Energen Corp.	EGN	26.80	37.31	$1,000	45.85	1,710.82	710.82	71.1
Entergy Corp.	ETR	67.39	14.84	$1,000	79.52	1,180.00	180.00	18.0
Exxon Mobil	XOM	67.89	14.73	$1,000	67.22	989.99	(10.01)	−1.0
Fair Isaac	FICO	10.95	91.32	$1,000	24.71	2,256.62	1,256.62	125.7
FedEx	FDX	35.77	27.96	$1,000	87.26	2,440.16	1,440.16	144.0
Fluor	FLR	33.24	30.08	$1,000	45.28	1,361.80	361.80	36.2
FMC Corp.	FMC	35.93	27.83	$1,000	59.47	1,655.16	655.16	65.5
FPL Group	FPL	45.33	22.06	$1,000	46.97	1,036.18	36.18	3.6
General Dynamics	GD	36.50	27.40	$1,000	73.94	2,026.31	1,026.31	102.6
General Mills	GIS	52.49	19.05	$1,000	72.25	1,376.71	376.71	37.7
Goodrich Corp.	GR	33.13	30.18	$1,000	71.20	2,148.46	1,148.46	114.9
Google	GOOG	337.84	2.96	$1,000	576.45	1,705.52	705.52	70.6
H.J. Heinz	HNZ	32.67	30.61	$1,000	46.36	1,419.04	419.04	41.9
Harris Corp.	HRS	31.41	31.84	$1,000	46.39	1,476.92	476.92	47.7
Hewlett-Packard	HPQ	29.03	34.45	$1,000	51.78	1,783.67	783.67	78.4
Honeywell Intl.	HON	26.83	37.27	$1,000	42.34	1,578.08	578.08	57.8
Hormel Foods	HRL	31.83	31.42	$1,000	41.63	1,307.89	307.89	30.8
Illinois Tool Works	ITW	27.80	35.97	$1,000	46.74	1,681.29	681.29	68.1
Intl. Business Machines	IBM	92.00	10.87	$1,000	125.62	1,364.99	364.99	36.5
Intl. Paper Co.	IP	5.69	175.75	$1,000	25.11	4,413.01	3,413.01	341.3
Iron Mountain	IRM	18.58	53.82	$1,000	25.64	1,379.98	379.98	38.0
Johnson & Johnson	JNJ	50.00	20.00	$1,000	64.29	1,285.80	285.80	28.6
Johnson Controls	JCI	11.38	87.87	$1,000	31.19	2,740.77	1,740.77	174.1
Kellogg Co.	K	38.93	25.69	$1,000	52.51	1,349.18	349.18	34.9

CHANGE IN PRICE 3/1/2009 THROUGH 3/10/2010

Company	Symbol	Price 3/1/09	Shares	Invested 3/1/09	Price	Mkt Value 3/10/10	$ Gain	% Gain
Kraft Foods	KFT	22.78	43.90	$1,000	29.38	1,289.73	289.73	29.0
Lowe's	LOW	15.84	63.13	$1,000	24.29	1,533.46	533.46	53.4
Lubrizol	LZ	27.49	36.38	$1,000	85.85	3,122.95	2,122.95	212.3
Marathon Oil	MRO	23.27	42.97	$1,000	31.49	1,353.24	353.24	35.3
McCormick & Co.	MKC	31.35	31.90	$1,000	38.10	1,215.31	215.31	21.5
McDonalds	MCD	52.25	19.14	$1,000	64.94	1,242.87	242.87	24.3
Medtronic	MDT	24.92	40.13	$1,000	44.63	1,790.93	790.93	79.1
Monsanto	MON	76.28	13.11	$1,000	71.11	932.35	(67.65)	
NIKE	NKE	41.53	24.08	$1,000	69.12	1,664.34	664.34	66.4
Norfolk Southern	NSC	27.41	36.48	$1,000	53.87	1,965.34	965.34	96.5
Northern Trust Corp.	NTRS	47.37	21.11	$1,000	54.03	1,140.35	140.35	14.0
Nucor	NUE	30.74	32.53	$1,000	45.03	1,464.87	464.87	46.5
Patterson	PDCO	18.07	55.34	$1,000	30.20	1,671.28	671.28	67.1
Paychex	PAYX	22.06	45.33	$1,000	31.79	1,441.07	441.07	44.1
Peet's Coffee & Tea	PEET	21.55	46.40	$1,000	40.00	1,856.15	856.15	85.6
PepsiCo	PEP	48.15	20.77	$1,000	64.43	1,338.39	338.39	33.8
Perrigo Co.	PRGO	20.09	49.78	$1,000	50.10	2,493.78	1,493.78	149.4
Piedmont Natural Gas	PNY	24.14	41.34	$1,000	26.96	1,116.82	116.82	11.7
Praxair	PX	56.75	17.62	$1,000	79.01	1,392.25	392.25	39.2
Raytheon	RTN	39.97	25.02	$1,000	57.10	1,428.57	428.57	42.9
Ross Stores	ROST	29.52	33.88	$1,000	52.07	1,763.89	763.89	76.4
Schlumberger	SLB	35.84	27.90	$1,000	64.20	1,791.29	791.29	79.1
Sigma-Aldrich	SIAL	31.63	31.62	$1,000	52.97	1,674.68	674.68	67.5
St. Jude Medical	STJ	33.16	30.16	$1,000	38.06	1,147.77	147.77	14.8
Staples	SPLS	15.95	62.70	$1,000	22.95	1,438.87	438.87	43.9
Starbucks	SBUX	9.15	109.29	$1,000	24.23	2,648.09	1,648.09	164.8
Stryker	SYK	33.67	29.70	$1,000	55.29	1,642.11	642.11	64.2
SYSCO	SYY	21.50	46.51	$1,000	28.41	1,321.40	321.40	32.1
Target	TGT	28.31	35.32	$1,000	52.64	1,859.41	859.41	85.9
Teva Pharmaceutical	TEVA	43.25	23.12	$1,000	60.94	1,409.02	409.02	40.9
The Boeing Co.	BA	31.44	31.81	$1,000	70.01	2,226.78	1,226.78	122.7
The Clorox Co.	CLX	48.59	20.58	$1,000	62.35	1,282.92	282.92	28.3
The Coca-Cola Co.	KO	40.85	24.48	$1,000	54.20	1,326.81	326.81	32.7
The Procter & Gamble Co.	PG	48.17	20.76	$1,000	63.01	1,308.08	308.08	30.8
The Southern Co.	SO	30.31	32.99	$1,000	32.36	1,067.63	67.63	6.8
TJX Companies	TJX	22.27	44.90	$1,000	41.87	1,880.11	880.11	88.0

▼ Appendix B: Up Cycle Performance (continued)

CHANGE IN PRICE 3/1/2009 THROUGH 3/10/2010

Company	Symbol	Price 3/1/09	Shares	Invested 3/1/09	Price	Mkt Value 3/10/10	$ Gain	% Gain
Tractor Supply Co.	TSCO	31.24	32.01	$1,000	57.79	1,849.87	849.87	85.0
United Parcel Service	UPS	41.19	24.28	$1,000	60.73	1,474.75	474.75	47.5
United Technologies	UTX	38.54	25.95	$1,000	71.79	1,862.74	862.74	86.3
UnitedHealth Group	UNH	19.65	50.89	$1,000	33.24	1,691.60	691.60	69.2
Valmont	VMI	42.68	23.43	$1,000	82.59	1,935.10	935.10	93.5
Varian Medical	VAR	30.51	32.78	$1,000	53.35	1,748.61	748.61	74.9
Verizon	VZ	28.53	35.05	$1,000	29.75	1,042.76	42.76	4.3
Vulcan Materials	VMC	41.41	24.15	$1,000	45.41	1,096.60	96.60	9.7
W.W. Grainger	BWW	61.46	16.27	$1,000	108.08	1,758.83	758.83	75.9
Walgreen	WAG	23.86	41.91	$1,000	34.27	1,436.30	436.40	43.6
Wells Fargo	WFC	12.10	82.64	$1,000	29.57	2,443.80	1,443.80	144.4

Total Securities Value: $162,884.11
Cash from Dividends: $2,665.00
Final 2010 Value: $165,549.11
Initial Investment in 100 Best: $100,000.00
Value of 100 Best on 3/10/2010: $165,549.11

Percentage Gain for 100 Best: 65.5%
S&P 500 SPDR ETF 3/1/2009: 100,000.00
S&P 500 SPDR ETF 3/10/2010: $155,511.97
Percentage Gain for S&P 500 SPDR ETF: 55.5%
% Difference in Gain: 18.1%

▼ Appendix C: Dividend and Yield

Company	Dividend	Yield%
Suburban Propane	3.36	7.3%
AT&T	1.68	7.0
Verizon	1.90	7.0
Duke Energy	0.96	6.1
Cincinnati Financial	1.58	6.0
Southern Company	1.82	5.7
General Mills	1.96	5.4
DuPont	1.64	4.8
Dominion Energy	1.83	4.7
Entergy	3.32	4.6
Conoco-Philips	2.20	4.4
Kimberly-Clark	2.64	4.4
PayChex	1.24	4.4
Alexander & Baldwin	1.26	4.2
FPL Group	2.00	4.1
Heinz	1.80	4.1

Company	Dividend	Yield%
Kraft Foods	1.16	4.1
Chevron	2.88	4.0
Abbott Laboratories	1.76	3.8
Johnson & Johnson	2.16	3.7
Clorox	2.20	3.5
Nucor	1.44	3.5
Coca-Cola	1.76	3.4
Sysco	1.00	3.4
Marathon Oil	1.00	3.3
McDonalds	2.20	3.3
Procter & Gamble	1.93	3.2
Campbell Soup	1.10	3.1
PepsiCo	1.92	3.1
Exxon Mobil	1.76	3.0
Air Products	1.96	2.9
Caterpillar	1.68	2.9

Company	Dividend	Yield%	Company	Dividend	Yield%
Honeywell	1.21	2.9	Patterson	0.40	1.4
J.M. Smucker	1.60	2.9	Ecolab	0.62	1.3
3M Company	2.10	2.8	Sigma-Aldrich	0.64	1.3
Baxter Intl.	1.16	2.8	Target	0.68	1.3
Boeing	1.16	2.8	TJX	0.60	1.3
Kellogg	1.50	2.8	Ross	0.64	1.2
Colgate-Palmolive	2.12	2.7	Stryker	0.60	1.2
McCormick & Co.	1.04	2.7	Teva Pharmaceuticals	0.65	1.2
UTX	1.70	2.6	Fluor	0.50	1.1
Norfolk Southern	1.36	2.5	Iron Mountain	0.25	1.1
Archer Daniels Midland	0.60	2.4	CVS	0.35	1.0
Dover	1.04	2.4	C.R. Bard	0.68	0.9
Praxair	1.80	2.4	Church & Dwight	0.56	0.9
Intl. Paper	0.50	2.3	FMC	0.50	0.9
Northern Trust	1.12	2.3	Oracle	0.20	0.9
Medtronic	0.82	2.2	Tractor Supply Co.	0.56	0.9
Monsanto	1.06	2.2	Valmont	0.66	0.9
W.W. Grainger	2.16	2.1	Apache	0.60	0.7
Becton, Dickinson	1.48	2.1	Hewlett-Packard	0.32	0.7
Deere & Co.	1.20	2.1	Wells Fargo	0.20	0.7
Hormel Foods	0.84	2.1	Dentsply	0.20	0.6
IBM	2.60	2.1	FedEx	0.44	0.6
Bunge	0.92	1.9	Fair Isaac	0.08	0.4
Harris	0.88	1.9	Perrigo	0.25	0.4
Johnson Controls	0.52	1.9	Apple	–	0.0
Walgreen	0.55	1.8	Bed, Bath, and Beyond	–	0.0
Lubrizol	1.44	1.7	CarMax	–	0.0
Staples	0.36	1.7	Chipotle	–	0.0
UnitedHealth	0.50	1.6	Google	–	0.0
Costco	0.82	1.5	NetApp	–	0.0
NIKE	1.08	1.5	Panera	–	0.0
Schlumberger	0.84	1.5	Peet's	–	0.0
Starbucks	0.40	1.5	Varian	–	0.0
Best Buy	0.56	1.4	St. Jude	–	0.0